# Lecture Notes in Computer Science       10418

*Commenced Publication in 1973*
Founding and Former Series Editors:
Gerhard Goos, Juris Hartmanis, and Jan van Leeuwen

## Editorial Board

More information about this series at http://www.springer.com/series/7410

Satoshi Obana · Koji Chida (Eds.)

# Advances in Information and Computer Security

12th International Workshop on Security, IWSEC 2017
Hiroshima, Japan, August 30 – September 1, 2017
Proceedings

 Springer

*Editors*
Satoshi Obana (iD)
Hosei University
Tokyo
Japan

Koji Chida
NTT Corporation
Tokyo
Japan

ISSN 0302-9743          ISSN 1611-3349   (electronic)
Lecture Notes in Computer Science
ISBN 978-3-319-64199-7          ISBN 978-3-319-64200-0   (eBook)
DOI 10.1007/978-3-319-64200-0

Library of Congress Control Number: 2017947500

LNCS Sublibrary: SL4 – Security and Cryptology

Printed on acid-free paper

This Springer imprint is published by Springer Nature
The registered company is Springer International Publishing AG
The registered company address is: Gewerbestrasse 11, 6330 Cham, Switzerland

# Preface

The 12th International Workshop on Security (IWSEC 2017) was held at the International Conference Center Hiroshima, in Hiroshima, Japan, during August 30 – September 1, 2017. The workshop was co-organized by the Technical Committee on Information Security in Engineering Sciences Society of the Institute of Electronics, Information and Communication Engineers and the Special Interest Group on Computer Security of Information Processing Society of Japan.

This year, the workshop received 37 submissions. Finally, 11 papers were accepted as regular papers, and three papers were accepted as short papers. Each submission was anonymously reviewed by at least three reviewers, and these proceedings contain the revised versions of the accepted papers. In addition to the presentations of the papers, the workshop also featured a poster session. The keynote speeches were given by Khaled El Emam and by Kazue Sako.

The best paper award was given to "On Quantum Related-Key Attacks on Iterated Even-Mansour Ciphers" by Akinori Hosoyamada and Kazumaro Aoki, and the best student paper award was given to "Not All Browsers Are Created Equal: Comparing Web Browser Fingerprintability" by Nasser Mohammed Al-Fannah and Wanpeng Li.

A number of people contributed to the success of IWSEC 2017. We would like to thank the authors for submitting their papers to the workshop. The selection of the papers was a challenging and dedicated task, and we are deeply grateful to the members of the Program Committee and the external reviewers for their in-depth reviews and detailed discussions.

Last but not least, we would like to thank the general co-chairs, Kazuto Ogawa and Masayuki Terada, for leading the local Organizing Committee, and we would also like to thank the members of the local Organizing Committee for their efforts to ensure the smooth running of the workshop.

May 2017

Satoshi Obana
Koji Chida

# IWSEC 2017
# 12th International Workshop on Security Organization

Hiroshima, Japan, August 30 – September 1, 2017

co-organized by

ISEC in ESS of IEICE

(Technical Committee on Information Security in Engineering Sciences Society
of the Institute of Electronics, Information and Communication Engineers)

and

CSEC of IPSJ

(Special Interest Group on Computer Security of Information
Processing Society of Japan)

## General Co-chairs

| | |
|---|---|
| Kazuto Ogawa | Japan Broadcasting Corporation, Japan |
| Masayuki Terada | NTT DOCOMO, Japan |

## Advisory Committee

| | |
|---|---|
| Hideki Imai | The University of Tokyo, Japan |
| Kwangjo Kim | Korea Advanced Institute of Science and Technology, Korea |
| Christopher Kruegel | University of California, Santa Barbara, USA |
| Günter Müeller | University of Freiburg, Germany |
| Yuko Murayama | Tsuda College, Japan |
| Koji Nakao | National Institute of Information and Communications Technology, Japan |
| Eiji Okamoto | University of Tsukuba, Japan |
| C. Pandu Rangan | Indian National Academy of Engineering, India |
| Kai Rannenberg | Goethe University Frankfurt, Germany |
| Ryoichi Sasaki | Tokyo Denki University, Japan |

## Program Co-chairs

| | |
|---|---|
| Satoshi Obana | HOSEI University, Japan |
| Koji Chida | NTT, Japan |

## Local Organizing Committee

| | |
|---|---|
| Hiroaki Anada | University of Nagasaki, Japan |
| Atsushi Fujioka | Kanagawa University, Japan |
| Takuya Hayashi | Kobe University, Japan |
| Takato Hirano | Mitsubishi Electric Corporation, Japan |
| Hiroyuki Inoue | Hiroshima City University, Japan |
| Akira Kanaoka | Toho University, Japan |
| Yutaka Kawai | Mitsubishi Electric Corporation, Japan |
| Takaaki Mizuki | Tohoku University, Japan |
| Ken Naganuma | Hitachi, Ltd., Japan |
| Yoshitaka Nakamura | Future University Hakodate, Japan |
| Tetsushi Ohki | Shizuoka University, Japan |
| Go Ohtake | Japan Broadcasting Corporation, Japan |
| Masakazu Soshi | Hiroshima City University, Japan |
| Yuji Suga | Internet Initiative Japan Inc., Japan |
| Yu Tsuda | National Institute of Information and Communications Technology, Japan |
| Sven Wohlgemuth | Hitachi, Ltd., Japan |
| Takumi Yamamoto | Mitsubishi Electric Corporation, Japan |
| Kan Yasuda | NTT, Japan |

## Program Committee

| | |
|---|---|
| Mohamed Abid | University of Gabes, Tunisia |
| Mitsuaki Akiyama | NTT, Japan |
| Elena Andreeva | KU Leuven, Belgium |
| Reza Azarderakhsh | Florida Atlantic University, USA |
| Josep Balasch | KU Leuven, Belgium |
| Gregory Blanc | Télécom SudParis, France |
| Olivier Blazy | Université de Limoges, France |
| Aymen Boudguiga | Institute for Technological Research SystemX, France |
| Kai-Chi Chang | National Center for Cyber Security Technology, Taiwan |
| Yue Chen | Florida State University, USA |
| Céline Chevalier | Université Panthéon-Assas, France |
| Sabrina De Capitani di Vimercati | DI - Università degli Studi di Milano, Italy |
| Herve Debar | Télécom SudParis, France |
| Itai Dinur | Ben-Gurion University, Israel |
| Josep Domingo-Ferrer | Universitat Rovira i Virgili, Catalonia |
| Oriol Farràs | Universitat Rovira i Virgili, Spain |
| Atsushi Fujioka | Kanagawa University, Japan |
| Dawu Gu | Shanghai Jiao Tong University, China |
| Roberto Guanciale | KTH Royal Institute of Technology, Sweden |
| Florian Hahn | SAP, Germany |
| Atsuo Inomata | Tokyo Denki University, Japan |

| | |
|---|---|
| Akira Kanaoka | Toho University, Japan |
| Hiroaki Kikuchi | Meiji University, Japan |
| Hyung Chan Kim | The Affiliated Institute of ETRI, Korea |
| Yuichi Komano | Toshiba Corporation, Japan |
| Noboru Kunihiro | The University of Tokyo, Japan |
| Maryline Laurent | Télécom SudParis, France |
| Heejo Lee | Korea University, South Korea |
| Hyung Tae Lee | Nanyang Technological University, Singapore |
| Zhou Li | RSA Labs., USA |
| Frédéric Majorczyk | DGA-MI/CentraleSupelec, France |
| Florian Mendel | Graz University of Technology, Austria |
| Bart Mennink | Radboud University, The Netherlands |
| Kirill Morozov | Tokyo Institute of Technology, Japan |
| Koichi Mouri | Ritsumeikan University, Japan |
| Ivica Nikolić | Nanyang Technological University, Singapore |
| Ryo Nojima | National Institute of Information and Communications Technology, Japan |
| Alexis Olivereau | CEA LIST, France |
| Kaan Onarlioglu | Northeastern University, USA |
| Thomas Peyrin | Nanyang Technological University, Singapore |
| Yusuke Sakai | National Institute of Advanced Industrial Science and Technology, Japan |
| Yu Sasaki | NTT, Japan |
| Dominique Schröder | Friedrich-Alexander Universität Erlangen-Nürnberg, Germany |
| Yannick Seurin | Agence Nationale de la Sécurité des Systèmes d'Information, France |
| Yuji Suga | Internet Initiative Japan Inc., Japan |
| Willy Susilo | University of Wollongong, Australia |
| Mio Suzuki | National Institute of Information and Communications Technology, Japan |
| Katsuyuki Takashima | Mitsubishi Electric Corporation, Japan |
| Mehdi Tibouchi | NTT, Japan |
| Giorgos Vasiliadis | Qatar Computing Research Institute HBKU, Greece |
| Cong Wang | City University of Hong Kong, Hong Kong, SAR China |
| Sven Wohlgemuth | Hitachi, Ltd., Japan |
| Pa Pa Yin Minn | Yokohama National University, Japan |
| Chung-Huang Yang | National Kaohsiung Normal University, Taiwan |
| Kan Yasuda | NTT, Japan |
| Maki Yoshida | National Institute of Information and Communications Technology, Japan |
| Rui Zhang | Chinese Academy of Sciences, China |

## Additional Reviewers

Arij Ben Amor
Avik Chakraborti
Christoph Egger
Lorenzo Grassi
Moeen Hasanalizadeh
Masahiro Ishii
Amandine Jambert
Sarra Jebri
Jeong Jihoon
Saqib Kakvi

Marc Kaplan
Thijs Laarhoven
Jason Legrow
Gaëtan Leurent
Bernardo Magri
Giulio Malavolta
Michele Minelli
María Naya-Plasencia
Sk. Md. Mizanur Rahman
Alfredo Rial

Atsushi Takayasu
Yang Tao
Thomas Unterluggauer
Yuting Xiao
Zhengyu Yang
Takanori Yasuda
Youngho Yoo
Qian Zhang

# Contents

## Cryptographic Protocols

## Public Key Cryptosystems (2)

# Post-quantum Cryptography

# On Quantum Related-Key Attacks on Iterated Even-Mansour Ciphers

Akinori Hosoyamada[✉] and Kazumaro Aoki

NTT Secure Platform Laboratories, 3-9-11, Midori-cho Musashino-shi,
Tokyo 180-8585, Japan
{hosoyamada.akinori,aoki.kazumaro}@lab.ntt.co.jp

**Abstract.** The impacts that quantum computers will have on cryptography have become more and more important to study for not only public key cryptography but also symmetric key cryptography. For example, at ISITA 2012, Kuwakado and Morii showed that an adversary with a quantum computer can recover keys of the Even-Mansour construction in polynomial time by applying Simon's algorithm. In addition, at CRYPTO 2016, Kaplan et al. showed that Simon's algorithm can also be used to perform forgery attacks against MACs and exponentially speedup a slide attack. This paper introduces a tool for finding the period of a function that is periodic up to constant addition and shows that a quantum adversary can use the tool to perform a related-key attack in polynomial time. Our quantum related-key attack is an extension of the quantum slide attack by Kaplan et al. against iterated Even-Mansour ciphers that are implemented on quantum circuits. Although the relationships among keys are strong, our algorithm can recover all the keys of a two-round iterated Even-Mansour cipher in polynomial time.

## 1 Introduction

Widely used public key cryptographic schemes, such as RSA, will become insecure when a practical quantum computer appears [14]. Since this threat was first reported, many researchers have been studying post-quantum public key cryptography. Moreover, NIST announced that they have initiated a process to standardize post-quantum public key cryptographic algorithms [11]. As for symmetric key cryptography, quantum computers will also threaten the security of existing schemes that are proved or expected to be secure in classical settings. For instance, Grover's algorithm [3] can reduce the time complexity for exhaustive key search against an $m$-bit key block cipher from $O(2^m)$ to $O(2^{m/2})$, but the complexity remains exponential and this algorithm seems to affect symmetric key cryptography less significantly than Shor's algorithm affects public key cryptography. Moreover, polynomial time quantum algorithms have recently been reported that break cryptographic schemes for not only public key cryptography but also symmetric key cryptography [5,7,8]. It is becoming more and more important to study how much quantum computers will affect current symmetric key schemes and how we can construct schemes that are secure even in the post-quantum era.

© Springer International Publishing AG 2017
S. Obana and K. Chida (Eds.): IWSEC 2017, LNCS 10418, pp. 3–18, 2017.
DOI: 10.1007/978-3-319-64200-0_1

In classical settings, an adversary requires exponential time to distinguish a three-round Feistel scheme from random permutations by using a chosen *plaintext* attack [9,16] and recover keys of (iterated) Even-Mansour ciphers by using a chosen ciphertext attack [1,2]. Kuwakado and Morii showed that an adversary with a quantum computer can break these schemes in polynomial time [7,8] by applying Simon's algorithm [15]. At CRYPTO 2016, Kaplan et al. showed that Simon's algorithm can also be applied to forgery attacks against MACs and a slide attack against iterated Even-Mansour ciphers the round keys of which are all the same [5]. These attacks assume that an adversary can query encryption oracles in an arbitrary quantum superposition of the inputs, and the model is called *Q2 model* [6]. Table 1 summarizes the attacks on $n$-bit block ciphers under the Q2 model. More recently, at FSE 2017, Kaplan et al. showed that the best attack against a symmetric key scheme in classical settings is not necessarily the best one in quantum settings if existing classical attacks are "quantized" [6]. For other quantum attacks, we refer to [4,12,13].

**Table 1.** Attacks on $n$-bit block ciphers under Q2 model

| Target | #Round | Condition | Goal | Algorithm | Time | Source |
|--------|--------|-----------|------|-----------|------|--------|
| Feistel | 3 | — | D | PF | $O(n)$ | [8] |
| EM | 1 | — | KR | PF | $O(n)$ | [7] |
| iEM | any | same subkeys | KR | PF | $O(n)$ | [5] |
| iEM | any | related-key | partial KR | PF+const | $O(n)$ | Sect. 5.1 |
| iEM | 2 | related-key | KR | PF+const | $O(n)$ ($2^{14}$ for $n = 128$) | Sects. 5.2 and 5.3 |

EM: Even-Mansour, iEM: iterated EM, KR: key recovery,
D: distinguishing, PF: period finding using Simon's Algorithm,
PF+const: PF extension for a function up to constant addition (Sect. 3)

After seeing the results of the key recovery attack against the Even-Mansour cipher by Kuwakado and Morii, a question naturally arises as to whether there is also a quantum algorithm that can recover keys of iterated Even-Mansour ciphers. The iterated Even-Mansour cipher, or key-alternating cipher, is a natural extension of the Even-Mansour cipher and can be considered as a model of AES [10]. The technique of Kuwakado and Morii cannot directly be applied to iterated Even-Mansour ciphers because Simon's algorithm cannot be applied directly to iterated Even-Mansour ciphers, and they referred to the question as an open problem in their paper [8]. The quantum slide attack by Kaplan et al. can be regarded as a partial answer to this open problem. They treated only iterated Even-Mansour ciphers the round keys of which are all the same. They constructed a period function by exploiting the slide properties and succeeded in applying Simon's algorithm.

In this paper, we consider iterated Even-Mansour ciphers the round keys of which are independent. First, we introduce a technical tool extending Simon's original algorithm and use it for our attack. The advantage of our tool is that it can find the period of function that is periodic up to constant addition. Second, we show that there is a polynomial time algorithm that can recover partial keys of iterated Even-Mansour ciphers, if allowed to access related-key quantum encryption oracles. Our related-key setting is an extension of the setting of the quantum slide attack by Kaplan et al. In particular, for two-round iterated Even-Mansour ciphers, our algorithm can recover the entire key with two related-key oracles, which gives another partial answer to the open problem above.

## 2   Preliminaries

This section describes notations and the attack model that we consider throughout this paper.

### 2.1   Notations

For a bit-string $x$, let $\bar{x}$ be the bitwise complement of $x$. We regard $\{0,1\}^n$ as an $n$-dimensional vector space over $\mathbb{Z}/2\mathbb{Z}$. For $x, y \in \{0,1\}^n$, let $x \cdot y$ denote the formal inner product of the two vectors. Denote $Span(v_1, v_2, \ldots, v_l)$ the vector space spanned by vectors $v_1, v_2, \ldots, v_l$ over $\mathbb{Z}/2\mathbb{Z}$. For $\phi : \{0,1\}^n \to \{0,1\}^n$ and $u \in \{0,1\}^n$, define $(\Delta_u \phi)(x)$ as $\phi(x) \oplus \phi(x \oplus u)$ and call $(\Delta_u \phi)(x)$, the differential of $\phi$. Define $\epsilon(\phi; w_1, w_2, \ldots, w_j) := \max_{t \notin Span(w_1, w_2, \ldots, w_j)} \Pr_x[\phi(x \oplus t) = \phi(x)]$, where $w_1, w_2, \ldots, w_j \in \{0,1\}^n$.

### 2.2   Attack Model

Classically, security against a chosen plaintext attack is considered in the model in which encryption oracles can be used by an adversary. This paper considers the model in which an adversary can use quantum encryption oracles. This model is used by Kuwakado and Morii [7,8], followed by Kaplan et al. [5]. In their paper on quantum differential and linear attacks, by Kaplan et al. call this model *Q2 model* [6].

Let $x, y$ be in $\{0,1\}^n$, and $b$ denote a bit. We assume that an adversary can use ordinary quantum gates, such as the Hadamard gate $H^{\otimes n} : |x\rangle \mapsto \frac{1}{\sqrt{2^n}} \sum_y (-1)^{x \cdot y} |y\rangle$, NOT gate $NOT : |x\rangle \mapsto |\bar{x}\rangle$, controlled-NOT gate $CNOT : |x\rangle|y\rangle \mapsto |x\rangle|x \oplus y\rangle$, and controlled-controlled NOT gate $CCNOT : |b\rangle|x\rangle|y\rangle \mapsto |b\rangle|x\rangle|y \oplus bx\rangle$, where $bx$ is the product of a scalar $b \in \{0,1\}$ and a vector $x \in \{0,1\}^n$. The controlled NOT gate corresponds to the XOR gate in a classical circuit. The controlled-controlled NOT gate is the modified controlled NOT gate that takes an additional input $b$ and branches processing depending on $b$ (Fig. 1).

For the function $\phi$, we call the quantum oracle $|x\rangle|y\rangle \mapsto |x\rangle|y \oplus \phi(x)\rangle$ the quantum oracle of $\phi$. We assume that an adversary can integrate the gate into his circuits (Fig. 2).

If $P$ is a public random permutation, we assume that an adversary can integrate the quantum gates of $P$ and $P^{-1}$, $P : |x\rangle|y\rangle \mapsto |x\rangle|y \oplus P(x)\rangle$ and

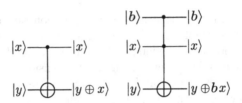

**Fig. 1.** *CNOT* and *CCNOT*.

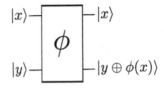

**Fig. 2.** Quantum oracle of $\phi$.

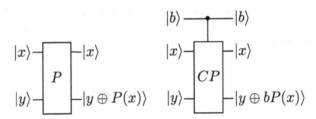

**Fig. 3.** *P* and controlled *P*.

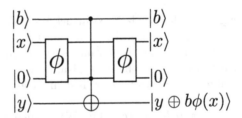

**Fig. 4.** Quantum circuit of $C\phi$.

$P^{-1} : |x\rangle|y\rangle \mapsto |x\rangle|y \oplus P^{-1}(x)\rangle$, and the controlled $P$ gate $CP : |b\rangle|x\rangle|y\rangle \mapsto |b\rangle|x\rangle|y \oplus bP(x)\rangle$, into his quantum circuits (Fig. 3).

We note that an adversary can construct a quantum circuit that calculates the controlled $\phi$, $C\phi : |b\rangle|x\rangle|y\rangle \mapsto |b\rangle|x\rangle|y \oplus b\phi(x)\rangle$ (Fig. 4), and $\Delta_u\phi$, the differential of $\phi$, if allowed to access the quantum oracle of $\phi$ (Fig. 5).

In the following, we refer to a quantum circuit that runs in polynomial time as an *efficient* quantum circuit. Similarly, we refer to a polynomial time quantum algorithm as an *efficient* algorithm.

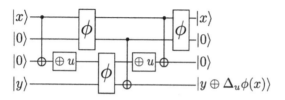

**Fig. 5.** Quantum circuit of $\Delta_u \phi$.

# 3   Simon's Algorithm and Its Extension

In this section, first, we overview Simon's algorithm for periodic functions and its extension by Kaplan et al. [5]. Second, we extend the algorithm further and introduce a tool for solving the problem of finding a period of a function that is periodic up to constant addition. To solve the problem, we use the differential of the function and make a double-periodic function.

Simon developed a quantum algorithm that efficiently solves the following problem [15].

*Problem 3.1.* Assume that there is a function $\phi : \{0,1\}^n \to \{0,1\}^n$ that satisfies $\phi(x \oplus s) = \phi(x)$ for some $s \in \{0,1\}^n$. Then, find $s$.

Simon's algorithm repeats a subroutine **SSub**. **SSub** operates a quantum circuit into which the quantum oracle of $\phi$ is integrated, measures the final quantum state, and outputs a vector $u \in \{0,1\}^n$ (Fig. 6). The distribution of the output $u$ is the same as uniform distribution on the set $\{u \in \{0,1\}^n | u \cdot s = 0\}$. We can find the orthogonal space of $s$ with high probability by repeating **SSub** $O(n)$ times, and then we can find $s$. For more details, see the original paper [15].

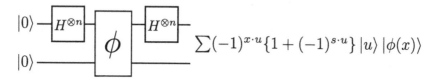

**Fig. 6.** Quantum circuit of **SSub**. $u$ runs over $\{0,1\}^n$. $x$ runs over a subset of $\{0,1\}^n$, which includes exactly one element of $\phi^{-1}(y)$ for $\forall y \in \phi(\{0,1\}^n)$.

Existing quantum attacks against symmetric key schemes using Simon's algorithm are performed with the following steps:

1. Make a periodic function $\phi$ with a period $s$ exploiting internal structures of a target scheme, here $s$ includes secret information. Sometimes $s$ itself is the secret key of the scheme.
2. Apply Simon's algorithm to $\phi$ and recover the secret information $s$.

In Simon's original paper, the additional condition

$$\phi(x) = \phi(y) \Rightarrow x = y \text{ or } y = x \oplus s \tag{1}$$

is assumed. This condition seems artificial and is rarely satisfied by functions constructed from symmetric key schemes. Kaplan et al. have overcome this problem. They proved that we can efficiently calculate $s$ by increasing the number of repetitions of **SSub** even if $\phi$ does not satisfy this condition, if $\epsilon(\phi; s)$, which indicates to what extent $\phi$ is far from the condition (1), is sufficiently small [5].

**Proposition 3.1. (Simon [15], Kaplan et al. [5]).** *Assume that there exists a positive number $p_0 < 1$, and $\epsilon(\phi, s) \le p_0$ is satisfied. Then we can find $s$ with probability at least $1 - (2(\frac{1+p_0}{2})^c)^n$ by repeating **SSub** $cn$ times.*

In the above arguments, we considered only functions that have domain sizes equal to their codomain size, but the above arguments are applicable to functions of arbitrary domain and codomain sizes.

**Our Tool.** In this paper, we seek to apply Simon's algorithm more broadly than those by Kaplan et al. Consider the following problem for periodic functions *up to constant addition.*

*Problem 3.2.* Assume that there is a function $\phi : \{0,1\}^n \to \{0,1\}^n$ and vectors $s, \gamma \in \{0,1\}^n$ that satisfy $\phi(x \oplus s) = \phi(x) \oplus \gamma$ for $\forall x \in \{0,1\}^n$. Then, find $s$ and $\gamma$.

We focus on the differential of $\phi$ to solve this problem. Take $u \in \{0,1\}^n$ arbitrarily. Then for $\forall w \in Span(s, u)$ and $\forall x \in \{0,1\}^n$,

$$(\Delta_u \phi)(x \oplus w) = (\Delta_u \phi)(x)$$

holds. In other words, $\Delta_u \phi$ is a double-periodic function with a double period $\{s, u\}$. More generally, consider a function $\psi : \{0,1\}^n \to \{0,1\}^n$ that has a double period $s, u \in \{0,1\}^n$, i.e. $\psi(x \oplus w) = \psi(x)$ holds for $\forall w \in Span(s, u)$ and $\forall x \in \{0,1\}^n$. When we operate **SSub** once for $\psi$, **SSub** outputs a vector that is orthogonal to $Span(s, u)$. We can prove the following proposition similarly as Proposition 3.1.

**Proposition 3.2.** *Let $\psi : \{0,1\}^n \to \{0,1\}^n$ be a function that has a double period $s, u \in \{0,1\}^n$. Assume that there exists a positive number $p_0 < 1$, and $\epsilon(\psi; s, u) \le p_0$ is satisfied. Then we can obtain $s$ and $u$ with probability at least $1 - (2(\frac{1+p_0}{2})^c)^n$, by operating **SSub** $cn$ times.*

Applying the above proposition for $\Delta_u \phi$, we obtain the following proposition, which can be used to solve Problem 2.

**Proposition 3.3.** *Assume that there exist $u \in \{0,1\}^n$ and a positive number $p_0 < 1$, and $\epsilon(\Delta_u \phi; s, u) \le p_0$ is satisfied. Then we can obtain $s$ and $\gamma$ with probability at least $1 - (2(\frac{1+p_0}{2})^c)^n$, by operating **SSub** $cn$ times.*

This proposition is our main technical tool, and we will utilize it later for performing related-key attacks.

# 4    Previous Work on Quantum Attacks Against Even-Mansour Schemes

In this section, we overview two quantum attacks: the key recovery attack against Even-Mansour cipher by Kuwakado and Morii [8], and the quantum slide attack against iterated Even-Mansour ciphers the round keys of which are all the same by Kaplan et al. [5].

Among recent attacks with quantum computers, those by Kuwakado and Morii [7,8], and Kaplan et al. [5], are such that an adversary can query encryption oracles in an arbitrary quantum superposition of the inputs. As is pointed out by Kaplan et al. [5], these attacks first construct a function with a period that contains secret information by exploiting the internal structure of cryptographic schemes, and apply Simon's algorithm [15] to efficiently calculate the period. In the following, $P$ denotes a public random permutation on $\{0,1\}^n$.

## 4.1    Key Recovery Attack Against Even-Mansour Cipher

Even-Mansour cipher $E^P_{k_1,k_2}$ is the cipher that is defined as

$$E^P_{k_1,k_2}(x) = P(x \oplus k_1) \oplus k_2,$$

where $(k_1, k_2)$ is the secret key. Let $D^P_{k_1,k_2}$ denote the decryption. Even and Mansour showed that an adversary has to query oracles at least $2^{n/2}$ times to recover keys when allowed to access oracles $P, P^{-1}, E^P_{k_1,k_2}$, and $D^P_{k_1,k_2}$ [2]. In contrast, Kuwakado and Morii showed that an adversary can recover the key of an Even-Mansour cipher in polynomial time, when allowed to access the quantum oracle $E^P_{k_1,k_2}$ [8]. The overview of the attack is as follows.

Define $f : \{0,1\}^n \to \{0,1\}^n$ as $f(x) = E^P_{k_1,k_2}(x) \oplus P(x)$. Then $f(x) = P(x \oplus k_1) \oplus P(x) \oplus k_2$ holds and $f$ has a period $k_1$. Hence we can find $k_1$ efficiently by using Simon's algorithm. Moreover, we can calculate $k_2$ with negligible costs, since $E^P_{k_1,k_2}(x) \oplus P(x \oplus k_1) = P(x \oplus k_1) \oplus k_2 \oplus P(x \oplus k_1) = k_2$ holds.

## 4.2    Quantum Slide Attack

Let $E_k$ be a cipher constructed by composing a function $F_k$ iteratively, where $k$ is the secret key. In classical settings, the slide attack is an attack against ciphers that have an iterative structure, such as $E_k$, with exponential time complexity. Let $P_k(x)$ denote $P(x \oplus k)$. Kaplan et al. showed that an adversary with a quantum computer can recover the key of an iterated Even-Mansour cipher the round keys of which are all the same, $E^P_k(x) = (P_k \circ P_k \circ \cdots \circ P_k)(x) \oplus k$, in polynomial time by applying a slide attack and Simon's algorithm [5]. They assumed that an adversary is allowed to access quantum oracle $E^P_k$. Define $f : \{0,1\}^{n+1} \to \{0,1\}^n$ as

$$f(b\|x) = \begin{cases} P(E^P_k(x)) \oplus x & (b = 0), \\ E^P_k(P(x)) \oplus x & (b = 1), \end{cases}$$

where $b \in \{0,1\}, x \in \{0,1\}^n$. The function $f$ can be implemented on efficient quantum circuits [5]. For arbitrary $x \in \{0,1\}^n$, we have

$$
\begin{aligned}
f(0\|x) &= P(E_k^P(x)) \oplus x \\
&= P(E_k^P(x)) \oplus k \oplus (x \oplus k) \\
&= E_k^P(P(x \oplus k)) \oplus (x \oplus k) \\
&= f(1\|(x \oplus k)) \\
&= f((0\|x) \oplus (1\|k)),
\end{aligned}
$$

thus $f$ has a period $1\|k$. Hence we can recover $k$ with Simon's algorithm (Fig. 7).

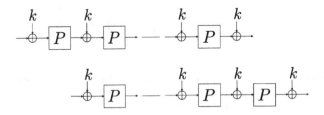

**Fig. 7.** Slide attack against iterated Even-Mansour cipher round keys of which are all the same.

*Remark 4.1.* The argument in Sect. 4.1 is not actually complete. Strictly speaking, we should evaluate $\epsilon(f; k_1)$ and apply Proposition 3.1 for calculating the period $k_1$ of $f$. Kaplan et al. strictly argued these problems in their paper [5] and showed that $\epsilon(f; k_1) < 1/2$ holds for $P$ without any second-order differential with probability greater than $1/2$. Similarly, they strictly argued these problems also for the quantum slide attack in Sect. 4.2.

## 5    Quantum Related-Key Attack

Let $E_k$ be a symmetric key block cipher. Assume an adversary is allowed to access (classical or quantum) oracles $E_k, E_{k'}$, where $k$ and $k'$ are different secret keys. A related-key attack is an attack in which the adversary does not know $k$ and $k'$ themselves, but knows a relationship that $k$ and $k'$ satisfy. Denote $P$ an $n$-bit public random permutation. Iterated Even-Mansour $E^P(x; k_1, k_2, \ldots, k_i)$ is defined as

$$
E^P(x; k_1, k_2, \ldots, k_i) = (P_{k_{i-1}} \circ \cdots \circ P_{k_2} \circ P_{k_1})(x) \oplus k_i,
$$

where $k_1, k_2, \ldots, k_i \in \{0,1\}^n$ are the secret keys and $P_k = P(x \oplus k)$. In the following, we assume that two keys $k = (k_1, k_2, \ldots, k_i), k' = (k_1', k_2', \ldots, k_i')$ satisfy the relationship $k_l' = k_{l+1}$ $(1 \le l \le i-1)$. For $i = 2$, an iterated Even-Mansour cipher corresponds to an original Even-Mansour cipher and we can perform the polynomial time attack described above, so we assume $i \ge 3$ in the following. We also assume that an adversary can query a superposition of inputs to quantum oracles.

## 5.1 Partial Key Recovery

This section shows that an adversary with a quantum computer can recover partial keys $k_1$ and $k_{i+1}$, if allowed to access quantum oracles $E^P(x; k_1, k_2, \ldots, k_i)$, $E^P(x; k_2, k_3, \ldots, k_{i+1})$. We abbreviate $E^P(x; k_1, k_2, \ldots, k_i)$ and $E^P(x; k_2, k_3, \ldots, k_{i+1})$ as $E_1(x)$ and $E_2(x)$, respectively (Fig. 8).

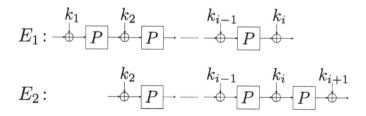

**Fig. 8.** Related-key attack considered in this paper.

Before describing the main claim in this section, we mention the security of $E_1$ and $E_2$. To prove the above claim, we construct a function $g$ that is periodic up to constant addition using $E_1, E_2, P$, and apply Proposition 3.3 to $\Delta_u g$. Here, $u$ is a fixed vector in $\{0, 1\}^{n+1}$. To apply Proposition 3.3, it is necessary to bound $\epsilon(\Delta_u g; s, u)$, where $s$ is the period of $g$. For bounding $\epsilon(\Delta_u g; s, u)$, we assume that $E_1$ and $E_2$ do not have specific linear dependencies that hold with high probability, i.e., the following condition is satisfied:

There are no $t_0, u_0 \in \{0, 1\}^n \setminus \{0^n, k_1\}$ that satisfy

$$\Pr_x[\Delta_{t_0}(\Delta_{u_0}(P \circ E_1))(x) = 0] \geq 1/4, \text{ or}$$
$$\Pr_x[\Delta_{t_0}(\Delta_{u_0}(E_2 \circ P))(x) = 0] \geq 1/4, \text{ or}$$
$$\Pr_x[\Delta_{u_0}(P \circ E_1)(x) = \Delta_{u_0}(E_2 \circ P)(x \oplus t_0)] \geq 1/4.$$

$E_1$ and $E_2$ are actually insecure if one of the above linear condition holds, regardless of whether a quantum computer exists or not. In addition, this condition is only satisfied with negligible probability, since the permutation $P$ is a random permutation.

The main claim in this section is as follows.

*Claim.* Let $P$ be an $n$-bit public random permutation. An adversary can recover $k_1$ and $k_{i+1}$ efficiently if allowed to access quantum oracles $E^P(x; k_1, k_2, \ldots, k_i)$, $E^P(x; k_2, k_3, \ldots, k_{i+1})$.

Define $g : \{0, 1\}^{n+1} \rightarrow \{0, 1\}^n$ as

$$g(b\|x) = \begin{cases} P(E_1(x)) \oplus x & (b = 0), \\ E_2(P(x)) \oplus x & (b = 1). \end{cases}$$

Before proving the above claim, we show the following lemma.

**Lemma 5.1.** *g is a periodic function with a period* $1\|k_1$ *up to constant addition. That is, the following equation holds for* $\forall b \in \{0,1\}, \forall x \in \{0,1\}^n$:

$$g((b\|x) \oplus (1\|k_1)) = g(b\|x) \oplus k_1 \oplus k_{i+1}.$$

*Proof.* For $x \in \{0,1\}^n$, we have

$$
\begin{aligned}
g(0\|x) &= P(E^P(x; k_1, k_2, \ldots, k_i)) \oplus x \\
&= E^P(P(x \oplus k_1); k_2, k_3, \ldots, k_{i+1}) \oplus k_{i+1} \oplus x \\
&= E^P(P(x \oplus k_1); k_2, k_3, \ldots, k_{i+1}) \\
&\qquad \oplus (x \oplus k_1) \oplus (k_1 \oplus k_{i+1}) \\
&= g(1\|(x \oplus k_1)) \oplus (k_1 \oplus k_{i+1}),
\end{aligned}
$$

which implies the claim of the lemma. □

Next, we prove the claim. Take $u_0 \in \{0,1\}^n \setminus \{0^n\}$ arbitrarily, and let $u$ be $0\|u_0$. We prove $\epsilon(\Delta_u g; 1\|k_1, u) < 1/2$ holds by contradiction. If we assume $\epsilon(\Delta_u g; 1\|k_1, u) \geq 1/2$ holds, then there exist $b_0 \in \{0,1\}$, $t_0 \in \{0,1\}^n$ that satisfy $b_0\|t_0 \in \{0,1\}^{n+1} \setminus Span((1\|k_1), u)$ and

$$\mathrm{Pr}_{b,x}[\Delta_u g((b\|x) \oplus (b_0\|t_0)) = \Delta_u g(b\|x)] \geq 1/2$$

holds. Therefore, we have

$$
\begin{aligned}
\mathrm{Pr}_x[\Delta_u g((0\|x) \oplus (b_0\|t_0)) &= \Delta_u g(0\|x)] \\
+ \mathrm{Pr}_x[\Delta_u g((1\|x) \oplus (b_0\|t_0)) &= \Delta_u g(1\|x)] \geq 1/2.
\end{aligned}
$$

If $b_0 = 0$, this implies that

$$
\begin{aligned}
\mathrm{Pr}_x[\Delta_{t_0}(\Delta_{u_0}(P \circ E_1))(x) = 0] \geq 1/4, \text{ or} \\
\mathrm{Pr}_x[\Delta_{t_0}(\Delta_{u_0}(E_2 \circ P))(x) = 0] \geq 1/4
\end{aligned}
$$

holds, which does not occur in our assumption. Moreover, if $b_0 = 1$ we have

$$
\begin{aligned}
\mathrm{Pr}_x[\Delta_{u_0}(E_2 \circ P)(x \oplus t_0) &= \Delta_{u_0}(P \circ E_1)(x)] \\
+ \mathrm{Pr}_x[\Delta_{u_0}(P \circ E_1)(x \oplus t_0) &= \Delta_{u_0}(E_2 \circ P)(x)] \geq 1/2,
\end{aligned}
$$

which implies

$$\mathrm{Pr}_x[\Delta_{u_0}(P \circ E_1)(x) = \Delta_{u_0}(E_2 \circ P)(x \oplus t_0)] \geq 1/4,$$

but this does not occur in our assumption. Thus, we have $\epsilon(\Delta_u g; 1\|k_1, u) < 1/2$. Moreover, $g$ can be implemented on the quantum circuit in Fig. 9. In accordance with the above arguments and Lemma 5.1, we can apply Proposition 3.3 to $g$. Thus, we can recover $k_1$ and $k_{i+1}$ efficiently, and the claim holds.

The algorithm **AlgPartial** that recovers subkeys $k_1, k_{i+1}$ is summarized below:

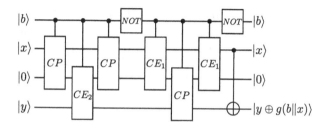

**Fig. 9.** Quantum circuit on which $g$ is implemented. Note that gate $CE_i$ ($i = 1, 2$) is constructed from oracle $E_i$ and $CCNOT$ gate as in Fig. 4.

## Algorithm **AlgPartial**

1. Choose $u_0 \in \{0, 1\}^n \setminus \{0^n\}$ arbitrarily, and let $u$ be $0 \| u_0$.
2. Construct the circuit that operates **SSub** for $\Delta_u g$.
3. Set $L$ as an empty list.
4. Repeat Step 5 while $|L| < n - 1$:
5. Operate **SSub** once and obtain a vector $v$ in $\{0, 1\}^{n+1}$. If $|L| = 0$ or $v$ is orthogonal to all the vectors in $L$, then add $v$ to $L$.
6. Find the vector space $V \subset \{0, 1\}^{n+1}$ spanned by the vectors that are orthogonal to all the elements in $L$ with a classical computer.
7. Find $1 \| k_1$ from $V$, and calculate $k_{i+1}$, and output $k_1, k_{i+1}$.

In the above algorithm, we can easily find $1 \| k_1$ from $V$ since $V = Span(u, 1 \| k_1)$. Moreover, we can easily calculate $k_{i+1}$ if we find $k_1$, since we have $k_{i+1} = g((b \| x) \oplus (1 \| k_1)) \oplus g(b \| x) \oplus k_1$ for $\forall b \in \{0, 1\}, \forall x \in \{0, 1\}^n$ by Lemma 5.1. This algorithm runs in polynomial time, and outputs the correct $k_1, k_{i+1}$ with high probability by Proposition 3.3.

### 5.2   Full Key Recovery for Two-Round Even-Mansour Cipher

This section shows that an adversary can recover all the keys of Two-round Even-Mansour cipher.

*Claim.* Let $P$ be an $n$-bit public random permutation. Suppose that $P$ has no second-order differential with a probability greater than $1/2$, and assume the same condition as we assumed for the claim in Sect. 5.1. Then, an adversary can recover $k_1, k_2, k_3, k_4$ in polynomial time if allowed to access quantum oracles $E^P(x; k_1, k_2, k_3)$, $E^P(x; k_2, k_3, k_4)$.

*Remark 5.1.* The condition in which $P$ has no second-order differential with probability greater than $1/2$ is necessary for applying the quantum key recovery attack against the Even-Mansour cipher (see Remark 4.1).

First, we can recover $k_1$ and $k_4$ in polynomial time by applying the algorithm **AlgPartial**. Then, we can construct an efficient quantum circuit on which

$E^P(x; k_2, k_3)$ is implemented, since we have $E^P(x; k_2, k_3) = E^P(P^{-1}(x) \oplus k_1; k_1, k_2, k_3)$. Hence we can apply the attack in Sect. 4.1 and obtain $k_2$ and $k_3$.

Figure 10 illustrates the quantum circuit on which $E^P(x; k_2, k_3)$ is implemented, where we abbreviate $E^P(x; k_1, k_2, k_3)$ and $E^P(x; k_2, k_3)$ as $E_1$ and $E_3$, respectively.

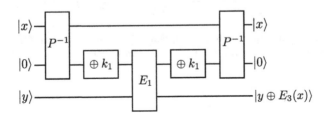

**Fig. 10.** Quantum circuit on which $E_3(x) = E^P(x; k_2, k_3)$ is implemented.

The algorithm **AlgFull** that recovers full keys is summarized below:

Algorithm **AlgFull**

1. Call **AlgPartial** and obtain $k_1$ and $k_4$.
2. Construct the circuit that operates **SSub** for $E^P(x; k_2, k_3) \oplus P(x)$ (Fig. 11).
3. Set $L$ as an empty list.
4. Repeat Step 5 while $|L| < n - 1$:
5. Operate **SSub** once and obtain a vector $v$ in $\{0, 1\}^n$. If $|L| = 0$ or $v$ is orthogonal to all the vectors in $L$, then add $v$ to $L$.
6. Find the vector space $V \subset \{0, 1\}^n$ spanned by the vectors that are orthogonal to all the elements in $L$ with a classical computer.
7. Find $k_2$ from $V$, calculate $k_3$, and output $k_1, k_2, k_3, k_4$.

In the above algorithm, we can easily find $k_2$ from $V$ since $V = \{0, k_2\}$. Moreover, we can easily calculate $k_3$ after we find $k_2$, since we have $k_3 = E^P(x; k_2, k_3) \oplus P(x \oplus k_2)$ for $\forall x \in \{0, 1\}^n$. This algorithm runs in polynomial time, and outputs correct $k_1, k_2, k_3, k_4$ with high probability.

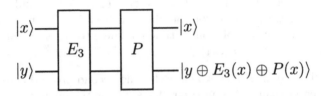

**Fig. 11.** Quantum circuit on which $E^P(x; k_2, k_3) \oplus P(x)$ is implemented.

*Remark 5.2.* Note that, if we want to efficiently recover full keys of $r$-round iterated Even-Mansour ciphers with only two oracles $E^P(x; k_1, k_2, \ldots, k_{r+1})$, $E^P(x; k_2, k_3, \ldots, k_{r+2})$ for $r \geq 3$ similarly to we did for $r = 2$, we need an efficient algorithm that recovers full keys of a $(r-1)$-round iterated Even-Mansour cipher with only *one* oracle $E^P(x; k_2, k_3, \ldots, k_{r+1})$. Since no such algorithm is known to exist, we can not claim that our algorithm can also be used to recover full keys for $r \geq 3$. On the other hand, if we are allowed to access $r$ quantum oracles, e.g. $E_1 := E^P(x; k_1, k_2, \ldots, k_{r+1})$, $E_2 := E^P(x; k_2, k_3, \ldots, k_{r+2}), \ldots, E_r := E^P(x; k_r, k_{r+1}, \ldots, k_{2r})$, and their inverses, then we can efficiently recover full keys $k_1, k_2, \ldots, k_{2r}$ as follows. For $1 \leq c \leq r - 1$, operate **AlgPartial** using two oracles $E_c$ and $E_{c+1}$ to recover $k_c, k_{c+r+1}$. Then we obtain partial keys $k_1, \ldots, k_{r-1}, k_{r+2}, \ldots, k_r$, and can simulate a quantum oracle $E^P(x; k_r, k_{r+1})$. Thus, we can also recover $k_r, k_{r+1}$ by applying the algorithm in Sect. 4.1. Eventually, we efficiently recover full keys $k_1, k_2, \ldots, k_{2r}$.

## 5.3   Estimating Time Complexity of AlgFull

In this section, we estimate the time complexity of **AlgFull** concretely under reasonable assumptions. In particular, we show that an adversary with a quantum computer can recover all the keys $k_1, k_2, k_3, k_4$ of a 128-bit two-round Even-Mansour cipher with a time complexity $2^{14}$ and probability higher than 99.9%.

Firstly, we describe our assumptions for time complexity of quantum operations. We treat an $n$-bit operation or an $(n+1)$-bit operation as a unit operation. That is, we regard the following quantum gates as taking a unit time:

- $(n + 1)$-bit Hadamard transformation $H^{\otimes n+1}$
- the XOR operation on two $n$-bit strings
- the encryption oracle $E : |x\rangle|y\rangle \mapsto |x\rangle|y \oplus E(x)\rangle$ since $E$ essentially operates an $n$-bit operation, although this is a $2n$-bit quantum gate
- $P$ and $CP$, where $CP$ is the controlled $P$ gate

We count the number of unit operations performed throughout the entire algorithm. We also assume that the time consumed by a unit operation is less than or equals to the time needed to perform encryption once followed by the classical convention. Finally, we estimate the upper bound of the time complexity of a quantum algorithm by the number of unit operations in the quantum circuit on which the algorithm is implemented, multiplied by the time needed to perform encryption once. We ignore the cost of performing 1-bit operations on quantum circuits, since these costs are negligible compared with the cost needed to operate one encryption. Moreover, solving linear equations in a classical computer requires less time than performing a few encryptions, since linear equations are solved only once or twice. Let $n = 128$ and we consider a 128-bit 2-round iterated Even-Mansour cipher in the following.

First, we estimate the time complexity of **AlgPartial**, which outputs $k_1$ and $k_4$. **AlgPartial** operates **SSub** on the function $\Delta_u g$ repeatedly, i.e., runs the circuit in Fig. 6 in which $\phi$ is replaced by $\Delta_u g$ and performs measurement over and over. Figure 9, shows that 13 operations are performed in calculating $g$ once. Here, we note that 3 operations are performed in calculating $CE_1$ or $CE_2$ (see Fig. 4). Thus, we can see that 44 operations are performed in calculating $\Delta_u g$ from Fig. 5. Eventually, 46 unit operations are performed during the subroutine **SSub** (see Fig. 6). **AlgPartial** repeats **SSub** until $|L|$, the number of elements in $L$, increases to 127. The probability that $|L|$ becomes 127 (which is the probability that **AlgPartial** succeeds at recovering $k_1$ and $k_4$) after repeating **SSub** for $129 \cdot c$ times is at least $1 - (2(\frac{1+p_0}{2})^c)^{129}$ by Proposition 3.3. $p_0$ can be set to $1/2$ from the arguments in Sect. 4.1. If we substitute 3 for $c$, then $(2(\frac{1+p_0}{2})^c)^{129} = (2(\frac{1+1/2}{2})^3)^{129} \le 3.1 \times 10^{-10}$ holds. Therefore, $|L|$ becomes 127 with a probability more than 99.9% and we can recover $k_1, k_4$ if **SSub** is repeated $3 \cdot 129$ times, and the total number of unit operations performed through **AlgPartial** is $46 \cdot 3 \cdot 129 \approx 2^{14}$.

Next, we estimate the total time complexity of **AlgFull**. **AlgFull** first operates **AlgPartial** to obtain $k_1, k_4$, the time complexity of which is $2^{14}$ from the above arguments. After that, **Algfull** operates **SSub** on the function $E^P(x; k_2, k_3) \oplus P(x)$ repeatedly to obtain $k_2, k_3$. Figures 10 and 11 show that unit operations are performed 6 times in calculating $E(x; k_2, k_3) \oplus P(x)$. Thus, 8 unit operations are performed during the subroutine **SSub**. Similarly to **AlgPartial**, $3 \cdot 128$ operations of **SSub** will recover $k_2$ and $k_3$ with probability more than 99.9%. Eventually, the time complexity of **AlgFull** becomes $(46+8) \cdot 3 \cdot 128 \approx 2^{14}$. Therefore **AlgFull** recovers $k_1, k_2, k_3, k_4$ with a time complexity $2^{14}$ and probability more than 99.9%.

*Remark 5.3.* Here we give a remark about qubits needed to run **AlgFull**. We note that the quantum circuit of **SSub** on $\Delta_u g$ and $E_3$ can be implemented using $(6n + 2)$-qubits and $3n$-qubits, respectively, and thus we can run **AlgFull** with $(5n+2)$-qubits. This is because quantum circuits illustrated above reset all ancilla qubits, and we can reuse the ancilla qubits in each quantum circuit. Efficient reuse of ancilla qubits increase time complexity a little since swap of qubits needs three $CCNOT$ gates (see Fig. 12), however, increased amount of complexity is negligible. For example, in Fig. 9, both $CE_1$ and $CE_2$ need additional $n$-qubits (see Fig. 4), but we can reuse them and $g$ can be implemented with $(4n + 1)$-qubits. In particular, **AlgFull** can be implemented with 770-qubits when $n = 128$.

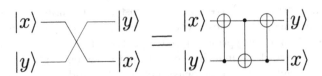

**Fig. 12.** Swap of qubits.

# 6   Conclusion

This paper has shown that there exists an algorithm that performs a related-key attack against an iterated Even-Mansour cipher, extending the quantum slide attack by Kaplan et al. In particular, we showed that the algorithm can recover all the keys of a two-round Even-Mansour cipher. For example, the attack against a 128-bit two-round Even-Mansour cipher succeeds with a time complexity of $2^{14}$ and a negligible memory complexity under reasonable assumptions. This can be regarded as a partial answer to the open problem of whether there exists a quantum algorithm that efficiently recovers keys of iterated Even-Mansour ciphers. We introduced a technical tool extending Simon's original algorithm and used it for our related-key attack. The advantage of our tool is that it can find the period of a function that is periodic up to a constant addition. A future task is to find algorithms that can recover keys of iterated Even-Mansour ciphers in weaker related-key conditions or a single-key setting.

# References

1. Chen, S., Steinberger, J.P.: Tight security bounds for key-alternating ciphers. IACR Cryptology ePrint Archive 2013, 222 (2013). http://eprint.iacr.org/2013/222
2. Even, S., Mansour, Y.: A construction of a cipher from a single pseudorandom permutation. J. Cryptology **10**(3), 151–162 (1997). https://doi.org/10.1007/s001459900025
3. Grover, L.K.: A fast quantum mechanical algorithm for database search. In: Proceedings of the Twenty-Eighth Annual ACM Symposium on Theory of Computing. STOC 1996, NY, USA, pp. 212–219 (1996). http://doi.acm.org/10.1145/237814.237866
4. Kaplan, M.: Quantum attacks against iterated block ciphers. CoRR abs/1410.1434 (2014). http://arxiv.org/abs/1410.1434
5. Kaplan, M., Leurent, G., Leverrier, A., Naya-Plasencia, M.: Breaking symmetric cryptosystems using quantum period finding. In: Proceedings of the Advances in Cryptology - CRYPTO 2016–36th Annual International Cryptology Conference, Part II, Santa Barbara, CA, USA, August 14–18, 2016, pp. 207–237 (2016). http://dx.doi.org/10.1007/978-3-662-53008-5_8
6. Kaplan, M., Leurent, G., Leverrier, A., Naya-Plasencia, M.: Quantum differential and linear cryptanalysis. IACR Trans. Symmetric Cryptol. **2016**(1), 71–94 (2016). http://tosc.iacr.org/index.php/ToSC/article/view/536
7. Kuwakado, H., Morii, M.: Quantum distinguisher between the 3-round Feistel cipher and the random permutation. In: Proceedings of the IEEE International Symposium on Information Theory, ISIT 13–18, 2010, Austin, Texas, USA, pp. 2682–2685 (2010). http://dx.doi.org/10.1109/ISIT.2010.5513654
8. Kuwakado, H., Morii, M.: Security on the quantum-type Even-Mansour cipher. In: Proceedings of the International Symposium on Information Theory and its Applications, ISITA 2012, Honolulu, HI, USA, October 28–31, 2012. pp. 312–316 (2012). http://ieeexplore.ieee.org/document/6400943/
9. Luby, M., Rackoff, C.: How to construct pseudo-random permutations from pseudo-random functions (abstract). In: Proceedings of the Advances in Cryptology - CRYPTO 1985, Santa Barbara, California, USA, August 18–22, 1985, p. 447 (1985). https://doi.org/10.1007/3-540-39799-X_34

10. NIST: Advanced encryption standard (AES) FIPS 197 (2001)
11. NIST: Submission requirements and evaluation criteria for the post-quantum cryptography standardization process (2016)
12. Rötteler, M., Steinwandt, R.: A note on quantum related-key attacks. Inf. Process. Lett. **115**(1), 40–44 (2015). http://dx.doi.org/10.1016/j.ipl.2014.08.009
13. Santoli, T., Schaffner, C.: Using Simon's algorithm to attack symmetric-key cryptographic primitives. Quantum Inf. Comput. **17**(1&2), 65–78 (2017). http://www.rintonpress.com/xxqic17/qic-17-12/0065-0078.pdf
14. Shor, P.W.: Polynomial-time algorithms for prime factorization and discrete logarithms on a quantum computer. SIAM J. Comput. **26**(5), 1484–1509 (1997). http://dx.doi.org/10.1137/S0097539795293172
15. Simon, D.R.: On the power of quantum computation. SIAM J. Comput. **26**(5), 1474–1483 (1997). http://dx.doi.org/10.1137/S0097539796298637
16. Treger, J., Patarin, J.: Generic attacks on Feistel networks with internal permutations. In: Proceedings of the Progress in Cryptology - AFRICACRYPT 2009, Second International Conference on Cryptology in Africa, Gammarth, Tunisia, June 21–25, 2009, pp. 41–59 (2009). http://dx.doi.org/10.1007/978-3-642-02384-2_4

# The Beauty and the Beasts—The Hard Cases in LLL Reduction

Saed Alsayigh[1]([⊠]), Jintai Ding[1], Tsuyoshi Takagi[2,3], and Yuntao Wang[4]

[1] Department of Mathematical Sciences, University of Cincinnati, Cincinnati, USA
alsayisd@mail.uc.edu, jintai.ding@gmail.com
[2] Institute of Mathematics for Industry, Kyushu University, Fukuoka, Japan
takagi@imi.kyushu-u.ac.jp
[3] CREST, Japan Science and Technology Agency, Kawaguchi, Japan
[4] Graduate School of Mathematics, Kyushu University, Fukuoka, Japan
y-wang@math.kyushu-u.ac.jp

**Abstract.** In this paper, we will systematically study who indeed are the hard lattice cases in LLL reduction. The "hard" cases here mean for their special geometric structures, with a comparatively high "failure probability" that LLL can not solve SVP even by using a powerful relaxation factor. We define the perfect lattice as the "Beauty", which is given by basis of vectors of the same length with the mutual angles of any two vectors to be exactly 60°. Simultaneously the "Beasts" lattice is defined as the lattice close to the Beauty lattice. There is a relatively high probability (e.g. 15.0% in 3 dimensions) that our "Beasts" bases can withstand the exact-arithmetic LLL reduction (relaxation factors $\delta$ close to 1), comparing to the probability (corresponding <0.01%) when apply same LLL on random bases from TU Darmstadt SVP Challenge. Our theoretical proof gives us a direct explanation of this phenomenon. Moreover, we give rational Beauty bases of 3 and 8 dimensions, an irrational Beauty bases of general high dimensions. We also give a general way to construct Beasts lattice bases from the Beauty ones. Experimental results show the Beasts bases derived from Beauty can withstand LLL reduction by a stable probability even for high dimensions. Our work in a way gives a simple and direct way to explain how to build a hard lattice in LLL reduction.

**Keywords:** Lattice · LLL reduction · Hard cases · Post-Quantum Cryptography

## 1 Introduction

As one of the compelling candidates in Post-Quantum Cryptography, Lattice-based cryptography is now a very hot topic due to all the versatile constructions based on the Learning With Errors (LWE) and the Ring Learning With Errors (RLWE) problems [10,17]. But to select a practical parameter, we must have a solid understanding on the hardness of the reduction algorithms. But as far

© Springer International Publishing AG 2017
S. Obana and K. Chida (Eds.): IWSEC 2017, LNCS 10418, pp. 19–35, 2017.
DOI: 10.1007/978-3-319-64200-0_2

as we know, now there is a clear gap between the theoretical estimation of the approximation factor and the case of experiments. By now, not much work has been done in this direction and this serious gap can be a real roadblock for us to move forward in this direction. However there are some of related works in other direction. These works aim to analyze the computational complexity of reduction algorithms in low dimensional bases, as in Semaev [18] and Nguyen, Stehlé [14] for more details. There are also some previous works on $\gamma$-unique SVP problem. Some practical evidence shows that unique SVP is potentially easier as $\gamma$ (the magnitude gap between the shortest and second independent shortest vector) becomes larger [5]. Much of the subsequent works concentrated on evaluating a more reasonable bound of $\gamma$, such that LLL reduction algorithm can derive a shortest vector successfully [8,11]. Oppositely, our work is to find "hard" cases, namely "Beasts", such that LLL can not find the shortest vector by a relatively high probability. In other words, our Beasts lattices give a potentiality to withstand a strong LLL reduction. Note that the reader should differentiate "hard" cases from the so-called "worst" cases concerning the computational complexity [1,14,16].

It is known that LLL can not guarantee a shortest vector even in the 3 dimensional lattices. In principle, when we do reduction to make the basis better and better, one reason we could not reach the best reduction is that in the LLL reduction process, we are essentially trying to do the best local reduction (2 vectors one time) to achieve the global reduction, which is very much related to local optimization and global optimization. Such a local method decides that there is a high probability that we will make the local decisions is not really right globally. What BKZ is doing is exactly to compensate such a defect, namely improve the global reduction by doing a better local reduction (instead of a local reduction in 2 dimension, a better reduction through searching in 3 or higher dimensions) [19]. For us, we want to find out what is really happening in such a local reduction. It turns out that the symmetry of the perfect lattice plays a key role here.

In this paper, we will open a new direction to look at this problem from a different angle, namely we will find out mathematically how we characterize the hard cases and explain from the point view of mathematical structure why they are hard. The reason behind is that we hope this will allow us first to fill the theoretical gap we mentioned above and further more this may give us new ideas on how to improve further the reduction algorithms. This is a direction which, we believe, was not explored before, and we do not know much about at the moment.

Our method is to start from low dimensional cases. Here through intuitive understanding and experiments, we realize that the key idea in low dimensions is related to the symmetry of the underlying lattice. By symmetry here, we mean the isometry group that keep the lattice invariant. We will first define a perfect lattice – bases vectors of 60° angles respectively with the same length, which is called "Beauty" in this paper. Then we can use this to explain that if we have a basis which is very close to the perfect lattice, which makes the decision to find the shortest very hard even with very high precision as the exact-arithmetic reduction. Namely there are many pretenders of "almost good basis" for the good basis, which comes from the weakness of selecting a non-optimal parameter $\delta$. This forms the barriers to find the good basis and therefore the shortest vector. Or even in more simple terms, there are many bases that could pass the LLL criterion to be a reduced basis. The "Beasts", namely the really hard cases, are the ones very near to the Beauty lattices.

It is practically impossible (in terms of probability) to randomly sample a good basis with the same length and close to 60° simultaneously, from the point of distribution. For this, we need some form of good probability experiments. We give a thorough analysis of 3 dimensional "Beauty" and "Beasts", which illuminate us how to construct higher dimensional cases. In experiments, we reduce our Beasts lattice bases using the exact-arithmetic LLL in NTL library. In our implementations, we consider the effects of some variable parameters of our constructed Beasts bases and LLL. Under the same condition, we also compare the failure probability for NTL rational LLL when it reduces random lattice bases from Darmstadt SVP Challenge. The experimental results show that our "Beasts" bases can keep a tough resistance to strong LLL (with relaxation factor $\delta$ close to 1), comparing with the random bases.

The paper is organized as follows. Section 2 covers notation and background on lattice and reduction algorithms. We give an explicit definition of Beauty and Beasts lattices in Sect. 3. In Sect. 4, the structures of the Beauty and the Beasts bases on 3 dimensional lattices are proposed, including the main theorem proof and experimental results. The exploratory structure of the Beauty and the Beasts bases for higher dimensional lattices and some experimental analysis are presented in Sect. 5. Finally some concluding remarks and future works are given in Section 6

## 2   Preliminaries

In this section we review some basic definitions and theorems related to some classical lattice algorithms.

### 2.1   Lattice Theory

Let linearly independent vectors set $(\mathbf{b}_1, \ldots, \mathbf{b}_n) \in \mathbb{R}^{n \times m}$ be a basis $B$ of lattice $L(\mathbf{b}_1, \ldots, \mathbf{b}_n) = \{\sum_{i=1}^{n} x_i \mathbf{b}_i, x_i \in \mathbb{Z}\}$. In our work, we use full-rank bases with row form vectors in lattice and we denote the $i$-th row vector of the basis by $B[i]$. The volume of $L$ is given by the volume of fundamental domain $\mathcal{F}(\mathbf{b}_1, \ldots, \mathbf{b}_n) = \{t_1 \mathbf{b}_1 + t_2 \mathbf{b}_2 + \cdots + t_n \mathbf{b}_n : 0 \leq t_i < 1\}$, which is equal to $\|\det(B)\|$. Generally if $B$ is a full-rank matrix and $U_i (i \in [1, \infty))$ are unimodular matrices, $U_i \cdot B$ gives infinitely many bases of $L(B)$ since $\det(U_i) = \pm 1$ give the same volume.

The Euclidean norm of a vector $\mathbf{b} \in \mathbb{R}^m$ is $\|\mathbf{b}\|$. The Gram-Schmidt Orthogonal (GSO) basis $(\mathbf{b}_1^*, \ldots, \mathbf{b}_n^*)$ is given by the following:

(a) $\mathbf{b}_1^* = \mathbf{b}_1$

(b) $\mathbf{b}_i^* = \mathbf{b}_i - \sum_{j=1}^{i-1} \mu_{ij} \mathbf{b}_j^*$ for all $2 \leq i \leq n$ where $\mu_{ij} = \frac{<\mathbf{b}_i, \mathbf{b}_j^*>}{\|\mathbf{b}_j^*\|^2} (1 \leq j < i \leq n)$

**The Gram-Schmidt Orthogonal (GSO) basis.** Let $(\mathbf{b}_1, \ldots, \mathbf{b}_n)$ be a basis of $\mathbb{R}^m$ and let $(\mathbf{b}_1^*, \ldots, \mathbf{b}_n^*)$ be its GSO basis then

(a) $< \mathbf{b}_i, \mathbf{b}_j^* >= 0 \quad \forall 1 \leq i < j \leq n.$

(b) $span(\mathbf{b}_1^*, \ldots, \mathbf{b}_k^*) = span(\mathbf{b}_1, \ldots, \mathbf{b}_k) \quad \forall 1 \leq k \leq n.$

(c) $\|\mathbf{b}_k^*\| \leq \|\mathbf{b}_k\| \quad \forall 1 \leq k \leq n.$

**Size-reduction.** A basis $(\mathbf{b}_1, \ldots, \mathbf{b}_d)$ is called size-reduced with factor $\eta \geq \frac{1}{2}$ if its GSO family satisfies $|\mu_{ij}| \leq \eta$ for all $1 \leq j < i \leq d$.

Here it's important to know that $\eta$ is usually $\frac{1}{2}$, but for the floating-point LLL one takes it at least slightly larger since the $\mu_{ij}$ will be known only approximately.

**$\delta$-reduction.** Let $(\mathbf{b}_1, \ldots, \mathbf{b}_n) \in \mathbb{R}_n^n$ be a basis of lattice $L$ and let $(\mathbf{b}_1^*, \ldots, \mathbf{b}_n^*)$ be its GSO basis then $(\mathbf{b}_1, \ldots, \mathbf{b}_n)$ is called $\delta$-reduced basis if it satisfies:

(1) $|\mu_{ij}| \leq \eta$ for all $1 \leq j < i \leq n$             (Size Condition)

(2) $\|\mathbf{b}_i^* + \mu_{i,i-1}\mathbf{b}_{i-1}^*\|^2 \geq \delta\|\mathbf{b}_{i-1}^*\|^2$ for all $2 \leq i \leq n$ where $\frac{1}{4} < \delta < 1$.   (Lovász Condition)

$\delta$ is called relaxation factor in LLL reduction algorithm.

**Minkowski's minima [13].** Let $L$ be a lattice with full-rank basis $(\mathbf{b}_1, \ldots, \mathbf{b}_n) \in \mathbb{R}^{n \times n}$. We denote the Euclidean norm of the shortest vector in $L$ as $\lambda_1(L)$. For all $1 \leq i \leq n$, Minkowski's $i$th minimum $\lambda_i(L)$ is defined as the minimum of $\max_{1 \leq j \leq i} \|\mathbf{b}_j\|$ over all $i$ linearly independent lattice vectors $(\mathbf{b}_1, \ldots, \mathbf{b}_n) \in L$.

**SVP and $\gamma$-unique SVP.** For a given basis $B \in \mathbb{R}^{n \times n}$, the Shortest Vector Problem (SVP) is to find the shortest non-zero vector in $L(B)$. It is called unique SVP, if $\lambda_1(L) \ll \lambda_2(L)$ is guaranteed in SVP. And the $\gamma$-unique SVP problem is scaling the bound by a positive multiple as $\gamma\lambda_1(L) < \lambda_2(L)$. The auxiliary condition can be seen as a bounded gap between the first Minkowski's minimum and the second Minkowski's minimum. It is known that if the gap is bigger, it is easier to find the shortest vector by a certain algorithm [5]. However, in our work we concentrate on constructing the hard bases with very small $\gamma$, such that by a high probability the LLL reduction can not find the shortest vector successfully.

## 2.2 Lattice Algorithms

**Lagrange's algorithm.** The Lagrange's algorithm can definitely solves the SVP in 2 dimensional lattice in polynomial time. Actually it finds a basis achieving the first two Minkowski's minima. In algorithmic principle the Lagrange's algorithm is similar to Euclids algorithm. Refer to [7] for more details.

**LLL reduction.** LLL reduction algorithm is a practical algorithm that is proved to terminate in a polynomial time and gives an $\delta$-reduced basis [9]. However that is proven when $\delta \in (\frac{1}{4}, 1)$ and in many applications they used $\eta$ slightly larger

---

**Algorithm 1.** LLL algorithm
___
**Input:** a basis $(\mathbf{b}_1, \ldots, \mathbf{b}_d)$ of L, and a constant $\delta \in (\frac{1}{4}, 1)$.
**Output:** the output basis $(\mathbf{b}_1, \ldots, \mathbf{b}_d)$ of L satisfies definition above for each $i$ from 2 to $d$.
1: $i \leftarrow 2$
2: **while** $i \leq d$ **do**
3:    $\mathbf{b}_i \leftarrow \mathbf{b}_i - \sum_{j=i-1}^{1} \lceil \mu_{i,j} \rfloor \mathbf{b}_j$
4:    **if** $\|\mathbf{b}_i^*\|^2 \geq (\delta - \mu_{i,i-1}^2)\|\mathbf{b}_{i-1}^*\|^2$ **then**
5:       $i \leftarrow i + 1$
6:    **else**
7:       $swap(\mathbf{b}_i, \mathbf{b}_{i-1})$
8:       $i \leftarrow \max\{2, i - 1\}$
9:    **end if**
10: **end while**

---

than $\frac{1}{2}$ to guarantee termination in a practical time. We use $\eta = \frac{1}{2}$ in our work. We present a simple implementation to LLL algorithm (Algorithm 1). $\lceil \cdot \rfloor$ denotes rounding a real number to its nearest integer.

Setting $\delta$ strictly smaller than 1 can guarantee a polynomial computational complexity of LLL, with respect to the magnitude of the initial basis and the dimension $n$. Also according to proof of [2], in the so-called "ideal" or "optimal" case of $\delta = 1$, LLL is still polynomial with respect to the magnitude of the basis, but it is still an open problem whether it is also polynomial in the dimension $n$. In our work we consider the general case with $\delta$ close to 1 but strictly smaller than 1.

Note that our work is easily confused from works in [3,14], which are trying to improve the LLL algorithm by using floating-point calculation or rounding technic, etc. We want to explore the hard cases for LLL from the geometrical structure of lattice bases, ignoring the efficiency of LLL so far. And also the new algorithm proposed in [18] is also a future work for us to modify our conjectures.

**Schnorr-Euchner's enumeration algorithm.** In 1994, Schnorr and Euchner proposed an enumeration algorithm to search the shortest vector of a lattice [19], which runs in exponential time and the cost is no more than $2^{O(n^2)}$. We denote it by "ENUM" in this paper. ENUM is the most efficient one in practice that can find the shortest vector successively in 100% but very heavy in high dimensions. There are some improvements for it as in [6]. However, we won't describe the details about ENUM here, because in our experiments we just modify if the LLL can produce a shortest vector by performing ENUM on the LLL-reduced basis.

## 3    The Beauty and the Beasts

**Definition of Beauty Lattice.** Let $B \in \mathbb{R}^{n \times n}$ be a full-rank basis then we say $L(B)$ is a *Beauty lattice* if its basis fulfils these two properties simultaneously:

1. its vectors are of the same length;
2. the angle between any two basis vectors is $60°$.

Example: In $\mathbb{R}^3$, the lattice generated by

$$B = \begin{pmatrix} 1 & 1 & 0 \\ 0 & 1 & 1 \\ 1 & 0 & 1 \end{pmatrix}$$

is a Beauty lattice.

The corresponding basis $B$ is called *Beauty basis*. In the following contents, we denoted the primitive $n$ dimensional Beauty bases by $Beauty_n$ if the integer components in bases vectors are 1. We can get infinite Beauty bases by multiplying any $P \in \mathbb{R}$ by $Beauty_n$. We can see the Beauty lattice in $\mathbb{R}^2$ graphically in Fig. 1.

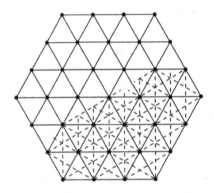

**Fig. 1.** The structure of Beauty lattices in $\mathbb{R}^2$.

It is folklore that for the symmetric property, the magnitudes of such basis vectors are all as same as the Minkowski's first minimum. In addition, the Beauty bases are already LLL reduced, namely the LLL algorithm will never fail to get the shortest vector on Beauty lattices.

Moreover, experiments show that if the first shortest vector is much shorter than the second one, then the lattice algorithms as LLL will succeed to reach the shortest vector with a much higher possibility [5]. Therefore we can conclude that in the low dimensions space, hard lattice or what we called the *Beast lattice* exist very close to the Beauty one.

**Definition of Beast Lattice.** A lattice $L(B)$ is called a *Beast lattice* if its basis vectors have the following two properties:

1. they are almost of the same length;
2. the angle between any two basis vectors is almost 60°.

We define the $n$ dimensional *Beasts basis* by denotion $Beasts_n$, which is generated from $Beauty_n$. Obviously there are infinitely many beasts bases around one Beauty basis. We will give a method to build the 3-dimensional beasts bases in Sect. 4.2 with concrete parameter settings and some theoretical proofs. In Sect. 5, we give the assessing structure for higher dimensional Beast bases.

**Two dimensional case.** Of course for two dimensional lattices, as the optimal cases of LLL ($\delta = 1$), definitely Lagrange's algorithm can find the vectors of Minkowski's minima for any structure of bases in polynomial time [7]. So our main focus in this paper is cases of 3 dimensions and higher.

## 4  Three Dimensional Case

In this section, we'll review the performance of classical rational LLL algorithm at first. Then we'll give our main theorem based on some theoretical analyses on a usual 3 dimensional Beasts lattices. And we simply evaluate the gap $\gamma = \lambda_2/\lambda_1$ in 3 dimensional Beasts. At last we show some experimental results to support our conjectures.

### 4.1  LLL Outputs a Shortest Vector?

As we know, the LLL algorithm gets stronger with the approximate factor $\delta$ asymptotically close to 1 in experiments. But for a given basis, it is folklore that LLL can not definitely output the shortest vector even when the dimension is 3. The Goldstein-Mayer bases [4] give us random bases in some sense. And it is used in Hermite Normal Form in the famous SVP Challenge operated by TU Darmstadt [20]. We generated 100,000 3 dimensional random bases from SVP Challenge and did some initial experiments using exact-arithmetic variants of LLL in NTL library [15]. Furthermore, we perform ENUM on the LLL reduced bases to check if the shortest vector is in the LLL reduced bases. We call LLL reduction "succeed" if the shortest one is in the output thereof. Figure 2 shows the number variety of LLL-failed cases in 3 dimensions using $\delta \in (0.25, 1)$.

### 4.2  Main Theorem

Now we will investigate why LLL reduction fails to get the shortest vector. We start our investigation within $\mathbb{R}^3$ – the 3 dimensional Beauty basis mentioned in Sect. 3. It obviously constitute a regular tetrahedron in 3 dimensional Euclidean space.

$$Beauty_3 = \begin{pmatrix} 1 & 1 & 0 \\ 0 & 1 & 1 \\ 1 & 0 & 1 \end{pmatrix}.$$

Note that to use a "strong" LLL, we set the parameter $\delta \in [0.9, 1)$. Although we do exam more than 100,000 random bases of $\mathbb{R}^3$ and found it almost succeed to get the shortest vectors, the reality is that LLL reduction can fail in a special cases. Our next theorem gives an examples of that failure cases:

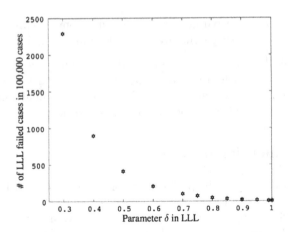

**Fig. 2.** The number of LLL failed cases in dimension 3 using same bases but different $\delta$.

Let $P$ be a big positive integer number and let $\epsilon_1, \epsilon_2, \epsilon_3$ and $\epsilon_4$ be very small positive integers fulfilling

$$\begin{cases} P \in [2^{x-1}, 2^x - 1] \ (x \in \mathbb{Z} \text{ and } x \ge y) \\ \epsilon_i \in [0, 2^y - 1] \qquad (y \in \mathbb{Z} \text{ and } y \ge 2) \\ \delta = 1 - 2^{-z} \qquad (z \in \mathbb{R} \text{ and } z \ge 3.32) \end{cases} \tag{1}$$

$$\epsilon_1 \ge \epsilon_2 > \epsilon_3 \ge \epsilon_4 \ge 0 \tag{2}$$

and

$$x - y - z \ge 1 \text{ and } y \le z. \tag{3}$$

Then the basis

$$Beasts_3 = \begin{pmatrix} P - \epsilon_1 & P - \epsilon_2 & 0 \\ 0 & P - \epsilon_3 & P - \epsilon_4 \\ P & 0 & P \end{pmatrix}$$

is a 3 dimensional Beasts basis which can withstand exact-arithmetic LLL reduction by a high potentiality. The failure probability of LLL to find the shortest vectors in dimension 3 is stably 15.0%, relatively random bases thereof is <0.01%. Note that for generality we apply stochastic disturbance $\epsilon_i$ on each element of first two vectors in $P \cdot Beauty_3$. Certainly one can subtract $\epsilon_i$ from all elements or from just one element of each vector. Experimental results are same for all these Beasts.

**Theorem 1.** Let $Beasts_3$ be the basis defined above and let $E$ be the unimodular matrix

$$E = \begin{pmatrix} 0 & -1 & 1 \\ 1 & -1 & 0 \\ 0 & 1 & 0 \end{pmatrix}.$$

then $EBeasts_3$ is an LLL reduced basis with $L(EBeasts_3) = L(Beasts_3)$, but the shortest vector is not in $EBeasts_3$.

**Proof.** Let $Beasts_3 = (\mathbf{b_1}, \mathbf{b_2}, \mathbf{b_3})^t$. At first, we declare that $\mathbf{b_1}$ is the shortest vector in $L(Beasts_3)$ and put the proof in Appendix A, for that in cases of constructed high Beasts bases, the first vector is definitely not the shortest one. Next we prove the second part of the theorem. Set

$$C = (\mathbf{c_1}, \mathbf{c_2}, \mathbf{c_3})^t = EB = (\mathbf{b_3} - \mathbf{b_2}, \mathbf{b_1} - \mathbf{b_2}, \mathbf{b_2})^t.$$

We have to show that $C$ satisfies the LLL conditions where

$$C = \begin{pmatrix} P & -(P - \epsilon_3) & \epsilon_4 \\ P - \epsilon_1 & \epsilon_3 - \epsilon_2 & -(P - \epsilon_4) \\ 0 & P - \epsilon_3 & P - \epsilon_4 \end{pmatrix}$$

First we will show that $C$ is size-reduced matrix then we'll show it satisfies Lovász condition. Note that in our work, we use $\eta = \frac{1}{2}$ for size reduction of LLL.

$$\left| \mu_{2,1}^C \right| = \left| \frac{< \mathbf{c_2}, \mathbf{c_1} >}{< \mathbf{c_1}, \mathbf{c_1} >} \right|$$

$$= \left| \frac{P(P - \epsilon_1) - (P - \epsilon_3)(\epsilon_3 - \epsilon_2) - (P - \epsilon_4)\epsilon_4}{P^2 + (P - \epsilon_3)^2 + \epsilon_4^2} \right|$$

$$= \left| \frac{P^2 - P\epsilon_3(\epsilon_2 - \epsilon_1)P + \epsilon_3(\epsilon_3 - \epsilon_2) + \epsilon_4(\epsilon_4 - P)}{2P^2 - 2P\epsilon_3 + \epsilon_4^2} \right|$$

$$\leq \frac{P^2 - P\epsilon_3}{2P^2 - 2P\epsilon_3}$$

$$\leq \frac{1}{2} = \eta$$

$$\left| \mu_{3,1}^C \right| = \left| \frac{< \mathbf{c_3}, \mathbf{c_1} >}{< \mathbf{c_1}, \mathbf{c_1} >} \right|$$

$$= \left| \frac{-(P - \epsilon_3)^2 + \epsilon_4(P - \epsilon_4)}{P^2 + (P - \epsilon_3)^2 + \epsilon_4^2} \right|$$

$$\leq \frac{P^2 - \epsilon_3 P}{2P^2 - 2\epsilon_3 P}$$

$$\leq \frac{1}{2} = \eta$$

To prove $|\mu_{3,2}^C| < \frac{1}{2}$, at first we need to get an approximate lower bound of $|\mu_{21}|$. Using the assumptions (1), (2) and (3), we get $x \geq 7$ and $|\mu_{21}| \geq 0.402$ can also be derived.

$$\left| \mu_{3,2}^C \right| = \left| \frac{< \mathbf{c_3}, \mathbf{c_2^*} >}{< \mathbf{c_2^*}, \mathbf{c_2^*} >} \right|$$

$$= \left| \frac{< \mathbf{c_3}, \mathbf{c_2} > - \mu_{21} < \mathbf{c_3}, \mathbf{c_1} >}{\|\mathbf{c_2} - \mu_{21}\mathbf{c_1}\|^2} \right|$$

$$= \left| \frac{(P - \epsilon_3)(\epsilon_3 - \epsilon_2) - (P - \epsilon_4)^2 + \mu_{21}(P - \epsilon_3)^2 - \mu_{21}\epsilon_4(P - \epsilon_4)}{(P - \epsilon_1 - \mu_{21}P)^2 + [\epsilon_3 - \epsilon_2 + \mu_{21}(P - \epsilon_3)]^2 + (P - \epsilon_4 + \mu_{21}\epsilon_4)^2} \right|$$

$$= \frac{1}{2} \left| \frac{(P - \epsilon_3)(\epsilon_3 - \epsilon_2) - (P - \epsilon_4)^2 + \mu_{21}(P - \epsilon_3)^2 - \mu_{21}\epsilon_4(P - \epsilon_4)}{[(P - \epsilon_3)(\epsilon_3 - \epsilon_2) - (P - \epsilon_4)^2 + \mu_{21}(P - \epsilon_3)^2 - \mu_{21}\epsilon_4(P - \epsilon_4)] + \zeta} \right|$$

We denote $\zeta$ the long remainders. From $P \geq 2^{x-1} \geq 2^{y+z} \geq 2^{y+4}$ we can get

$$\frac{\epsilon_1}{P} < \frac{2^y - 1}{2^{x-1}} < \frac{2^y - 1}{2^{y+4}} < \frac{1}{16}\left(1 - \frac{1}{2^y}\right) < \frac{1}{16}. \tag{4}$$

Hence we can get the following lower bound of $|\mu_{21}|$ as:

$$|\mu_{21}| = \left| \frac{< \mathbf{c_2}, \mathbf{c_1} >}{< \mathbf{c_1}, \mathbf{c_1} >} \right|$$

$$= \left| \frac{P(P - \epsilon_1) + (\epsilon_2 - \epsilon_3)(P - \epsilon_3) - \epsilon_4(P - \epsilon_4)}{P^2 + (P - \epsilon_3)^2 + \epsilon_4^2} \right|$$

$$= \left| \frac{P^2 + (\epsilon_2 - \epsilon_1 - \epsilon_3 - \epsilon_4)P + \epsilon_3^2 - \epsilon_2\epsilon_3 + \epsilon_4^2}{2P^2 - 2P\epsilon_3 + \epsilon_3^2 + \epsilon_4^2} \right|$$

$$> \frac{P^2 - 3\epsilon_1 P - \epsilon_1^2}{2P^2 + 2\epsilon_1^2}$$

$$= \frac{1}{2} \cdot (1 - \frac{2\epsilon_1^2}{P^2 + \epsilon_1^2} - \frac{3P\epsilon_1}{P^2 + \epsilon_1^2})$$

$$> \frac{1}{2} - (\frac{\epsilon_1}{P})^2 - \frac{3}{2}\frac{\epsilon_1}{P}$$

$$> \frac{1}{2} - (\frac{1}{16})^2 - \frac{3}{2} \cdot \frac{1}{16}$$

$$\approx 0.402$$

Using this result, we compute $\zeta > 0$ and finally we can derive $|\mu_{3,2}^C| \leq \frac{1}{2} = \eta$. During the all proof we omit some factors since we assumed that the epsilons' values are very small respect to $P$ value. So the omitted value doesn't affect in the sum value.

Next we want to show that the vectors of $C$ also satisfy Lovász condition. From Gram-Schmidt theorem, we have

$$\|\mathbf{b_1} - \mathbf{b_2}\|^2 = \|(\mathbf{b_1} - \mathbf{b_2})^*\|^2 + (\mu_{2,1}^C)^2\|(\mathbf{b_3} - \mathbf{b_2})^*\|^2.$$

Hence we can get

$$\|(\mathbf{b_1} - \mathbf{b_2})^*\|^2 = \|\mathbf{b_1} - \mathbf{b_2}\|^2 - (\mu_{2,1}^C)^2\|(\mathbf{b_3} - \mathbf{b_2})^*\|^2. \tag{5}$$

Now we should proof that $\|(\mathbf{b_1} - \mathbf{b_2})^*\|^2 - \delta\|\mathbf{b_3} - \mathbf{b_2}\|^2 \geq 0$ as follows.

$$\|(\mathbf{b_1} - \mathbf{b_2})^*\|^2 - \delta\|\mathbf{b_3} - \mathbf{b_2}\|^2$$
$$= ((P - \epsilon_1)^2 + (\epsilon_3 - \epsilon_2)^2 + (P - \epsilon_4)^2) - \delta(P^2 + (P - \epsilon_3)^2 + \epsilon_4^2) \tag{6}$$
$$= 2(1 - \delta)P^2 + 2(\delta\epsilon_3 - \epsilon_1 - \epsilon_4)P + \epsilon_1^2 + (\epsilon_3 - \epsilon_2)^2 + (1 - \delta)\epsilon_4 - \delta\epsilon_3^2.$$

Note that $z$ should take big value such that $\delta \to 1$. We consider the dominative part of Eq. (6). Finally, using our assumption (1) and (2), and from formula (5), we can get

$$\|(\mathbf{b_1} - \mathbf{b_2})^*\|^2 = \|\mathbf{b_1} - \mathbf{b_2}\|^2 - (\mu_{2,1}^C)^2\|(\mathbf{b_3} - \mathbf{b_2})^*\|^2$$
$$\geq \delta\|\mathbf{b_3} - \mathbf{b_2}\|^2 - (\mu_{2,1}^C)^2\|(\mathbf{b_3} - \mathbf{b_2})^*\|^2$$
$$\geq \delta\|\mathbf{b_3} - \mathbf{b_2}\|^2 - (\mu_{2,1}^C)^2\|\mathbf{b_3} - \mathbf{b_2}\|^2$$
$$\geq (\delta - (\mu_{2,1}^C)^2)\|\mathbf{b_3} - \mathbf{b_2}\|^2.$$

Similarly, we have the equation:

$$\|\mathbf{b}_3\|^2 = \|\mathbf{b}_3^*\|^2 + (\mu_{3,1}^C)^2\|(\mathbf{b}_3 - \mathbf{b}_2)^*\|^2 + (\mu_{3,2}^C)^2\|(\mathbf{b}_1 - \mathbf{b}_2)^*\|^2$$

and we can proof that it satisfies the Lovász condition by our assumptions above.

Therefore $C$ satisfies $\mu_{i,j}^C \leq \eta$ and Lovász condition too. Hence $C$ is LLL reduced and by the construction process we know that $\|C[i]\| > Beasts_3[1] = \lambda_1[L]$, for $\forall i \in \{1,2,3\}$.

Finally, it is easy to see that $EBeasts_3$ is a basis for $L(Beasts_3)$ therefore $L(EBeasts_3) = L(Beasts_3)$. $\qquad\square$

Theorem 1 means that even if we apply a strong LLL reduction to $EBeasts_3$, LLL fails to get the shortest vector in our parameter setting. (1), (2) and (3) are the most important conditions in our theoretical proof. Moreover, the theoretical conjecture perfectly matches our experimental results.

Moreover, using the condition (4): $\frac{\epsilon_2}{P} \leq \frac{\epsilon_1}{P} \leq \frac{1}{16}$, we can easily get the gap between $\lambda_1$ and $\lambda_2$ in our $Beasts_3$ bases:

$$\gamma = \frac{\lambda_2}{\lambda_1} \leq \frac{\sqrt{2P^2}}{\sqrt{(P-\epsilon_1)^2 + (P-\epsilon_2)^2}} \leq \sqrt{\frac{2P^2}{2P^2 - 2(\epsilon_1+\epsilon_2)P}} = \frac{1}{\sqrt{1-\frac{\epsilon_1+\epsilon_2}{P}}} \leq \sqrt{\frac{8}{7}} \approx 1.069.$$

## 4.3   Experimental Results in 3 Dimensional Beasts Lattices

In our experiments, we implemented our main program using C++ language and calculated the random unimodular matrices from Magma computational algebra system [12]. About the size of $x$, we also follow the strategy of TU Darmstadt SVP Challenge [20], which takes the size of entries of $n$ dimensional random lattice basis as $10 \cdot n$ bits. In our experiments, we also considered the size of entries and constructing technique in unimodular matrices. The experimental results show that with the size of entries increasing, the chance for LLL to find the shortest vector is bigger. Since we compare the performance of our Beasts bases with the randomly generated bases from SVP Challenge, where both original elements are $10 \cdot n$ bits length, the elements in unimodular matrices should be as small as possible (as size smaller than $n$ and close to 0). Because in LLL reductions, sometimes the shortest vector in the reduced basis is not in the first position, for the sake of fairness, we use ENUM algorithm to check if the shortest one is in the whole reduced bases or not.

Now we will show two experimental results. The first one is when we apply the 100,000 unimodular matrices to randomize 100,000 generated Beasts bases, the LLL (with $\delta \to 1$) fails to solve SVP by 15.0% probability under our parameters' assumption (1), (2) and (3). And this failure probability will become 18.3% if we apply the unimodular matrices on the same Beasts basis again. However for random bases generated from TU Darmstadt SVP Challenge [20], this failure probability is <0.01% for $\delta \in [0.9,1)$. This result means our constructed 3 dimensional Beasts lattice can withstand powerful LLL much better than random lattices.

The second experiment is on the failed cases as $EBeasts_3$ in our main theorem. In Table 1, we can see that under our parameters' assumption (1), (2) and (3), the failed cases will keep a stable probability that LLL can not find the shortest vector with $\delta \to 1$. Simultaneously this result validates that the LLL failed cases are all LLL reduced as what we proved on $EBeasts_3$.

**Table 1.** Some experimental results using our constructed 3-dimensional Beast bases. Note that we call LLL failed if the shortest vector was not in the LLL-reduced basis.

| $x$ | $y$ | $z$ | $\delta$ | LLL failed prob. |
|---|---|---|---|---|
| 10 | 2 | 6.64 | $1 - 10^{-2}$ | 100% |
| 20 | 2 | 16.6 | $1 - 10^{-5}$ | 100% |
| 30 | 9 | 19.9 | $1 - 10^{-6}$ | 100% |
| 30 | 5 | 23.25 | $1 - 10^{-7}$ | 100% |
| 30 | 2 | 26.5 | $1 - 10^{-8}$ | 100% |

Here the parameter $y$ is the critical value to make sure the LLL fail by 100%. Corresponding to the relaxation factor $\delta$ closer to 1 means our Beast bases can withstand a stronger LLL reduction.

## 5   High Dimensional Cases

In this section, we will study the hard cases in higher dimensions. We extend the 3 dimensional Beasts, keeping their two properties, which is the basis vectors are almost the same length and their angles are almost 60°. At first we observe the performance of LLL reduction in high dimensions. Then we give a rational version of 8 dimensional Beauty basis and a general irrational Beauty for higher dimensional bases. Easily we can build the corresponding Beasts bases from these Beauty bases. According with our conjectures in dimension 3, our experimental results show that the constructed Beast bases are stronger than random lattices to resist LLL reduction.

### 5.1   Success Probability of LLL in High Dimensions

Similar to the experiments in Sect. 4.1, we also did experiments for higher dimensions until 32. For each dimension, we used 100,000 random bases generated from TU Darmstadt SVP Challenge [20] and we fixed $\delta = 0.99$ in our experiments. From Fig. 3 we can see that the exact-arithmetic LLL can solve SVP by an extremely high success probability within 15 dimensions.

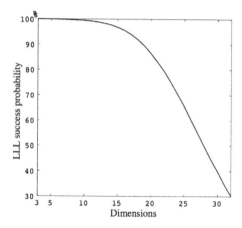

**Fig. 3.** Experimental results of random bases generated from TU Darmstadt SVP Challenge.

## 5.2   Build 8 Dimensional Beasts from Rational Beauty Bases

Our defined Beauty bases is a configuration of vectors in the Euclidean space fulfilling certain geometrical properties, namely vectors are sampled from the isometry group. Root system is known as a group somehow satisfying the symmetric property. Observation from the simple roots for root system $E_8$ in the odd coordinate inspired us to exploit a rational Beauty basis with integral vectors (with elements equal to 1) and components $1/2$, see $Beauty_8$ as follows.

$$
Beauty_8 = \begin{pmatrix}
1 & 1 & 0 & 0 & 0 & 0 & 0 & 0 \\
1 & 0 & 1 & 0 & 0 & 0 & 0 & 0 \\
\vdots & \vdots & \vdots & \ddots & \vdots & \vdots & \vdots & \vdots \\
1 & 0 & 0 & 0 & 0 & 0 & 0 & 1 \\
\frac{1}{2} & \frac{1}{2} & \frac{1}{2} & \frac{1}{2} & \frac{1}{2} & \frac{1}{2} & \frac{1}{2} & \frac{1}{2}
\end{pmatrix} \in \mathbb{Q}^{8 \times 8}.
$$

Following the 3 dimensional cases, we construct Beast bases as $Beasts_8$. The parameter settings carry forward the conditions (1), (2) and (3). Simultaneously extend $i \in [1, 4]$ to $i \in [1, 22]$ as $\epsilon_1 \geq \epsilon_2 > \epsilon_3 \geq \epsilon_4 \cdots \geq \epsilon_{22}$.

$$
Beasts_8 = \begin{pmatrix}
P - \epsilon_1 & P - \epsilon_2 & 0 & 0 & 0 & 0 & 0 & 0 \\
P - \epsilon_3 & 0 & P - \epsilon_4 & 0 & 0 & 0 & 0 & 0 \\
\vdots & \vdots & \vdots & \ddots & \vdots & \vdots & \vdots & \vdots \\
P - \epsilon_{13} & 0 & 0 & 0 & 0 & 0 & 0 & P - \epsilon_{14} \\
\lceil \frac{P}{2} \rceil - \epsilon_{15} & \lceil \frac{P}{2} \rceil - \epsilon_{16} & \lceil \frac{P}{2} \rceil - \epsilon_{17} & \lceil \frac{P}{2} \rceil - \epsilon_{18} & \lceil \frac{P}{2} \rceil - \epsilon_{19} & \lceil \frac{P}{2} \rceil - \epsilon_{20} & \lceil \frac{P}{2} \rceil - \epsilon_{21} & \lceil \frac{P}{2} \rceil - \epsilon_{22}
\end{pmatrix}.
$$

## 5.3  How to Build Beasts in General High Dimensions

Start from 3 dimensional cases, we want to add vector to get a Beauty lattice basis in $\mathbb{R}^4$. By basic calculation, we can easily get,

$$Beauty_4' = \begin{pmatrix} 1 & 1 & 0 & 0 \\ 0 & 1 & 1 & 0 \\ 1 & 0 & 1 & 0 \\ \frac{1}{2} & \frac{1}{2} & \frac{1}{2} & \frac{\sqrt{5}}{2} \end{pmatrix}.$$

We denote the $Beauty_n'$ to distinguish from the rational bases. Analogously using $Beasts_n'$ to stand the Beasts generated from $Beauty_n'$. By construction, we can get a full-rank Beauty lattice generated by the basis as follows.

$$Beauty_n' = \begin{pmatrix} 1 & 1 & 0 & 0 & 0 & 0 & \cdots & 0 & \cdots & 0 \\ 0 & 1 & 1 & 0 & 0 & 0 & \cdots & 0 & \cdots & 0 \\ 1 & 0 & 1 & 0 & 0 & 0 & \cdots & 0 & \cdots & 0 \\ \frac{1}{2} & \frac{1}{2} & \frac{1}{2} & \frac{\sqrt{5}}{2} & 0 & 0 & \cdots & 0 & \cdots & 0 \\ \frac{1}{2} & \frac{1}{2} & \frac{1}{2} & \frac{1}{2\sqrt{5}} & \sqrt{\frac{6}{5}} & 0 & \cdots & 0 & \cdots & 0 \\ \vdots & \vdots & \vdots & \vdots & \vdots & \vdots & \vdots & \vdots & \vdots \\ \frac{1}{2} & \frac{1}{2} & \frac{1}{2} & \frac{1}{2\sqrt{5}} & \sqrt{\frac{1}{30}} & \cdots & \frac{1}{\sqrt{i(i-1)}} & \sqrt{\frac{i+1}{i}} & \cdots & 0 \\ \vdots & \vdots & \vdots & \vdots & \vdots & \vdots & \vdots & \vdots & \vdots \\ \frac{1}{2} & \frac{1}{2} & \frac{1}{2} & \frac{1}{2\sqrt{5}} & \sqrt{\frac{1}{30}} & \cdots & \cdots & \frac{1}{\sqrt{n(n-1)}} & \sqrt{\frac{n+1}{n}} \end{pmatrix} \in \mathbb{R}^{n \times n}$$

Hence we know now how to build a Beauty lattice which can be easily converted to a hard lattice as the following:

1. Pick a large integer $P$.
2. Multiply $Beauty_n$ by the integer $P$ and round it to the ceiling integer.
3. Subtract a random matrix $\Sigma = [\epsilon_{ij}]$ where $\epsilon_{ij}$ sufficient small integer.

Or we can simply take the form from the following basis. Parameter settings follow the 3 dimensional cases in our main theorem in Sect. 4.2 and $\epsilon_1 \geq \epsilon_2 > \epsilon_3 \geq \epsilon_4 \cdots \geq \epsilon_n$.

$$Beasts_m' = \begin{pmatrix} P - \epsilon_{11} & P - \epsilon_{12} & 0 & 0 & 0 & \cdots & 0 & \cdots 0 \\ 0 & P - \epsilon_{22} & P - \epsilon_{23} & 0 & 0 & \cdots & 0 & \cdots 0 \\ P & 0 & P & 0 & 0 & \cdots & 0 & \cdots 0 \\ \lceil \frac{P}{2} \rceil - \epsilon_{41} & \lceil \frac{P}{2} \rceil - \epsilon_{42} & \lceil \frac{P}{2} \rceil - \epsilon_{43} & \lceil P\frac{\sqrt{5}}{2} \rceil - \epsilon_{44} & 0 & \cdots & 0 & \cdots 0 \\ \vdots & \vdots & \vdots & \vdots & \vdots & & \vdots & \vdots \\ \lceil \frac{P}{2} \rceil - \epsilon_{i1} & \lceil \frac{P}{2} \rceil - \epsilon_{i2} & \lceil \frac{P}{2} \rceil - \epsilon_{i3} & \lceil \frac{P}{2\sqrt{5}} \rceil - \epsilon_{i4} & \cdots & \lceil \frac{P}{\sqrt{i(i-1)}} \rceil - \epsilon_{i,i-1} & \lceil P\sqrt{\frac{i+1}{i}} \rceil - \epsilon_{i,i} & \cdots 0 \\ \vdots & \vdots & \vdots & \vdots & \vdots & \vdots & \vdots & \vdots \\ \lceil \frac{P}{2} \rceil - \epsilon_{n1} & \lceil \frac{P}{2} \rceil - \epsilon_{n2} & \lceil \frac{P}{2} \rceil - \epsilon_{n3} & \lceil \frac{P}{2\sqrt{5}} \rceil - \epsilon_{n4} & \cdots & \cdots & \lceil P\sqrt{\frac{n+1}{n}} \rceil - \epsilon_{n,n} \end{pmatrix}$$

## 5.4  Experimental Results of High Dimensional Cases

As same as the procedure in Sect. 4.3, we generate 100,000 bases for each dimension and randomize them by equal amount of unimodular matrices from Magma [12]. The bit length $x$ of $P$ is also set as $x = 10 \cdot n$. The parameter settings

**Table 2.** Some experimental results of higher dimensional Beast bases. Parameter settings $x = 10 \cdot n$, $z = log_2(1 - \delta)^{-1}$ and $y$ are under the conditions in Theorem 1.

| Dim $n$ | LLL failure prob. on the random bases | | | LLL failure prob. on the $Beasts'_n$ | | |
|---|---|---|---|---|---|---|
| | Ex1. $\delta = 1 - 10^{-1}$ | Ex2. $\delta = 1 - 10^{-2}$ | Ex3. $\delta = 1 - 10^{-3}$ | Ex1. $\delta = 1 - 10^{-1}$ | Ex2. $\delta = 1 - 10^{-2}$ | Ex3. $\delta = 1 - 10^{-3}$ |
| 4 | 0.057% | 0.035% | 0.022% | 30.3% | 30.3% | 30.3% |
| 5 | 0.129% | 0.068% | 0.048% | 39.4% | 39.4% | 39.4% |
| 6 | 0.240% | 0.107% | 0.103% | 40.5% | 40.5% | 40.5% |
| 7 | 0.350% | 0.173% | 0.157% | 43.5% | 43.5% | 43.5% |
| 8 | 0.542% | 0.256% | 0.229% | 47.2% | 47.2% | 47.2% |
| 9 | 0.79% | 0.400% | 0.359% | 50.7% | 50.7% | 50.7% |
| 10 | 1.14% | 0.507% | 0.485% | 53.2% | 53.2% | 53.2% |

fulfil the above sections respectively. Note that for all cases we perform ENUM algorithm to check if the shortest one is in the reduced bases or not.

At first, the LLL ($\delta \in [0.9, 1)$) failure probability solving SVP on $Beasts_8$ expanded lattices is stably 48.4%. However for the same magnitudes of vectors in TU Darmstadt SVP Challenge generated random lattices, the LLL failure probability is $\leq 0.542\%$, see Table 2.

Simultaneously Table 2 also shows that the $Beasts'_n$ bases constructed from irrational $Beauty'_n$ possess a comparative high probability to withstand exact-arithmetic version of LLL reduction with relaxation factor $\delta \in [0.9, 1)$. Moreover the LLL failure probability keep stable with the increasing of $\delta$, which means LLL becomes more powerful. Especially the close result for $Beasts_8$ (48.4%) and $Beasts'_8$ (47.2%) give a support for our conjecture of Beasts bases.

# 6    Conclusions

We studied the hard cases in LLL reduction, as we called them "Beasts", whose vectors fulfilling two properties: 1. the vectors are almost the same length; 2. the angles of the vectors are almost 60°. They are generated from the corresponding "Beauty" bases "exactly" instead of "almost". Our experimental results showed the randomized Beasts bases have a potentiality to withstand the LLL reduction. We started from 3 dimensional cases and gave a complete theoretical proof for this phenomenon. We also give a 8 dimensional rational Beauty and the general irrational Beauty for dimensions higher than 3. Comparing with the same magnitude of TU Darmstadt SVP Challenge random bases, our generated Beasts can stably withstand the exact-arithmetic LLL with relaxation factor $\delta \in [0.9, 1)$. However, we can't assert categorically that the Beasts are only our constructions. So it is an intriguing open problem if there are other hard cases in LLL reduction.

# A  Supplementary proof in main theory

Let $Beasts_3 = (\mathbf{b_1}, \mathbf{b_2}, \mathbf{b_3})^t$. We prove that $\mathbf{b_1}$ is the shortest vector in $L(Beasts_3)$, i.e. $\|\mathbf{b_1}\| = (\lambda_1(L)) \leq \|a\mathbf{b_1} + b\mathbf{b_2} + c\mathbf{b_3}\|$ for any coefficients set $(a, b, c) \in \mathbb{Z}^3 \backslash \{(0,0,0)\}$. We observe any non-zero vector $\mathbf{b} = a\mathbf{b_1} + b\mathbf{b_2} + c\mathbf{b_3}$ in $L(Beasts_3)$. The square norm of $\mathbf{b}$ is as

$$
\begin{aligned}
\|\mathbf{b}\|^2 &= \|a\mathbf{b_1} + b\mathbf{b_2} + c\mathbf{b_3}\|^2 \\
&= [a(P - \epsilon_1) + cP]^2 + [a(P - \epsilon_2) + b(P - \epsilon_3)]^2 + [b(P - \epsilon_4) + cP]^2 \\
&\geq (a(P - \epsilon_1) + c(P - \epsilon_1))^2 + [a(P - \epsilon_2) + b(P - \epsilon_2)]^2 + [b(P - \epsilon_1) + c(P - \epsilon_1)]^2 \\
&= [(a + b)^2 + (b + c)^2](P - \epsilon_1)^2 + (a + b)^2 (P - \epsilon_2)^2.
\end{aligned}
$$

Since $a, b$, and $c$ are integers and not equal to 0 at the same time, the smallest case for the right side of inequality is when

$$a = b = 0 \text{ and } |c| = 1.$$

However in this case $\|\mathbf{b}\| = \|\mathbf{b_3}\| > \|\mathbf{b_1}\|$ satisfying our theorem. So we consider a "looser" condition for the right side as

$$a + b = 0 \text{ and } |c| \in \mathbb{Z}_{>1}^+.$$

From it we derive

$$
\begin{aligned}
\|\mathbf{b}\|^2 &\geq [(c - a)^2 + (c + a)^2](P - \epsilon_1)^2 \\
&\geq 4(P - \epsilon_1)^2 \\
&= (P - \epsilon_1)^2 + (P - \epsilon_2)^2 + 3(P - \epsilon_1)^2 - (P - \epsilon_2)^2 \\
&= \|\mathbf{b_1}\|^2 + 2P(P - 3\epsilon_1 + \epsilon_2) + 3\epsilon_1^2 - \epsilon_2^2.
\end{aligned}
$$

From the inequality (4) we get $P - 3\epsilon_1 > 0$. Hence

$$
\begin{aligned}
\|\mathbf{b}\|^2 &\geq \|\mathbf{b_1}\|^2 + 2P(P - 3\epsilon_1 + \epsilon_2) + 3\epsilon_1^2 - \epsilon_2^2 \\
&\geq \|\mathbf{b_1}\|^2
\end{aligned}
$$

for $\epsilon_1 \geq \epsilon_2$. We finish the proof of $\|\mathbf{b_1}\| = \lambda_1(L)$.

# References

1. Akhavi, A.: Worst-case complexity of the optimal LLL algorithm. In: Gonnet, G.H., Viola, A. (eds.) LATIN 2000. LNCS, vol. 1776, pp. 355–366. Springer, Heidelberg (2000). doi:10.1007/10719839_35
2. Akhavi, A.: The optimal LLL algorithm is still polynomial in fixed dimension. Theor. Comput. Sci. 297(1–3), 323 (2003)
3. Bi, J., Coron, J.-S., Faugère, J.-C., Nguyen, P.Q., Renault, G., Zeitoun, R.: Rounding and chaining LLL: finding faster small roots of univariate polynomial congruences. In: Krawczyk, H. (ed.) PKC 2014. LNCS, vol. 8383, pp. 185–202. Springer, Heidelberg (2014). doi:10.1007/978-3-642-54631-0_11
4. Goldstein, D., Mayer, A.: On the equidistribution of Hecke points. Forum Mathematicum 15(2), 165–189 (2003)

5. Gama, N., Nguyen, P.Q.: Predicting lattice reduction. In: Smart, N. (ed.) EURO-CRYPT 2008. LNCS, vol. 4965, pp. 31–51. Springer, Heidelberg (2008). doi:10.1007/978-3-540-78967-3_3

6. Gama, N., Nguyen, P.Q., Regev, O.: Lattice enumeration using extreme pruning. In: Gilbert, H. (ed.) EUROCRYPT 2010. LNCS, vol. 6110, pp. 257–278. Springer, Heidelberg (2010). doi:10.1007/978-3-642-13190-5_13

7. Lagrange, L.: "Recherches d'arithmétique". Nouv. Mém. Acad. (1773)

8. Luzzi, L., Othman, G.R., Belfiore, J.C.: Augmented lattice reduction for MIMO decoding. IEEE Trans. Wireless Commun. 9(9), 2853–2859 (2010)

9. Lenstra, A.K., Lenstra Jr., H.W., Lovász, L.: Factoring polynomials with rational coefficients. Math. Ann. 261(4), 515–534 (1982)

10. Lyubashevsky, V., Peikert, C., Regev, O.: On ideal lattices and learning with errors over rings. In: Gilbert, H. (ed.) EUROCRYPT 2010. LNCS, vol. 6110, pp. 1–23. Springer, Heidelberg (2010). doi:10.1007/978-3-642-13190-5_1

11. Luzzi, L., Stehlé, D., Ling, C.: Decoding by embedding: correct decoding radius and DMT optimality. IEEE Trans. Inf. Theory 59(5), 2960–2973 (2013)

12. Magma computational algebra system. http://magma.maths.usyd.edu.au/magma/

13. Minkowski, H.: Geometrie der Zahlen (1910)

14. Nguyen, P.Q., Stehlé, D.: Low-dimensional lattice basis reduction revisited. ACM Trans. Algorithms 5(4) (2009)

15. Victor Shoup's NTL library. http://www.shoup.net/ntl/

16. Nguyen, P.Q., Vallée, B. (eds.): The LLL Algorithm - Survey and Applications. Information Security and Cryptography. Springer, Berlin Heidelberg (2010)

17. Regev, O.: On lattices, learning with errors, random linear codes, and cryptography. In: STOC 2005, pp. 84–93 (2005)

18. Semaev, I.: A 3-dimensional lattice reduction algorithm. In: Silverman, J.H. (ed.) CaLC 2001. LNCS, vol. 2146, pp. 181–193. Springer, Heidelberg (2001). doi:10.1007/3-540-44670-2_13

19. Schnorr, C.P., Euchner, M.: Lattice basis reduction: improved practical algorithms and solving subset sum problems. Math. Program. 66(1–3), 181–199 (1994)

20. TU Darmstadt lattice challenge. http://www.latticechallenge.org/

# System Security (1)

# Simple Infeasibility Certificates for Attack Trees

Ahto Buldas[1,2], Aleksandr Lenin[1,2,3(✉)],
Jan Willemson[1,3], and Anton Charnamord[2]

[1] Cybernetica AS, Mäealuse 2/1, Tallinn, Estonia
`aleksandr.lenin@cyber.ee`
[2] Tallinn University of Technology, Ehitajate Tee 5, Tallinn, Estonia
[3] Software Technology and Applications Competence Centre, Tallinn, Estonia

**Abstract.** We introduce infeasibility certificates, compact and easily verifiable proofs that no profitable attacks exist in the considered system model. We introduce computational methods for generation and validation of such proofs using an enhanced weight reduction technique. A new method for obtaining adversarial expenses by approximating an interval within which this value resides, is an interesting approach to tackle NP-complete tasks and allows to obtain values that require extensive computations in reasonable time.

## 1 Introduction

Attack trees are regularly used to perform cost-benefit analysis [2–4,11,13,15] to determine if the considered system model is sufficiently protected from rational profit-oriented adversaries. In these models, the adversarial profit as well as the expenses, related to preparing and launching single attack steps, are known to adversaries. If the profit exceeds expenses, the considered system is vulnerable, as it is profitable to attack it. The objective of the defender is to deploy security measures in a way that will make the attack process unprofitable for attackers. According to the rationality assumption, non-profitability of attacking is considered to be sufficient to hold rational attackers away from the considered system.

An attack tree is a hierarchical description of targeted attacks driven by a common goal. It is a tree-like structure where every leaf corresponds to an elementary attack step, annotated with corresponding cost to prepare and launch the attack step. In a more formal setting, an attack tree is a monotone Boolean function $\Phi(x_1, x_2, \ldots, x_n)$, the arguments of which are assigned with their corresponding weights (costs). The goal of an attacker is to satisfy $\Phi$ in the cheapest possible way. We denote by $w(\Phi)$ the minimal cost required to satisfy $\Phi$.

Existing analysis techniques like the improved failure-free model [3], approach the problem from the adversarial point of view, providing evidence about

The research leading to these results has received funding from the European Regional Development Fund through Estonian Centre of Excellence in ICT Research (EXCITE) and the Estonian Research Council under Institutional Research Grant IUT27-1.

S. Obana and K. Chida (Eds.): IWSEC 2017, LNCS 10418, pp. 39–55, 2017.
DOI: 10.1007/978-3-319-64200-0_3

feasibility of attacking by searching for the cheapest satisfying assignment to $\Phi$ the total weight of which does not exceed a certain threshold $T$. In this paper we study the same problem from the defender's perspective and aim at providing evidence about infeasibility of attacking, which is equivalent to showing that no profitable attacks exist in the model. In other words, we need to show that $w(\Phi) > K$, where $K$ is the adversarial profit.

Calculating $w(\Phi)$ is computationally expensive, as we need to consider every possible solution to find the cheapest one. We take a different approach and approximate the interval within which $w(\Phi)$ is determined. This provides us with a reasonable approximation of $w(\Phi)$ and lets us obtain the result in a much more efficient way, compared to calculating $w(\Phi)$ directly. We obtain this interval by approximating the upper $w_u(\Phi)$ and lower $w_l(\Phi)$ bounds of $w(\Phi)$ using genetic algorithms.

If $w_l(\Phi) > K$, attacking is infeasible, and this is what we need to achieve by deploying security measures. On the contrary, when $w_u(\Phi) < K$ attacking is profitable. If $K$ lies somewhere between $w_l(\Phi)$ and $w_u(\Phi)$, it is not possible to make reliable conclusions about feasibility of attacking, this situation would require more detailed analysis. Relying just on $w_l(\Phi)$ is insufficient – we need to obtain both bounds of $w(\Phi)$ to be able to estimate the relative error $\delta = \frac{w_u(\Phi)-w_l(\Phi)}{w_u(\Phi)}$ of the method. If the relative error is big then it might be that security expenses are way too high. The less the relative error is, the less unnecessary investments we probably make. We study how well $w_l(\Phi)$ approximates $w(\Phi)$ given a specific computational method that computes $w_l(\Phi)$ for the Boolean function $\Phi$. The better it does, the more precise estimation of $w(\Phi)$ we can obtain. It turned out that there are cases when $w_l(\Phi)$ equals $w(\Phi)$ so that the estimation is exact, but this is not always the case. Apart from the computational method presented in this paper, there exist other methods which can be used to obtain $w_l(\Phi)$, e.g. [8].

We need to be able to prove to the auditors that the values $w_u(\Phi)$ and $w_l(\Phi)$ are correctly calculated. Given $w_u(\Phi)$, it is easy to prove that this value is indeed an upper bound. To prove it, it is sufficient to present any satisfying solution with weight $w_u(\Phi)$, as there exists efficient algorithm that calculates the weight of a given solution. For $w_l(\Phi)$, in general, such a compact proof does not exist.

Therefore we introduce infeasibility certificates that are compact and easily verifiable proofs $\xi$ that the number $w_l(\Phi)$ is indeed a lower bound of the unknown value $w(\Phi)$. In practice, all we need to do in order to verify the feasibility of attacking, is to calculate the value of $w_l(\Phi)$ from the Boolean function $\Phi$ and a certificate $\xi$, and compare the obtained value to the adversarial profit $K$. If $w_l(\Phi) > K$, attacking is unprofitable. Infeasibility certificates may be used, for instance, to show auditors that the system is reasonably protected against rational profit-oriented adversaries. Such a certificate provides a proof that can be verified in a very time-efficient manner, even though the generation of such a certificate may be computationally expensive and take several days.

The outline of this paper is the following. Section 2 outlines the state of the art, Sect. 3 introduces efficient way to calculate adversarial expenses by means of the weight reduction method. Section 4 introduces infeasibility certificates, and their usage is demonstrated in Sect. 5 on a simple example. Section 6 provides relevant theorems and proofs. Section 2 outlines empirical evidence collected throughout the experiments studying the quality of approximation. Section 6 discusses some open questions.

## 2    Notation and Definitions

Let $X = \{x_1, x_2, \ldots\}$ be a fixed set of independent Boolean variables. For Boolean disjunction and conjunction operations, we use the conventional addition $(x_1 + x_2)$ and multiplication $x_1 x_2$, respectively. We use the notation $\Phi(X)$ to denote a Boolean function that may depend on any finite set of the Boolean variables in $X$. By $\Phi(x_1, x_2, \ldots, x_n)$, we mean a Boolean function that may depend on the variables $x_1, x_2, \ldots, x_n$, but not on any other variable in $X$. By a *conjunction* we mean any conjunction of a finite set of Boolean variables in $X$; for example $x_{i_1} x_{i_2} \ldots x_{i_k}$. By a *min-term* of a boolean function $\Phi(X)$, we mean any conjunction $\mu$ which implies the truth of $\Phi$, i.e. for which $\mu \models \Phi(X)$. By a weight function $w$, we mean any function $w \colon X \to \mathbb{R}^+$ which for any variable $x \in X$ returns a non-negative real number $w(x)$. Weight functions can be extended to all Boolean functions as follows:

– $w(\mu) = w(x_1) + \ldots + w(x_n)$, if $\mu = x_1 x_2 \ldots x_n$;
– $w(\Phi) = \min\{w(\mu) \colon \mu$ is a min-term of $\Phi\}$ for any Boolean function $\Phi$.

A min-term $\mu$ of $\Phi$ is a *cheapest min-term* if $w(\mu) = w(\Phi)$. The question of whether there exist feasible (to adversary) attacks against a system can be formalised in terms of the Weighted Monotone Satisfiability (WMSAT) problem.

**Definition 1.** *The* WMSAT *language consists of triples* $(\Phi, w, t)$, *where* $\Phi$ *is a monotone Boolean formula (AND/OR-formula),* $w$ *is a function that to every variable in* $\Phi$ *associates a weight* $w(z)$, *and* $t$ *is a real number (threshold) so that there is a min-term* $\mu$ *of* $\Phi$ *with* $w(\mu) \leq t$, *where* $w(\mu)$ *is the sum of all* $w(z)$ *such that* $z$ *is a variable in* $\mu$.

In practical context, $X = (\Phi, w, t)$ represents possible attacks against the system (via the monotone Boolean function $\Phi$), their costs (via the weight function $w$), as well as the estimated income of an adversary (via the threshold value $t$). It is known that the WMSAT problem is NP-complete [3, 14]:

**Theorem 1.** *The Weighted Monotone Satisfiability Problem is NP-complete.*

*Proof.* We will show that the Vertex Cover problem can be polynomially reduced to the WMSAT problem. Let $\mathcal{G}$ be the graph with a vertex set $\{v_1, \ldots, v_m\}$. We define a Boolean function $\mathcal{F}(x_1, \ldots, x_m)$ as follows. For each edge $(v_i, v_j)$ of $\mathcal{G}$ we define the clause $\mathcal{C}_{ij} = x_i \vee x_j$. The Boolean function $\mathcal{F}(x_1, \ldots, x_m)$ is defined as the conjunction of all $\mathcal{C}_{ij}$ such that $(v_i, v_j)$ is an edge of $\mathcal{G}$. Let the weight $w_i$ of each $x_i$ be equal to 1. It is obvious that $\mathcal{G}$ has a vertex cover $\mathcal{S}$ of size $|\mathcal{S}| < \mathcal{P}$ iff the monotone Boolean function $\mathcal{F}(x_1, \ldots, x_m)$ has a satisfying assignment with a total weight less than $\mathcal{P}$. □

For any language $L \in \mathbf{NP}$, there is an efficient (poly-time) verification algorithm $V(X, \mu)$, such that for every $X$ $X \in L \Leftrightarrow \exists \mu: V(X, \mu) = 1$. From the view-point of attack-trees and security, what one really wants is a proof $\xi$ (of size polynomial in $|X|$) that $X \notin$ WMSAT, which in the attack tree language means that there are no attacks with the cost less (or equal) than $t$. So, ideally we would like to have a poly-time verification algorithm $W$ such that for every $X = (\Phi, w, t)$ $X \notin$ WMSAT $\Leftrightarrow \exists \xi: W(X, \xi) = 1$, but the existence of such $W$ would imply $\mathbf{NP} = \mathbf{coNP}$ which, as the complexity theorists tend to believe, is not true. Hence, it is a very little hope to find such a $W$. We still may have an efficient verifier $W$ that works for some instances $X$, i.e. we only have the right-to-left implication.

**Definition 2.** *A* partial infeasibility verifier *for a language $L$ is a poly-time computable function $W$ such that for every $X: X \notin L \Leftarrow \exists \alpha: W(X, \alpha) = 1$ . Any $\alpha$ such that $W(X, \alpha) = 1$ is called an* infeasibility certificate *for $X$.*

In the practical attack-tree context, $L =$ WMSAT and $\alpha$ is a proof that $X$ is not in WMSAT which in practical context means that there exist no feasible attacks against the system. Practical usability of $W$ depends on for how many useful $X$-s the function $W$ works, as well as on the size of $\alpha$.

## 3   Related Work

### 3.1   Attack Tree Semantics

The idea of analyzing security using the so-called attack trees was popularized by Schneier in [18], who suggested to use attack trees as a convenient hierarchical representation of an attack scenario. The model of Buldas *et al.* [2] is remarkable for introducing the multi-parameter approach to the quantitative security risk analysis. The model assumes rational adversaries who behave fully adaptively and are always trying to maximize their average outcome. The authors state that in order to assess security it is sufficient to assess adversarial utility. Their model introduced a novel way to think about security and gave start to multi-parameter quantitative security analysis. Jürgenson and Willemson have shown that Buldas *et al.* model is inconsistent with Mauw-Oostijk foundations [15] and introduced the so-called parallel model [11] and the serial model [12] which provided more reliable results, however in neither models the adversary behaved in a fully adaptive way. Also, these models were intractable from the computational point of view, which is why Jürgenson and Willemson developed genetic approximation methods [13]. All the previously described models tried to approach the problem of estimating adversarial expenses from above considering only the upper bound of adversarial expenses. Buldas-Stepanenko fully adaptive model [4] was the first model which tried to take a different view on the problem and aimed at estimating adversarial expenses from below considering lower bounds of expenses. Their failure-free model is similar to the fully adaptive model with the only difference that in the failure-free model success probabilities of the attack steps are equal to 1. The most significant contribution of the paper [4] is the upper bounds ideology by which the models should estimate adversarial utility from above, trying to avoid false-positive security results. The improved failure-free model [3] improves the Buldas-Stepanenko failure-free model [4] by eliminating the force-failure states. In the improved model the adversarial behavior more fully conforms to the upper bounds ideology introduced in [4]. It turned out that the elimination of the force failure states has made the model computationally easier. The authors show that finding an optimal strategy in the new model is NP-complete and introduced the cost reduction and propagation methods to get an estimation of the lower bound of adversarial expenses.

## 3.2   Infeasibility Certificates

Here we list several possible methods that could be used to certify infeasibility of a WMSAT instance.

There exist satisfiability modulo theories (SMT) solvers, like Z3 [16], which can generate proofs of unsolvability for infeasible SMT instances. A WMSAT instance may be encoded as an SMT instance and an infeasibility proofs may be obtained from the solvers, however these proofs cannot be easily verified and require proof assistants, such as Coq [7], to verify them. Additionally, the performance of solving WMSAT instances encoded as SMT instances is questionable. Infeasibility of a system of linear equations may be certified by an infeasibility certificate the existence of which follows from the Range/kernel theorem [5] for complex domain and from the Farkas' lemma [6] for the real domain. We can represent the WMSAT problem in the form of a system of linear equations with real coefficients and theoretically generate an infeasibility certificate for it. However, in practice this approach is inefficient, as this involves converting an arbitrary propositional Boolean formula $\Phi$ into CNF, which is computationally expensive, and besides that, the size of the matrix $A$ of coefficients of linear constraint inequalities $(A \cdot x \geqslant b$ in the canonical representation of LP) grows exponentially in the number of variables in $\Phi$. Two notable results from semialgebraic geometry and convex optimization, Hilbert's Nullstellensatz [19] and Stengle's Positivstellensatz [20,21], state that for every infeasible system of polynomial equations and inequalities there exist a simple algebraic identity that directly certifies the infeasibility of the system. Nullstellensatz deals with polynomial equations in complex variables, and has been studied for the 3-colorability problem [8]. Nullstellensatz seems not to fit well for certifying infeasibility of a WMSAT instance, as it cannot be encoded as a system of polynomial equations. Positivstellensatz deals with arbitrary systems of polynomial equations and inequalities and therefore is a promising approach. Generating a Positivstellensatz infeasibility certificate is a convex feasibility problem. Finding bounded degree solutions to the Positivstellensatz is a semideinite problem. This gives a hierarchy of syntactically verifiable certificates, the validity of which may be easily checked. However, solving semidefinite programs (SDPs) is NP-hard for quartic and higher degree polynomials [1,10]. A computational tractable replacement for this is to apply sum-of-squares (SOS) relaxation to obtain an optimization problem over affine families of polynomials, subject to SOS constraints. It is known that SOS programs may be solved in polynomial time [9,17]. This approach provides a computational method to generate a bounded degree Positivstellensatz infeasibility certificates for given WMSAT instances in polynomial time, and is therefore a promising solution, which will be considered for future research. In this paper we focus on computational methods for generating and verifying infeasibility certificates for WMSAT instances, which use attack trees and does not require any conversions between attack trees and other equivalent representations, e.g. systems of polynomials.

## 4    Efficient Adversarial Expenses Calculation

An attack tree shown on the left-hand side in Fig. 1a corresponds to the Boolean function $\phi(x,y,z) = (x+z)(z+y)$, where logical conjunction is denoted as multiplication, and logical disjunction is denoted as sum. Each argument of the function is annotated with a weight. Let the arguments have the following weights: $w(x) = 2, w(z) = 6$, and $w(y) = 4$.

In order to find $w(\phi)$ we need to find the weight of the cheapest satisfying assignment. $\phi$ has five min-terms: $(xz),(zy),(xy),(xzy)$, and $(z)$. Hence, $w(\phi) =$ $\min\{w(xz), w(zy), w(xy), w(xzy), w(z)\} = \min\{8, 10, 6, 12, 6\} = 6$. Calculating the weight of the function this way is computationally expensive for large trees and not quite practical. The tree structure of an attack tree facilitates the usage

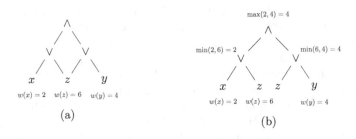

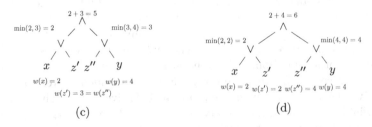

**Fig. 1.** Adversarial expenses calculation: an attack tree (a), propagation method (b), cost reduction (c) and (d).

of the efficient propagation methods [3,14] that allow to calculate $w_l(\phi)$ in time $\mathcal{O}(n)$, where $n$ is the number of attack tree nodes.

**Definition 3.** *A propagation method is a pair $(\bigwedge, \bigvee)$ of real-valued binary operations such that for every two Boolean functions $F$ and $G$:*

$$\bigwedge(w(F), w(G)) \leqslant w(FG) \quad and \quad \bigvee(w(F), w(G)) \leqslant w(F + G)$$

For instance, the pair $(\max, \min)$ is a propagation method, because

$$\max(w(F), w(G)) \leqslant w(FG) \quad and \quad \min\{w(F), w(G)\} = w(F + G)$$

However, it can be seen in Fig. 1b that the max operator is a very rough estimation of $w(\phi)$ and one could think of using $(+, \min)$ instead. The problem is that this is not a propagation method because it is possible that $w(F) + w(G) > w(FG)$. However, we are able to convert the function $FG$ into a function $F'G'$ for which $(+, \min)$ is a propagation method in terms of Definition 3. This can be done by using the technique known as weight reduction [3,14]. The rule $w(F) + w(G) \leqslant w(FG)$ holds only if $F$ and $G$ have no common variables. The weight reduction technique eliminates the common variables in the following way. If $z$ is a common variable of $F$ and $G$, then we first replace $z$ with new independent variables $z'$ in $F$ and $z''$ in $G$, and define the weights so that $w(z') + w(z'') = w(z)$. It can be shown that $w(F'G') \leqslant w(FG)$ according to Theorem 4.5.5 in [14]. The functions $F'$ and $G'$ now have one less common variable, and we can repeat the procedure with other common variables.

As the Boolean function in Fig. 1b contains a common variable $z$, and therefore the propagation method $(+, \min)$ cannot be applied directly, and weight reduction must be done first. The common variable $z$ is substituted with its independent copies $z \mapsto z'$ and $z \mapsto z''$, and their corresponding weights are distributed in a way that $w(z') + w(z'') = w(z)$. This distribution may be done in a variety of ways, as illustrated in Fig. 1c and d, both representing the reduced function $\phi(x, z', z'', y) = (x + z')(z'' + y)$. Independently on how we distribute weights, the rule $w(z') + w(z'') = w(z)$ must hold. In the case of a symmetric distribution $w(z') = 3 = w(z'')$ the result is underestimated, as can be seen in Fig. 1c, however, asymmetric distribution $w(z) = 2$ and $w(z'') = 4$ produces the exact result for $w(\phi)$ as can be seen in Fig. 1d. Thus, the choice of a distribution sets the precision with which the exact result can be approximated.

The main idea behind weight reduction is that every instance of the common variable in a Boolean formula is substituted with an independent copy of this variable with reduced weight. The sum of the weights of the reduced variables must never exceed the initial weight of the common variable, thus guaranteeing that this method will not over-estimate the weight of the function, according to Theorem 4.5.5 in [14]. We will show that in the case of Boolean functions with 1 common variable, the result is always exact. We refer the reader to Theorem 4 for details. If the Boolean function contains 2 or more common variables, this does not hold due to the existence of the so-called reduction defect. For example, the function $(vc + auz)(uy + bz)$ with unit costs for its variables, always has a reduction defect.

## 4.1    Infeasibility Certificates for WMSAT

In this subsection we present a method of constructing infeasibility certificates for WMSAT that uses weight reduction and propagation described above. The certificate $\alpha$ consists of instructions for a complete weight reduction of $\Phi$. For any conjunction-type sub-formula $\Psi = FG$ of $\Phi$ for any common variable $z$ of $F$ and $G$ we have to describe how we distribute the weight of $z$ between $F$ and $G$. For this, we have to define a real number $\alpha_{\Psi,z} \in [0,1]$ which means that if the weight of $z$ was $w$, then it will be redefined to $\alpha w$ in $F$ and $(1 - \alpha)w$ in $G$. We call a pair $(\Psi, z)$ a *decision point* of $\Phi$. All the values $\alpha_{\Psi,z}$ together form a *certificate*. Formally, the certificate is a function $\alpha$ that assigns to each decision point $(\Psi, z)$ of $\Phi$ a real number $\alpha(\Psi, z)$ from the unit interval $[0, 1]$.

**Definition 4.** *By a decision point of a Boolean formula $\Phi$ we mean a pair $(\Psi, z)$ where $\Psi$ is a conjunction-type sub-formula $FG$ of $\Phi$ so that $z$ is a common variable of $F$ and $G$. The set of all decision points of $\Phi$ is denoted by $\mathcal{D}(\Phi)$.*

**Definition 5.** *By a certificate for a Boolean formula $\Phi$ we mean a function $\alpha \colon \mathcal{D}(\Phi) \to [0, 1]$.*

As described above, the certificate consists of instructions how to weight-reduce $(\Phi, w)$ to $(\Phi', w')$ so that the propagation method $(+, \min)$ computes the exact value of $w'(\Phi')$ that of course may be smaller than $w(\Phi)$.

## 4.2    Computational Methods

The algorithm Desp that for a Boolean formula $\Phi$ computes the list $\mathcal{D} = \mathcal{D}(\Phi)$ of decision points. The list $\mathcal{D}$ is initially empty.

---

**Algorithm 4.1.** Algorithm Desp($\Phi$) for generating a list of decision points.

---

**Data:** Boolean formula $\Phi$
**Result:** A list $\mathcal{D}$ of decision points

1   **if** $\Phi = z$ *(an atomic variable)* **then**
2     |   **return** $\{z\}$;
3   **else if** $\Phi \in \{FG, F + G\}$
4     |   $S_F := \mathsf{Desp}(F)$ and $S_G := \mathsf{Desp}(G)$;
5     |   **if** $\Phi = FG$ **then**
6     |     |   **forall** $z \in S_F \cap S_G$ **do**
7     |     |     |   append $(\Phi, z)$ to $\mathcal{D}$;
8     |   **return** $S_F \cup S_G$;

---

The evaluation algorithm Eval that applies the propagation method $(+, \min)$ to the weight-reduced Boolean formula $\Phi'$ (and computes $w'(\Phi')$) can be defined as

**Algorithm 4.2.** Algorithm $\mathsf{Eval}^\alpha(\Phi, \mathcal{A})$ : for evaluating the weight reduced Boolean function $\Phi'$.

**Data:** Boolean formula $\Phi$
**Result:** Lower bound of $w(\Phi)$

1  **if**  $\Psi = z$ *(an atomic variable)* **then**
2  $\quad$ **return** $w(z) \cdot \prod_{(z,\beta) \in \mathcal{A}} \beta$;

3  **if**  $\Psi = F + G$ **then**
4  $\quad$ **return** $\min\{\mathsf{Eval}^\alpha(F, \mathcal{A}), \mathsf{Eval}^\alpha(G, \mathcal{A})\}$;

5  **if**  $\Psi = FG$ **then**
6  $\quad$ $\mathcal{A}_F := \mathcal{A}_G = \mathcal{A}$;
7  $\quad$ **forall**  $(\Psi, z) \in \mathcal{D}$ **do**
8  $\quad\quad$ append $(z, \alpha(z))$ to $\mathcal{A}_F$;
9  $\quad\quad$ append $(z, 1 - \alpha(z))$ to $\mathcal{A}_G$;
10 $\quad$ **return** $\mathsf{Eval}^\alpha(\Psi, \mathcal{A}_F) + \mathsf{Eval}^\alpha(\Psi, \mathcal{A}_G)$;

follows. It uses the list of decision points $\mathcal{D}$, and the weight function $w$ as global parameters and $\alpha$ as an oracle. The input parameters are a Boolean function $\Phi$ and an adjustment list $\mathcal{A}$ which is needed for adjusting the weight function $w$.

The verification algorithm $W(X, \alpha)$, given a triple $X = (\Phi, w, t)$ and the certificate $\alpha$ is shown in Algorithm 4.3.

**Algorithm 4.3.** Algorithm $W((\Phi, w, t), \alpha)$ for verifying the infeasibility certificate $\alpha$.

**Data:** Boolean formula $\Phi$
**Result:** 1 or 0

1  Compute the decision list $\mathcal{D}$ using $\mathsf{Desp}(\Phi)$;
2  Compute $\ell = \mathsf{Eval}(\Phi, ())$, where $()$ is the empty list;
3  **if**  $\ell > t$ **then**
4  $\quad$ **return** 1;

5  **else**
6  $\quad$ **return** 0;

## 5   Analysis

The more close is $\ell = w'(\Phi')$ to the exact value $w(\Phi)$, the more valuable is the result. We show (Theorem 1) that if $\Phi = FG$ and $z$ is the only common variable of $F$ and $G$, then we can divide the weight $w(z)$ of $z$ between $F$ and $G$ such that the resulting modified function $F'G'$, where $z$ is replaced with $z'$ in $F'$ and with $z''$ in $G'$ has the same weight than the original function, i.e. $w'(F'G') = w(FG)$.

This means that if in all conjunction type sub-formulae $FG$ of $\Phi$ the sub-formulae $F$ and $G$ do not have more than one common variable, the certificate $\alpha$ can be chosen so that $\mathsf{Eval}^\alpha(\Phi,\mathcal{A}) = w(\Phi)$, i.e. the lower bound is exact.

Unfortunately, as we show in Theorem 3 that this property does not generalise to the case of more than one common variable. We show that if $F$ and $G$ contain two common variables, then it might be that $\mathsf{Eval}^\alpha(\Phi,\mathcal{A}) < w(\Phi)$ for every possible certificate $\alpha$, i.e. the *reduction defect* $\delta = w(\Phi) - \max_\alpha \mathsf{Eval}^\alpha(\Phi,\mathcal{A})$ is positive.

Theorem 2 gives necessary and sufficient conditions for the positive reduction defect for a single decision point reduction and shows that the defect a single decision point $(\Psi, z)$ may create is upper bounded by $w(z)/2$.

As the weight function $w$ is uniquely defined by its values $w(x_1), w(x_2), \dots$ on the Boolean variables, we denote by $w_{\xi_1,\xi_2,\dots}$ the weight function $w$ for which $\xi_1 = w(x_1), \xi_2 = w(x_2), \dots$ Hence, for any Boolean function $\Phi$, we can define a real-valued function $f_\Phi(\xi_1, \xi_2, \dots) = w_{\xi_1,\xi_2,\dots}(\Phi)$. It is easy to see that $f_\Phi$ is continuous, because $w(\mu)$ is a continuous function of the weights, the number of min-terms is finite, and for any continuous functions $f(X)$ and $g(X)$, the function $\varphi(X) = \min\{f(X), g(X)\}$ is also continuous.

## 5.1   The Case of One Common Variable

For convenience, we add additional variables $z, z', z'', \dots, y_1, y_2, \dots$ to $X$. Let $F(x_1, \dots, x_n, z)$ and $G(z, y_1, \dots, y_m)$ be monotone Boolean functions. Let $z$ be the only common variable in $F$ and $G$. Let $F'(x_1, \dots, x_n, z')$ and $G'(z'', y_1, \dots, y_m)$ be the modified Boolean functions where $z$ has been replaced with $z'$ and $z''$, respectively. Note that $F'$ and $G'$ have no common variables. We always assume that $w(z) = w(z') + w(z'')$ even if we change the values of $w(z')$ and $w(z'')$. Thereby, we use a parameter $\alpha \in [0,1]$ so that $w(z') = \alpha w(z)$ and $w(z'') = (1-\alpha)w(z)$. By $w_\alpha$, we mean a weight function that behaves exactly like $w$, but for which $w(z') = \alpha w(z)$ and $w(z'') = (1-\alpha)w(z)$. A min-term $\mu$ of a Boolean function $\Phi$ is said to be $\alpha$-*cheapest* if $w_\alpha(\mu) = w_\alpha(\Phi)$.

**Lemma 1.** $w_\alpha(F') + w_\alpha(G') = w_\alpha(F'G') \le w(FG)$ *for any* $\alpha \in [0,1]$.

*Proof.* As $F'$ and $G'$ have no common variables, we have that $w_\alpha(F'G') = w_\alpha(F') + w_\alpha(G')$. For any min-term $\mu$ of $FG$, there is a min-term $\mu'$ of $F'G'$ obtained from $\mu$ by replacing $z$ with $z'z''$. From $w(z) = w(z') + w(z'')$ it follows that $w_\alpha(\mu') = w_\alpha(\mu)$. Hence, $w_\alpha(F'G') \le w(FG)$.                  $\square$

For any conjunction $\mu$, we define two subsets of the unit interval $I = [0,1]$:

$$\mathcal{O}_{F,\mu} = \{\alpha \in I : w_\alpha(\mu) > w_\alpha(F')\} \quad \text{and} \quad \mathcal{O}_{G,\mu} = \{\alpha \in I : w_\alpha(\mu) > w_\alpha(G')\}$$

For any Boolean function $\Phi$, let $\mathsf{M}_z(\Phi)$ denote the set of all min-terms of $\Phi$ that contain $z$, and $\mathsf{M}_{\bar{z}}(\Phi)$ the set of all min-terms of $\Phi$ without $z$.

$$\mathcal{O}_F = \bigcap_{\mu \in \mathsf{M}_{\bar{z}}(F)} \mathcal{O}_{F,\mu} = \{\alpha \in I : \text{All } \alpha\text{-cheapest min-terms of } F' \text{ contain } z'\}$$

$$\mathcal{O}_G = \bigcap_{\mu \in \mathsf{M}_{\bar{z}}(G)} \mathcal{O}_{G,\mu} = \{\alpha \in I : \text{All } \alpha\text{-cheapest min-terms of } G' \text{ contain } z''\}$$

$$\mathcal{U}_F = \bigcap_{\mu \in \mathsf{M}_z(F)} \mathcal{O}_{F,\mu} = \{\alpha \in I : \text{No } \alpha\text{-cheapest min-term of } F' \text{ contains } z'\}$$

$$\mathcal{U}_G = \bigcap_{\mu \in \mathsf{M}_z(G)} \mathcal{O}_{G,\mu} = \{\alpha \in I : \text{No } \alpha\text{-cheapest min-term of } G' \text{ contains } z''\}$$

**Lemma 2.** *In terms of topology, $\mathcal{O}_F, \mathcal{O}_G, \mathcal{U}_F, \mathcal{U}_G$ ore open subsets of $I$.*

*Proof.* As $f_\mu(\alpha) = w_\alpha(\mu) - w_\alpha(F')$ and $g_\mu(\alpha) = w_\alpha(\mu) - w_\alpha(G')$ are continuous functions, $\mathcal{O}_{F,\mu} = f_\mu^{-1}[(0,\infty)]$, and $\mathcal{O}_{G,\mu} = g_\mu^{-1}[(0,\infty)]$, the sets $\mathcal{O}_{F,\mu}$ and $\mathcal{O}_{G,\mu}$ as pre-images of an open set $(0,\infty)$ are open. As finite intersections of open sets, the sets $\mathcal{O}_F, \mathcal{O}_G, \mathcal{U}_F, \mathcal{U}_G$ must also be open. $\square$

**Lemma 3.** *If $\mathcal{U}_F \cup \mathcal{U}_G \neq I$, then $w_\alpha(F'G') = w(FG)$ for an $\alpha \in I$.*

*Proof.* Let $\alpha \in I \setminus (\mathcal{U}_F \cup \mathcal{U}_G)$, i.e. there are $\alpha$-cheapest min-terms $\mu_F$ and $\mu_G$ of $F'$ and $G'$, respectively, such that $\mu_F = x_{i_1} x_{i_2} \dots x_{i_k} z'$ and $\mu_G = y_{j_1} y_{j_2} \dots y_{j_m} z''$. Hence, $\mu = x_{i_1} x_{i_2} \dots x_{i_k} z y_{j_1} y_{j_2} \dots y_{j_m}$ is a min-term of $FG$ and

$$\begin{aligned} w_\alpha(F'G') &= w_\alpha(F') + w_\alpha(G') = w_\alpha(\mu_F) + w_\alpha(\mu_G) \\ &= w(x_{i_1} \dots x_{i_k}) + w_\alpha(z') + w_\alpha(z'') + w(y_{j_1} \dots y_{j_m}) \\ &= w(x_{i_1} \dots x_{i_k}) + w(z) + w(y_{j_1} \dots y_{j_m}) = w(\mu) \geq w(FG) \ , \end{aligned}$$

and hence $w_\alpha(F'G') = w(FG)$ by Lemma 1. $\square$

**Lemma 4.** *If $\mathcal{O}_F \cup \mathcal{O}_G \neq I$, then $w_\alpha(F'G') = w(FG)$ for an $\alpha \in I$.*

*Proof.* Let $\alpha \in I \setminus (\mathcal{O}_F \cup \mathcal{O}_G)$, i.e. there are $\alpha$-cheapest min-terms $\mu_F$ and $\mu_G$ of $F'$ and $G'$, respectively, such that $\mu_F = x_{i_1} x_{i_2} \dots x_{i_k}$ and $\mu_G = y_{j_1} y_{j_2} \dots y_{j_m}$. Hence, $\mu = x_{i_1} x_{i_2} \dots x_{i_k} y_{j_1} y_{j_2} \dots y_{j_m}$ is a min-term of $FG$ and

$$w_\alpha(F'G') = w_\alpha(\mu_F) + w_\alpha(\mu_G) = w(\mu_F) + w(\mu_G) = w(\mu) \geq w(FG) \ ,$$

and hence $w_\alpha(F'G') = w(FG)$ by Lemma 1. $\square$

**Lemma 5.** *If $\mathcal{O}_F \cup \mathcal{O}_G = I$ and $\mathcal{O}_F$ or $\mathcal{O}_G$ is empty, then $w_\alpha(F'G') = w(FG)$ for an $\alpha \in I$.*

*Proof.* By $\mathcal{O}_F \cup \mathcal{O}_G = I$, for any $\alpha \in I$, either: (a) all $\alpha$-cheapest min-terms of $F'$ contain $z'$, or (b) all $\alpha$-cheapest min-terms of $G'$ contain $z''$.

If $\mathcal{O}_F = \emptyset$, then this means that for every $\alpha \in I$ there is an $\alpha$-cheapest min-term of $F'$ without $z'$ contradicting (a), and hence (b) is true. Take $\alpha = 0$ and let $\mu_F = x_{i_1} x_{i_2} \ldots x_{i_k}$ be an $\alpha$-cheapest min-term of $F'$ and $\mu_G$ be an $\alpha$-cheapest min-term of $G'$. This also means that $\mu = \mu_F \mu_G$ is a min-term of $FG$, whereas $w(\mu) = w(\mu_F) + w(\mu_G)$. As $w_\alpha(\mu_F) = w(\mu_F)$ and by the choice of $\alpha$, we have $w_\alpha(\mu_G) = w(\mu_G)$, we have

$$w_\alpha(F'G') = w_\alpha(\mu_F) + w_\alpha(\mu_G) = w(\mu_F) + w(\mu_G) = w(\mu) \geq w(FG) \ ,$$

and hence, $w_\alpha(F'G') = w(FG)$ by Lemma 1.

If $\mathcal{O}_G = \emptyset$, then this means that for every $\alpha \in I$ there is an $\alpha$-cheapest min-term of $G'$ without $z''$ contradicting (b), and hence (a) is true. Take $\alpha = 1$ and let $\mu_G = y_{j_1} y_{j_2} \ldots y_{j_m}$ be an $\alpha$-cheapest min-term of $G'$ and $\mu_F$ be an $\alpha$-cheapest min-term of $F'$. This also means that $\mu = \mu_F \mu_G$ is a min-term of $FG$, whereas $w(\mu) = w(\mu_F) + w(\mu_G)$. As $w_\alpha(\mu_G) = w(\mu_G)$ and by the choice of $\alpha$, we have $w_\alpha(\mu_F) = w(\mu_F)$, we have

$$w_\alpha(F'G') = w_\alpha(\mu_F) + w_\alpha(\mu_G) = w(\mu_F) + w(\mu_G) = w(\mu) \geq w(FG) \ ,$$

and hence, $w_\alpha(F'G') = w(FG)$ by Lemma 1.     $\square$

**Lemma 6.** *If $\mathcal{U}_F \cup \mathcal{U}_G = I$ and $\mathcal{U}_F$ or $\mathcal{U}_G$ is empty, then $w_\alpha(F'G') = w(FG)$ for an $\alpha \in I$.*

*Proof.* By $\mathcal{U}_F \cup \mathcal{U}_G = I$, for any $\alpha \in I$, either: (a) no $\alpha$-cheapest min-term of $F'$ contains $z'$, or (b) no $\alpha$-cheapest min-term of $G'$ contains $z''$.

If $\mathcal{U}_F = \emptyset$, then for every $\alpha \in I$ there is an $\alpha$-cheapest min-term of $F'$ with $z'$ contradicting (a), and hence (b) is true. Take $\alpha = 1$ and let $\mu_F = x_{i_1} x_{i_2} \ldots x_{i_k} z'$ be an $\alpha$-cheapest min-term of $F'$ and $\mu_G$ be an $\alpha$-cheapest min-term of $G'$. Also, $\mu = \mu_F \mu_G$ is a min-term of $FG$, whereas $w(\mu) = w(\mu_F) + w(\mu_G)$. As $w_\alpha(\mu_G) = w(\mu_G)$ ($\mu_G$ does not contain $z''$) and by the choice of $\alpha$, we have $w_\alpha(\mu_F) = w(\mu_F)$, we have $w_\alpha(F'G') = w_\alpha(\mu_F) + w_\alpha(\mu_G) = w(\mu_F) + w(\mu_G) = w(\mu) \geq w(FG)$, and hence, $w_\alpha(F'G') = w(FG)$ by Lemma 1.

If $\mathcal{U}_G = \emptyset$, then for every $\alpha \in I$ there is an $\alpha$-cheapest min-term of $G'$ with $z''$ contradicting (b), and hence (a) is true. Take $\alpha = 0$ and let $\mu_G = y_{j_1} y_{j_2} \ldots y_{j_m} z''$ be an $\alpha$-cheapest min-term of $G'$ and $\mu_F$ be an $\alpha$-cheapest min-term of $F'$. This also means that $\mu = \mu_F \mu_G$ is a min-term of $FG$, whereas $w(\mu) = w(\mu_F) + w(\mu_G)$. As $w_\alpha(\mu_F) = w(\mu_F)$ ($\mu_F$ does not contain $z'$) and by the choice of $\alpha$, we have $w_\alpha(\mu_G) = w(\mu_G)$, we have $w_\alpha(F'G') = w_\alpha(\mu_F) + w_\alpha(\mu_G) = w(\mu_F) + w(\mu_G) = w(\mu) \geq w(FG)$, and hence, $w_\alpha(F'G') = w(FG)$ by Lemma 1.     $\square$

**Theorem 2.** *There is $\alpha \in I$, so that $w_\alpha(F'G') = w(FG)$.*

*Proof.* Assume on the contrary that the statement is false. Then by the lemmas above, $\mathcal{O}_F \cup \mathcal{O}_G = I$, $\mathcal{U}_F \cup \mathcal{U}_G = I$ and all $\mathcal{O}_F, \mathcal{O}_G, \mathcal{U}_F, \mathcal{U}_G$ are non-empty. As $I$ is connected, we have $\mathcal{O}_F \cap \mathcal{O}_G \neq \emptyset$ and $\mathcal{U}_F \cap \mathcal{U}_G \neq \emptyset$.

If there is a cheapest min-term of $FG$ that contains $z$ and $\mu = x_{i_1} x_{i_2} \ldots x_{i_k} z y_{j_1} y_{j_2} \ldots y_{j_m}$ is such a min-term, and $\alpha \in \mathcal{U}_F \cap \mathcal{U}_G$, then no $\alpha$-cheapest min-terms of $F'$ and $G'$ contain $z'$ or $z''$ and hence $w_\alpha(F') = w(F)$ and $w_\alpha(G) = w(G)$. As $\mu_F = x_{i_1} x_{i_2} \ldots x_{i_k} z'$ and $\mu_G = z'' y_{j_1} y_{j_2} \ldots y_{j_m}$ are min-terms of $F'$

and $G'$, respectively (but not $\alpha$-cheapest, as they contain $z'$ and $z''$), then we have a contradiction:

$$w(FG) = w_\alpha(\mu_F) + w_\alpha(\mu_G) > w_\alpha(F') + w_\alpha(G') = w(F) + w(G) \geq w(FG) \ .$$

If no cheapest min-term of $FG$ contains $z$, and $\alpha \in \mathcal{O}_F \cap \mathcal{O}_G$, then all $\alpha$-cheapest min-terms of $F'$ and $G'$ contain $z'$ or $z''$. Let $\mu_F = x_{i_1} x_{i_2} \ldots x_{i_k} z'$ and $\mu_G = z'' y_{j_1} y_{j_2} \ldots y_{j_m}$ be $\alpha$-cheapest min-terms of $F'$ and $G'$, respectively. As then $\mu = x_{i_1} x_{i_2} \ldots x_{i_k} z y_{j_1} y_{j_2} \ldots y_{j_m}$ is a min-term of $FG$ (but not the cheapest, as it contains $z$), we again have a contradiction: $w_\alpha(F'G') = w_\alpha(\mu_F) + w_\alpha(\mu_G) = w(\mu) > w(FG) \geq w_\alpha(F'G')$.    $\square$

## 5.2   Two or More Common Variables

Let $z$ be any common variable of $F$ and $G$, such that $F = F_0 + z\partial F$ and $G = G_0 + z\partial G$, where $\partial F, \partial G, F_0, G_0$ do not depend on $z$. The functions $\partial F$ and $\partial G$ are the so-called *Boolean derivatives* $\partial F = \frac{\partial}{\partial z} F$ and $\partial G = \frac{\partial}{\partial z} G$. Let $F' = F_0 + z'\partial F$ and $G' = G_0 + z''\partial G$, where $w(z') + w(z'') = w(z); w(z') = \alpha w(z)$ and $w(z'') = (1-\alpha)w(z)$, where $\alpha \in [0,1]$; and $m_0 = \min\{w(F_0 G_0), w(z\partial F\partial G)\}$. As

$$FG = (F_0 + z\partial F)(G_0 + z\partial G) = F_0 G_0 + z\partial F\partial G + zG_0\partial F + zF_0\partial G$$
$$F'G' = (F_0 + z'\partial F)(G_0 + z''\partial G) = F_0 G_0 + z'z''\partial F\partial G + z'G_0\partial F + z''F_0\partial G$$

and $w(z'z''\partial F\partial G) = w(z\partial F\partial G)$, we have

$$w(FG) = \min\{w(F_0 G_0), w(z\partial F\partial G), w(zG_0\partial F), w(zF_0\partial G)\}$$
$$= \min\{m_0, w(zG_0\partial F), w(zF_0\partial G)\}$$
$$w(F'G') = \min\{w(F_0 G_0), w(z\partial F\partial G), w(z'G_0\partial F), w(z''F_0\partial G)\}$$
$$= \min\{m_0, w(z'G_0\partial F), w(z''F_0\partial G)\} \ .$$

The difference $\delta = w(FG) - \max_\alpha w(F'G')$ is called the *reduction defect*. It is non-negative, as $w(FG) \geq w(F'G')$.

**Theorem 3.** *The reduction defect $\delta$ is non-zero ($\delta > 0$) if and only if the following inequalities hold:*

$$\mid w(G_0\partial F) - w(F_0\partial G) \mid < w(z) < 2m_0 - w(G_0\partial F) - w(F_0\partial G) \ , \qquad (1)$$

*and has upper bound* $\delta \leq \frac{w(z)}{2} - \frac{1}{2} \mid w(G_0\partial F) - w(F_0\partial G) \mid \leq \frac{w(z)}{2}$ *.*

*Proof.* Note that $\delta$ is non-zero if and only if for any $\alpha$:

$$m' = \min\{w(z'G_0\partial F), w(z''F_0\partial G)\} < \min\{w(zG_0\partial F), w(zF_0\partial G)\} \qquad (2)$$
$$m' < m_0 = \min\{w(F_0 G_0), w(z\partial F\partial G)\} \qquad (3)$$

The quantity $m_1(\alpha) = \min\{w(z'G_0\partial F), w(z''F_0\partial G)\}$ gains maximum if $w(z'G_0\partial F) = w(z''F_0\partial G)$. We study two cases: (a) $w(G_0\partial F) \geq w(F_0\partial G)$ and (b) $w(G_0\partial F) \leq w(F_0\partial G)$.

From (a), it follows that the maximum occurs if

$$w(z) - 2w(z') = w(z'') - w(z') = w(G_0 \partial F) - w(F_0 \partial G) \ ,$$

i.e. if $w(z') = w_0 = \frac{w(z)}{2} - \frac{1}{2}(w(G_0 \partial F) - w(F_0 \partial G))$. Hence,

$$M = \max_\alpha m_1(\alpha) = \max_\alpha \min\{w(z'G_0 \partial F), w(z''F_0 \partial G)\} = w_0 + w(G_0 \partial F)$$

$$= \frac{w(z)}{2} - \frac{1}{2}(w(G_0 \partial F) - w(F_0 \partial G)) + w(G_0 \partial F)$$

$$= \frac{w(z)}{2} + \frac{1}{2}(w(G_0 \partial F) + w(F_0 \partial G)) \ .$$

Considering that $\min\{w(zG_0 \partial F), w(zF_0 \partial G)\} = w(z) + w(F_0 \partial G)$ and $\mid w(G_0 \partial F) - w(F_0 \partial G) \mid = w(G_0 \partial F) - w(F_0 \partial G)$ by (a), the conditions (2) and (3) transform to

$$\frac{w(z)}{2} + \frac{1}{2}(w(G_0 \partial F) + w(F_0 \partial G)) < w(z) + w(F_0 \partial G)$$

$$\frac{w(z)}{2} + \frac{1}{2}(w(G_0 \partial F) + w(F_0 \partial G)) < m_0 \ ,$$

which is equivalent to (1). The reduction defect is:

$$\delta = w(FG) - \max_\alpha w(F'G') = \min\{m_0, w(zG_0 \partial F), w(zF_0 \partial G)\} - M$$

$$\leq \min\{w(zG_0 \partial F), w(zF_0 \partial G)\} - M$$

$$= w(z) + w(F_0 \partial G) - \frac{w(z)}{2} - \frac{w(G_0 \partial F) + w(F_0 \partial G)}{2}$$

$$= \frac{w(z)}{2} - \frac{1}{2}(w(G_0 \partial F) - w(F_0 \partial G)) = \frac{w(z)}{2} - \frac{1}{2} \mid w(G_0 \partial F) - w(F_0 \partial G) \mid \ .$$

From (b), it follows that the maximum occurs if

$$w(z) - 2w(z'') = w(z') - w(z'') = w(F_0 \partial G) - w(G_0 \partial F) \ ,$$

i.e. if $w(z'') = w_0' = \frac{w(z)}{2} - \frac{1}{2}(w(F_0 \partial G) - w(G_0 \partial F))$. Hence,

$$M = \max_\alpha m_1(\alpha) = \max_\alpha \min\{w(z'G_0 \partial F), w(z''F_0 \partial G)\} = w_0' + w(F_0 \partial G)$$

$$= \frac{w(z)}{2} - \frac{1}{2}(w(F_0 \partial G) - w(G_0 \partial F)) + w(F_0 \partial G)$$

$$= \frac{w(z)}{2} + \frac{1}{2}(w(F_0 \partial G) + w(G_0 \partial F)) \ .$$

As $\min\{w(zG_0 \partial F), w(zF_0 \partial G)\} = w(z) + w(G_0 \partial F)$ and $\mid w(G_0 \partial F) - w(F_0 \partial G) \mid = w(F_0 \partial G) - w(G_0 \partial F)$ by (b), the conditions (2) and (3) transform to

$$\frac{w(z)}{2} + \frac{1}{2}(w(G_0 \partial F) + w(F_0 \partial G)) < w(z) + w(G_0 \partial F)$$

$$\frac{w(z)}{2} + \frac{1}{2}(w(G_0 \partial F) + w(F_0 \partial G)) < m_0 \ ,$$

which is equivalent to (1). The reduction defect is:

$$\delta \leq w(z) + w(G_0 \partial F) - \frac{w(z)}{2} - \frac{w(G_0 \partial F) + w(F_0 \partial G)}{2}$$

$$= \frac{w(z)}{2} - \frac{1}{2}\left(w(F_0 \partial G) - w(G_0 \partial F)\right)$$

$$= \frac{w(z)}{2} - \frac{1}{2}\left| w(F_0 \partial G) - w(G_0 \partial F) \right| \quad .$$

$\square$

**Theorem 4.** *There are $F$ and $G$ with two common variables and a suitable distribution weights, so that the weight reduction always has a defect.*

*Proof.* Let $F = vx + auz$ and $G = uy + bz$, i.e. the common variables are $z$ and $u$. Assume that all weights are equal to 1. Hence, $w(FG) = w(xyvu + xvbz + ayuz + abuz) = \min\{w(xyvu), w(xvbz), w(ayuz), w(abuz)\} = 4$. If $w(u') + w(u'') = w(u)$ and $w(z') + w(z'') = w(z)$, we have $F'G' = (vx + au'z')(u''y + bz'') = vxyu'' + xvbz'' + ayu'u''z' + abuz'z''$. Hence,

$$w(F'G') = \min\{w(vxyu''), w(xvbz''), w(ayu'u''z'), w(abuz'z'')\}$$
$$\leq \min\{w(xvbz''), w(ayu'u''z')\} = \min\{w(xvbz''), w(ayuz')\}$$
$$= \min\{w(xvb) + w(z''), w(ayu) + w(z')\}$$
$$= 3 + \min\{w(z'), w(z'')\} \leq 3.5 \quad .$$

$\square$

# 6   Conclusions and Open Questions

The results show that the new method is applicable in practice, as real-life attack trees tend to be flat with relatively small number of decision points, which makes it possible to generate infeasibility certificates for such trees. Even the relative error is close to 0.5 may be acceptable in practice because the attack tree parameters often cannot be measured with high precision.

Theorem 2 may be pessimistic in its assessment because it considers a particular way of choosing the certificate. For any decision point $(\Psi, z)$ it tries to choose $\alpha(\Psi, z)$ so that it minimizes the defect of a single step of the reduction. Global methods of choosing the values of $\alpha$ may obtain better results than what can be achieved by minimizing the local reduction defects. More precise estimations of reduction defect would be in place.

# References

1. Ahmadi, A.A., Olshevsky, A., Parrilo, P.A., Tsitsiklis, J.N.: NP-hardness of deciding convexity of quartic polynomials and related problems. Math. Program. **137**(1), 453–476 (2013)
2. Buldas, A., Laud, P., Priisalu, J., Saarepera, M., Willemson, J.: Rational choice of security measures via multi-parameter attack trees. In: Lopez, J. (ed.) CRITIS 2006. LNCS, vol. 4347, pp. 235–248. Springer, Heidelberg (2006). doi:10.1007/11962977_19
3. Buldas, A., Lenin, A.: New efficient utility upper bounds for the fully adaptive model of attack trees. In: Das, S.K., Nita-Rotaru, C., Kantarcioglu, M. (eds.) GameSec 2013. LNCS, vol. 8252, pp. 192–205. Springer, Cham (2013). doi:10.1007/978-3-319-02786-9_12
4. Buldas, A., Stepanenko, R.: Upper bounds for adversaries' utility in attack trees. In: Grossklags, J., Walrand, J. (eds.) GameSec 2012. LNCS, vol. 7638, pp. 98–117. Springer, Heidelberg (2012). doi:10.1007/978-3-642-34266-0_6
5. Blekherman, G., Parrilo, P.A., Thomas, R.R.: Semidefinite Optimization and Convex Algebraic Geometry. Society for Industrial and Applied Mathematics, Philadelphia (2012)
6. Boyd, S., Vandenberghe, L.: Convex Optimization. Cambridge University Press, New York (2004)
7. Corbineau, P.: A declarative language for the Coq proof assistant. In: Miculan, M., Scagnetto, I., Honsell, F. (eds.) TYPES 2007. LNCS, vol. 4941, pp. 69–84. Springer, Heidelberg (2008). doi:10.1007/978-3-540-68103-8_5
8. De Loera, J.A., Lee, J., Malkin, P.N., Margulies, S.: Computing infeasibility certificates for combinatorial problems through hilbert's nullstellensatz. J. Symb. Comput. **46**(11), 1260–1283 (2011)
9. Helton, J.W., Nie, J.: Semidefinite representation of convex sets. Math. Program. **122**(1), 21–64 (2010)
10. Hillar, C., Lim, L.-H.: Most tensor problems are np-hard. J. ACM **60**(6), 4:51–45:39 (2013)
11. Jürgenson, A., Willemson, J.: Computing exact outcomes of multi-parameter attack trees. In: Meersman, R., Tari, Z. (eds.) OTM 2008. LNCS, vol. 5332, pp. 1036–1051. Springer, Heidelberg (2008). doi:10.1007/978-3-540-88873-4_8
12. Jürgenson, A., Willemson, J.: Serial model for attack tree computations. In: Lee, D., Hong, S. (eds.) ICISC 2009. LNCS, vol. 5984, pp. 118–128. Springer, Heidelberg (2010). doi:10.1007/978-3-642-14423-3_9
13. Jürgenson, A., Willemson, J.: On fast and approximate attack tree computations. In: Kwak, J., Deng, R.H., Won, Y., Wang, G. (eds.) ISPEC 2010. LNCS, vol. 6047, pp. 56–66. Springer, Heidelberg (2010). doi:10.1007/978-3-642-12827-1_5
14. Lenin, A.: Reliable and Efficient Determination of the Likelihood of Rational Attacks. TUT Press, Tallinn (2015)
15. Mauw, S., Oostdijk, M.: Foundations of attack trees. In: Won, D.H., Kim, S. (eds.) ICISC 2005. LNCS, vol. 3935, pp. 186–198. Springer, Heidelberg (2006). doi:10.1007/11734727_17
16. de Moura, L., Bjørner, N.: Z3: an efficient SMT solver. In: Ramakrishnan, C.R., Rehof, J. (eds.) TACAS 2008. LNCS, vol. 4963, pp. 337–340. Springer, Heidelberg (2008). doi:10.1007/978-3-540-78800-3_24
17. Prajna, S., Papachristodoulou, A., Seiler, P., Parrilo, P.A.: Sostools: Sum of squares optimization toolbox for matlab (2004)

18. Schneier, B.: Attack trees. Dr. Dobb's J. Softw. Tools **24**(12), 21–22, 24, 26, 28–29, December 1999
19. Smith, K.E., Kahanpää, L., Kekäläinen, P., et al.: An Invitation to Algebraic Geometry. Universitext. Springer Science + Business Media, New York (2000)
20. Stengle, G.: A nullstellensatz and a positivstellensatz in semialgebraic geometry. Math. Ann. **207**, 87–98 (1974)
21. Stengle, G.: A nullstellensatz and positivstellensatz in semialgebraic geometry. Math. Ann. **207**, 87–97 (1994)

# Enhanced TLS Handshake Authentication with Blockchain and Smart Contract (Short Paper)

Bingqing Xia[1,2], Dongyao Ji[1,2(✉)], and Gang Yao[1,2]

[1] State Key Lab of Information Security,
Institute of Information Engineering of Chinese Academy of Sciences, Beijing, China
jidongyao@iie.ac.cn
[2] School of Cyber Security, University of Chinese Academy of Sciences,
Beijing, China

**Abstract.** Transport Layer Security (TLS) is the main standard designed for secure connections over the Internet. Security of TLS connections against active Man-in-the-Middle attacks relies on correctly validating public-key certificates during TLS handshake authentication. Although Certificate Transparency (CT) and further improved CT system—IKP mitigated the certificate authentication issues from the perspective of monitoring CA misbehavior, less attentions have been paid to consider the misbehavior of domain in using certificates during TLS handshake authentication. One misusing case is that domains refuse to use the certificates in Certificate Transparency Log for their own profits, the other is that a malicious domain impersonates the real one to deceive clients. In order to defend against domain's misbehaviors in using certificates, we propose ETDA system based on IKP and CT aiming to enhance the security of TLS protocol from a novel perspective. ETDA is a blockchain-based system enforcing the automatic punishments in response to domain misbehavior and compensations to the client during TLS handshake authentication. The decentralized nature and incentives mechanism of ETDA provide an effective approach to prevent domains from sending invalid certificates to clients. We implement this system through Ethereum platform and Game Theory, which proved to be both technically and economically feasible.

**Keywords:** TLS Handshake Protocol · Certificate transparency · Ethereum blockchain · Smart contract · Game Theory

## 1  Introduction

Transport Layer Security (TLS) are protocols designed to provide confidentiality, authenticity, and integrity over the Internet [1]. TLS clients receive digital

This work was supported by the National Key Research and Development Program of China, No. 2016YFB0800503.

S. Obana and K. Chida (Eds.): IWSEC 2017, LNCS 10418, pp. 56–66, 2017.
DOI: 10.1007/978-3-319-64200-0_4

certificates when they request to establish secure connections to domains. They verify them using the embedded public keys of CAs in their browsers or operating system certificate trust stores. Specifically, with a rogue certificate, the adversary may be able to conduct a TLS man-in-the-middle (MITM) attack between the end user and a fake website. Since the rogue certificate is technically valid and trusted, there will not be automated detection or security warnings generated for such an attack. In order to immediately identify a rogue certificate (including bogus or self-signed certificate), Certificate Transparency (CT) was proposed to provide a publicly logged and audited certificates facility for checking the validity of certificates [2]. A supplementary system Revocation Transparency [3] was also proposed. And a further improved CT system—IKP [4] infrastructure initially improved the log-based PKI based on blockchain and smart contract by offering automatic responses to CA misbehaviors and incentives for those who help detect misbehaviors. Unfortunately, despite these benefits, TLS handshake still suffers from several problems. First, responding to domain misbehavior takes time and requires manual effort in CT. Second, IKP fails to consider the misbehavior of domain in using certificates during TLS handshake authentication. Finally, there is no way to overcome denial of service attack [5].

In this paper, we try to solve these problems by applying blockchain and smart contract based on CT and IKP. Smart contracts are agreements between mutually distrusting participants, which are automatically enforced by the consensus mechanism of the blockchain without relying on a trusted authority [6]. The security of TLS protocol largely depends on whether the client has authenticated the received certificates, thus surveillance over domain's certificates sent to clients during the TLS handshake is also significant. In this paper, we present an enhanced TLS handshake domain authentication framework ETDA, a supplement to IKP. ETDA system relies on a decentralized entity that handles the definition and evaluation of domain misbehavior in certificates during the TLS handshake authentication and automatically executes pre-defined reactions to this misbehavior, which enhances the security of TLS handshake protocol and provides a new application scenario for blockchain research.

In summary, we make the following contributions:

1. We design and propose an enhanced TLS handshake domain authentication framework ETDA, including Client Check Policies and Domain Reactions Polices.
2. We demonstrate through a game theoretic analysis that ETDA system punishes domain misbehavior and compensates client, which proved to be feasible economically.
3. We implement this system through Ethereum platform, which proved to be feasible technically.

## 2    Background

In this section, we provide the background required to understand ETDA including TLS handshake authentication and smart contract on blockchain.

**TLS handshake authentication:** The full TLS handshake protocol allows domain and client to authenticate each other. In this paper, we only consider the widely used version where clients authenticate domains(a.com)which mainly depends on the certificate provided by domains. Whether the certificate is valid or not is the key component during TLS handshake authentication [7].

**Smart Contract on Blockchain:** Blockchain is basically an append-only data structure maintained by the nodes of a peer-to-peer network. It was initially introduced for Bitcoin payments [8]. Implementing smart contracts on blockchains is also a prominent topics. Smart contracts are user-defined programs that are automatically executed and enforced by the consensus protocol of the blockchain [9]. A smart contract is identified by an address (a 160-bit identifier), which allows users to create and invoke a smart contract by posting a transaction including payments (in Ether) and input data to the contract address. Since resided on blockchain, The program code of a smart contract can not be tampered once the contract is created to avoid the interference of malicious behavior to normal execution of contract. In this paper, we apply Ethereum Blockchain as the smart contract platform which supports stateful contracts where values can persist on the blockchain to be used in various invocations. For detailed information, please refer to [10,11].

## 3   ETDA Framework

In this section, we first propose the framework of ETDA system in Fig. 1. In general, ETDA system extends the traditional TLS ecosystem where domains interact with clients by carrying out TLS handshake with Ethereum blockchain. Then we illustrate the main components and functions of ETDA as well as explicit description of Client Check Policy and Domain Reaction Policy respectively.

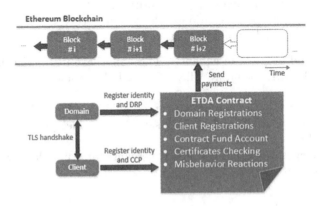

**Fig. 1.** Framework of ETDA

## 3.1   Components and Functions

We illustrate the following four main components in ETDA and functions:

**Domains.** Domains send certificates to clients during TLS handshake and issue Domain Reaction Policies (DRPs), which take effect if a domain sends an invalid certificate to clients, acting as a sort of payments insurance policy against domains misbehaviors. To participate in ETDA, domains should register identity information and DRPs in Ethereum blockchain.

**Clients.** Clients receive certificates from domains in TLS handshake protocol and issue Client Check Policies (CCPs), which publicize criterion to determine whether the certificates are valid. Clients also purchase DRPs from domains to obtain incentives for compensations if the certificate proved invalid. To join ETDA, clients should register identity and CCPs in Ethereum blockchain.

**ETDA Contract.** ETDA Contract provides different functions related to the operations of each entity in ETDA and contains the logic to execute the operations. It owns a contract fund account which maintains its own balance to escrow funds and provide rewards. Since based on blockchain, the contract is shared for all entities joining the blockchain once the contract is publicized.

**Ethereum Blockchain.** It is a decentralized platform providing incentive nature and a transaction framework to participants. We design smart contracts to realize incentives mechanism of punishing the misbehaving domains and compensating the clients automatically based on Ethereum Blockchain.

## 3.2   Client Check Policies (CCPs)

A CCP is issued by a client to check the validity of a domain's certificate. We design the contents of CCPs including: (1) *Client Name*, to identify client for which CCP is active. (2) *Payment Address*, to authenticate client's identities and receive payments. (3) *Valid From*, to denote start date of CCP's validity. (4) *Valid To*, to denote the expire date of CCP's validity. (5) *Version Number*, to denote version of CCP. (6) *Check Contract*, specified as a smart contract address to determine certificate validity.

Specifically, Check Contract is an Ethereum account on blockchain that provides a function *check* which takes in serialized bytes of a public-key certificate and returns a Boolean value representing certificate validity. We leverage Certificate Transparency (CT) Certificate Logs [2] as the checking criterion to check invalid certificates. The check policy can be interpreted as:

> **If** the certificate hasn't been logged in the Certificate Transparency Logs
>    and the domain is the one who sends the certificate,
> **then** the domain is deemed to have misbehaved.

### 3.3 Domain Reaction Polices (DRPs)

A DRP is issued by a domain in response to its misbehavior in certificates. Similar to CCP, we design the contents of DRPs including: (1) *Domain Name*, to identify who sends certificates to clients during TLS handshake, (2) *Issuer*, the primary domain who issued the DRP. In particular, the primary domain is responsible for the certificate misbehaviors for all of its subdomains, for example a.com is responsible for the certificate errors for c.a.com et. (3) *Payment address*, to authenticate domain's identity and send payments, (4) *Valid From*, to denote start date of DRPs validity, (5) *Valid To*, to denote expiration date of DRP's validity. (6) *Version Number*, to denote version of CCP corresponding to DRP. (7) *Reaction contract*, smart contract in response to domain's misbehaviors.

Reactions Contract is also a contract account on Ethereum which provides a method *trigger* in response to domain's misbehaviors in using certificates. The DRP itself also contains two methods including *terminate* and *expire* through the ETDA contract. The *terminate* method can be called by a client if the domain misbehaves in certificate and executes after *trigger* method. The *expire* method can be called by the domain once the DRP has expired. In general, a DRP contains a domain's commitment denoting that:

> **If** a domain (for example a.com) sends an invalid certificate to a client, **then** it will pay X *Ether* and the client who detects it will get Y *Ether*.

## 4 ETDA Operations

We take an in-depth look at the main operations of ETDA in this section and specify three entities involved in operations: (1) the client, who we denote as C, (2) the domain, which we denote as D, (3) the contract fund account, which we denote as CF. We use these abbreviations in the following sections as well.

### 4.1 Registrations

Each domain interacting with clients in TLS protocol should register its identity and a DRP in ETDA contract. When registering identity information, D sends a transaction which contains the D's certificate and corresponding certificate link containing the trusted root as well as signature information signed with private key which corresponds to the public key in certificate to ETDA contract. Therefore, the ETDA contract can determine domain's identity. In this way, an account for a registering domain D is created. D generates a pair of public key and private key $(PK_{D-account}, SK_{D-account})$ to control this account.

During TLS handshake, D sends a certificate appending with the signature information signed with the private key for manipulating its account. We denote the signature information as $SIG_{SK_{D-account}}(Cert, D, sid)$, which binds the certificate *Cert* with the D's identity information $D$ and a session number $sid$ to ensure that when D misuses the certificate, it fails to deny the misbehavior. Similarly, C should register its identity in ETDA contract. We denote the registration fees of D and C as $r_D$ and $r_C$ respectively.

## 4.2   Purchasing DRPs

If C choose to check a certificate from D, then C should purchase a DRP issued by D. We denote the fee for purchasing the DRP as $p$ which is transferred from C to D who issued the DRP. Besides, $g_D$ and $g_C$ are denoted as gas fees [10] paid to the contract fund account (CF). These gas fees restrict the execution steps of transactions to prevent from *denial-of-service* attacks where adversaries try to overwhelm the network with over-consumption of resources.

## 4.3   Certificates Checking

C can check D's certificate by executing the certificate check contract. If the certificate hasn't been logged in the CT Logs and D is the one who sends the certificate, then the certificate is deemed to be invalid. We present this checking algorithm written in smart contract in Solidity as a *check* method, where the output is true that denotes the certificate invalid and triggers the DRP's reaction contract. The detection algorithm is as follows:

---
**Algorithm 1.** *Check* Method in Certificate Check Contract
---
1: **procedure** Certificate_checking check()
2: Input: certificate Cert , $SIG_{SK_{D-account}}()$
3:      List $\leftarrow$ get CT_Logs
4:      look up Cert in List
5:      **if** (Cert not in List) and (Verify($SIG_{SK_{D-account}}()$)=true) **then**
6:           output: true
7:      **end if**
8: **end procedure**

---

## 4.4   Misbehaviors Reactions

Once a CCP determines a D's certificate to be invalid, the reaction contract of DRP is triggered to execute a series of payments automatically. We realize this incentives mechanism through a Game Theoretic model whose core idea is Nash Equilibrium [12]. We specify the following three kinds of payments:

**Misbehavior payment, m:** is the fund paid to C from D who sends an invalid certificate. It aims at compensating C for security risks it will suffer in TLS protocol. The amount of m depends on the severity of the misbehavior. We assume two kinds of misbehavior payments: (1) internal misbehavior payment, $m_i$, which is caused by a registered domain in Ethereum, (2) external misbehavior payment, $m_e$, which is caused by an un-registered domain.

**Termination Payment, t:** is the fund split between C and D if C terminates the DRP before *Valid To* date of DRP. It compensates C for lost trust in D due to the misbehavior of D and the cost of purchasing a new DRP. To guarantee that C can receive some minimum amount of funds, we set a parameter $\delta$. And the split amount of the termination payout is proportional to the amount of time left in the DRP's validity. We denote the total amount of termination payment is $t$, which is split for C as $t_C$, and D as $t_D$ $(t = t_C + t_D)$ and the proportion of the termination as $\theta$ $(0 \leq \theta \leq 1)$. Then we observe:

$$t_C = \delta + \theta(t - \delta) \tag{1}$$
$$t_D = (1 - \theta)(t - \delta) \tag{2}$$

And we remark:

$$\delta \leq t_C \leq t \tag{3}$$
$$0 \leq t_D \leq t - \delta \tag{4}$$

**Contract Fund Payment, f:** is the fund paid to contract fund account aiming to replenish the contract fund to ensure that it owns enough funds to continue its operation. Therefore, we design contract fund payments to compensate for any losses that the contract fund may suffer which will occur with high probability. We denote the total amount as S $(S = m+t+f)$ and a proportion $\alpha$ $(0 < \alpha < 1)$ of the total amount $(\alpha I)$ is escrowed in the contract to ensure the availability of these funds. The algorithm of *trigger* method is as follows:

---
**Algorithm 2.** *Trigger* Method in Domain Reaction Contract
---
1: **procedure** Misbehavior_reaction trigger()
2: Input: Certificate_checking check()=true
3:        Client ← Domain $m$ *Ether*
4:        Contract_Fund ← Domain $f$ *Ether*
5: **end procedure**

---

In particular, ETDA contract maintains a mapping between C and a list of their corresponding active DRPs. When C purchase a new DRP, ETDA contract adds the new DRP to C's current DRP list. This scheme ensures the DRP to every single instance of D's misbehavior is unambiguous. In summary, we combine the two operations of the certificate checking and the misbehavior reaction, and present Algorithm 3 which handles an invalid certificate.

---
**Algorithm 3.** ETDA contract handling an invalid certificate
---
1: **procedure** $ETDA\_contract$
2: Input: certificate Cert, Client address C
3:        D← get certificate_owner name from Cert
4:        $SIG_{SK_{D-account}}()$ ← get D's signature information from D
5:        CCP← get CCP from C
6:        $Check\_contract$ ← get check contract address from CCP
7:        **if** $Check\_contract$.check(Cert, $SIG_{SK_{D-account}}()$) **then**
8:                $DRP\_list$ ← look up DRP list for D
9:                DRP ← get reaction contract address from $DRP\_list[0]$
10:               DRP.trigger($check\_contract$.check())
11:               delete DRP from $DRP\_list$
12:               terminate()
13:        **end if**
14: **end procedure**

---

# 5    Payments Analysis

In this section, we analyze the payments between different entities in different scenarios. First, we provide a general analysis of a list of payments in response to each action in ETDA. Then we provide explicit analysis for different scenarios to determine what constraints to set to guarantee that entities benefit from behaving correctly and get punished for misbehaving with Game Theory approach.

## 5.1    General Analysis

We summarize the different payment flows between different entities for the main operations in Table 1 and classify the domains misbehaviors into two categories: **(1) DRP-issuer scenario.** D is the issuer of the DRP. If D misbehaves, we call it internal misbehavior as illustrated in Sect. 4. **(2) non-DRP-issuer scenario.** omain is not the issuer of the DRP and we denote the issuer as R. We note that an external misbehavior can only occur in non-DRP-issuer scenario.

We propose the following principles for payment designs: (1) Domains who internally misbehave lose money. (2) Domains who externally misbehave cannot profit. (3) Clients profit from internal misbehaviors. In particular, The domain may purposely misbehave in order to trigger DRP and then collude with the entities who receive positive funds to gain profits after summing their rewards. Therefore we must guarantee that no possible collusion attacks can result in the profits for the misbehaving domain.

## 5.2    DRP-issuer Scenario

For DRP-issuer scenario, we assume C has purchased a DRP and appropriate fees has been sent. Table 2 presents how payments transfer between different entities in response to scenarios of whether D misbehaves or not.

We observe that if D misbehaves, D should pay additional $m_i + t_C + f$ as punishment than it would otherwise and C will be rewarded $m_i + t_C$ as compensation. To guarantee C to profit, we set $m_i + t_C > p$. By Eq. 3 which is $\delta \leq t_C$, we set the constraint $p < m_i + \delta$ and to guarantee D to lose money for its misbehavior, we set $p < m_i + \delta + f$. However, this constraint is subsumed by the previous constraint $p < m_i + \delta$, which sets a tighter bound on $p$. To avoid collusion attacks, we observe that C profits If D misbehaves. The total rewards of D and C is -f. Thus D cannot profit from colluding with C. To sum up, the constraint based on Game Theory is: $p < m_i + \delta$.

## 5.3    non-DRP-issuer Scenario

In this scenario, we consider whether or not D registers in ETDA contract respectively as Tables 3 and 4 present.

**non-DRP-issuer scenario where D registers.** From Table 3, we observe that C has the same rewards as in the DRP-issuer scenario. Therefore we set

**Table 1.** Payments for various events

| Event | From | To | Amount |
|---|---|---|---|
| Register Domain | D | CF | $r_D$ |
| Register Client | C | CF | $r_C$ |
| Issue (purchase) DRP | D | CF | $\alpha S + g_D$ |
| | C | CF | $p + g_C$ |
| | CF | D | $p$ |
| Detect internal misbehavior (DRP-issuer) | CF | C | $m_i + t_C$ |
| | CF | D | $\alpha S - t_C - f$ |
| Detect internal misbehavior (non-DRP-issuer) | CF | C | $m_i + t_C$ |
| | CF | R | $\alpha S - t_C$ |
| | D | CF | $m_i + f$ |
| Detect external misbehavior (non-DRP-issuer) | CF | C | $m_e + t_C$ |
| | CF | R | $\alpha S - t_C$ |
| Terminate DRP | CF | C | $t_C$ |
| | CF | D | $\alpha S - t_C$ |
| Expire DRP | CF | D | $\alpha S$ |

**Table 2.** Rewards in the DRP-issuer scenario

| Entities | Events | | |
|---|---|---|---|
| | C | D | CF |
| Behave | $-p$ | $p$ | 0 |
| Misbehave | $-p + m_i + t_C$ | $p - m_i - t_C - f$ | $f$ |

the same constraint as $p < m_i + \delta$. For R who is the issuer of DRP and has not misbehaved, it should still profit for the DRP purchase fee. Therefore we set $p > t_C$. And by Eq. 3 which is $t_C \leq t$, we set the tighter constraint $p > t$. For D, it should pay additional fee $r_D$ for the registration. If D misbehaves, while D still faces penalty as in the DRP-issuer scenario, it receives $p + r_D$ less rewards than it behaves. Similarly, considering collusion attacks, we add the rewards of C, R and D. The sum $-f - r_D$ still ends up with a negative rewards to avoid collusion attack. To sum up, the constraints are: $t < p < m_i + \delta$.

**non-DRP-issuer scenario where D does not register.** From Table 4, we observe that R has the same rewards as in the non-DRP-issuer scenario where D registers. Since D has not registered in ETDA, it does not need to pay anything and fails to have sufficient funds to pay C, then ETDA contract's CF replenish D's absence funds and pay the appropriate rewards to C. Since that D does not need to pay anything, colluding with any entity with positive reward results in profits. Colluding with R will definitely bring D profits but the profits is less than

**Table 3.** Rewards in the domain-registered non-DRP-issuer scenario

| Entities | Events | | | |
|---|---|---|---|---|
| | C | R | D | CF |
| Behave | $-p$ | $p$ | $-r_D$ | $r_D$ |
| Misbehave | $-p + m_i + t_c$ | $p - t_c$ | $-r_D - m_i - f$ | $f + r_D$ |

the collusion rewards if D behaves. According to Game Theory, misbehaving is not the better strategy, which enforces D to choose the better choice, namely is to behave. If D colludes with C, the total sum of D and C is $-p + m_e + t_C$, therefore, we must set the constraint $p \geq m_e + t_C$ to ensure this reward is non-positive. Combining Eq. 3, we set a tighter constraint $p \geq m_e + t$. Under this constraint, we observe that C will have to lose money which seems unreasonable. However, C still obtains a higher reward than the case that D behaves. Therefore, checking D's misbehavior is the better strategy for C. To sum up, the constraint set based on Game Theory is: $p \geq m_e + t$.

**Table 4.** Rewards in the domain-unregistered non-DRP-issuer scenario

| Entities | Events | | | |
|---|---|---|---|---|
| | C | R | D | CF |
| Behave | $-p$ | $p$ | 0 | 0 |
| Misbehave | $-p + m_e + t_C$ | $p - t_c$ | 0 | $-m_e$ |

## 6    Conclusion

On the basis of CT and IKP, we proposed ETDA: a system for detecting and automatically responding to Domain misbehavior with smart contracts on Ethereum Blockchain. This provides a novel way for enhancing the security of TLS handshake authentication protocols. One merit of our method is that it can provide the power to restrict the error behavior of the domain. Besides, our experience suggests that reward and punishment mechanism based on Game Theory may be more suitable to repel the concrete attack scenarios.

## References

1. Rescorla, E.: The Transport Layer Security (TLS) Protocol Version 1.3-draft-ietf-tls-tls13-20, April 2017. https://tools.ietf.org/html/draft-ietf-tls-tls13-20
2. Laurie, B., Langley, A., Kasper, E. Certificate Transparency, June 2013. http://tools.ietf.org/pdf/rfc6962.pdf, IETF RFC 6962
3. Laurie, B., Kasper, E.: Revocation Transparency (2012). http://sump2.links.org/RevocationTransparency.pdf

4. Matsumoto, S., Reischuk, R.: IKP: Turning a PKI Around with Blockchains. Cryptology ePrint Archive: Report 2016/1018
5. Aura, T., Nikander, P., Leiwo, J.: DOS-resistant authentication with client puzzles. In: Christianson, B., Malcolm, J.A., Crispo, B., Roe, M. (eds.) Security Protocols 2000. LNCS, vol. 2133, pp. 170–177. Springer, Heidelberg (2001). doi:10.1007/3-540-44810-1_22
6. Luu, L., Chu, D., Olickel, H., Saxena, P., Hober, A.: Making smart contracts smarter. In: Proceedings of the 2016 ACM SIGSAC Conference on Computer and Communications Security, pp. 254–269, October 2016
7. Bhargavan, K., Lavaud, A., Fournet, C., Pironti, A., Strub, P.: Triple handshakes and cookie cutters: breaking and fixing authentication over TLS. In: IEEE Symposium on Security and Privacy (SP), pp. 98–113 (2014)
8. Nakamoto, S.: Bitcoin: A pee-to-peer electronic cash system (2008)
9. Delmolino, K., Arnett, M., Kosba, A., Miller, A., Shi, E.: Step by step towards creating a safe smart contract: lessons and insights from a cryptocurrency lab. In: Clark, J., Meiklejohn, S., Ryan, P.Y.A., Wallach, D., Brenner, M., Rohloff, K. (eds.) FC 2016. LNCS, vol. 9604, pp. 79–94. Springer, Heidelberg (2016). doi:10.1007/978-3-662-53357-4_6
10. Ethereum Foundation. Ethereum's white paper (2014). https://github.com/ethereum/wiki/White-Paper
11. Bonneau, J.: EthIKS: using ethereum to audit a CONIKS key transparency log. In: Clark, J., Meiklejohn, S., Ryan, P.Y.A., Wallach, D., Brenner, M., Rohloff, K. (eds.) FC 2016. LNCS, vol. 9604, pp. 95–105. Springer, Heidelberg (2016). doi:10.1007/978-3-662-53357-4_7
12. Weibull, J.: Evolutionary Game Theory. MIT Press, Cambridge (1995)

# Public Key Cryptosystems (1)

# Multipurpose Public-Key Encryption

Rui Zhang[1,2] and Kai He[1,2(✉)]

[1] State Key Laboratory of Information Security,
Institute of Information Engineering,
Chinese Academy of Sciences, Beijing 100093, China
{r-zhang,hekai}@iie.ac.cn
[2] School of Cyber Security, University of Chinese Academy of Sciences,
Beijing 100049, China

**Abstract.** We propose a new type of public-key schemes, that simultaneously satisfies selective opening (SO) security, key-dependent message (KDM) security and leakage-resilience. Our construction can be instantiated under the quadratic residuosity (QR) assumption or Paillier's decisional composite residuosity (DCR) assumption. With the decisional Diffie-Hellman (DDH) assumption holding on a subgroup of QR or DCR group, the instantiated encryption schemes enjoy key-privacy in addition.

**Keywords:** Public key encryption · Selective opening · KDM-security · Leakage resilience · Key privacy

## 1 Introduction

In practice, an encryption scheme is usually used as module or library. Take a popular software library OpenSSL as an example, which has been used for various purposes such as secure communication, file encryption or by other upper protocols.

However, an application designer may not be so aware of what exactly the security threat is for his encryption module in a real information system, to name a few, key dependent message security (KDM) [3], leakage resilience [16] and key privacy [1] were proposed for various applications where encryption is used. Hence, it is desirable that an encryption scheme can work in many practical scenarios, such that application designers can make fewer mistakes by taking an encryption module from a *standard* library. To solve this dilemma, we introduce a new primitive of public key encryption, called multipurpose PKE, which should provide a number of functionalities, in particular, the following ones:

**Semantic Security.** The classical notion of semantic security [10] for public-key encryption (PKE) guarantees that an efficient attacker with access to the public encryption-key must not be able to find two messages such that it can distinguish between an encryption of one message and an encryption of the other (indistinguishability under chosen plaintext attack, in short, IND-CPA). Numerous candidate public-key encryption schemes that meet this definition

S. Obana and K. Chida (Eds.): IWSEC 2017, LNCS 10418, pp. 69–84, 2017.
DOI: 10.1007/978-3-319-64200-0_5

have been presented over the years, both under specific hardness assumptions (like the hardness of factoring) and under general assumptions (such as the existence of injective one-way trapdoor functions). On the other hand, with wide adoptions of PKE in various scenarios, IND-CPA security no longer suffices.

**Selective Opening (SO) Security.** An adversary may view some encryptions and then choose to corrupt a certain fraction of the users, thus revealing the decryptions of those users' messages and the randomness used to encrypt them. Lossy encryption was proposed by Bellare, Hofheinz and Yilek [2] to achieve selective opening security w.r.t. this kind of corruption attack. SO-security ensures that the messages sent from those uncorrupted parties remain secure. Fehr, Hofheinz, Kiltz and Wee [9] also examines the case of CCA cryptosystems that are selective opening secure. In their work, they show how to adapt the non-committing encryption and the hash proof systems of [8], to provide CCA security in the selective opening setting.

**Key-Dependent Message (KDM) Security.** "Key cycle" usage may happen in careless key management, for example a backup system may store the backup encryption key on disk and then encrypt the entire disk, including the key, and backup the result. Another example is the BitLocker disk encryption utility (used in Windows Vista) where the disk encryption key can end up on disk and be encrypted along with the disk contents. KDM-security was proposed for this setting. An encryption scheme is key-dependent message secure if it is secure even the plaintext depends on the secret keys. Due to its extensive usefulness in protocol design and analysis [3,7], hard disk encryption [4], achieving KDM-security was widely studied in recent years. Lu, Li and Jia [14] achieved KDM-CCA security by enhancing a chosen ciphertext secure scheme based on the high entropy hash proof system with three tools: a key-dependent message encoding, an entropy filter and an authenticated encryption secure against related-key attacks. Kitagawa, Matsuda, Hanaoka and Tanaka [13] showed that Fujisaki-Okamoto construction satisfies KDM-CCA security.

**Leakage-Resilience.** Leakage-resilient cryptography was motivated by side-channel attacks such as cold boot attacks [11], in which a significant fraction of the secret key $sk$ is leaked to the adversary. Naor and Segev [16] presented public-key encryption schemes that are resilient to leakage rate of $1 - o(1)$ in the bounded leakage model. Qin and Liu [17] proposed a novel approach to achieve leakage-resilient CCA security by replacing the universal hash proof system in Naor and Segev's HPS-based framework with a new primitive called one-time lossy filter. This results in efficient constructions of LR-CCA secure PKE schemes based on the DDH and DCR assumptions with leakage rate $1/2 - o(1)$.

**Key-Privacy (Anonymity).** Bellare, Boldyreva, Desai and Pointcheval [1] formulated a security requirement called key-privacy or anonymity which asks that the encryption provides privacy of the key under which the encryption was performed. It asks that an eavesdropper in possession of a ciphertext not be able to tell which specific key, out of a set of known public keys, is the one under which the ciphertext was created. Thus key-privacy prevents any eavesdropper from tracing the ciphertext and learning who receives the plaintext, which provides her extra information that could be used for next step of her attack. Ideally, we would like to be able to prove that popular and existing schemes have the anonymity property (rather than having to design new schemes).

## 1.1 Related Work

Bellare, Boldyreva, Desai and Pointcheval [1] proved that the ElGamal encryption and the Cramer-Shoup encryption are key-private, so these schemes are "dual-purpose". In [5] Brakerski and Goldwasser constructed a scheme having KDM-security, leakage resilience and auxiliary-input (which can be viewed as a specific form of key-leakage) security, which also can be viewed as "dual-purpose". However, to the best of our knowledge, no encryption scheme provides all the security notions described above simultaneously.

## 1.2 Our Contributions

In this paper, we propose a new and generic construction of PKE that achieves selective opening (SO) security, $n$-key-dependent message (KDM) security (semantic security) and leakage-resilience. To achieve this goal, we introduce a new tool, called enhanced smooth projective hashing (ESPH), which is a variant of the smooth projective hashing [18]. It is worth mentioning that smooth projective hashing has been used to construct a number of applications, however, $n$-KDM-security cannot be proven directly from the smooth projective hashing and it is not clear whether the scheme [18] is SO-secure or key-private, either.

Therefore, we enhance the smooth projective hashing with four additional properties which are range orthogonality, $\kappa$-leakage smoothness, hashing key homomorphism and lossy evaluation. We remark that these properties can easily be fulfilled by simple and natural constructions from different classical assumptions, which is also a generalization of observations on instantiations of smooth projective hashing.

In particular, we show how to construct ESPH from QR and DCR assumptions. Instantiations with DCR enjoy shorter parameters and make the cryptosystems feasible and practical. Technically we find that if the public keys and the range of the smooth projective hashing have some group structure and the subgroup assumption holds on the public key group, those invalid public keys, which are not in the subgroup, behave exactly like lossy keys in lossy encryption. Moreover, we describe the secret key homomorphism in the sense of smooth projective hashing, then we prove $n$-KDM-security by this secret key homomorphism together with 1-KDM-security. We summarize these features as lossy evaluation and hashing key homomorphism. Range orthogonality is an observation on range of QR/DCR type smooth projective hashing, and it helps us to describe smoothness more precisely. $\kappa$-leakage smoothness is an abstraction of smoothness in

BHHO-like [4] smooth projective hashing. This feature implies leakage-resilience directly. Key privacy comes from an additional DDH assumption in subgroups naturally.

## 2    Preliminary

In this section we review some useful notations, lemmas and notions.

**Notations.** We denote by $[n]$ a set $\{1, 2, \ldots, n\}$ for any integer $n \in \mathbb{N}$. We denote the process of picking $x$ randomly according to the uniform distribution over a finite $S$ by $x \xleftarrow{\$} S$. Statistical distance between two random variables $X$ and $Y$ with Support $\Omega$ is defined as $\Delta(X; Y) = \frac{1}{2}\sum_{s \in \Omega}|\Pr[X = s] - \Pr[Y = s]|$. A function $f : \mathbb{N} \to \mathbb{R}_{\geq 0}$ is said to be negligible, if for all $c$, there exists $N$ such that $f(\lambda) < 1/\lambda^c$ for all $\lambda > N$. We denote a negligible function by $\mathsf{negl}(\cdot)$. For ensembles of random variable $\{X(\lambda)\}_{\lambda \in \mathbb{N}}$ and $\{Y(\lambda)\}_{\lambda \in \mathbb{N}}$, we say that they are $\mathsf{negl}(\lambda)$-close or $X(\lambda) \approx_s Y(\lambda)$ if $\Delta(X(\lambda); Y(\lambda)) = \mathsf{negl}(\lambda)$. We write $X(\lambda) \approx_c Y(\lambda)$ if for all probabilistic polynomial time (PPT) distinguisher $D$ there is a negligible function $\mathsf{negl}(\cdot)$ such that: $|\Pr[D(1^\lambda, X(\lambda))] - \Pr[D(1^\lambda, Y(\lambda))]| \leq \mathsf{negl}(\lambda)$.

### 2.1    Simplified Leftover Hash Lemma

We use the following lemma which is an immediate corollary of the leftover hash lemma and explicitly appears in [4,5].

**Lemma 1.** Let $\mathcal{H}$ be a 2-universal hash family from a set $\mathcal{X}$ to a set $\mathcal{Y}$. Then the distribution $(H, H(x))$ is $\sqrt{\frac{|\mathcal{Y}|}{4|\mathcal{X}|}}$-close to uniform distribution on $\mathcal{H} \times \mathcal{Y}$, where $H \xleftarrow{\$} \mathcal{H}$ and $x \xleftarrow{\$} \mathcal{X}$.

**Lemma 2.** Let $\mathcal{H}$ be a 2-universal hash family from a set $\mathcal{X}$ to a set $\mathcal{Y}$. Let $f : \mathcal{X} \to \mathcal{Z}$ be some functions. Then the distribution $(H, H(x), f(x))$ is $\sqrt{\frac{|\mathcal{Y}||\mathcal{Z}|}{4|\mathcal{X}|}}$-close to $(H, y, f(x))$, where $H \xleftarrow{\$} \mathcal{H}$, $x \xleftarrow{\$} \mathcal{X}$, and $y \xleftarrow{\$} \mathcal{Y}$.

### 2.2    Security Under Selective Opening

We adopt the indistinguishability-based definition of encryption secure against a selective opening adversary from [12]. We define two games, a real and an ideal game which should be indistinguishable to any efficient adversary. The key point to notice is that the adversary receives both the messages and the randomness for her selection.

$\mathcal{M}$ denotes a $n$-message sampler outputting a $n$-vector $\boldsymbol{m} = (m_1, \ldots, m_n)$ of messages whereas $\mathcal{M}_{|I, \boldsymbol{m}[I]}$ denotes an algorithm that conditionally resamples another random $n$-vector $\boldsymbol{m}' = (m_1', \ldots, m_n')$ such that $m_i' = m_i$ for each $i \in I \subset [n]$. If such a resampling can be done efficiently for all $I, m$, then $\mathcal{M}$ is said to support efficient conditional resampling.

**Definition 1.** *A public key cryptosystem* $(\mathbf{G}, \mathbf{E}, \mathbf{D})^1$ *is indistinguishable under selective openings (IND-SO-CPA secure) if, for any message sampler* $\mathcal{M}$ *supporting efficient conditional resampling and any PPT adversary* $\mathcal{A} = (\mathcal{A}_1, \mathcal{A}_2)$, *we have*

$$|\Pr[\mathrm{Exp}_{\mathcal{A}}^{\text{ind-so-real}} = 1] - \Pr[\mathrm{Exp}_{\mathcal{A}}^{\text{ind-so-ideal}} = 1]| < \mathsf{negl}(\lambda)$$

*for security parameter* $\lambda$, *and where the experiments* IND-SO-Real *and* IND-SO-Ideal *are defined as follows:*

$\mathrm{Exp}_{\mathcal{A}}^{\text{ind-so-real}}$

$\boldsymbol{m} = (m_1, \ldots, m_n) \xleftarrow{\$} \mathcal{M}$

$r_1, \ldots, r_n \xleftarrow{\$} \mathsf{coins}(\mathbf{E})$

$(I, st) \xleftarrow{\$} \mathcal{A}_1(\mathbf{E}(m_1; r_1), \ldots, \mathbf{E}(m_n; r_n))$

$b \xleftarrow{\$} \mathcal{A}_2(st, (m_i, r_i)_{i \in I}, \boldsymbol{m})$

$\mathrm{Exp}_{\mathcal{A}}^{\text{ind-so-ideal}}$

$\boldsymbol{m} = (m_1, \ldots, m_n) \xleftarrow{\$} \mathcal{M}$

$r_1, \ldots, r_n \xleftarrow{\$} \mathsf{coins}(\mathbf{E})$

$(I, st) \xleftarrow{\$} \mathcal{A}_1(\mathbf{E}(m_1; r_1), \ldots, \mathbf{E}(m_n; r_n))$

$\boldsymbol{m}' = (m_1', \ldots, m_n') \xleftarrow{\$} \mathcal{M}_{|I, \boldsymbol{m}[I]}$

$b \xleftarrow{\$} \mathcal{A}_2(st, (m_i, r_i)_{i \in I}, \boldsymbol{m}')$

### 2.3   $n$-KDM Security

We adopt the $n$-KDM-security definition from [4]. Informally, KDM-security implies that the adversary cannot distinguish the encryption of a key-dependent message from an encryption of 0. We define key-dependence relative to a fixed set of functions $\mathcal{F}$. Let $n > 0$ be an integer and let $\mathcal{F}$ be a finite set of functions $\mathcal{F} := \{f : \mathcal{SK}^n \to \mathcal{M}\}$. For each function $f \in \mathcal{F}$ we require that $|f(z)|$ is the same for all inputs $z \in S^n$ (i.e. the output length is independent of the input). We define KDM-security with respect to $\mathcal{F}$ using the following game that takes place between a challenger and an adversary $\mathcal{A}$. For an integer $n > 0$ and a security parameter $\lambda$ the game proceeds as follows:

**Init.** The challenger chooses a random bit $b \xleftarrow{\$} \{0, 1\}$ and runs $\mathbf{G}(1^\lambda, n)$ to obtain $(pk_1, sk_1), \ldots, (pk_n, sk_n)$. It sends the vector $(pk_1, \ldots, pk_n)$ to $\mathcal{A}$.
**Queries.** The adversary repeatedly issues queries where each query is of the form $(i, f)$ with $1 \leq i \leq n$ and $f \in \mathcal{F}$. The challenger responds by setting

$$y \leftarrow f(sk_1, \ldots, sk_n) \in \mathcal{M}, c \leftarrow \begin{cases} \mathbf{E}(pk_i, y) & \text{if } b = 0 \\ \mathbf{E}(pk_i, 0^{|y|}) & \text{if } b = 1 \end{cases}$$

and sends $c$ to $\mathcal{A}$.
**Finish.** Finally, the adversary outputs a bit $b' \in \{0, 1\}$.

We say that $\mathcal{A}$ is a $\mathcal{F}$-KDM adversary and that $\mathcal{A}$ wins the game if $b = b'$. Let $W$ be the event that $\mathcal{A}$ wins the game and define $\mathcal{A}$'s advantage as

$$\mathrm{Adv}_{\mathcal{A}}^{\text{ind-kdm},\mathcal{F}}(\lambda) := |\Pr[W] - \frac{1}{2}|.$$

---

[1] In the sender selective opening scenario all messages are sent to one receiver, therefore we omit receiver's public key in $\mathbf{E}$ for simplicity.

**Definition 2.** *We say that a public-key encryption scheme* $(\mathbf{G}, \mathbf{E}, \mathbf{D})$ *is n-KDM with respect to* $\mathcal{F}$ *if* $\mathrm{Adv}_{\mathcal{A}}^{\mathrm{ind\text{-}kdm},\mathcal{F}}(\lambda)$ *is a negligible function of* $\lambda$ *for any adversary* $\mathcal{A}$ *that runs in expected polynomial time in* $\lambda$.

## 2.4   Leakage Resilience

We adopt the definition from [16] and we consider leakages in single key setting.

Formally, for a public-key encryption scheme $(\mathbf{G}, \mathbf{E}, \mathbf{D})$ we denote by $\mathcal{SK}$ and $\mathcal{PK}$ the sets of secret keys and public keys that are produced by $\mathbf{G}(1^\lambda)$. That is, $\mathbf{G}(1^\lambda) \to \mathcal{SK} \times \mathcal{PK}$ for every $\lambda \in \mathbb{N}$. The leakage oracle, denoted $\mathcal{LO}(sk)$, takes as input a function $f : \mathcal{SK} \to \{0,1\}^*$ and outputs $f(sk)$. We say that an oracle machine $\mathcal{A}$ is a $\kappa$-key-leakage adversary if the sum of output lengths of all the functions that $\mathcal{A}$ submits to the leakage oracle is at most $\kappa(\lambda)$.

**Definition 3.** *A public-key encryption scheme* $(\mathbf{G}, \mathbf{E}, \mathbf{D})$ *is semantically secure against* $\kappa(\lambda)$-*key-leakage attacks if for any probabilistic polynomial-time* $\kappa(\lambda)$-*key-leakage adversary* $\mathcal{A} = (\mathcal{A}_1, \mathcal{A}_2)$ *it holds that*

$$\mathrm{Adv}_{\mathcal{A}}^{\mathrm{ind\text{-}lr},\mathcal{LO}}(\lambda) := |\Pr[\mathrm{Exp}_{\mathcal{A}}^{\mathrm{ind\text{-}lr},\mathcal{LO}}(0) = 1] - \Pr[\mathrm{Exp}_{\mathcal{A}}^{\mathrm{ind\text{-}lr},\mathcal{LO}}(1) = 1]|$$

*is negligible in* $\lambda$, *where* $\mathrm{Exp}_{\mathcal{A}}^{\mathcal{LO}}(b)$ *is defined as follows:*

$$\begin{aligned}
&\mathrm{Exp}_{\mathcal{A}}^{\mathrm{ind\text{-}lr},\mathcal{LO}}(b) \\
&\quad (pk, sk) \leftarrow \mathbf{G}(1^\lambda) \\
&\quad (m_0, m_1, st) \leftarrow \mathcal{A}_1^{\mathcal{LO}(sk)}(pk) \ \text{s.t.} \ |m_0| = |m_1| \\
&\quad c \leftarrow \mathbf{E}(pk, m_b) \\
&\quad b' \leftarrow \mathcal{A}_2(st, c) \\
&\quad \text{Output } b'
\end{aligned}$$

# 3   Enhanced Smooth Projective Hashing and Multipurpose Encryption

In this section, we introduce our main contributions: enhanced smooth projective hashing and a generic construction of multipurpose encryption from ESPH.

## 3.1   Enhanced Smooth Projective Hashing

We adopt the notations of smooth projective hashing from [18] with some additional properties which are: range orthogonality, $\kappa$-leakage smoothness, hashing key homomorphism and lossy evaluation.

**Setup.** Fix a family of groups $\mathcal{G}_{pp}$ indexed by a public parameter $pp$. We require that $pp$ be efficiently samplable along with a secret parameter $sp$ given a security parameter $1^\lambda$, and assume that all algorithms are given $pp$ as part of its input. We omit $pp$ henceforth whenever the context is clear. We consider subgroups $\mathcal{G}_{\mathrm{YES}}$ of $\mathcal{G}$ and we use $\mathcal{G}_{\mathrm{NO}}$ to denote $\mathcal{G} \backslash \mathcal{G}_{\mathrm{YES}}$. We require that each of these groups (or sets) $\mathcal{G}, \mathcal{G}_{\mathrm{YES}}, \mathcal{G}_{\mathrm{NO}}$ be efficiently samplable given $pp$, and that given the secret parameter $sp$, we can efficiently verify membership in $\mathcal{G}_{\mathrm{YES}}$.

**Subgroup Membership Assumption.** We consider a computational assumption pertaining to the group $\mathcal{G}$, which we refer to the subgroup membership assumption. The assumption states that the uniform distributions over $\mathcal{G}_{\text{YES}}$ and $\mathcal{G}$ are computationally indistinguishable, even given $pp$.

**Homomorphic Projective Hashing.** Fix a public parameter $pp$. We consider a family of hash functions $\{\Lambda_{hk} : \mathcal{G} \rightarrow \mathcal{K}\}$ indexed by a hashing key $hk$. We require that $\Lambda_{hk}(\cdot)$ be efficiently computable (by a 'private evaluation' algorithm), and $hk$ be efficiently samplable. In addition, we require that both $\mathcal{G}$ and $\mathcal{K}$ are groups, and that $\Lambda_{hk}(\cdot)$ is a group homomorphism, that is, for all $hk$ and all $C_0, C_1 \in \mathcal{G}$, we have $\Lambda_{hk}(C_0) \cdot \Lambda_{hk}(C_1) = \Lambda_{hk}(C_0 \cdot C_1)$.[2] We say that $\Lambda_{hk}(\cdot)$ is projective if there exists a projection map $\mu(\cdot)$ defined on $hk$ such that $\mu(hk)$ determines the behavior of $\Lambda_{hk}$ on inputs from $\mathcal{G}_{\text{YES}}$. Specifically, we require that there exists an efficient public evaluation algorithm Pub that on input $\mu(hk)$ and randomness $r$ used to sample $C$, outputs the value $\Lambda_{hk}(C)$.

**Range Orthogonality.** We require that $\mathcal{K} = \mathcal{K}_0 \times \mathcal{K}_1$ and for all $C \in \mathcal{G}_{\text{YES}}$, $\Lambda_{hk}(C) \in \mathcal{K}_0$.

**$\kappa$-Leakage Smoothness.** We say that $\Lambda_{hk}(\cdot)$ is $\kappa$-leakage smooth if the behavior of $\Lambda_{hk}$ on $\mathcal{G}_{\text{NO}}$ is completely undetermined, even knowing $\kappa$-bits of $hk$. That is, for all $C \in \mathcal{G}_{\text{NO}}$ and functions $f : hk \mapsto z \in \{0,1\}^{\kappa}$, the following distributions are statistically close:

$$(pk, \Lambda_{hk}(C), f(hk)) \quad \text{and} \quad (pk, \Lambda_{hk}(C) \cdot K, f(hk))$$

where $hk$ is random, $pk = \mu(hk)$ and $K \overset{\$}{\leftarrow} \mathcal{K}_1$. We also say that $\Lambda_{hk}(\cdot)$ is average-case smooth where we relax the requirement for smoothness to hold for a random $C \in \mathcal{G}$ [16]. That is, the following distributions are statistically close:

$$(pk, C, \Lambda_{hk}(C), f(hk)) \quad \text{and} \quad (pk, C, \Lambda_{hk}(C) \cdot K, f(hk))$$

where $hk$ is random, $pk = \mu(hk)$, $C \overset{\$}{\leftarrow} \mathcal{G}$ and $K \overset{\$}{\leftarrow} \mathcal{K}_1$.

**Hashing Key Homomorphism.** We require that given $\mu(hk)$, a binary relation $R$ such that $(hk, hk') \in R$, $C \in \mathcal{G}$, and $\Lambda_{hk}(C)$, $\mu(hk')$ and $\Lambda_{hk'}(C)$ can be efficiently computed. Additionally, if $(hk_1, hk_2) \in R_{1,2}$ and $(hk_1, hk_3) \in R_{1,3}$, the binary relation $R_{2,3}$ such that $(hk_2, hk_3) \in R_{2,3}$ can be efficiently computed with $R_{1,2}$ and $R_{1,3}$.

This property has been used to prove $n$-KDM-security in [4,5,15] explicitly or implicitly. Here we abstract it in the language of smooth projective hashing.

**Lossy Evaluation.** We require that $\mu(hk)$ also lies in a group, namely, $\mu(hk) \in \mathcal{G}'$. $\mathcal{G}'$ is also determined by $pp$ and subgroup membership assumption also

---

[2] Since the homomorphism, $\forall hk$, $\Lambda_{hk}(1_{\mathcal{G}}) \mapsto 1_{\mathcal{K}}$.

holds on $\mathcal{G}'$. Specifically, for all $hk$, $C \in \mathcal{G}_{\text{YES}}$ with corresponding randomness $r$ and for $pk \in \mathcal{G}'_{\text{NO}}$, the following distributions are statistically close:

$$(C, \text{Pub}(pk, r) \cdot K_0) \quad \text{and} \quad (C, \text{Pub}(pk, r) \cdot K_1)$$

given $K_0, K_1 \in \mathcal{K}_1$. Again, $sp$ can be used to verify membership of $\mathcal{G}'_{\text{YES}}$. Moreover, for $pk \in \mathcal{G}'_{\text{NO}}$, given $C, \text{Pub}(pk, r)$, $K_0$, $K_1$ and $sp$, an equivalent randomness $r'$ for $C$ such that $\text{Pub}(pk, r) \cdot K_0 = \text{Pub}(pk, r') \cdot K_1$ can be efficiently computed.

## 3.2  Generic Construction of Multipurpose Encryption

Starting with a family of projective hash functions $\{\Lambda_{hk_i} : \mathcal{G} \to \mathcal{K}\}_{i \in [n]}$, we may derive a semantically secure public-key encryption scheme $\mathcal{E} = (\mathbf{G}, \mathbf{E}, \mathbf{D})$. The message space is $\mathcal{M}$, and we require an homomorphic injective map $\phi : \mathcal{M} \to \mathcal{K}_1$ which is efficiently computable and invertible.

Here we emphasize that $\phi$ is homomorphic[3] since later on, we will use this homomorphism to answer KDM queries related to multiple secret keys.

- $\mathbf{G}(1^\lambda, n)$: Sample public parameters $pp$, a series of uniform hashing key $\{hk_i\}_{i \in [n]}$ and compute $\{pk_i := \mu(hk_i)\}_{i \in [n]}$. Output $pp$ which would be used as an implicit input for the following algorithms, and the key pairs

$$\{pk_i, sk_i | pk_i := \mu(hk_i), sk_i := hk_i\}_{i \in [n]}$$

- $\mathbf{E}(pk_i, m)$: Sample $C \xleftarrow{\$} \mathcal{G}_{\text{YES}}$ with randomness $r$, output the ciphertext

$$(C, \text{Pub}(pk_i, r) \cdot \phi(m))$$

- $\mathbf{D}(sk_i, (C, \psi))$: Output the plaintext

$$\phi^{-1}(\Lambda_{sk_i}(C)^{-1} \cdot \psi)$$

Correctness follows by the correctness of projective hashing. Though very similar to the IND-CPA version of Cramer-Shoup scheme, the efficiency of this scheme depends on the underlying assumption of ESPH and we discuss it after giving the instantiations.

In the following analysis, we show that our scheme is "somewhat flexible", which means some functions are optional. SO-security could be achieved by using more random bits (depends on the instantiation), and higher leakage rate could be reached by longer parameter. On the other way, a fraction of randomness could be saved by not being SO-secure, and short parameter could be enjoyed with lower leakage rate.

## 4  Security Analysis

In this section, we show the construction we proposed is SO-secure, $n$-KDM-secure and leakage resilient. As for key-privacy, since it is related to specific assumptions, we discuss it after we give the instantiations.

---

[3] Since we view $\mathcal{M}$ as an additive group, we require that $\phi(0) = 1_\mathcal{K}$.

## 4.1  Security Under Selective Opening

**Theorem 1.** *Suppose* $\{\Lambda_{hk_i}(\cdot)\}_{i\in[n]}$ *is a family of projective hash functions that is average-case smooth and lossy evaluable, and the subgroup membership is hard (w.r.t.* $\mathcal{G}$ *vs* $\mathcal{G}_{\text{YES}}$ *and* $\mathcal{G}'_{\text{YES}}$ *vs* $\mathcal{G}'_{\text{NO}}$*). Then, the encryption scheme* $(\mathbf{G}, \mathbf{E}, \mathbf{D})$ *described in Sect. 3.2 is IND-SO-CPA secure.*

It has been shown in [2,12] that lossy encryption is IND-SO-CPA secure. To show that $(\mathbf{G}, \mathbf{E}, \mathbf{D})$ is IND-SO-CPA, it is sufficient to show that $(\mathbf{G}, \mathbf{E}, \mathbf{D})$ implies a lossy encryption scheme.

*Proof.* Additionally, we have to define injective key generation and lossy key generation.

- $\mathbf{G}(1^\lambda, \text{inj})$ outputs $(pk, sk)$ besides $pp$, keys generated by $\mathbf{G}(1^\lambda, \text{inj})$ are called injective keys.
- $\mathbf{G}(1^\lambda, \text{lossy})$ outputs keys $(pk_{\text{lossy}}, sk_{\text{lossy}})$ besides $pp$, keys generated by $\mathbf{G}(1^\lambda, \text{lossy})$ are called lossy keys.

Let $\mathbf{G}(1^\lambda, 1)$ be $\mathbf{G}'(1^\lambda, \text{inj})$ and let sampling $pk_{\text{lossy}} \xleftarrow{\$} \mathcal{G}'_{\text{NO}}$ and setting $sk_{\text{lossy}} = \perp$ be lossy key generation $\mathbf{G}'(1^\lambda, \text{lossy})$.
Now we show that $(\mathbf{G}', \mathbf{E}, \mathbf{D})$ fits the requirements of lossy encryption.

**Correctness on injective keys.** For all plaintexts $m \in \mathcal{M}$,

$$\Pr[(pk, sk) \xleftarrow{\$} \mathbf{G}'(1^\lambda, \text{inj}); r \xleftarrow{\$} \text{coins}(\mathbf{E}) : \mathbf{D}(sk, \mathbf{E}(pk, m; r)) = m] = 1.$$

This property is implied by the correctness of $(\mathbf{G}, \mathbf{E}, \mathbf{D})$.
**Indistinguishability of keys.** In lossy mode, public keys are computationally indistinguishable from those in the injective mode. Specifically, if proj : $(pk, sk) \to pk$ is the projection map, then

$$\{\text{proj}(\mathbf{G}'(1^\lambda, \text{inj}))\} \approx_c \{\text{proj}(\mathbf{G}'(1^\lambda, \text{lossy}))\}.$$

This property is implied by the underlying subgroup membership assumption.
**Lossiness of lossy keys.** If $(pk_{\text{lossy}}, sk_{\text{lossy}}) \xleftarrow{\$} \mathbf{G}'(1^\lambda, \text{lossy})$, then for all $m_0, m_1 \in \mathcal{M}$, the following distributions are statistically close:

$$\mathbf{E}(pk_{\text{lossy}}, m_0; \text{coins}(\mathbf{E})) \quad \text{and} \quad \mathbf{E}(pk_{\text{lossy}}, m_1; \text{coins}(\mathbf{E})).$$

This property is a direct result of lossy evaluation.
**Openability.** Suppose that $(pk_{\text{lossy}}, sk_{\text{lossy}}) \xleftarrow{\$} \mathbf{G}'(1^\lambda, \text{lossy})$ and $r \xleftarrow{\$} \text{coins}(\mathbf{E})$, then for all $m_0, m_1 \in \mathcal{M}$, with overwhelming probability, there exists $r' \in \text{coins}(\mathbf{E})$ such that $\mathbf{E}(pk_{\text{lossy}}, m_0; r) = \mathbf{E}(pk_{\text{lossy}}, m_1; r')$. In other words, there is an (unbounded) algorithm opener that can open a lossy ciphertext to any arbitrary plaintext with all but negligible probability.

This property is also a direct result of lossy evaluation. Since $r'$ can be efficiently computed given $sp$, $(\mathbf{G}', \mathbf{E}, \mathbf{D})$ is semantic secure under selective opening (IND-SO-CPA) [2,12].

Since lossy key generation is useless in the real scheme and $\mathbf{G}$ generates $n$ key pairs independently, $(\mathbf{G}, \mathbf{E}, \mathbf{D})$ is IND-SO-CPA secure.

## 4.2  $n$-KDM Security

**Theorem 2.** *Suppose* $\{\Lambda_{hk_i}(\cdot)\}_{i \in [n]}$ *is a family of projective hash functions that is average-case smooth, homomorphic and hashing key homomorphic, and the subgroup membership is hard (w.r.t.* $\mathcal{G}$ *vs* $\mathcal{G}_{YES}$*). Then, the encryption scheme* $(\mathbf{G}, \mathbf{E}, \mathbf{D})$ *described in Sect. 3.2 is* $n$*-KDM-secure with respect to* $\mathcal{F}$ *where* $\mathcal{F} = \{f_{e_1,\ldots,e_n,k} : (sk_1,\ldots,sk_n) \mapsto \phi^{-1}(k \cdot \prod_{i \in [n]} \Lambda_{sk_i}(e_i))|e_i \in \mathcal{G}_{NO}, k \in \mathcal{K}_1\}.$

In the following proof, we show that $(\mathbf{G}, \mathbf{E}, \mathbf{D})$ is 1-KDM-secure firstly. Then we show that with the help of additional properties form ESPH, we can "reduce" $n$-KDM-security to 1-KDM-security.

*Proof.* In the 1-KDM game, $\mathcal{F}$ degenerates to $\mathcal{F} = \{f_{e,k} : sk \mapsto \phi^{-1}(k \cdot \Lambda_{sk}(e)\}$ and $\mathbf{G}(1^{\lambda}, 1) \rightarrow (pk = \mu(hk), sk = hk)$. Since in the query phase the adversary only queries polynomial times, to show that $(\mathbf{G}, \mathbf{E}, \mathbf{D})$ is 1-KDM-secure, it is sufficient to show that:

1. On each query of $\mathcal{A}$,

$$(pk, sk, \mathbf{E}(pk, f_{e,k}(sk))) \approx_c (pk, sk, (C \cdot e^{-1}, \mathsf{Pub}(pk, r) \cdot k)),$$

thus $\mathbf{E}(pk, f_{e,k}(sk))$ could be generated without knowing $sk$.

2.
$$(pk, (C \cdot e^{-1}, \mathsf{Pub}(pk, r) \cdot k)) \approx_c (pk, \mathbf{E}(pk, 0^{|m|})).$$

The first point could be proved due to the hybrid transitions from [18, Sect. 4] as below:

$$\mathbf{E}(pk, f_{e,k}(sk); r)$$

$$= (C, \mathsf{Pub}(pk, r) \cdot \Lambda_{sk}(e) \cdot k) \qquad\qquad : C \xleftarrow{\$} \mathcal{G}_{YES}, \text{ randomness } r$$

$$= (C, \Lambda_{sk}(C) \cdot \Lambda_{sk}(e) \cdot k) \qquad\qquad : C \xleftarrow{\$} \mathcal{G}_{YES}, \text{ via projective property}$$

$$\approx_c (C, \Lambda_{sk}(C) \cdot \Lambda_{sk}(e) \cdot k) \qquad\qquad : C \xleftarrow{\$} \mathcal{G}, \text{ via subgroup membership}$$

$$= (C, \Lambda_{sk}(C \cdot e) \cdot k) \qquad\qquad\qquad : C \xleftarrow{\$} \mathcal{G}, \text{ since } \Lambda_{sk} \text{ is homomorphic}$$

$$= (C \cdot e^{-1}, \Lambda_{sk}(C) \cdot k) \qquad\qquad\qquad\qquad : C \xleftarrow{\$} \mathcal{G}, \text{ since } e \in \mathcal{G}$$

$$\approx_c (C \cdot e^{-1}, \Lambda_{sk}(C) \cdot k) \qquad\qquad\qquad\qquad\qquad : C \xleftarrow{\$} \mathcal{G}_{YES}$$

$$= (C \cdot e^{-1}, \mathsf{Pub}(pk, r) \cdot k) \qquad : C \xleftarrow{\$} \mathcal{G}_{YES}, \text{ randomness } r, \text{ via projective}$$

Note that the above transition does not rely on smoothness, and therefore everything goes through even if we append $(pk, sk)$ to the view.

Note that the result of the public evaluation $\mathsf{Pub}(pk, r)$ is determined by $r$ rather than $C$ and $C \cdot e^{-1} \in \mathcal{G}_{NO}$, the second point could be proved due to subgroup membership assumption together with smoothness.

Let $pk$ in the 1-KDM game be $pk_1$, then the simulator randomly generates binary relation $R_{1,2}, \ldots, R_{1,n}$ and generate $pk_2, \ldots, pk_n$ with $R_{1,2}, \ldots, R_{1,n}$.

We require that $f \in \mathcal{F}$ is additive. Namely, $f(sk_1, \ldots, sk_n) = f_1(sk_1) + \cdots + f_n(sk_n)$.[4] Then, to answer $(i, f)$, the simulator simulates $\mathbf{E}(pk_j, f_j(sk_j))_{j \in [n]}$ in the first step by 1-KDM-security. Secondly, the simulator computes $\mathbf{E}(pk_i, f_j(sk_j))_{j \in [n] \setminus \{i\}}$ with $\mathbf{E}(pk_j, f_j(sk_j)), R_{1,i}, R_{1,j}$ by hashing key homomorphism. Note that $\mathbf{E}(pk_i, \cdot)$ is a homomorphic encryption since $\Lambda_{sk_i}(\cdot)$ is homomorphic. Finally the simulator transforms the ciphertext $\mathbf{E}(pk_i, f_j(sk_j))_{j \in [n]}$ into $\mathbf{E}(pk_i, f(sk_1, \ldots, sk_n))$.

We "reduce" $n$ secret keys to one secret key $sk_1 = sk$, thus we reduce $n$-KDM to 1-KDM by secret key and ciphertext homomorphism.

Again we emphasize that this technique has been used to prove $n$-KDM security in [4, 5, 15] explicitly or implicitly.

## 4.3   Leakage Resilience

**Theorem 3.** *Suppose $\{\Lambda_{hk_i}(\cdot)\}_{i \in [n]}$ is a family of projective hash functions that is average-case $\kappa$-leakage smooth, and the subgroup membership is hard (w.r.t. $\mathcal{G}$ vs $\mathcal{G}_{\mathrm{YES}}$). Then, the encryption scheme $(\mathbf{G}, \mathbf{E}, \mathbf{D})$ described in Sect. 3.2 is $\kappa$-leakage-resilient w.r.t. $sk_i, i \in [n]$.*

It can be easily seen that Theorem 3 follows as a direct conclusion of $\kappa$-leakage smoothness. In fact, Theorem 3 for the original hash proof system based encryption scheme and QR/DCR implementation has been proven in [16] and [5] respectively. Here we just state it in the language of ESPH rather than specific computational assumptions.

*Proof.* For $pk = \mu(sk), |f(sk)| \leq \kappa$, Theorem 3 is implied by the following hybrid transitions:

$$(pk, \mathbf{E}(pk, m_0; r), f(sk))$$

$$= (pk, C, \mathsf{Pub}(pk, r), f(sk)) \qquad\qquad : C \xleftarrow{\$} \mathcal{G}_{\mathrm{YES}}, \text{ randomness } r$$

$$= (pk, C, \Lambda_{sk}(C) \cdot \phi(m_0), f(sk)) \qquad : C \xleftarrow{\$} \mathcal{G}_{\mathrm{YES}}, \text{ via projective property}$$

$$\approx_c (pk, C, \Lambda_{sk}(C) \cdot \phi(m_0), f(sk)) \qquad : C \xleftarrow{\$} \mathcal{G}, \text{ via subgroup membership}$$

$$\approx_s (pk, C, \Lambda_{sk}(C) \cdot \phi(m_1), f(sk)) \qquad : C \xleftarrow{\$} \mathcal{G}, \text{ via } \kappa\text{-leakage smoothness}$$

$$\approx_c (pk, \mathbf{E}(pk, m_1; r), f(sk)) \qquad\qquad\qquad\qquad \text{by reversing the hybrids}$$

---

[4] In fact, since the homomorphism of $\phi$, the function class $\mathcal{F}$ we described in Theorem 2 fits this requirement.

# 5    Instantiations from QR and DCR

Most of this section is copied verbatim from [18, Sect. 7] except minor changes to fit our new requirement.

We utilize the subgroup indistinguishability framework of Brakerski and Goldwasser [5] (also [8, Sect. 7.4.2]). We consider a family of finite commutative groups $\mathbb{G}$ that is generated by two elements $g, h$ of co-prime order (thus $|\mathbb{G}| = \text{ord}(g) \cdot \text{ord}(h)$); we use $\mathbb{G}_0$ to denote $\langle g \rangle$. We will require the following additional properties:

- Given the public description of $\mathbb{G}$, we may compute $\text{ord}(h)$ and a good approximation $a$ for $\text{ord}(g)$ (so that the uniform distributions over $[a]$ and over $\text{ord}(g)$ are statistically close).
- Computing discrete log with respect to $h$ is easy.
- The uniform distributions over $\mathbb{G}_0$ and $\mathbb{G}$ are computationally indistinguishable, given $g, h$.
- Given a randomly selected element in $\mathbb{G}_0$, it is invertible with overwhelming probability.

**Instantiation from QR.** Fix a Blum integer $N = PQ$ for $\lambda$-bit safe primes $P, Q \equiv 3 \pmod 4$ (such that $P = 2p + 1$ and $Q = 2q + 1$ for primes $p, q$). Let $\mathbb{J}_N$ denote the subgroup of $\mathbb{Z}_N^*$ with Jacobi symbol $+1$, and let $\mathbb{QR}_N$ denote the subgroup of quadratic residues. The QR assumption states that the uniform distributions over $\mathbb{QR}_N$ and $\mathbb{J}_N \backslash \mathbb{QR}_N$ are computationally indistinguishable. That is, we may take $\mathbb{G}$ and $\mathbb{G}_0$ to be $\mathbb{J}_N$ and $\mathbb{QR}_N$ respectively. Observe that $\mathbb{J}_N$ is isomorphic to $\mathbb{QR}_N \times (\pm 1)$ and that $|\mathbb{J}_N| = 2pq = 2|\mathbb{QR}_N|$. We can then sample $g$ by squaring a random element in $\mathbb{Z}_N^*$ and fix $h$ to be $-1$. Note that $|\mathbb{QR}_N| = pq = N/4 - \mathcal{O}(\sqrt{N})$, which we may approximate by $N/4$.

**Instantiation from DCR.** Again, fix a Blum integer $N = PQ$ for $\lambda$-bit safe primes $P, Q \equiv 3 \pmod 4$ (such that $P = 2p + 1$ and $Q = 2q + 1$ for primes $p, q$). Let $\mathbb{QR}_{N^2}$ denote the subgroup of quadratic residues of $\mathbb{Z}_{N^2}^*$, so $|\mathbb{QR}_{N^2}| = Npq$. Let $\mathbb{SCR}_{N^2}$ denote the subgroup of $N$-th residues of $\mathbb{QR}_{N^2}$. Then, $\mathbb{QR}_{N^2} = \mathbb{SCR}_{N^2} \times \langle 1 + N \rangle$. Roughly speaking, the DCR assumption states that the uniform distributions over $\mathbb{SCR}_{N^2}$ and $\mathbb{QR}_{N^2}$ are computationally indistinguishable. We may take $\mathbb{G}$ and $\mathbb{G}_0$ to be $\mathbb{QR}_{N^2}$ and $\mathbb{SCR}_{N^2}$ respectively. We can sample a random generator $g$ of $\mathbb{G}_0$ as follows: pick $x \xleftarrow{\$} \mathbb{Z}_{N^2}^*$ and set $g := x^{2N}$. In addition, we can fix $h := N + 1$. Note that $|\mathbb{G}_0| = pq = N/4 - \mathcal{O}(\sqrt{N})$, which we may approximate by $N/4$.

**Setup.** Sample a random group $\mathbb{G}$ along with generators $g$ and $h$. In addition, sample $\boldsymbol{p} \xleftarrow{\$} \mathbb{Z}_{\text{ord}(g)}^\ell$. Output

$$pp := (\mathbb{G}, g^{\boldsymbol{p}}, h) \quad \text{and} \quad sp := (\text{ord}(g), \boldsymbol{p})$$

The subgroup indistinguishability problem is given by:

$$\mathcal{G}_{\text{YES}} := \{g^{r\boldsymbol{p}} : r \in \mathbb{Z}_{\text{ord}(g)}\} \subseteq \mathbb{G}_0^{\ell}$$
$$\text{and} \quad \mathcal{G} := \{h^{\boldsymbol{d}} \cdot g^{r\boldsymbol{p}} : \boldsymbol{d} \in \mathbb{Z}_{\text{ord}(h)}^{\ell}, r \in \mathbb{Z}_{\text{ord}(g)}\} \subseteq \mathbb{G}^{\ell}$$

where the group operation over $\mathbb{G}^{\ell}$ is the natural one given by coordinate-wise product. The uniform distributions over $\mathcal{G}_{\text{YES}}$ and $\mathcal{G}$ are computationally indistinguishable under subgroup indistinguishability as shown in [5]. (The reduction is fairly straight-forward: it essentially takes the challenge $(x, g, h)$ where either $x \xleftarrow{\$} \mathbb{G}_0$ or $x \xleftarrow{\$} \mathbb{G}$ and computes $(g^{\boldsymbol{p}'}, x^{\boldsymbol{p}'})$ where $\boldsymbol{p}' \xleftarrow{\$} \mathbb{Z}_{|\mathbb{G}|}^{\ell}$.) The subgroup membership can be verified with the help of $\text{ord}(g)$. Since $\text{ord}(g) = pq$, let $(p_1, \ldots, p_l) = \boldsymbol{p}$, $p_i$ is invertible with overwhelming probability. We can even distinguish $\boldsymbol{c} \in \mathcal{G}_{\text{YES}}$ from $h^{\boldsymbol{d}} \cdot g^{\boldsymbol{a}}$ using $sp$, where $\boldsymbol{d} \xleftarrow{\$} \mathbb{Z}_{\text{ord}(h)}^{\ell}$, $\boldsymbol{a} \xleftarrow{\$} \mathbb{Z}_{\text{ord}(g)}^{\ell}$. This could be used to check the well-formedness of ciphertexts. The subgroup indistinguishability problem in lossy evaluation part is given by:

$$\mathcal{G}'_{\text{YES}} := \mathbb{G}_0 \quad \text{and} \quad \mathcal{G}' := \mathbb{G}$$

which can be viewed as the above version with shrunk $\ell$.

**Hashing.** The hashing key is given by a column vector $\boldsymbol{s} \xleftarrow{\$} \mathbb{Z}_{\text{ord}(h)}^{\ell}$.

$$\mu(g^{\boldsymbol{p}}, \boldsymbol{s}) := g^{\boldsymbol{p}^{\mathsf{T}} \boldsymbol{s}} \in \mathbb{G}$$

Private and public evaluation are given by:

$$\Lambda_{\boldsymbol{s}}(\boldsymbol{c}) := \boldsymbol{c}^{\boldsymbol{s}} \in \mathbb{G} \quad \text{and} \quad \text{Pub}(g^{\boldsymbol{p}^{\mathsf{T}} \boldsymbol{s}}, r) := (g^{\boldsymbol{p}^{\mathsf{T}} \boldsymbol{s}})^r$$

where $\boldsymbol{c} = (c_1, \ldots, c_{\ell}) \in \mathbb{G}^{\ell}$, $\boldsymbol{s} = (s_1, \ldots, s_{\ell})$ and $\boldsymbol{c}^{\boldsymbol{s}} := \prod_{i=1}^{\ell} c_i^{s_i}$. Clearly, $\Lambda_{\boldsymbol{s}}(\cdot)$ is a group homomorphism. The projective property simply follows from the fact that $g^{(r\boldsymbol{p})^{\mathsf{T}} \boldsymbol{s}} = g^{r\boldsymbol{p}^{\mathsf{T}} \boldsymbol{s}} = (g^{\boldsymbol{p}^{\mathsf{T}} \boldsymbol{s}})^r$.

**Range orthogonality.** Let $\mathcal{K}_0 = \langle g \rangle$, $\mathcal{K}_1 = \langle h \rangle$, range orthogonality follows immediately.

**$\kappa$-leakage smoothness.** To establish average-case smoothness, first observe that:

$$\Lambda_{\boldsymbol{s}}(h^{\boldsymbol{d}} \cdot g^{r\boldsymbol{p}}) \bmod \mathbb{G}_0 = h^{\boldsymbol{d}^{\mathsf{T}} \boldsymbol{s}}$$

The leftover hash lemma tells us that $\boldsymbol{d}^{\mathsf{T}} \boldsymbol{s}$ is statistically close to uniform over $\mathbb{Z}_{\text{ord}(h)}$. More precisely, for $\frac{2^{\kappa}}{\text{ord}(h)^{\ell-1}} \leq \text{negl}(\lambda)$ and any function $f : hk \mapsto z \in \{0, 1\}^{\kappa}$, the following distributions are statistically close:

$$(\boldsymbol{p}, \boldsymbol{p}^{\mathsf{T}} \boldsymbol{s} \bmod \text{ord}(g), \boldsymbol{d}, \boldsymbol{d}^{\mathsf{T}} \boldsymbol{s} \bmod \text{ord}(h), f(\boldsymbol{s}))$$
$$\text{and} \quad (\boldsymbol{p}, \boldsymbol{p}^{\mathsf{T}} \boldsymbol{s} \bmod \text{ord}(g), \boldsymbol{d}, d', f(\boldsymbol{s}))$$

where $\boldsymbol{s} \xleftarrow{\$} \mathbb{Z}_{\text{ord}(h)}^{\ell}$, $\boldsymbol{d} \xleftarrow{\$} \mathbb{Z}_{\text{ord}(h)}^{\ell}$, $d' \xleftarrow{\$} \mathbb{Z}_{\text{ord}(h)}$. Note that $|\text{ord}(h)| = |2\lambda|$ under DCR assumption, for $\ell \geq 2$, the distributions above are statistically close under DCR assumption with the leakage rate at $1 - \frac{1}{\mathcal{O}(1)}$, where $s \xleftarrow{\$}$ $\mathbb{Z}^\ell_{\mathrm{ord}(h)}, d \xleftarrow{\$} \mathbb{Z}^\ell_{\mathrm{ord}(h)}, d' \xleftarrow{\$} \mathbb{Z}_{\mathrm{ord}(h)}{}^5$. Average-case smoothness follows readily, since $g^{\boldsymbol{p}^{\mathrm{T}}\boldsymbol{s}}$ is completely determined by $\boldsymbol{p}^{\mathrm{T}}\boldsymbol{s} \bmod \mathrm{ord}(g)$.

**Hashing key homomorphism.** First we define a binary relation $R_{\boldsymbol{v}}$: $(\boldsymbol{s}, \boldsymbol{s}') \in R_{\boldsymbol{v}}$ if and only if $\boldsymbol{s} + \boldsymbol{v} = \boldsymbol{s}' \bmod \mathrm{ord}(g)$. Then $\mu(\boldsymbol{s}') = \mu(\boldsymbol{s}) \cdot g^{\boldsymbol{p}^{\mathrm{T}}\boldsymbol{v}}$ and $\Lambda_{\boldsymbol{s}'}(c) = \Lambda_{\boldsymbol{s}}(c) \cdot c^{\boldsymbol{v}}$, which means hashing key homomorphism follows.

**Lossy evaluation.** To illustrate this property, it is sufficient to show that for fixed $a \in \mathbb{Z}^*_{\mathrm{ord}(g)}$ and $c \in \mathcal{G}_{\mathrm{YES}}$, $\mathsf{Pub}(g^a \cdot h, r)$ can be viewed as $\mathsf{Pub}(g^a \cdot h, r') \cdot h^m$ for any $m \in \mathbb{Z}_{\mathrm{ord}(h)}$. Let $r' = r + k \cdot \mathrm{ord}(g)$, $r'$ is a equivalent witness for $c$, but $\mathsf{Pub}(g^a \cdot h, r') = g^{ar} \cdot h^{r + k \cdot \mathrm{ord}(g)}$ so $m = -k \cdot \mathrm{ord}(g)$. Since $\mathrm{ord}(g)$ and $\mathrm{ord}(h)$ are relatively prime, $\forall m \in \mathbb{Z}_{\mathrm{ord}(h)}, \exists k \in \mathbb{Z}_{\mathrm{ord}(h)}$ such that $m \equiv -k \cdot \mathrm{ord}(g) \bmod \mathrm{ord}(h)$. Then lossy evaluation follows. Note that given $\mathsf{Pub}(g^a, r)$ and $m$, $r'$ can be efficiently computed using $\mathrm{ord}(g)$.

**Class $\mathcal{F}$.** The message space $\mathcal{M} = \mathbb{Z}_{\mathrm{ord}(h)}$ and $\phi(m) = h^m$. Observe that for all $\boldsymbol{a} \in \mathbb{Z}^\ell, c \in \mathbb{Z}$ (such that $\boldsymbol{a}^{\mathrm{T}}\boldsymbol{s} + c \in \mathbb{Z}_{\mathrm{ord}(h)}$ for all $\boldsymbol{s} \in \mathbb{Z}^\ell_{\mathrm{ord}(h)}$):

$$\Lambda_{\boldsymbol{s}}(h^{\boldsymbol{a}}) \cdot h^c = h^{\boldsymbol{a}^{\mathrm{T}}\boldsymbol{s}+c} = \phi(\boldsymbol{a}^{\mathrm{T}}\boldsymbol{s} + c).$$

That is, the resulting scheme is $\mathcal{F}$-KDM-secure for $\mathcal{F} = \{(\boldsymbol{s}_1, \ldots, \boldsymbol{s}_n) \mapsto \sum_{i=1}^n \boldsymbol{a}_i^{\mathrm{T}}\boldsymbol{s}_i + c_i | \boldsymbol{a}_i \in \mathbb{Z}^\ell, c_i \in \mathbb{Z}\}$, i.e. affine functions of the bits (or modular polynomials of degree at most 1, w.r.t. DCR assumption) of the secret keys.

**Key-Privacy.** For $g^{\boldsymbol{p}} = (g^{p_1}, \ldots, g^{p_\ell})$, $\boldsymbol{c} = (c_1, \ldots, c_\ell) \in \mathcal{G}_{\mathrm{YES}}, \mu(\boldsymbol{s}) = g^{\boldsymbol{p}^{\mathrm{T}}\boldsymbol{s}}$ and $\Lambda_{\boldsymbol{s}}(c)$, note that $(g, g^r, \mu(\boldsymbol{s}), \Lambda_{\boldsymbol{s}}(c))$ is DDH tuple, where $r$ is the witness of $c$. So if DDH assumption holds on $\mathbb{G}_0$, $(\mathbf{G}, \mathbf{E}, \mathbf{D})$ makes a key-private encryption scheme. The proof could be analogized to [1, Appendix A].

Note that $N = PQ = (2p+1)(2q+1)$, suppose that DDH assumption holds on $\mathbb{QR}_P$ and $\mathbb{QR}_Q$ or $\mathbb{SCR}_{P^2}$ and $\mathbb{SCR}_{Q^2}$, then by Chinese remainder theorem, DDH assumption holds on $\mathbb{G}_0$ for QR instantiation or DCR instantiation respectively. Thus even adversaries obtain $sp$ or factors of $N$, they have negligible advantages to distinguish $\mathbf{E}(pk_i, m)$ from $\mathbf{E}(pk_j, m)$, where $i, j \in [n]$.

## 6    Conclusion

Since the instantiation from DCR assumption makes a multi-bit encryption scheme and has shorter parameters ($\ell \geq 2$), in Table 1 we compare it with the IND-CPA encryption scheme instantiated by the original DCR based projective hashing from [8, Sect. 8.2.1].

We conclude that with a marginal cost we obtained our encryption scheme. Note that IND-SO-CCA security seems not easily to be derived from the smooth projective hashing based encryption schemes. On the contrast, IND-KDM-CCA and IND-LR-CCA could be reached using general transforms in [6, 16]. Furthermore, those two transforms are compatible! Unfortunately the IND-SO-CCA

---

[5] Higher leakage rate could be obtained by lengthening $\ell$ instead of $\lambda$.

**Table 1.** Comparison between schemes under the DCR assumption.

| Scheme | Size (**el**) $[pp, pk, sk, ct]$ | Computation cost (**ex**) [Enc, Dec] | Random bits [Enc] | SO | $n$-KDM | LR |
|---|---|---|---|---|---|---|
| CPA-CS | 1, 1, 1, 2 | 3, 1 | $2\lambda - 2$ | No | No | No |
| Our construction | 2, 1, 2, 3 | 4, 2 | $4\lambda - 2$ | Yes | Yes | Yes |

[a] Abbreviations: CPA-CS = IND-CPA version of Cramer-Shoup scheme, **el** = group element, **ex** = group element exponentiation.
[b] $pp$ can be shared among all users.

transform proposed in [12] is not compatible with above ones, so achieving multipurpose and IND-CCA secure encryption schemes would be our future work.

**Acknowledgments.** We would like to thank Yang Tao, Gaosheng Tan and the anonymous reviewers for their helpful discussions and comments. This work was partially supported by National Natural Science Foundation of China (No. 61632020, 61472416 and 61602468) and Key Research Project of Zhejiang Province (No. 2017C01062).

# References

1. Bellare, M., Boldyreva, A., Desai, A., Pointcheval, D.: Key-privacy in public-key encryption. In: Boyd, C. (ed.) ASIACRYPT 2001. LNCS, vol. 2248, pp. 566–582. Springer, Heidelberg (2001). doi:10.1007/3-540-45682-1_33
2. Bellare, M., Hofheinz, D., Yilek, S.: Possibility and impossibility results for encryption and commitment secure under selective opening. In: Joux, A. (ed.) EUROCRYPT 2009. LNCS, vol. 5479, pp. 1–35. Springer, Heidelberg (2009). doi:10.1007/978-3-642-01001-9_1
3. Black, J., Rogaway, P., Shrimpton, T.: Encryption-scheme security in the presence of key-dependent messages. In: Nyberg, K., Heys, H. (eds.) SAC 2002. LNCS, vol. 2595, pp. 62–75. Springer, Heidelberg (2003). doi:10.1007/3-540-36492-7_6
4. Boneh, D., Halevi, S., Hamburg, M., Ostrovsky, R.: Circular-secure encryption from decision Diffie-Hellman. In: Wagner, D. (ed.) CRYPTO 2008. LNCS, vol. 5157, pp. 108–125. Springer, Heidelberg (2008). doi:10.1007/978-3-540-85174-5_7
5. Brakerski, Z., Goldwasser, S.: Circular and leakage resilient public-key encryption under subgroup indistinguishability. In: Rabin, T. (ed.) CRYPTO 2010. LNCS, vol. 6223, pp. 1–20. Springer, Heidelberg (2010). doi:10.1007/978-3-642-14623-7_1
6. Camenisch, J., Chandran, N., Shoup, V.: A public key encryption scheme secure against key dependent chosen plaintext and adaptive chosen ciphertext attacks. In: Joux, A. (ed.) EUROCRYPT 2009. LNCS, vol. 5479, pp. 351–368. Springer, Heidelberg (2009). doi:10.1007/978-3-642-01001-9_20
7. Camenisch, J., Lysyanskaya, A.: An efficient system for non-transferable anonymous credentials with optional anonymity revocation. In: Pfitzmann, B. (ed.) EUROCRYPT 2001. LNCS, vol. 2045, pp. 93–118. Springer, Heidelberg (2001). doi:10.1007/3-540-44987-6_7
8. Cramer, R., Shoup, V.: Universal hash proofs and a paradigm for adaptive chosen ciphertext secure public-key encryption. In: Knudsen, L.R. (ed.) EUROCRYPT 2002. LNCS, vol. 2332, pp. 45–64. Springer, Heidelberg (2002). doi:10.1007/3-540-46035-7_4

9. Fehr, S., Hofheinz, D., Kiltz, E., Wee, H.: Encryption schemes secure against chosen-ciphertext selective opening attacks. In: Gilbert, H. (ed.) EUROCRYPT 2010. LNCS, vol. 6110, pp. 381–402. Springer, Heidelberg (2010). doi:10.1007/978-3-642-13190-5_20

10. Goldwasser, S., Micali, S.: Probabilistic encryption. J. Comput. Syst. Sci. **28**(2), 270–299 (1984)

11. Halderman, J.A., Schoen, S.D., Heninger, N., Clarkson, W., Paul, W., Calandrino, J.A., Feldman, A.J., Appelbaum, J., Felten, E.W.: Lest we remember: cold boot attacks on encryption keys. In: van Oorschot, P.C. (ed.) USENIX, pp. 45–60 (2008)

12. Hemenway, B., Libert, B., Ostrovsky, R., Vergnaud, D.: Lossy encryption: constructions from general assumptions and efficient selective opening chosen ciphertext security. In: Lee, D.H., Wang, X. (eds.) ASIACRYPT 2011. LNCS, vol. 7073, pp. 70–88. Springer, Heidelberg (2011). doi:10.1007/978-3-642-25385-0_4

13. Kitagawa, F., Matsuda, T., Hanaoka, G., Tanaka, K.: On the key dependent message security of the fujisaki-okamoto constructions. In: Cheng, C.-M., Chung, K.-M., Persiano, G., Yang, B.-Y. (eds.) PKC 2016. LNCS, vol. 9614, pp. 99–129. Springer, Heidelberg (2016). doi:10.1007/978-3-662-49384-7_5

14. Lu, X., Li, B., Jia, D.: KDM-CCA security from RKA secure authenticated encryption. In: Oswald, E., Fischlin, M. (eds.) EUROCRYPT 2015. LNCS, vol. 9056, pp. 559–583. Springer, Heidelberg (2015). doi:10.1007/978-3-662-46800-5_22

15. Malkin, T., Teranishi, I., Yung, M.: Efficient circuit-size independent public key encryption with KDM security. In: Paterson, K.G. (ed.) EUROCRYPT 2011. LNCS, vol. 6632, pp. 507–526. Springer, Heidelberg (2011). doi:10.1007/978-3-642-20465-4_28

16. Naor, M., Segev, G.: Public-key cryptosystems resilient to key leakage. In: Halevi, S. (ed.) CRYPTO 2009. LNCS, vol. 5677, pp. 18–35. Springer, Heidelberg (2009). doi:10.1007/978-3-642-03356-8_2

17. Qin, B., Liu, S.: Leakage-resilient chosen-ciphertext secure public-key encryption from hash proof system and one-time lossy filter. In: Sako, K., Sarkar, P. (eds.) ASIACRYPT 2013. LNCS, vol. 8270, pp. 381–400. Springer, Heidelberg (2013). doi:10.1007/978-3-642-42045-0_20

18. Wee, H.: KDM-security via homomorphic smooth projective hashing. In: Cheng, C.-M., Chung, K.-M., Persiano, G., Yang, B.-Y. (eds.) PKC 2016. LNCS, vol. 9615, pp. 159–179. Springer, Heidelberg (2016). doi:10.1007/978-3-662-49387-8_7

# Secure Certificateless Proxy Re-encryption Without Pairing

Veronika Kuchta[1(✉)], Gaurav Sharma[1], Rajeev Anand Sahu[1],
Tarunpreet Bhatia[2], and Olivier Markowitch[1]

[1] Universite Libre de Bruxelles, Brussels, Belgium
veronika.kuchta@ulb.ac.be
[2] Thapar University, Patiala, India

**Abstract.** A Proxy Re-encryption (PRE) is a cryptographic scheme for delegation of decryption rights. In a PRE scheme, a *semi-honest* proxy agent of Bob re-encrypts the ciphertext, on the message intended for Alice, on behalf of Bob, without learning anything about the message. The PRE schemes are useful in the scenarios where data are desired to be shared with the authorized users over the cloud. For such important applications, in this paper, we present an efficient and secure proxy re-encryption scheme. To avoid the overhead due to certification and to get rid of the key escrow issue of identity-based setting, we construct our scheme on the certificateless setting. The scheme has been proved secure in random oracle model under the standard assumption, the hardness of the computational Diffie-Hellman problem (CDHP). Moreover, as we device a pairing-free construction, our scheme is significantly more efficient than the best available scheme.

**Keywords:** Certificateless proxy re-encryption · Secure data sharing · Computational Diffie-Hellman (CDH) problem · Random oracle model

## 1 Introduction

Proxy re-encryption enables the semi-trusted proxy server to re-encrypt the ciphertext encrypted under Alice's public key to another ciphertext encrypted under Bob's public key. The re-encryption is processed by the server, after receiving a re-encryption key generated by Alice for Bob, without being able to access the original content. This property changes the whole game as per the needs of end-to-end encryption in cloud based applications like Dropbox, Box, Slack while not losing out the efficiency and collaboration features. Such solutions assure the users a secure experience of sharing encrypted files on cloud without any third party getting access to the user's encryption keys.

A weaker re-encryption scheme is one in which the proxy possesses both the keys (public as well as private) simultaneously. One key decrypts a plaintext, while the other encrypts it. Since the goal of a secure re-encryption system is to avoid revealing either of the keys or the underlying plaintext to the proxy, this

S. Obana and K. Chida (Eds.): IWSEC 2017, LNCS 10418, pp. 85–101, 2017.
DOI: 10.1007/978-3-319-64200-0_6

method is not ideal. On the other hand proxy re-encryption allows a strong foundation for the features of secure collaboration, public transportation privacy [13], private email forwarding and encrypted storage [2]. With cloud sharing taking over the traditional teamwork systems, a new concern being raised is the security aspect of these collaborations especially when there is sensitive data at stake. Proxy re-encryption takes the responsibility of keeping any unintended third party at bay from such data. Email being the most widely used medium of data sharing often has been a victim of prying eyes. Proxy re-encryption ensures only that the intended recipient holds the data, which was meant for it. It also reduces the over-reliance on passwords generally associated with emails. The convenient assistance provided by cloud storage by making data mobile has darkly eclipsed the fact that in reality there is no cloud, rather all data is at some strangers computer which in fact is an open invitation for security breach.

The foundation of classical public key cryptosystem includes certificate management and hence, is being considered computationally expensive. The introduction of identity-based approach shifted the paradigm. Here, the public key is directly associated with the identity of the user and therefore, no further need of certificates. The evolution of certificateless public key cryptography was suggested by Al-Riyami [1], which eliminated the problem of key escrow in identity-based cryptosystems. The need of proxy re-encryption in various recently developed real-time applications leads to combination of the concept of certificateless and proxy re-encryption. The implementation of CLPRE in these applications can securely transfer the sensitive data without revealing it to any intermediate device. A lightweight CLPRE can be a strong solution for the devices with constrained resources.

## 1.1 Related Work

The notion of proxy re-encryption was introduced in [4] where a bidirectional proxy re-encryption scheme was proposed. However, it suffers from collusion attack where receiver colludes with proxy to get sender's secret key. [2] proposed first unidirectional PRE scheme which prevents collusion attack but achieves only chosen plaintext attack. Keeping in mind, the difficulty of public key certificate management in traditional public key encryption (PKE) [5,7,14,16,17] and the key escrow problem in the ID-based public key encryption (ID-PKE) [8,11,14,15,20,21,24] into perspective, it naturally trickles down to a pressing need of investigating PRE in the certificateless public key encryption (CL-PKE) setting. To take maximum benefit of traditional PKE and ID-PKE without the associated cons and their corresponding criticisms, the introduction of primitive of PRE into CL-PKE by [23] came into existence, thus proposing the first concrete certificateless proxy re-encryption scheme. Leveraging the identity of a user as a component of its public key, CLPRE eliminates the key escrow problem in ID-PKE, without needing to use the certificates for guaranteeing the authenticity of public keys in traditional PKE.

Thereafter, [25] leverages cloud resources and proposed CLPRE scheme for data sharing in public cloud. They further enhanced it to multi-proxy CLPRE in which multiple proxy servers are deployed in different cloud providers and randomized CLPRE in which randomizing re-encryption key for better security and robustness. Xu's scheme was proved vulnerable by [12] and they extended [3] scheme to a more robust replayable chosen-ciphertext attack (RCCA) CLPRE scheme. But it relies on expensive pairing operations. [26] proposed single hop unidirectional chosen plaintext secure scheme CLPRE1 and chosen ciphertext secure scheme CLPRE2 without pairing based on computational Diffie-Hellman (CDH) assumption. In comparison to [23] and [25], their scheme provides shortest re-encryption key making it more efficient but their scheme relies on weaker security model. [22] breaks the confidentiality of [26] and extended [7] to certificateless setting and proposed CCA secure CLPRE scheme based on exponential cryptosystem. For efficiency comparison, they selected pairing based [12]. [19] proposed strongly CCA secure CLPRE without bilinear pairing. They compared their scheme with existing schemes based on computation cost and communication overhead. Unfortunately, the scheme is vulnerable to same confidentiality attack, presented by [22]. From the above discussion, it can be concluded that the only secure scheme remaining is [22].

## 1.2  Our Contribution

In this paper, we present an efficient and secure proxy re-encryption scheme. To avoid the overhead due to certification and to get rid of the key escrow issue of identity-based setting, we construct our scheme on the certificateless setting. The denial of decryption attack in original certificateless encryption scheme motivates to adopt the certificateless model, given by [3]. The scheme has been proved secure in random oracle model under the standard assumption, the hardness of the computational Diffie-Hellman problem (CDHP). Moreover, as we device a pairing-free construction, our scheme is significantly more efficient than the available best scheme on the same setup [22]. In contrast to the scheme in [22], we provide a significant improvement in the computational efficiency. The scheme in [22] requires to perform several pre-calculations during the key generation procedure which increases the memory costs and makes the construction less efficient. We achieve a significant reduction of the pre-calculated values during the key generation procedure which makes our scheme especially lightweight and memory efficient. Furthermore, unlike the theoretical comparison of [22], we obtain the precise operation times for various computations on a practical setup with standard parameters, and compare the schemes in the view of total operation time. We also consider the size of ciphertexts between the schemes and show that our scheme is more efficient than [22], in all the views.

## 1.3  Road Map

Rest of the paper is organized as follows: in Sect. 2, we introduce necessary notations, definitions and hardness assumption for the security. In Sect. 3, we define the CLPRE and formalize a security model for it. The proposed CLPRE scheme is described in Sect. 4. The security analysis and efficiency comparison have been presented in Sects. 5 and 6 respectively, followed by the conclusion in Sect. 7.

## 2    Preliminaries

In this section, we introduce computational problems and hardness assumptions. We rely on the standard definitions used for security of cryptographic schemes [10].

**Definition 1 (Computational Diffie-Hellman Problem (CDHP)).** Let $G$ be a multiplicative cyclic group with generator $g$. Let $CDH : G \times G \to G$ be a map defined by

$$CDH(X,Y) = Z \text{ where } X = g^a, Y = g^b \text{ and } Z = g^{ab}.$$

The *computational Diffie-Hellman problem* (CDHP) is to evaluate $CDH(X,Y)$ given $X, Y \xleftarrow{\$} G$ without the knowledge of $a, b \in \mathbb{Z}_q^*$. (Note that obtaining $a \in \mathbb{Z}_q^*$, given $g, X \in G$ is solving the discrete logarithm problem (DLP).)

**Definition 2 (Computational Diffie-Hellman Assumption).** Given a security parameter $\lambda$, let $\langle q, G, g, X, Y, \rangle \leftarrow \mathfrak{G}(\lambda)$. The *computational Diffie-Hellman assumption* (CDHA) states that for any PPT algorithm $\mathcal{A}$ which attempts to solve CDHP, its *advantage*

$$\mathbf{Adv}_{\mathfrak{G}}(\mathcal{A}) := Prob[\mathcal{A}(q, G, g, X, Y) = CDH(X,Y)]$$

is negligible in $\lambda$. We say that the $(t, \epsilon)$-*CDH assumption* holds in group $G$ if there is no algorithm which takes at most $t$ running time and can solve CDHP with at least a non-negligible advantage $\epsilon$.

## 3    Certificateless Proxy Re-encryption Scheme

In this section we present the formal definition of a certificateless proxy re-encryption (CLPRE) scheme and formalize a security model for it.

### 3.1    Certificateless Proxy Re-encryption

In a CLPRE scheme we have the following scenario: We consider a cloud storage application where many different users store their encrypted data. Assume, user $\mathbb{A}$ wants to share her data with user $\mathbb{B}$, without sharing her individual secret key. The idea of certificateless proxy re-encryption is that user $\mathbb{A}$ provides her encrypted data with a re-encryption key to the cloud service provider. This encrypted data under user $\mathbb{A}$'s public key $pk_\mathbb{A}$ can be re-encrypted by a proxy $\mathbb{P}$ to a data of user $\mathbb{B}$ under his public key $pk_\mathbb{B}$. The secret which is required for the decryption procedure, is generated as a combination of partial secret key provided by the KGC and of the user's secret key and results in user's full secret and public values.

For a fixed security parameter $\lambda$, the eleven algorithms of our CLPRE scheme work as provided in the description below. Note that indices $i$ and $j$ indicate different user's. Later in the construction of the scheme we use letters $\mathbb{A}$ and $\mathbb{B}$ to indicate the difference of users, where $\mathbb{A}$ denotes the user who uploads the encrypted data and $\mathbb{A}$ is the user who can download the re-encrypted cloud data.

**Setup$(1^\lambda)$:** On input security parameter $1^\lambda$, this PPT algorithm run by the Key Generation Center (KGC) outputs master secret key and master public key $msk, mpk$ and public parameters $params$.

**PartKeyExtr$(params, msk, ID)$:** On input public parameters $params$, master secret key $msk$ and the user's identity $ID$ this PPT algorithm outputs the partial secret key $psk_{ID}$ and the partial public key $ppk_{ID}$.

**KeyGen$(params, ppk, ID)$:** On input public parameters $params$, partial public key $ppk_{ID}$ and user's identity $ID$, this PPT algorithm outputs user's secret key $sk_{ID}$ and user's public key $pk_{ID}$.

**SetPrivatValue$(params, sk_{ID}, psk_{ID})$:** On input public parameters $params$, user's secret key $sk_{ID}$, partial secret key $psk_{ID}$, this PPT algorithm outputs users secret value $SK_{ID} = (psk_{ID}, sk_{ID})$.

**SetPublicValue$(params, pk_{ID}, ppk_{ID})$:** On input public parameters $params$, user's public key $pk_{ID}$, partial public key $ppk_{ID}$, this PPT algorithm outputs users public value $PK_{ID} = (ppk_{ID}, pk_{ID})$.

**ReEncKey$(params, ID_i, ID_j, SK_{ID_i}, PK_{ID_j})$:** This PPT algorithm is run by the user with $ID_i$. On input public parameters $params$, identities $ID_i, ID_j$, secret and public values $sk_{ID_i}$ and $pk_{ID_j}$ it outputs a re-encryption key $RK_{i \to j}$.

**PubKeyVer$(params, psk_{ID}, PK_{ID})$:** On input public parameters $params$, partial secret key $psk_{ID}$ and public value $PK_{ID}$ it outputs either 1 or $\perp$.

**Encrypt$(params, ID_i, PK_{ID_i}, m)$:** This PPT algorithm is run by the user who uploads the data. The algorithm takes as input the public parameters $params$, the identity of user $ID_i$, the public value $PK_{ID_i}$ and a message $m$ from the message space $\mathcal{M}$. It outputs a first level ciphertext $C$.

**ReEncrypt$(params, ID_i, ID_j, C, RK_{i \to j})$:** This PPT algorithm is run by the proxy user. On input public parameters $params$, user's identities $ID_i, ID_j$, a first level ciphertext $C$ and a re-encryption key $RK_{i \to j}$ it outputs a second level ciphertext $C'$ or an error symbol $\perp$.

**Decrypt 1$(params, ID_i, C, SK_{ID_i})$:** The deterministic algorithm is run by the user. On input public parameters $params$, user's identity $ID_i$, a first level ciphertext $C$ and user's secret value $SK_{ID_i}$ it outputs either $m \in \mathcal{M}$ or $\perp$.

**Decrypt 2$(params, ID_j, C', SK_{ID_j})$:** The deterministic algorithm is run by the user. On input public parameters $params$, user's identity $ID_j$, a second level ciphertext $C'$ and user's secret value $SK_{ID_j}$ it outputs either $m \in \mathcal{M}$ or $\perp$.

## 3.2    Security Model for CLPRE Scheme

In this section we present the security model of our CLPRE scheme which is called "indistinguishability against chosen ciphertext attacks" - IND-CCA.

The original security notion of an certificateless proxy re-encryption scheme is defined for two types of adversaries, $\mathcal{A}_I$ and $\mathcal{A}_{II}$, where the first type adversary $\mathcal{A}_I$ does not have access to the master key of key generation center, and second type adversary $\mathcal{A}_{II}$ does have the access. In the following paragraphs we provide only the definition of type-I-adversary. We refer to the full version of our paper for the full proof of both types of adversary.

## 3.3  IND-CCA Security of First Level Ciphertext Against $\mathcal{A}_I$

Let $\mathcal{A}_I$ be Type-I adversary against our CLPRE scheme. We assume that $\mathcal{A}_I$ interacts with the challenger $\mathcal{C}$, where $\mathcal{C}$ keeps history of received queries and sent answers by generating lists with corresponding answers.

**Initialization:** Challenger sets the list of corrupted identities **CI** and the list which consists of the current public keys **PK**. At the beginning the **CI** list is empty and the list **PK** contains $PK_{ID_i}$ corresponding to the identities $ID_i$.

**Phase-I:** Challenger $\mathcal{C}$ runs **Setup**$(\lambda)$ on input security parameter $\lambda$, to generate master key $mk$ and parameters $param$. $\mathcal{C}$ gives $param$ to $\mathcal{A}_I$ but keeps $msk$ secret. In the next lines we describe the responses for received queries.

**Partial Key Extract Queries:** On input $ID$, challenger runs **PartKeyExtr** algorithm to generate the partial public key $ppk_{ID}$ and partial private key $psk_{ID}$. $\mathcal{C}$ returns these keys to the adversary.

**Private Key Extract Queries:** On input $ID$, the challenger runs partial key extract algorithm, $ppk_{ID}, psk_{ID} \leftarrow$ **PartKeyExtr**$(param, mk, ID)$ and algorithm for setting the secret value $(sk_{ID}, pk_{ID}) \leftarrow$ **KeyGen**$(param, ID)$. The challenger generates the private key $SK_{ID} \leftarrow$ **SetPrivatValue**$(param, psk_{ID}, sk_{ID})$ and gives it to $\mathcal{A}_I$.

**Public Key Queries:** On Input $ID$, challenger $\mathcal{C}$ runs the partial key extract algorithm to obtain the partial key: $(ppk_{ID}, psk_{ID}) \leftarrow$ **PartKeyExtr**$(param, mk, ID)$. Furthermore it runs $(sk_{ID}, pk_{ID}) \leftarrow$ **KeyGen**$(param, ID)$. The challenger computes the public key $PK_{ID} \leftarrow$ **SetPublicValue**$(param, ppk_{ID}, pk_{ID})$ and gives it to $\mathcal{A}_I$.

**Re-Encryption Key Queries:** On input two identities $(ID_i, ID_j)$, the challenger runs re-encrypt key generation algorithm $rk_{i \rightarrow j} \leftarrow$ **ReEncKey**$(ID_i, ID_j, param, SK_{ID_i}, PK_{ID_j})$, where $ID_i$ denotes the identity of user $i$ and $PK_{ID_j}^{(c)}$ is the current public key of user $j$.

**Re-Encryption Queries:** On input $(ID_i, ID_j, C)$, where $C$ is first level ciphertext, the challenger computes the re-encryption key $rk_{i \rightarrow j} \leftarrow$ **ReEncKey**$(ID_i, ID_j, param, SK_{ID_i}, PK_{ID_j})$. Using this key, $\mathcal{C}$ computes re-encryption $C' \leftarrow$ **ReEncrypt**$(ID_i, ID_j, param, C, rk_{i \rightarrow j})$ and returns $C'$ to $\mathcal{A}_I$.

**Decryption1 Queries:** On input $(ID, C)$, the challenger runs **Decrypt1** $(param, sk_{ID}, C)$, using the private key $sk_{ID}$ which is an inversion of the current public key $pk_{ID}^{(c)}$, where $C$ is the first level ciphertext. The challenger returns either message $M$ or $\bot$.

**Decryption2 Queries:** On input $(ID, C)$, the challenger runs **Decrypt2** $(param, sk_{ID}, C)$, using the private key $sk_{ID}$ which is an inversion of the current public key $pk_{ID}^{(c)}$, where $C$ is the second level ciphertext. The challenger returns either message $M$ or $\perp$.

**Public Key Replacement:** On input $(ID_i, pk_{ID_i})$, the adversary $\mathcal{A}_I$ replaces the old public key of $ID_i$ with the new public key $pk'$.

**Challenge:** $\mathcal{A}_I$ outputs a challenge identity $ID^*$ which has not been queried before during the described queries, and two messages $(M_0, M_1)$ it wants to be challenged on. As another restriction, note that the challenge identity does not belong to the list of corrupted identities **CI**. Challenger picks a random bit $\delta \xleftarrow{r} \{0,1\}$ and computes $C_\delta \leftarrow$ **Encrypt**$(ID^*, param, PK_{ID^*}, M_\delta)$, where $PK_{ID^*}^{(c)}$ is the current public key of the challenge identity.

**Phase-II:** $\mathcal{A}_I$ issues queries as in Phase-I. Before we describe the differences and restrictions to Phase I, we define a challenge derivative, which is a result of re-encryption of the challenge ciphertext. We determine the following notes:
- $(ID^*, C^*)$ is a derivative of itself.
- If some $(ID_i, C_i)$ is a challenge derivative and the adversary received the ciphertext $C_j \leftarrow$ **ReEncrypt** after issuing an re-encrypt query on input $(ID_i, ID_j, C_i)$, then $(ID_j, C_j)$ is a challenge derivative.
- If some $(ID_i, C_i)$ is a challenge derivative and the adversary received the re-encrypt key $rk_{i \to j} \leftarrow$ **ReEncKey** after issuing an re-encrypt key query on input $(ID_i, ID_j)$, and after querying for re-encryption $C_j \leftarrow$ **ReEncrypt**$(ID_i, ID_j, param, C_i, rk_{i \to j})$, then $(ID_j, C_j)$ is a challenge derivative.

In contrast to Phase-I, $\mathcal{A}_I$ **cannot** issue the following queries:

**Private Key Extract query:** On input $ID_i$, if there is a pair $(ID_i, C_i)$ which is a derivative of $(ID^*, C^*)$, or $ID_i = ID_*$, the challenger returns $\perp$.

**Re-Encryption Key query:** On input $(ID_i, ID_j)$, if $ID_i = ID^*$ and the second one $ID_j$ has been corrupted by the adversary, $\mathcal{C}$ returns $\perp$.

**Re-Encryption queries:** On input $(ID_i, ID_j, C_{ID_i})$ if $(ID_i, C_{ID_i})$ is a derivative of $(ID^*, C^*)$, and $ID_j$ is corrupted by $\mathcal{A}_I$, the challenger returns $\perp$.

**Decryption1 queries:** On input $(ID, C)$, if $(ID, C)$ is a derivative of $(ID^*, C^*)$, the challenger returns $\perp$.

**Decryption2 queries:** On input $(ID, C)$, if $(ID, C)$ is a derivative of $(ID^*, C^*)$, the challenger returns $\perp$.

**Guess:** Adversary $\mathcal{A}_I$ returns a guess $\delta' \xleftarrow{r} \{0,1\}$ and wins the game if $\delta = \delta'$.

**Definition 3.** *Our CLPRE scheme is secure against Type-I adversary in the first level ciphertext security game, if for any running time t, there is an adversary who makes at most $q_{pk}$ public key queries, at most $q_{pke}$ partial key extract queries, at most $q_{sk}$ private key extract queries, at most $q_{rek}$ re-encryption key queries, at most $q_{re}$ re-encryption queries, at most $q_{de1}$ and $q_{de2}$ decryption queries for the original ciphertext and re-encrypted ciphertext respectively, and has a negligible advantage in winning the game, i.e. $\mathbf{Adv}_{CLPRE, \mathcal{A}_I, \mathbf{first}}^{IND-CCA} \leq \epsilon.$*

## 4   Proposed Scheme

We present here our efficient and secure CLPRE scheme. As described in Sect. 3, our construction consists of the following eleven algorithms:

**Setup**($1^\lambda$): In the setup phase, the KGC on input security parameter $\lambda$, chooses the system's master secret $msk = s \in \mathbb{Z}_q^*$, computes master public key $mpk := y = g^s$ and system's public parameters $params = (G, q, y, g, m, n, H_1, H_2, H_3, H_4, H_5, H_6, H_7)$, where $G = <g>$ is a cyclic group of prime order $q$. $m$ and $n$ are bitlength and $H_i$, $i = 1, ..7$ are cryptographic hash functions as defined below:

$H_1 : \{0,1\}^* \times G \to \mathbb{Z}_q^*$          $H_5 : G^4 \to \mathbb{Z}_q^*$
$H_2 : \{0,1\}^* \times G^3 \to \mathbb{Z}_q^*$        $H_6 : \{0,1\}^m \times \{0,1\}^n \times \{0,1\}^* \times G^2 \to \mathbb{Z}_q^*$
$H_3 : G^4 \times \{0,1\}^* \to \mathbb{Z}_q^*$        $H_7 : G \to \{0,1\}^{m+n}$
$H_4 : G^2 \times \{0,1\}^* \times \{0,1\}^* \to \mathbb{Z}_q^*$.

**PartKeyExtr**($params, msk, ID$):   On input public parameters $params = (G, q, y, g, m, n, H_1, H_2, H_3, H_4, H_5, H_6, H_7)$, master secret key $msk = s$ and user $\mathbb{A}$'s identity $ID_\mathbb{A}$, the KGC randomly selects $\alpha_{\mathbb{A},11}, \alpha_{\mathbb{A},12}, \beta \in \mathbb{Z}_q^*$ and computes

$$a_{\mathbb{A},11} = g^{\alpha_{\mathbb{A},11}}, \quad a_{\mathbb{A},12} = g^{\alpha_{\mathbb{A},12}}, \quad a_2 = g^\beta.$$

The KGC also computes

$$x_{\mathbb{A},11} = \alpha_{\mathbb{A},11} + sH_1(ID_\mathbb{A}, a_{\mathbb{A},11}), \quad x_{\mathbb{A},12} = \alpha_{\mathbb{A},12} + sH_1(ID_\mathbb{A}, a_{\mathbb{A},12}),$$
$$x_2 = \beta + sH_2(ID_\mathbb{A}, a_{\mathbb{A},11}, a_{\mathbb{A},12}, a_2).$$

This algorithm outputs partial private key $psk = (x_{\mathbb{A},11}, x_{\mathbb{A},12})$ and partial public key $ppk = (a_{\mathbb{A},11}, a_{\mathbb{A},12}, a_2, x_2)$.

**KeyGen**($params, ppk, ID$): The algorithm takes as input public parameters $params$, partial public key $ppk = (a_{\mathbb{A},11}, a_{\mathbb{A},12}, a_2, x_2)$ and user $\mathbb{A}$'s identity $ID_\mathbb{A}$. The KGC randomly selects $z_{\mathbb{A}1}, z_{\mathbb{A}2}, \gamma \in Z$ and computes:

$$u_{\mathbb{A}1} = g^{z_{\mathbb{A}1}}, \quad u_{\mathbb{A}2} = g^{z_{\mathbb{A}2}}, \quad a_3 = g^\gamma, \quad t = \gamma + x_2 H_3(ID_\mathbb{A}, u_{\mathbb{A}1}, u_{\mathbb{A}2}, a_2, a_3).$$

Finally, it outputs user secret key $sk_\mathbb{A} = (z_{\mathbb{A}1}, z_{\mathbb{A}2})$ and user public key $pk_\mathbb{A} = (u_{\mathbb{A}1}, u_{\mathbb{A}2}, t, a_3)$ and communicate to the user through a secure channel.

**SetPrivatValue**($params, sk, psk$): On input public parameters, user $\mathbb{A}$'s secret key $sk_\mathbb{A} = (z_{\mathbb{A}1}, z_{\mathbb{A}2})$ and partial secret key $psk = (x_{\mathbb{A},11}, x_{\mathbb{A},12})$. The user $\mathbb{A}$, after receiving the above values, set its private key by computing:

$$SK_\mathbb{A} = (z_{\mathbb{A}1}, z_{\mathbb{A}2}, x_{\mathbb{A},11}, x_{\mathbb{A},12})$$

**SetPublicValue**($params, pk, ppk$): On input public parameters, user $\mathbb{A}$'s public key $pk_\mathbb{A} = (u_{\mathbb{A}1}, u_{\mathbb{A}2}, t, a_3)$ and partial public key $ppk = (a_{\mathbb{A},11}, a_{\mathbb{A},12}, a_2, x_2)$. Also, the public key as $PK_\mathbb{A} = (u_{\mathbb{A}1}, u_{\mathbb{A}2}, a_{\mathbb{A},11}, a_{\mathbb{A},12}, a_2, x_2, t, a_3)$

**ReEncKey**$(params, ID_\mathbb{A}, ID_\mathbb{B}, SK_\mathbb{A}, PK_\mathbb{B})$: On input public parameters $params$, user $\mathbb{A}$'s identity $ID_\mathbb{A}$ and his secret value $SK_\mathbb{A} = (z_{\mathbb{A}1}, z_{\mathbb{A}2}, x_{\mathbb{A},11}, x_{\mathbb{A},12})$, user $\mathbb{B}$'s identity $ID_\mathbb{B}$ and user $\mathbb{A}$'s public value $PK_\mathbb{A} = (u_{\mathbb{A}1}, u_{\mathbb{A}2}, a_{\mathbb{A},11}, a_{\mathbb{A},12}, a_2, x_2, t, a_3)$, the original user $\mathbb{A}$ computes re-encryption key as follows:

$$t_{\mathbb{B}i} = a_{\mathbb{B},1i} y^{H_1(ID_\mathbb{B},\ a_{\mathbb{B},1i})} \text{ for } i \in \{1, 2\}, \quad t_{\mathbb{A}\mathbb{B}} = H_4(t_{\mathbb{B}1}{}^{z_{\mathbb{A}1}}, u_{\mathbb{B}1}{}^{x_{\mathbb{A},11}}, ID_\mathbb{A}, ID_\mathbb{B}),$$
$$RK_{\mathbb{A}\to\mathbb{B}} = (x_{\mathbb{A},11} + z_{\mathbb{A}1}) + (x_{\mathbb{A},12} + z_{\mathbb{A}2}) H_5(u_{\mathbb{A}1}, u_{\mathbb{A}2}, a_{\mathbb{A},11}, a_{\mathbb{A},12})$$

**PubKeyVer**$(params, psk, PK)$: On input public parameters $params$, partial secret key $psk = (x_{\mathbb{A},11}, x_{\mathbb{A},12})$ and public value $PK_\mathbb{A} = (u_{\mathbb{A}1}, u_{\mathbb{A}2}, a_{\mathbb{A},11}, a_{\mathbb{A},12}, a_2, x_2, t, a_3)$, the partial private keys, partial public keys and public keys can be verified as follows:

$$g^{x_{\mathbb{A},11}} = a_{\mathbb{A},11} y^{H_1(ID_\mathbb{A},\ a_{\mathbb{A},11})}, \quad g^{x_{\mathbb{A},12}} = a_{\mathbb{A},12} y^{H_1(ID_\mathbb{A},\ a_{\mathbb{A},12})},$$
$$g^{x_2} = a_2 y^{H_2(ID_\mathbb{A}, a_{\mathbb{A},11}, a_{\mathbb{A},12}, a_2)},$$
$$g^t = a_3 a_2^{H_3(ID_\mathbb{A}, u_{\mathbb{A}1}, u_{\mathbb{A}2}, a_2, a_3)} y^{H_2(ID_\mathbb{A}, a_{\mathbb{A},11}, a_{\mathbb{A},12}, a_2) H_3(ID_\mathbb{A}, u_{\mathbb{A}1}, u_{\mathbb{A}2}, a_2, a_3)}.$$

**Encrypt**$(params, ID_\mathbb{A}, PK_\mathbb{A}, m)$: The algorithm takes as input public parameters $params$, sender's identity $ID_\mathbb{A}$, his public value $PK_\mathbb{A} = (u_{\mathbb{A}1}, u_{\mathbb{A}2}, a_{\mathbb{A},11}, a_{\mathbb{A},12}, a_2, x_2, t, a_3)$. To encrypt a message $M \in \{0,1\}^m$, user $\mathbb{A}$ computes:

$$C_1 = g^r, C_2 = (M\|\sigma) \oplus H_7\left(\left(t_{\mathbb{A}1} u_{\mathbb{A}1} (t_{\mathbb{A}2} u_{\mathbb{A}2})^{H_5(u_{\mathbb{A}1}, u_{\mathbb{A}2}, a_{\mathbb{A},11}, a_{\mathbb{A},12})}\right)^r\right)$$

and stores the ciphertext $C = (C_1, C_2)$ in the cloud.
We note that $r = H_6(M, \sigma, ID_\mathbb{A}, u_{\mathbb{A}1}, u_{\mathbb{A}2})$, and $\sigma \in \{0,1\}^n$.

**ReEncrypt**$(params, ID_\mathbb{A}, ID_\mathbb{B}, C, RK_{\mathbb{A}\to\mathbb{B}})$: The algorithm is run by the proxy user and takes as input public parameters $params$, users identities $ID_\mathbb{A}, ID_\mathbb{B}$, ciphertext $C$ and re-encryption key $RK_{\mathbb{A}\to\mathbb{B}}$. To generate re-encrypted ciphertext for user $\mathbb{B}$, the proxy agent $\mathbb{P}$ computes:

$$C_1' = C_1{}^{RK_{\mathbb{A}\to\mathbb{B}}}, \quad C_2' = C_2.$$

$C' = (C_1', C_2')$ is the re-encrypted ciphertext of the message $M \in \{0,1\}^m$.

**Decrypt1**$(params, ID_\mathbb{A}, C, SK_\mathbb{A})$: On input $params$, user's identity $ID_\mathbb{A}$, first level ciphertext $C$ and $\mathbb{A}$'s secret value $SK_\mathbb{A} = (z_{\mathbb{A}1}, z_{\mathbb{A}2}, x_{\mathbb{A},11}, x_{\mathbb{A},12})$, user $\mathbb{A}$ performs the following computation to decrypt the ciphertext $C$ and retrieves the message $M$:

$$(M\|\sigma) = C_2 \oplus H_7\left(C_1^{(x_{\mathbb{A},11}+z_{\mathbb{A}1})+(x_{\mathbb{A},12}+z_{\mathbb{A}2})H_5(u_{\mathbb{A}1}, u_{\mathbb{A}2}, a_{\mathbb{A},11}, a_{\mathbb{A},12})}\right)$$

and verify using $C_1 = g^r$ where $r = H_6(M, \sigma, ID_\mathbb{A}, u_{\mathbb{A}1}, u_{\mathbb{A}2})$.

**Decrypt2**$(params, ID_\mathbb{B}, C', SK_\mathbb{B})$: On input public parameters $params$, user's identity $ID_\mathbb{B}$, second level ciphertext $C'$ and $\mathbb{B}$'s secret value $SK_\mathbb{B} = (z_{\mathbb{B}1}, z_{\mathbb{B}2}, x_{\mathbb{B},11}, x_{\mathbb{B},12})$, the user $\mathbb{B}$ computes message $M$ from the re-encrypted ciphertext $C'$ as follows:

$$(M\|\sigma) = C_2' \oplus H_7\left((C_1')^{\frac{1}{t_{\mathbb{B}\mathbb{A}}}}\right), \text{ where } t_{\mathbb{B}\mathbb{A}} = H_4(u_{\mathbb{A}1}{}^{x_{\mathbb{B},11}}, t_{\mathbb{A}1}{}^{z_{\mathbb{B}1}}, ID_\mathbb{A}, ID_\mathbb{B}).$$

**Correctness:** The correctness of decryption can be realized as follows:

$$t_{AB} = H_4(t_{B1}{}^{z_{A1}}, u_{B1}{}^{x_{A,11}}, ID_A, ID_A)$$
$$= H_4(a_{B,11}{}^{z_{A1}} y^{H_1(ID_B, a_{B,11}) z_{A1}}, g^{z_{B1} x_{11}}, ID_B, ID_B)$$
$$= H_4(u_{A1}{}^{x_{B,11}}, t_{A1}{}^{z_{B1}}, ID_A, ID_B) = t_{BA}.$$

# 5   Analysis of the Proposed Scheme

In this Section, we analyze the security of our proposed scheme. Note that due to page limits we are not able to provide the corresponding proofs for the type-II adversary. The full security proof will be presented in the full version of this paper. Here we focused on the first type adversary only and prove the chosen ciphertext security of first level ciphertext. To address the security analysis, we precisely prove the following Theorem 1. In order to generalize the identities of the different users, we use indices $i$ and $j$.

## 5.1   Security Against a Type-I Adversary

**Theorem 1.** *Our certificateless proxy re-encryption (CLPRE) scheme is IND-CCA secure in the random oracle model, assuming that the underlying CDH assumption is hard to solve.*

*Proof.* Let $\mathcal{A}$ be an adversary against $IND - CCA$ security of our CLPRE. We show how to construct from $\mathcal{A}$ an adversary $\mathcal{B}$ against the CDH problem.

**Initialization:** Algorithm $\mathcal{B}$ is given the instance of CDH problem. It sets $y = g^a$ and defines the master secret key as $msk = a$. It sends the public parameters $params = (p, q, \mathbb{G}, y, H_1, H_2, H_3, H_4, H_5, H_6, H_7)$ to $\mathcal{A}$, where the hash functions $H_1, \ldots, H_7$ are simulated by the random oracle controlled by $\mathcal{B}$. Whenever $\mathcal{A}$ queries random oracles $H_i, i \in \{1, \ldots, 7\}$, $\mathcal{B}$ simulates them as follows.

$H_1$ **oracle queries:** Challenger $\mathcal{B}$ generates a $H_1$-List of entries $(\langle ID_i, a_{i,11}\rangle, \chi_1)$, where $\chi_1$ is the corresponding $H_1$ value and $i$ indicates the index of user's identity. After receiving a query from $\mathcal{A}$ on input $(ID_i, a_{i,11})$, $\mathcal{B}$ checks the $H_1$ list on the corresponding value. If found, it returns $\chi_1$ to $\mathcal{A}$. If not, it chooses a random $\chi_1' \in \mathbb{Z}_q^*$, returns it to $\mathcal{A}$ and adds $(\langle ID_i, a_{i,11}\rangle, \chi_1')$ to the $H_1$-List.

$H_2$ **oracle queries:** $\mathcal{B}$ generates a $H_2$-List of entries $(\langle ID_i, a_{i,11}, a_{i,12}, a_2\rangle, \chi_2)$, where $\chi_2$ is the corresponding $H_2$ value. After receiving a query from $\mathcal{A}$ on input $(ID_i, a_{i,11}, a_{i,12}, a_2)$, $\mathcal{B}$ checks the $H_2$ list on the corresponding value. If found, it returns $\chi_2$ to $\mathcal{A}$. If not, it chooses a random $\chi_2' \in \mathbb{Z}_q^*$, returns it to $\mathcal{A}$ and adds $(\langle ID_i, a_{i,11}\rangle, \chi_2')$ to the $H_2$-List.

$H_3$ **oracle queries:** $\mathcal{B}$ generates a $H_3$-List of entries $(\langle ID_i, u_{i,1}, u_{i,2}, a_2, a_3\rangle, \chi_3)$, where $\chi_3$ is the corresponding $H_3$ value. After receiving a query from $\mathcal{A}$ on input $(ID_i, u_{i,1}, u_{i,2}, a_2, a_3)$, $\mathcal{B}$ checks the $H_3$ list on the corresponding value. If found, it returns $\chi_3$ to $\mathcal{A}$. If not, it chooses a random $\chi_3' \in \mathbb{Z}_q^*$, returns it to $\mathcal{A}$ and adds $(\langle ID_i, u_{i,1}, u_{i,2}, a_2, a_3\rangle, \chi_3')$ to the $H_3$-List.

$H_4$ **oracle queries:** $\mathcal{B}$ generates a $H_4$-List of entries $(\langle t_j^{z_{i,1}}, u^{x_{i,11}}, ID_i, ID_j \rangle,$ $\chi_4)$, where $\chi_4$ is the corresponding $H_4$ value. After receiving a query from $\mathcal{A}$ on input $(t_j^{z_{i,1}}, u_j^{x_{i,11}}, ID_i, ID_j)$, $\mathcal{B}$ checks the $H_4$ list on the corresponding value. If found, it returns $\chi_4$ to $\mathcal{A}$. If not, it chooses a random $\chi'_4 \in \mathbb{Z}_q^*$, returns it to $\mathcal{A}$ and adds $(\langle t_j^{z_{i,1}}, u_j^{x_{i,11}}, ID_i, ID_j \rangle, \chi'_4)$ to the $H_4$-List.

$H_5$ **oracle queries:** $\mathcal{B}$ generates a $H_5$-List of entries $(\langle u_{i,1}, u_{i,2}, a_{i,11}, a_{i,12} \rangle, \chi_5)$, where $\chi_5$ is the corresponding $H_5$ value on input $ID_i, a_{i,11}$. On receiving a query from $\mathcal{A}$ on input $(u_{i,1}, u_{i,2}, a_{i,11}, a_{i,12})$, $\mathcal{B}$ checks the $H_5$ list on the corresponding value. If found, it returns $\chi_5$ to $\mathcal{A}$. If not, it chooses an $\chi'_5 \in \mathbb{Z}_q^*$, returns it to $\mathcal{A}$ and adds $(\langle u_{i,1}, u_{i,2}, a_{i,11}, a_{i,12} \rangle, \chi'_5)$ to the $H_5$-List.

$H_6$ **oracle queries:** $\mathcal{B}$ generates a $H_6$-List of entries $(\langle M, \sigma, ID_i, u_{i,1}, u_{i,2} \rangle, \chi_6)$, where $\chi_6$ is the corresponding $H_6$ value. After receiving a query from $\mathcal{A}$ on input $(M, \sigma, ID_i, u_{i,1}, u_{i,2})$, $\mathcal{B}$ checks the $H_6$ list on the corresponding value. If found, it returns $\chi_6$ to $\mathcal{A}$. If not, it chooses an $\chi' \in \mathbb{Z}_q^*$, returns it to $\mathcal{A}$ and adds $(\langle M, \sigma, ID_i, u_{i,1}, u_{i,2} \rangle, \chi'_6)$ to the $H_6$-List.

$H_7$ **oracle queries:** $\mathcal{B}$ generates a $H_7$-List of entries $(\langle A \rangle, \chi_7)$, where $\chi_7$ is the corresponding $H_7$ value. On receiving a query from $\mathcal{A}$ on input $A$, $\mathcal{B}$ checks the $H_7$-List on the corresponding value. If found, it returns $\chi_7$ to $\mathcal{A}$. If not, it chooses an $\chi'_7 \in \mathbb{Z}_q^*$, returns it to $\mathcal{A}$ and adds $(\langle A \rangle, \chi'_7)$ to the $H_7$-List.

**Phase-I:** $\mathcal{A}$ issues distinct queries corresponding to the security game in Section (1.1.1). In the following paragraphs we describe the simulation of the corresponding answers by algorithm $\mathcal{B}$. Assume there is a list for each oracle, i.e., **PKE-List, PrK-List, PuK-List, ReK-List, ReE-List, De1-List, De2-List**, which contains all possible answers. We assume that these lists are controlled by $\mathcal{B}$.

**Partial Key Extract queries:** On input $ID_i$, algorithm $\mathcal{B}$ checks the **PKE-List** consisting of entries $(ID_i, \langle x_{i,11}, x_{i,12}, a_{i,11}, a_{i,12}, a_2, x_2 \rangle, \langle \alpha_{i,11}, \alpha_{i,12}, \beta \rangle)$. If the corresponding entry is in the list, $\mathcal{B}$ returns $\langle x_{i,11}, x_{i,12}, a_{i,11}, a_{i,12}, a_2, x_2 \rangle$. Otherwise $\mathcal{B}$ picks random $\alpha_{\tilde{i},11}, \alpha_{\tilde{i},12}, \tilde{\beta} \xleftarrow{r} (\mathbb{Z}_q^*)^3$ and computes $a_{\tilde{i},11} = g^{\alpha_{\tilde{i},11}}$, $a_{\tilde{i},12} = g^{\alpha_{\tilde{i},12}}$, $\tilde{a}_2 = g^{\tilde{\beta}}$. After computing the values, $\mathcal{B}$ queries the random oracle $H_1$ on input $(ID_i, \tilde{a}_\iota)$, where $i \in \{(11), (12)\}$ and obtains $(\langle ID_i, \tilde{a}_\iota \rangle, \chi_{1_\iota}) \in H_1$-List. $\mathcal{B}$ picks a random value $\rho \leftarrow \mathbb{Z}_q^*$ and computes $x_{i,11} = \alpha_{\tilde{i},11} + \rho\chi_{1_\iota}$. It queries $H_2$ oracle on input $(\langle ID_i, a_{\tilde{i},11}, a_{\tilde{i},12}, \tilde{a}_2 \rangle)$ and receives $(\langle ID_i, a_{\tilde{i},11}, a_{\tilde{i},12}, \tilde{a}_2 \rangle, \chi_2)$. $\mathcal{B}$ computes then $x_2 = \tilde{\beta} + \rho\chi_2$. It returns $\langle x_{i,11}, x_{i,12}, a_{i,11}, a_{i,12}, a_2, x_2 \rangle$ to $\mathcal{A}$.

**Public Key queries:** On Input $ID_i$, algorithm $\mathcal{B}$ checks the **PuK-List**, which consists of the entries $(\langle ID_i, u_{i,1}, u_{i,2}, a_{i,11}, a_{i,12}, a_2, x_2, a_3, t \rangle, coin)$. $\mathcal{B}$ checks whether the corresponding entry is in the list. If so, it returns the required public key $\langle ID_i, u_{i,1}, u_{i,2}, a_{i,11}, a_{i,12}, a_2, x_2, a_3, t \rangle$ to $\mathcal{A}$. Otherwise if the above mentioned query does not appear in the **PuK-List**, $\mathcal{B}$ picks a $coin \in \{0,1\}$, with the probability $Pr[coin = 0] = \tau$ and runs the previously described simulation of partial key extract queries to obtain the partial key $\langle x_{i,11}, x_{i,12}, x_2, a_{i,11}, a_{i,12}, x_2 \rangle$.

If $coin = 0$, pick random values $z_{\tilde{i},1}, z_{\tilde{i},2}, \tilde{\beta}, \tilde{\gamma}, \tilde{s} \in \mathbb{Z}_q^*$ and compute $\tilde{u}_1 = g^{\tilde{z}_1}, \widetilde{u_2} = g^{\tilde{z}_2}, \tilde{a}_2 = g^{\tilde{\beta}} + \tilde{s}H_2(ID_i, a_{i,11}, a_{i,12}, \tilde{a}_2), \tilde{a}_3 = g^{\tilde{\gamma}}$. It queries the $H_3$

oracle on input $(ID_i, \widetilde{u_{i,1}}, \widetilde{u_{i,2}}, \tilde{a}_2, \tilde{a}_3)$, and receives the corresponding hash value as simulated above. It sets: $\tilde{t} = \gamma + x_2 H_3(ID_i, \widetilde{u_{i,1}}, \widetilde{u_{i,2}}, \tilde{a}_2, \tilde{a}_3)$. $\mathcal{B}$ adds the tuple $(ID_i, x_{i,11}, x_{i,12}, \widetilde{z_{i,1}}, \widetilde{z_{i,2}}, \tilde{\gamma})$ to **PrK**-List and the corresponding pubic key tuple $(\langle ID_i, \widetilde{u_{i,1}}, \widetilde{u_{i,2}}, a_{i,11}, a_{i,12}, \tilde{a}_2, x_2, \tilde{a}_3, \tilde{t}\rangle, coin)$ to **PuK**-List. It gives the following public key $pk = \langle ID_i, \widetilde{u_{i,1}}, \widetilde{u_{i,2}}, a_{i,11}, a_{i,12}, \tilde{a}_2, x_2, \tilde{a}_3, \tilde{t}\rangle$ to the adversary $\mathcal{A}$. The public key computed above is identically distributed to the output of the **SetPublicValue** algorithm, which is $(g^{z_{i,1}}, g^{z_{i,2}}, g^{\alpha_{i,11}}, g^{\alpha_{i,12}}, x_2, t, g^\gamma)$, where $z_{i,1}, z_{i,2}, \alpha_{i,11}, \alpha_{i,12}, \gamma$ are uniformly and randomly chosen from $\mathcal{Z}_q^*$ where the public values $x_2 = \beta + sH_2(ID_i, a_{i,11}, a_{i,12}, a_2)$, and $t = \gamma + x_2 H_3(ID_i, u_{i,1}, u_{i,2}, a_2, a_3)$ are independently distributed since $H_2, H_3$ are random oracles.

We also show that the simulated public key passes the public key verification procedure: $g^{\tilde{t}} = \tilde{a}_3 \tilde{a}_2^{H_3(\cdot)} g^{aH_2(\cdot)H_3(\cdot)}$.

If $coin = 1$, $\mathcal{B}$ picks $\widetilde{z_{i,1}}', \widetilde{z_{i,2}}', \tilde{\beta}', \tilde{\gamma}', \tilde{s}' \in \mathcal{Z}_q^*$ and computes $\widetilde{u_{i,1}} = g^{\widetilde{z_{i,1}}}, \widetilde{u_{i,2}} = g^{\widetilde{z_{i,2}}}, \tilde{a}_2 = g^{\tilde{\beta}'}, x_2 = \tilde{\beta}' + \tilde{s}' H_2(ID_i, a_{i,11}, a_{i,12}, \tilde{a}_2), a_3 = g^{\tilde{\gamma}'}$. $\mathcal{B}$ adds the tuples $(ID_i, x_{i,11}, x_{i,12}, \widetilde{z_{i,1}}, \widetilde{z_{i,2}}, \tilde{\gamma})$ to **PrK**-List and $(\langle ID_i, u_{i,1}, u_{i,2}, a_{i,11}, a_{i,12}, a_2, a_3, t\rangle, coin)$ to **PuK**-List and gives the public key $\langle ID_i, u_{i,1}, u_{i,2}, a_{i,11}, a_{i,12}, x_2, a_3, t\rangle$ to the adversary $\mathcal{A}$.

**Private Key Extract queries:** On input $ID$, $\mathcal{B}$ checks the **PrK**-List, which consists of the entries $(\langle ID, x_{11}, x_{12}, z_1, z_2\rangle, coin)$. If $coin = 0$, $\mathcal{B}$ checks whether the corresponding entry is in the **PrK**-list. If so, it returns the required secret key. If $coin = 1$, $\mathcal{B}$ rejects, meaning that the public key for an $ID$ has been replaced by the adversary $\mathcal{A}$. Otherwise, $\mathcal{B}$ aborts the simulation.

**Re-Encryption Key queries:** On input $(ID_i, ID_j)$, $\mathcal{B}$ searches the **ReK**-List, which consists of the entries $(\langle ID_i, ID_j\rangle, rk_{i\to j}, t_{j1}, t_{j2}, \theta)$. If $\mathcal{B}$ finds the corresponding value on input $(ID_i, ID_j)$, it returns the re-encryption key to $\mathcal{A}$. Otherwise it runs the simulation for public key queries described above to generate $(\langle ID_j, u_{j,1}, u_{j,2}, a_{j,11}, a_{j,12}, a_2, x_2, a_3, t\rangle, coin)$, where $a_{j,11}$ denotes the public key of user $ID_j$. If $coin = 0$, $\mathcal{B}$ runs the simulation of private key as described above to obtain $\langle ID_i, x_{i,11}, x_{i,12}, z_{i,1}, z_{i,2}\rangle$. Furthermore it computes $t_j = a_{j,11} g^{aH_1(ID_j, a_{j,11})}$. Using the values $t_j$ and $rk_{i\to j}$, $\mathcal{B}$ computes the value $H_4(t_j^{z_{i,1}}, u_{j,1}^{x_{i,11}}, ID_i, ID_j)$. It gives $rk_{i\to j}$ to $\mathcal{A}$. It sets $\theta = 1$ and updates the value in the **ReK**-List. Otherwise, if $coin = 1$, $\mathcal{B}$ aborts the simulation.

**Re-Encryption queries:** On input $(ID_i, ID_j, C)$, where $C$ is first level ciphertext, $\mathcal{B}$ checks the **PuK**-List on input $(\langle ID_i, u_{i,1}, u_{i,2}, a_{i,11}, a_{i,12}, a_2, x_2, a_3, t\rangle, coin)$. If $coin = 0$, and the public key is the current public key which has not been modified by $\mathcal{A}$, then $\mathcal{B}$ runs the simulation of re-encrypt key generation to obtain the re-encryption key $rk_{i\to j}$. It computes the re-encryption **ReEncrypt**$(ID_i, ID_j, param, C, rk_{i\to j})$. Otherwise, if $coin = 1$, $\mathcal{B}$ picks a random $\sigma \xleftarrow{r} \{0,1\}^n$ and sets $C_1 = g^b$. Then it computes $t_i = a_{i,11} g^{aH_1(ID_i, a_{i,11})}$ and generates $H_7((t_{i1}u_{i1}(t_{i2}u_{i2})^{H_5(u_{i,1}, u_{i,2}, a_{i,11}, a_{i,12})} \cdot u_{i,1})^r)$. $\mathcal{B}$ computes the second component of the ciphertext by doing $C_2 = (M||\sigma) \oplus H_7(C_1)$. Upon receiving the re-encryption key from the simulation above, $\mathcal{B}$ re-encrypts $C$ by calculating $C_1' = C_1^{rk_{i\to j}}$ and $C_2' = C_2$.

**Decryption1 queries:** On input $(ID_i, C)$, where $C$ is the first level ciphertext, $\mathcal{B}$ first recovers $(\langle ID_j, u_{j,1}, u_{j,2}, a_{j,11}, a_{j,12}, a_2, x_2, a_3, t \rangle, coin)$. $\mathcal{B}$ runs the simulation of private key extraction to recover $(\langle ID_j, x_{j,11}, x_{j,12}, z_{j,1}, z_{j,2} \rangle, coin)$. Using this secret key $sk_{ID_j}$, $\mathcal{B}$ picks a random $\sigma \xleftarrow{r} \{0,1\}^n$ and searches for the $H_6(\cdot, \sigma, u_{i,1}, u_{i,2})$ value in the $H_6$-List. It calculates the following value $C_2 \oplus H_7(C_1^{(x_{i,11}+z_{i,1})+(x_{i,12}+z_{i,2})H_5(u_{i,1},u_{i,2},a_{i,11},a_{i,12})})$ and gives the result to $\mathcal{A}$.

**Decryption2 queries:** On input $(ID, C')$, where $C' = (C'_1, C'_2)$ is the second level ciphertext, $\mathcal{B}$ first recovers $(\langle ID, u_1, u_2, a_{j,11}, a_{j,12}, a_2, x_2 a_3, t \rangle, coin)$ from the $PuK$-List. If $coin = 0$, $\mathcal{B}$ runs the simulation of private key extraction to recover the following tuple $(\langle ID_i, x_{i,11}, x_{i,12}, z_{i,1}, z_{i,2} \rangle, coin)$. It runs the re-encryption key simulation to generate $t_{ji}$ and computes then $C'_2 \oplus H_7(C_1'^{1/t_{ji}})$. $\mathcal{B}$ returns it to $\mathcal{A}$. Otherwise it computes the ciphertext as described in the Decryption1 query and generates the corresponding re-encryption using the re-encryption key simulated as showed above.

**Public Key Replacement:** On input $(ID_i, pk_{ID_i})$, whenever the adversary $\mathcal{A}$ wants to replace the old public key of $ID_i$ with the new public key $pk'$, $\mathcal{B}$ checks the validity of the new key. If the check fails, $\mathcal{B}$ returns $\perp$. Otherwise it updates the **CPK**-List with the new key.

**Challenge:** $\mathcal{A}$ outputs a challenge identity $ID^*$ which has not been queried before, and two messages $(M_0, M_1)$ it wants to be challenged on. Note also that the challenge identity does not belong to the list of corrupted identities **CI**. $\mathcal{B}$ recovers $(\langle ID_i, u_{i,1}, u_{i,2}, a_{i,11}, a_{i,12}, a_2, a_3, t \rangle, coin)$ from the $PuK$-List. If $coin = 0$ it aborts. Otherwise, if $coin = 1$, $\mathcal{B}$ picks a random $\sigma \xleftarrow{r} \{0,1\}^n$ and sets $C^*_1 = g^r = g^b$ (assuming that $r = b$). $\mathcal{B}$ computes the second component of the ciphertext as follows $C_2 = (M||\sigma) \oplus H_7(g^b) = (M||\sigma) \oplus H_7(C^*_1)$. Since according to the encryption procedure the following equation holds: $C_2 = (M||\sigma) \oplus H_7\left(\left(t_{i1}u_{i1}(t_{i2}u_{i2})^{H_5}\right)^r\right)$, where $t_{i1} = a_{i,11}g^{aH_1(\cdot)}$, we have

$$C^*_2 = (M||\sigma) \oplus H_7(C^*_1) = (M||\sigma) \oplus H_7\left(\left(t_{i,1}u_{i,1}(t_{i,2}u_{i,2})^{H_5}\right)^r\right)$$

$$= (M||\sigma) \oplus H_7\left(\left(a^b_{i,11}g^{abH_1}u^b_{i,1}a^b_{i,12}g^{abH_1 H_5}u^{bH_5}_{i,1}\right)\right).$$

**Phase-II:** $\mathcal{A}$ issues queries as in Phase-I. Due to page limit we skip the detailed description, where the queries of all the above mentioned oracles are answered as before considering the restrictions defined in the security game in Sect. 1.1.1.

**Guess:** Finally $\mathcal{A}$ outputs a guess $\delta'$ of $\delta$. $\mathcal{B}$ picks a random tuple $(X, H_7(X))$ from the $H_7$-List. In order to extract $g^{ab}$ from $X = a^b_{i,11}u^b_{i1}g^{abH_1(1+H_5)}a^b_{i,12}u^{H_5}_{i1}$ it performs the following computation: $a^b_{i,1\kappa} = g^{\alpha_{i,1\kappa}b}$ for $\kappa \in \{1,2\}$ and $u^b_{i1} = g^{z_{i,1}b}$, where $\alpha_{i,11}$ and $z_{i,1}$ are randomly guessed from $\mathbb{Z}^*_q$. The guess probability of the correct values $\alpha_{i,11}, z_{i,1}$ reduce success probability by $1/(q-1)^2$, where $q - 1 = |\mathbb{Z}^*_q|$. By performing the following conversion $a^{bH_5}_{i,1\kappa} = (g^b)^{\alpha_{i,11}H_5}$, and $u^b_{i,\kappa} = g^{z_{i,\kappa}b}$

where $g^b$ is the instance of CDH problem. Furthermore it computes $X' = \left(\frac{X}{(g^b)^{(\alpha_{i,11}+z_{i,1})+(\alpha_{i,12}+z_{i,2})H_5}}\right)^{1/(H_1 H_5)}$. It outputs $X'$ as CDH solution.

**Analysis:** It is obvious that the simulations of $H_1, \ldots, H_7$ are perfect as long as $\mathcal{A}$ does not query the $H_7$ oracle on $X^b$. Note that the corresponding value of $coin$ in case of challenge identity is 1. If during the re-encryption key generation queries on input $(ID_i, ID_j)$, $ID_i \neq ID^*$, the corresponding $coin$ value is 0. If any of these conditions does not hold, $\mathcal{B}$ aborts the simulation. It holds $Pr[\neg Abort] \geq (1-\pi) \cdot \pi^{q_{pk}+q_{pke}+q_{sk}+q_{rek}+q_{re}+q_{de1}+q_{de2}}$. The simulation of re-encryption queries is also perfect, if the adversary submits valid ciphertexts. Assume there is a polynomial time algorithm $\mathcal{D}$ distinguishing between correctly computed re-encryption keys and incorrectly formed keys in the simulation. Let $D$ denote this even and $Pr[D] = \tau$. Furthermore we assume either $\mathcal{A}$ querying $H_7$ on input $X^b$ or event D happening given that simulation does not abort. Let $E$ denote this event. It holds $Pr[\delta' = \delta | \neg E] = 1/2$ and $Pr[\delta' = \delta] = Pr[\delta' = \delta | \neg E]Pr[\neg E] + Pr[\delta' = \delta | E]Pr[E] \leq 1/2(1 + Pr[E])$ and $Pr[\delta' = \delta] \geq 1/2(1 - Pr[E])$. Let $\nu$ be the advantage for the $\mathcal{A}$ adversary. It holds $\nu = |Pr[\delta' = \delta] - 1/2| \leq 1/2Pr[E] = 1/2\frac{1}{Pr[\neg Abort]}(Pr[ask\ H_7] + \tau)$. It holds $Pr[ask\ H_7] \geq 2\nu \left(1/(q-1)^2\right)(1-\pi) \cdot \pi^{q_{pk}+q_{pke}+q_{sk}+q_{rek}+q_{re}+q_{de1}+q_{de2}} - \tau$. It is obvious that $\mathcal{B}$ can solve CDH problem if $H_7$ will be queried on $X^b$. $\square$

## 6    Efficiency Analysis Details

In this section we compare the efficiency of our CLPRE scheme with the best known scheme [22] and show that our scheme is more efficient in the view of computation and operation time than the existing scheme. To compute the operation time and to achieve the 1024-bit RSA level security, we use MIRACL [18], a standard cryptographic library. The hardware platform is: Pantium IV 3 GHZ processor with 512 M bytes memory. Operating system is Windows XP. Further, we refer to [9] where the operation time (OT) for various cryptographic operations have been obtained. Precisely, the OT for one exponentiation in cyclic group $G$ is 5.31 milisecond (ms). We ignore other operations in the analysis since their computation cost is trivial, for example one general hash function takes $<0.001$ ms which is negligible with compare to the time taken by the exponentiation. To evaluate the total operation time, we use the method followed in [6,9]. In each of the algorithms: **PartKeyExtr, PrivKeyExtr, SetPublicValue, ReEncKey, Encrypt, ReEncrypt, Decrypt 1, Decrypt 2** we compare the total number of exponentiations, ciphertext size and the consequent total operation time (OT).

*Remark 1.* In the Table 1, $t$ is the string of bitlength $m+n$. Also, in the ciphertext size, we compare size of ciphertext $C$ in **Encrypt** algorithm only, for both the schemes, as in both the schemes the size of re-encrypted ciphertext $C'$ is of the same size that of $C$ in the corresponding schemes.

**Table 1.** Efficiency comparison

| Algorithms | Scheme [22] | Our scheme |
|---|---|---|
| **PartKeyExtr** | $3t_{exp}$ | $3t_{exp}$ |
| **PrivKeyExtr** | $2t_{exp}$ | $3t_{exp}$ |
| **SetPublicValue** | $2t_{exp}$ | $0$ |
| **ReEncKey** | $2t_{exp}$ | $2t_{exp}$ |
| **Encrypt** | $4t_{exp}$ | $3t_{exp}$ |
| **ReEncrypt** | $t_{exp}$ | $t_{exp}$ |
| **Decrypt 1** | $2t_{exp}$ | $2t_{exp}$ |
| **Decrypt 2** | $4t_{exp}$ | $3t_{exp}$ |
| Ciphertext size | $3\ log(q) + t$ | $log(q) + t$ |
| Total OT (in ms) | 106.2 | 90.27 |

# 7  Conclusion

In this paper, we have proposed an efficient certificateless proxy re-encryption scheme without pairing. Our scheme is secure in random oracle model under the standard assumption, the hardness of the computational Diffie-Hellman problem (CDHP). In the computational cost perspective, our scheme is more efficient than the existing best scheme in the similar setup. The proposed scheme is best suitable for application for data sharing to the authorized users over the cloud.

# References

1. Al-Riyami, S.S., Paterson, K.G.: Certificateless public key cryptography. In: International Conference on the Theory and Application of Cryptology and Information Security, pp. 452–473. Springer (2003)
2. Ateniese, G., Kevin, F., Green, M., Hohenberger, S.: Improved proxy re-encryption schemes with applications to secure distributed storage. ACM Trans. Inform. Syst. Secur. (TISSEC) **9**(1), 1–30 (2006)
3. Baek, J., Safavi-Naini, R., Susilo, W.: Certificateless public key encryption without pairing. In: Zhou, J., Lopez, J., Deng, R.H., Bao, F. (eds.) ISC 2005. LNCS, vol. 3650, pp. 134–148. Springer, Heidelberg (2005). doi:10.1007/11556992_10
4. Blaze, M., Bleumer, G., Strauss, M.: Divertible protocols and atomic proxy cryptography. In: Nyberg, K. (ed.) EUROCRYPT 1998. LNCS, vol. 1403, pp. 127–144. Springer, Heidelberg (1998). doi:10.1007/BFb0054122
5. Canetti, R., Hohenberger, S.: Chosen-ciphertext secure proxy re-encryption. In: Proceedings of the 14th ACM Conference on Computer and Communications Security, pp. 185–194. ACM (2007)
6. Cao, X., Kou, W., Xiaoni, D.: A pairing-free identity-based authenticated key agreement protocol with minimal message exchanges. Inf. Sci. **180**(15), 2895–2903 (2010)

7. Chow, S.S.M., Weng, J., Yang, Y., Deng, R.H.: Efficient unidirectional proxy re-encryption. In: Bernstein, D.J., Lange, T. (eds.) AFRICACRYPT 2010. LNCS, vol. 6055, pp. 316–332. Springer, Heidelberg (2010). doi:10.1007/978-3-642-12678-9_19

8. Chu, C.-K., Tzeng, W.-G.: Identity-based proxy re-encryption without random oracles. In: Garay, J.A., Lenstra, A.K., Mambo, M., Peralta, R. (eds.) ISC 2007. LNCS, vol. 4779, pp. 189–202. Springer, Heidelberg (2007). doi:10.1007/978-3-540-75496-1_13

9. Debiao, H., Jianhua, C, Jin, H.: An id-based proxy signature schemes without bilinear pairings. annals of telecommunications-annales des télécommunications 66(11–12), 657–662 (2011)

10. Dutta, R., Barua, R., Sarkar, P.: Pairing-based cryptographic protocols: A survey. IACR Cryptology ePrint Archive 2004, 64 (2004)

11. Green, M., Ateniese, G.: Identity-based proxy re-encryption. In: Katz, J., Yung, M. (eds.) ACNS 2007. LNCS, vol. 4521, pp. 288–306. Springer, Heidelberg (2007). doi:10.1007/978-3-540-72738-5_19

12. Guo, H., Zhang, Z., Zhang, J., Chen, C.: Towards a secure certificateless proxy re-encryption scheme. In: Susilo, W., Reyhanitabar, R. (eds.) ProvSec 2013. LNCS, vol. 8209, pp. 330–346. Springer, Heidelberg (2013). doi:10.1007/978-3-642-41227-1_19

13. Heydt-Benjamin, T.S., Chae, H.-J., Defend, B., Fu, K.: Privacy for public transportation. In: Danezis, G., Golle, P. (eds.) PET 2006. LNCS, vol. 4258, pp. 1–19. Springer, Heidelberg (2006). doi:10.1007/11957454_1

14. Liang, K., Liu, J.K., Wong, D.S., Susilo, W.: An efficient cloud-based revocable identity-based proxy re-encryption scheme for public clouds data sharing. In: Kutyłowski, M., Vaidya, J. (eds.) ESORICS 2014. LNCS, vol. 8712, pp. 257–272. Springer, Cham (2014). doi:10.1007/978-3-319-11203-9_15

15. Liang, K., Susilo, W., Liu, J.K., Wong, D.S.: Efficient and fully CCA secure conditional proxy re-encryption from hierarchical identity-based encryption. Comput. J. 58, 2778–2792 (2015)

16. Libert, B., Vergnaud, D.: Unidirectional chosen-ciphertext secure proxy re-encryption. In: Cramer, R. (ed.) PKC 2008. LNCS, vol. 4939, pp. 360–379. Springer, Heidelberg (2008). doi:10.1007/978-3-540-78440-1_21

17. Lu, Y., Li, J.: A pairing-free certificate-based proxy re-encryption scheme for secure data sharing in public clouds. Future Gener. Comput. Syst. 62, 140–147 (2016)

18. MIRACL. Multiprecision integer and rational arithmetic cryptographic library. http://certivox.org/display/EXT/MIRACL

19. Qin, Z., Wu, S., Xiong, H.: Strongly secure and cost-effective certificateless proxy re-encryption scheme for data sharing in cloud computing. In: Wang, Y., Xiong, H., Argamon, S., Li, X.Y., Li, J.Z. (eds.) BigCom 2015. LNCS, vol. 9196, pp. 205–216. Springer, Cham (2015). doi:10.1007/978-3-319-22047-5_17

20. Shao, J., Cao, Z.: CCA-secure proxy re-encryption without pairings. In: Jarecki, S., Tsudik, G. (eds.) PKC 2009. LNCS, vol. 5443, pp. 357–376. Springer, Heidelberg (2009). doi:10.1007/978-3-642-00468-1_20

21. Shao, J., Cao, Z.: Multi-use unidirectional identity-based proxy re-encryption from hierarchical identity-based encryption. Inf. Sci. 206, 83–95 (2012)

22. Srinivasan, A., Pandu Rangan, C.: Certificateless proxy re-encryption without pairing. IACR Cryptology ePrint Archive, 2014:933 (2014)

23. Sur, C., Jung, C.D., Park, Y., Rhee, K.H.: Chosen-ciphertext secure certificateless proxy re-encryption. In: Decker, B., Schaumüller-Bichl, I. (eds.) CMS 2010. LNCS, vol. 6109, pp. 214–232. Springer, Heidelberg (2010). doi:10.1007/978-3-642-13241-4_20

24. Wang, L., Wang, L., Mambo, M., Okamoto, E.: New identity-based proxy re-encryption schemes to prevent collusion attacks. In: Joye, M., Miyaji, A., Otsuka, A. (eds.) Pairing 2010. LNCS, vol. 6487, pp. 327–346. Springer, Heidelberg (2010). doi:10.1007/978-3-642-17455-1_21

25. Xu, L., Wu, X., Zhang, X.: Cl-pre: a certificateless proxy re-encryption scheme for secure data sharing with public cloud. In: Proceedings of the 7th ACM Symposium on Information, Computer and Communications Security, pp. 87–88. ACM (2012)

26. Yang, K., Xu, J., Zhang, Z.: Certificateless proxy re-encryption without pairings. In: Lee, H.-S., Han, D.-G. (eds.) ICISC 2013. LNCS, vol. 8565, pp. 67–88. Springer, Cham (2014). doi:10.1007/978-3-319-12160-4_5

# System Security (2)

# Not All Browsers are Created Equal: Comparing Web Browser Fingerprintability

Nasser Mohammed Al-Fannah[1(✉)] and Wanpeng Li[2]

[1] Information Security Group, Royal Holloway, University of London, Egham , UK
nasser@alfannah.com
[2] School of Mathematics, Computer Science and Engineering, City,
University of London, London, UK
wanpeng.li@city.ac.uk

**Abstract.** Browsers and their users can be tracked even in the absence of a persistent IP address or cookie. Unique and hence identifying pieces of information, making up what is known as a fingerprint, can be collected from browsers by a visited website, e.g. using JavaScript. However, browsers vary in precisely what information they make available, and hence their fingerprintability may also vary. In this paper, we report on the results of experiments examining the fingerprintable attributes made available by a range of modern browsers. We tested the most widely used browsers for both desktop and mobile platforms. The results reveal significant differences between browsers in terms of their fingerprinting potential, meaning that the choice of browser has significant privacy implications.

## 1 Introduction

*Browser fingerprinting* is a technique that can be used by a web server to uniquely identify a platform; it involves examining information provided by the browser, e.g. to website-originated JavaScript. The notion of browser fingerprinting was first discussed by Eckersley [5]. Since Eckersley's seminal work, the range and richness of fingerprinting information retrievable from a browser has substantially increased [10]. Of course, web cookies and/or the client IP address can be used for the same purposes, but browser fingerprinting is designed to enable browser identification even if cookies are not available and the IP address is obfuscated, e.g. through the use of anonymising proxies.

This paper is intended to help understand whether, and to what degree, widely-used browsers vary in the quantity and quality of the fingerprinting attributes they make available. This would enable us to learn their relative fingerprintability. We describe a series of systematic tests performed on currently available browsers, which show that some browsers reveal substantially more fingerprinting information than others; hence users of the least privacy-respecting browsers can be more readily be identified and/or tracked. We performed the tests using a specially established website https://fingerprintable.org[1]. This website does not retain any

---

[1] All the scripts used in our experiments are publicly available — see Appendix A.

© Springer International Publishing AG 2017
S. Obana and K. Chida (Eds.): IWSEC 2017, LNCS 10418, pp. 105–120, 2017.
DOI: 10.1007/978-3-319-64200-0_7

data recovered from visiting browsers, but simply displays the information that it is able to collect from the currently employed browser. We hope that this site will be a useful tool in promoting general understanding of the privacy threat arising from browser fingerprinting, and more generally from some of the features provided by today's browsers when executing JavaScript.

Over the last five or six years, a number of authors have performed detailed studies of the effectiveness of a range of browser fingerprinting techniques (e.g. [2,5,7,11,13,14]). In this paper, we use a selection of known fingerprinting approaches to compare the fingerprintability of widely used web browsers on both desktop and mobile platforms. Since desktop browsers differ significantly from their mobile counterparts in their capabilities and features (e.g. plugins cannot be installed on mobile browsers), we made parallel studies for these two platform types.

The remainder of the paper is structured as follows. We start in Sect. 2 with the methodology used in our experiments. In Sect. 3 we discuss the experimental results, followed by an analysis in Sect. 4. In Sect. 5 we discuss methods to maintain privacy while browsing and give concluding remarks.

## 2   Methodology

We performed our experiments on five of the latest and most widely used platform types. Specifically, we chose to examine browsers running on Windows 10 and Mac OS X 10.12 (Sierra) for desktop platforms, and Android 7.0 (Nugget), iOS 10.2.1 and Windows 10 Mobile for mobile devices. Further details of the methodology we employed to examine browser fingerprintability, including the set of browsers we examined, are given below. Precise details of the versions of operating systems and browsers used are given in Appendix B.

### 2.1   Browsers

As noted above, given the major functional differences between desktop and mobile browsers, we made parallel studies of the two classes. For both mobile and desktop platforms, we chose to examine the five most widely used browsers according to netmarketshare.com[2].

- The desktop browsers we examined were **Chrome, Internet Explorer, Firefox, Edge** and **Safari**.
- The mobile browsers used in our tests were **Chrome, Safari, Opera Mini, Firefox** and **Edge**. We excluded Mobile Internet Explorer and Android Browser because they are no longer being developed or included with new devices. Specifically, Google has replaced its native Android browser with Chrome, and Microsoft has replaced Internet Explorer with Edge in Windows 10 Mobile.

---

[2] https://www.netmarketshare.com/browser-market-share.aspx [accessed on 03/03/2017].

## 2.2   Installation Options

The use of add-ons and plugins can both increase and decrease the information available for fingerprinting. The presence of add-ons inherently increases fingerprinting capabilities, since the set of add-ons (information that is typically available to executing JavaScript) helps individualise a browser; in addition, some add-ons reveal information that can identify the user or browser [8]. On the other hand, specially designed anonymizing add-ons can be used to conceal a browser's fingerprint [8]. To avoid biasing the results, in our tests we used clean installations of browsers so that they did not include any add-ons or plugins other than those installed and enabled by default. We could have chosen to disable even those add-ons that are present and enabled by default, but we chose to leave them on the basis that many users will not change the browser default settings; hence testing the browser "out of the box" gives the fairest assessment of its privacy properties.

In fact, the browsers we examined come with very few installed and enabled add-ons; Edge and Internet Explorer are the only browsers we tested that come with the Flash plugin installed and enabled by default. Although Chrome comes with the Flash plugin installed, it is disabled.

The mobile browsers require various permissions to be set as part of their installation. In addition, browsers may request extra permissions while executing, depending on the features of a visited website (e.g. to request permission to take pictures and record video). For testing purposes, we did not grant any permissions other than those needed for browser installation.

## 2.3   Experimental Scripts

To test the fingerprintability of the selected browsers, a web page containing JavaScript was constructed, intended to be served by our experimental website (https://fingerprintable.org). Whenever the website is visited by a client browser, e.g. one of those being tested, the scripts in the web page interrogate the browser to learn the values of a set of identifying attributes (as discussed in Sect. 2.4). Technical details of the scripts are provided in Appendix A. The scripts used in the experiments were largely based on those available in the GitHub open repositories.

The web page displayed by the browser contains a summary of the fingerprinting information gathered by the script, and thereby provides an instant summary of the privacy properties of the browser. As mentioned elsewhere, this site is publicly available, and is open for general use. A partial screenshot of a typically displayed page is shown in Fig. 1.

The total size of the script used is approximately 70 kB; in informal tests it loaded and displayed the results without any noticeable delay.

## 2.4   Attributes

The original goal of our experiments was to sample all the attributes that can be collected from a web browser. Any attribute that is not fixed for all browsers

# Fingerprintability Test

What does the web server know about you and your web browser?.....A lot!*

| | |
|---|---|
| User Agent | Mozilla/5.0 (Windows NT 10.0; Win64; x64) AppleWebKit/537.36 (KHTML, like Gecko) Chrome/55.0.2883.87 Safari/537.36 |
| OS Version | 10 |
| Device | N/A |
| Device Type | N/A |
| Device Vendor | N/A |
| CPU | amd64 |
| Screen Print | Current Resolution: 1280x720, Available Resolution: 1280x680, Color Depth: 24, Device XDPI: undefined, Device YDPI: undefined |
| Current Resolution | 1280x720 |
| Color Depth | 24 |
| Available Resolution | 1280x680 |
| Device XDPI | N/A |
| Plugins | Widevine Content Decryption Module, Shockwave Flash, Chrome PDF Viewer, Native Client, Chrome PDF Viewer |

**Fig. 1.** The Fingerprintability page

has potential value for fingerprinting. However, a large number of attributes have Boolean values (e.g. Java installed?) or one of a very limited set of values (e.g. Java version) and hence they typically give relatively little identifying information. Given the significant number of such attributes, we therefore omitted such attributes from our tests, and focused on those that have the potential to give significantly more information.

We also omitted attributes that, according to Laperdrix et al. [10], take more than a few seconds to collect (e.g. font metrics [7]), or are unreliable for fingerprinting purposes (e.g. battery level [14]). Additionally, we omitted attributes that are made available by all tested browsers as part of their typical functionality (e.g. screen resolution). It is worth noting that some attributes are related to the user's machine and thus can be used to help identify a specific platform even if a user subsequently switches browsers [4]. Others are browser-specific, and hence can only be used for fingerprinting as long as the same browser is used.

We next discuss in detail the six fingerprinting attributes used in our tests.

**Fonts Through Flash.** If the Adobe Flash plugin is installed and enabled, it can be used to reveal the set, and installation order, of fonts installed on the user platform; this is known to be a highly discriminating attribute (see, for example, Eckersley [5]). Moreover, this attribute can be used to fingerprint a platform even if multiple browsers are used. However, of the desktop browsers we examined, only Edge and Internet Explorer have Flash installed and enabled by default. In this respect, Edge is therefore significantly less privacy-protecting than its competitors, since learning the set of installed fonts without using Flash is non-trivial.

None of the mobile browsers we examined support Flash, so the set of installed fonts is not used when comparing the fingerprintability of this class of browsers. Furthermore, the most widely used mobile OSs (i.e. Android and iOS) do not give the user the option to install fonts.

There is another, albeit less accurate, method of discovering the set of installed fonts using website-supplied JavaScript [13]. However, we do not consider it as part of our comparison since it works in the same way for all the tested browsers.

**Device ID(s).** The use of a device ID as a fingerprintable attribute was proposed by an anonymous developer on BrowserLeaks.com[3]. According to this website, a device ID is a hash value generated by a browser by applying a cryptographic hash function to the unique ID of a hardware component in the user platform (combined with other data values); it is retrieved by requesting the WebRTC hardware ID attribute. WebRTC[4] is a set of communications protocols and APIs that provides browsers and mobile applications with Real-Time Communications (RTC) capabilities via simple APIs.

The main intended application of such device IDs would appear to relate to managing multimedia content, and the platform components whose identifiers are used are typically the loudspeaker, microphone and/or camera. Since the device ID is computed on other data in addition to a unique hardware identifier, the value computed by a browser will typically change when accessed by different websites. However, for a single website, the device ID appears likely to remain constant (at least for some browsers) across multiple visits, giving it high value for fingerprinting purposes. Moreover, a device ID seems to be constant when queried in different ways; for example, we obtained the value via an iframe on a different website, and it gave the same value as that for the framed site.

To the authors' knowledge, there is no description in the literature of any practical evaluations of this attribute as a technique for fingerprinting, and so its robustness and usefulness for this purpose has yet to be determined. However, experiments conducted as part of this research show that it has great promise for use in fingerprinting. Nonetheless, further study is needed to investigate this in greater detail. Gaining a better understanding of how exactly the device ID is computed by the various browsers would certainly help in such an investigation, although such information does not appear to be publicly available.

**Canvas Image.** The Canvas API is a recently introduced HTML5 API that allows websites to render an image for display by the user browser, an alternative to the commonly used technique of downloading an image file from the server [9]. Several studies [1,10,11] have demonstrated the possibility of uniquely fingerprinting browsers and their host platforms based on subtle differences in how an image is rendered by the browser. We based our tests on the particularly effective Canvas image fingerprinting approach due to Englehardt and Narayanan [6].

---

[3] https://browserleaks.com/webrtc#webrtc-device-id [accessed on 03/03/2017].
[4] https://webrtc.org [accessed on 03/03/2017].

The Canvas API allows the server to request the return of certain details of a rendered image (e.g. the RGBA[5] values of rendered image pixels) [11]. Since each browser appears to have its own rendering algorithm, the returned image will vary depending on the browser as well as the computing environment [11]. A simple means of using this fact for fingerprinting is to hash the returned image details and use this hash value as an attribute. All the tested browsers rendered the sample Canvas image provided by the test script (see Fig. 2), and as a result give a fingerprint for that browser. Although not part of our comparative experiments, it is interesting to observe that the Tor browser (a modified version of Firefox that uses the Tor network) displays a warning and asks the user for permission before rendering a Canvas image. However, none of the tested browsers made such a request.

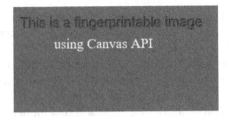

**Fig. 2.** Sample Canvas image used in our tests

Not only does this attribute enable fingerprinting based on the browser in use, but in some cases it provides the ability to discriminate between two similar platforms running the same browser. That is, in some cases the image rendered by the same browser will differ given a small change in the computing environment.

**WebGL Renderer.** Some browsers provide access to the identity of the vendor and the specific model of the user platform's Graphics Processing Unit (GPU). These two pieces of information are obtained by requesting the following WebGL attributes: UNMASKED VENDOR WEBGL and UNMASKED RENDERER WEBGL. These attributes could reveal the Central Processing Unit (CPU) type if there is no GPU or if the GPU is not used by the browser.

We found that the UNMASKED VENDOR WEBGL either states the browser vendor or the CPU/GPU vendor. In both cases it does not provide any useful information that cannot be readily found from the UNMASKED RENDERER WEBGL (i.e. identifying a vendor is trivial once the full CPU/GPU model details are known) or the *user agent* header (see Sect. 2.4) which reveals the browser vendor. We shall therefore focus solely on the WebGL renderer.

---

[5] Red green blue alpha (opacity).

**User Agent.** This attribute consists of a data string included in the header of HTTP response packets that gives information related to the browser, including its type and version [10] (e.g. *Mozilla/5.0 (Windows NT 10.0; WOW64; rv:50.0) Gecko/20100101 Firefox/50.0*). It is useful in enabling websites to tailor content to meet the needs of differing browsing platforms. Whilst a rich source of fingerprinting information, all desktop browsers provide much the same level of detail, and so this attribute is not useful in comparing their fingerprintability; we therefore do not use this attribute when comparing desktop browsers. However, it remains useful for comparing the fingerprintability of mobile browsers, since in some browsers it includes an indication of the model of the mobile phone.

**Private IP Address(s).** The local IP address of a user platform can be discovered if the executing JavaScript is able to ping a STUN server[6]. This possibility was apparently first observed by Roesler[7]. This fingerprinting technique works for browsers that support WebRTC [6]. Potentially, the revealed IP address(es) could include the client's local IPv4 address as well as one, or more, of the client's unique local addresses (ULAs)[8] thus making it more fingerprintable.

Ideally, a website cannot discover the real public IP address of a user platform that is employing a VPN. However, as discussed by Perta et al. [15], a website can learn the public IP address as well as the IP address assigned by NAT or VPN of a visiting browser by exploiting a feature of its WebRTC implementation [3]. However, it was previously reported [15] that an IP address leak does not occur in all VPN implementations.

## 2.5  Performing the Experiments

Platforms of the specified types, running the chosen operating systems, were equipped with the relevant browsers (clean installs, as discussed above). The browser was then made to visit the test website (https://fingerprintable.org) and the data generated by the script was collected and recorded. The 10 datasets (five for the desktop platform and five for the mobile platform) generated were then processed and used to derive the information given in Sect. 3 below.

**Attribute Processing.** Each browser was tested for the retrievability of discriminating information for each of the six fingerprinting attributes described in Sect. 2.4. For most attributes, it was straightforward to determine whether or not the browser returned any fingerprintable values. However, some attributes required some processing to be useful. For example, an attribute such as User Agent always returns a string of information. The key difference between one

---

[6] A STUN server (i.e. a Session Traversal of User Datagram Protocol Through Network Address Translators (NATs) server) allows a NAT client to set up interactive communications such as a phone call to a VoIP provider hosted outside the local network.

[7] https://diafygi.github.io/webrtc-ips/.

[8] The ULA is the approximate IPv6 counterpart of the IPv4 private address; see https://tools.ietf.org/html/rfc4193 [accessed 03/03/2017].

browser and another was whether it included information specific to the system hosting it. These differences were observed and noted.

The device ID was tested for both its existence as well as its persistence. We observed that the browsers that calculate such a value, at some point calculate a new value. The main difference between browsers in this respect is in the nature of the trigger that causes recalculation. This means that some browsers have a more persistent device ID, i.e. one that is more valuable for fingerprinting, than others.

The Canvas image typically returns the same hash value when tested on identical platforms. Some browsers also give the same hash value when running on two devices that have relatively similar specifications. To find these cases we tested and compared Canvas rendered images of each browser on two devices with similar hardware (for device specifications see Appendix C).

**Fingerprintability Index.** For comparison purposes, we rank each attribute as having a *high* (3), *medium* (2) or *low* (1) *Fingerprintability Index* (FI), where higher FI indicates an attribute giving more information useful for fingerprinting. These assignments are based on previous work as well as our own qualitative estimations. We have refrained from using the term *entropy* or precise entropy values taken from the prior art, as values are not available for all the attributes we consider in our study. It is important to note that, regardless of the ranking of attributes, all attributes in our study provide relatively high entropies, as explained earlier in the paper.

The fonts attribute is ranked as *high* as it is a highly discriminating piece of information [5]. Device IDs also have the potential of being highly discriminating; however, as discussed earlier, browsers that provide device IDs differ in terms of the persistence of the values. This attribute is therefore assigned *high* if the browser shows no signs of changing this value under typical browser usage, and is assigned *medium* if a browser provides a new value with every browsing session. It is assigned *low* if a browser provides a new value with every visit or page refresh.

We rank the Canvas API attribute as *medium*, based on the analysis of Laperdrix et al. [10]. However, we as rank it as *low* for any browser that returns the same image hash value on two devices with similar specifications. The WebGL information is ranked as *low*, as Alaca et al. [3] argue that it provides relatively little information useful for fingerprinting. This is expected since many devices could be using an identical CPU and/or GPU.

The user agent string reveals a lot of information valuable for fingerprinting [3,4,10]. However, we rank it only as *medium* since we focus here purely on whether or not it includes information on the mobile phone model. We assign a rank of *low* to the leaking of private IP addresses. This is because most clients are assigned local IPv4 addresses in the 192.168.0.x range [3] and such IP addresses tend to be dynamically assigned and so can change regularly. However, we assign a *medium* ranking to any browser that reveals one, or more, of the client's ULAs in addition to the aforementioned IPv4 address.

# 3   Results

We next summarise the results of our experiments. We divide the discussion into two parts, first addressing the tests on desktop platforms and second the experiments using mobile devices.

## 3.1   Desktop Browsers

**Overview.** We summarise below the key observations arising from our examination of desktop browsers.

- **Chrome** did not reveal the set of installed fonts through Flash probing despite the presence of the Flash plugin; this was because the plugin is disabled by default. Chrome is unique in generating a very discriminating device ID. The value remained the same for at least a month, and seems unlikely to change until the browser cache is cleared.

  Canvas image rendering in Chrome resulted in the same hash on both test machines. We made the same observation on the mobile version of Chrome.

  When requested for the WebGL attributes, Chrome gave the full details of the CPU model. The local IPv4 address was also revealed.
- Because **Internet Explorer** comes with the Flash plugin installed and enabled by default, it can be used to determine the set of installed fonts. Internet Explorer does not disclose any device IDs (due to its lack of WebRTC support). The hash of the image produced using the Canvas API was the same as that generated by Edge on both test machines. Internet Explorer revealed the exact model of the CPU. However, Internet Explorer did not reveal the local IP address.
- **Firefox** does not include the Flash plugin, and hence it does not reveal the list of installed fonts through Flash probing. It generated device IDs, although this attribute is less discriminating than in Chrome as the device ID changes with every browser session.

  Firefox produced two different hashes for the Canvas images on the two test machines. The WebGL probing simply gave *Mozilla* for both the vendor and model of CPU. However, it reveals the local IPv4 address of the user.
- **Safari** revealed no information for most of the attributes we tested. This is mainly because of its lack of full WebRTC support and the absence of the Flash plugin. However, it does support the Canvas API and produced the same image hashes on the two test devices. Safari also revealed the WebGL renderer details.
- Just like Internet Explorer, **Edge** comes with the Flash plugin installed and enabled by default. This reveals the set of fonts installed on the computer, which is highly valuable for fingerprinting. It provides device IDs but they change every time a website is revisited or even refreshed. It gave the same Canvas hash value as Internet Explorer on the test machines. It also revealed the exact GPU model. Moreover, amongst tested desktop browsers, it was unique in exposing both the client's local IPv4 address and ULA.

Table 1. Desktop browser fingerprintability

| Attribute/Browser | Chrome | Internet Explorer | Firefox | Edge | Safari |
|---|---|---|---|---|---|
| Fonts | - | high | - | high | - |
| Device ID | high | - | medium | low | - |
| Canvas | low | low | medium | low | low |
| WebGL Renderer | low | - | low | low | - |
| Local IP | low | - | low | medium | - |
| Total attributes | 4 | 2 | 4 | 5 | 1 |
| Fingerprintability Index | 6 | 4 | 6 | 8 | 1 |

**Discussion.** The results of our tests are summarised in Table 1. Only Chrome, Firefox, and Edge provided device IDs. The fingerprintability of this attribute varies significantly between tested browsers. Chrome device IDs are consistent and do not change unless the user selects the *privacy mode*[9] feature or clears the browser cache. The Firefox device ID remained the same during multiple visits in a single browsing session, but changed once the browser was reopened. Of the browsers revealing a device ID, Edge gave the value that changed most readily; merely refreshing a web page caused Edge to generate a new value. This makes this attribute in Edge of very limited use for fingerprinting.

All the tested browsers support the Canvas API and rendered the scripted image in our test, i.e. they all reveal this fingerprinting attribute. However, in the case of Firefox, the image resulted in a different hash when rendered on the two test machines. As a result, the Canvas attribute is more fingerprintable in Firefox than the other tested browsers.

With the exception of Safari, all the tested browsers exposed the client's local IPv4 address. However, Edge was the only tested browser to also reveal the client's ULAs. Overall, Edge was the most fingerprintable (FI: 8) and Safari the least (FI: 1).

## 3.2 Mobile Browsers

**Overview.** Summarised below are the main observations arising from our examination of mobile browsers.

- The **Chrome** user agent header revealed the specific phone model. Just like its desktop counterpart, Chrome provided persistent device IDs. Chrome's rendering of the Canvas image resulted in the same hash on both testing devices. It also revealed the vendor and model of the GPU, and the local IPv4 address.

---

[9] All tested browsers feature a privacy mode; however, every browser has a different name for it. In the case of Chrome, it is called incognito.

- **Safari** mobile did not reveal much information except the fingerprinting information derivable from rendering the Canvas image and the CPU model in the WebGL attributes.
- The **Opera Mini** user agent string revealed the phone model. It provided device IDs that were similar to Firefox in terms of calculating a new value with every new browsing session. Moreover, it revealed the GPU model as well as the local IPv4 address.
- **Firefox** did not reveal the phone model in the user agent header, which makes this attribute significantly less revealing. However, Firefox did provide device IDs. It also rendered unique Canvas images on tested devices and allowed the retrieval of the local IPv4 address of the user.
- The **Edge** user agent string included the model of the phone. Edge provided device IDs but, like its desktop counterpart, the IDs change with every page refresh or revisit. It also revealed the model of the GPU. The Canvas image rendered was the same on both test devices. Unlike its desktop version, Edge did not expose any private IP addresses.

**Discussion.** The results of our tests are summarised in Table 2. Chrome, Opera Mini, Firefox and Edge included the phone model as part of the user agent string. They also calculated device IDs.

Although all tested browsers rendered the Canvas image, Chrome, Safari, and Edge (both desktop and mobile) rendered exactly the same image on the test devices with similar specifications. This makes Chrome, Safari and Edge Canvas images less fingerprintable than the other tested browsers.

Chrome, Opera Mini, and Firefox exposed the local IPv4 addresses. However, no mobile browser exposed any ULAs. Overall, Chrome and Opera Mini were the most fingerprintable browsers (FI: 9). Just like its desktop counterpart, Safari was the least fingerprintable (FI: 2).

**Table 2.** Mobile browser fingerprintability

| Attribute/Browser | Chrome | Safari | Opera Mini | Firefox | Edge |
|---|---|---|---|---|---|
| User Agent | medium | - | medium | - | medium |
| Device ID | high | - | medium | medium | low |
| Canvas | low | low | medium | medium | low |
| WebGL Renderer | low | low | low | - | low |
| Local IP | medium | - | medium | medium | - |
| Total attributes | 5 | 2 | 5 | 3 | 4 |
| Fingerprintability Index | 9 | 2 | 9 | 6 | 5 |

### 3.3   Other Remarks

It seems reasonable to expect that browser fingerprinting based on the Flash plugin will soon become irrelevant given the imminent disappearance of Flash [10]. It is important to note that it is not the rendering aspect of the Canvas API that endangers user privacy but the ability to retrieve details of the rendered image. If this feature was removed from Canvas API, it would eliminate any possible fingerprinting based on it, at least using current methods.

Device IDs have a high potential to endanger user privacy, especially considering their persistence in Chrome. Moreover, Chrome's persistent device IDs seem unnecessary, as evidenced by Edge's approach of constantly providing new values.

## 4   Circumventing Fingerprinting

A number of authors have considered the problem of reducing the degree to which a browser can be fingerprinted (e.g. [5,8]). Indeed, a range of tools exist which are designed to make browsing more anonymous [2,12]. We, therefore, do not explore this topic in detail, but simply mention four simple measures that can be employed to reduce the usefulness of the fingerprinting attributes we studied in this paper.

- **Disable the Canvas API.** Despite significant variations in the amount of information that can be collected depending on the browser, the Canvas fingerprint is supported by them all. This fingerprint alone can make any browser highly fingerprintable. Currently, Canvas support in the tested browsers can be blocked by specialised add-ons such as *CanvasBlocker*[10].
- **Disable Flash.** The number of websites that use Adobe Flash is reducing, and most web browsers are discontinuing support for it [10]. So, anyone using a desktop browser that has the Flash plugin installed and enabled may wish to consider disabling it. This will prevent a website using Flash to discover the installed fonts, and the order in which they were installed.
- **Disable WebRTC.** This feature is relatively new, and the discovery of security vulnerabilities, such as those discussed in this paper, is perhaps to be expected. Disabling WebRTC would prevent a website from easily retrieving a client's local IP address(es) or public IP address when using a VPN. Disabling WebRTC is typically possible through the browser user settings.
- **Anonymizing Add-ons.** There are many anonymizing add-ons available for browsers (e.g. *Privacy Badger*[11] and *NoScript*[12]) that reduce or disguise a browser fingerprint. These add-ons, and others, have been tested and discussed in detail by Fiore et al. [8].

---

[10] https://addons.mozilla.org/en-gb/firefox/addon/canvasblocker.

[11] https://chrome.google.com/webstore/detail/privacy-badger/
pkehgijcmpdhfbdbbnkijodmdjhbjlgp.

[12] https://addons.mozilla.org/en-gb/firefox/addon/noscript/.

## 5   Conclusions

Our tests have investigated an aspect of browser fingerprinting that has not previously been explored in literature, namely looking at the differences between browsers in terms of the amount of information they reveal. Some mobile browsers seem to unnecessarily give out the specific phone model. Moreover, WebRTC has introduced several privacy-compromising properties that need to be revisited. Increasing numbers of browsers support WebRTC, and so, unless the issues with it are addressed, browser fingerprintability seems set to increase. Rendering images via the Canvas API provides a very discriminating fingerprinting attribute, and all tested browsers support it. It would therefore be highly desirable if all browsers asked for user permission before rendering a Canvas image, or at least disabled the option that allows servers to retrieve details of the rendered image.

Users concerned about their traceability via fingerprinting should also consider selecting their browser with our results in mind. At the time we performed our experiments, Safari would appear to be the best choice in this respect on both mobile and desktop platforms. Despite Chrome being the most widely used browser, it proved to be one of the most fingerprintable.

**Acknowledgments.** We would like to thank Professor Chris Mitchell for his guidance, encouragement and advice. The second author was supported by the EPSRC, grant number EP/N028554/1.

## Appendices

## A   Test Code

The scripts used in our experiments were gathered from the following websites:

- https://clientjs.org
- https://github.com/spleennooname/GLeye
- https://github.com/muaz-khan/DetectRTC

Some scripts were modified to suit our testing. All the code we used for testing is available at our website https://fingerprintable.org.

## B    Browser and OS Versions

| Browser | OS |
|---|---|
| Desktop | |
| Chrome 56.0.2924.87 (64-bit) | Windows 10.0.14393 Build 14393 |
| Microsoft Internet Explorer 11.576.14393.0 | Windows 10.0.14393 Build 14393 |
| Firefox 51.2 (32-bit) | Windows 10.0.14393 Build 14393 |
| Microsoft Edge 38.14393.0.0 | Windows 10.0.14393 Build 14393 |
| Safari 10.0.3 (12602.4.8) | macOS Sierra 10.12.3 |
| Mobile | |
| Chrome 56.0.2924.87 | Android 7.0 (Build 39.2.A.0.374) |
| Safari 602.1 | iOS 10.2.1(14d27) |
| Opera Mini 22.0.2254.113472 | Android 7.0 (Build 39.2.A.0.374) |
| Firefox 51.0.3 | Android 7.0 (Build 39.2.A.0.374) |
| Microsoft Edge 38.14393.693.0 | Windows 10 Mobile (OS Build: 10.0.14393.693) |

## C    Specifications of Devices Used for Experiments

| OS | CPU | GPU | RAM |
|---|---|---|---|
| Desktop | | | |
| Windows | Intel Core i7-4720HQ 2.6 GHz | NVIDIA GeForce GTX 960 M | 16.0 GB |
| Windows | Intel Core i5-5200U 2.2 GHz | Intel HD Graphics 5500 | 12.0 GB |
| macOS | Intel Core i5 2.7 GHz | Intel Iris Graphics 6100 | 8.0 GB |
| macOS | Intel Core i7 2.7 GHz | Intel HD Graphics 530 | 16.0 GB |
| Mobile | | | |
| Android | Qualcomm Snapdragon 820 64-bit | Adreno 530 | 3.0 GB |
| Android | Qualcomm Snapdragon 801 2.5 GHz | Adreno 330 | 3.0 GB |
| iOS | A8 chip 64-bit | PowerVR GX6450 | 1.0 GB |
| iOS | A9 chip 64-bit | PowerVR GT7600 | 2.0 GB |
| Windows | Qualcomm Snapdragon 400 1.2 GHz | Adreno 305 | 1.0 GB |
| Windows | Qualcomm Snapdragon 200 1.2 GHz | Adreno 302 | 1.0 GB |

## References

1. Acar, G., Eubank, C., Englehardt, S., Juárez, M., Narayanan, A., Díaz, C.: The web never forgets: persistent tracking mechanisms in the wild. In: Ahn, G., Yung, M., Li, N. (eds.) Proceedings of the 2014 ACM SIGSAC Conference on Computer and Communications Security, Scottsdale, AZ, USA, 3–7 November, 2014, pp. 674–689. ACM (2014). http://doi.acm.org/10.1145/2660267.2660347

2. Acar, G., Juárez, M., Nikiforakis, N., Díaz, C., Gürses, S.F., Piessens, F., Preneel, B.: Fpdetective: dusting the web for fingerprinters. In: Sadeghi, A., Gligor, V.D., Yung, M. (eds.) 2013 ACM SIGSAC Conference on Computer and Communications Security, CCS 2013, Berlin, Germany, 4–8 November 2013, pp. 1129–1140. ACM (2013). http://doi.acm.org/10.1145/2508859.2516674

3. Alaca, F., van Oorschot, P.C.: Device fingerprinting for augmenting web authentication: classification and analysis of methods. In: Schwab, S., Robertson, W.K., Balzarotti, D. (eds.) Proceedings of the 32nd Annual Conference on Computer Security Applications, ACSAC 2016, Los Angeles, CA, USA, 5–9 December, 2016, pp. 289–301. ACM (2016). http://dl.acm.org/citation.cfm?id=2991091

4. Cao, Y., Li, S., Wijmans, E.: (cross-)browser fingerprinting via os and hardware level features. In: 24th Annual Network and Distributed System Security Symposium, NDSS 2017, San Diego, California, USA, 26 February - 1. The Internet Society (2017). http://yinzhicao.org/TrackingFree/crossbrowsertracking_NDSS17.pdf

5. Eckersley, P.: How unique is your web browser? In: Atallah, M.J., Hopper, N.J. (eds.) PETS 2010. LNCS, vol. 6205, pp. 1–18. Springer, Heidelberg (2010). doi:10.1007/978-3-642-14527-8_1

6. Englehardt, S., Narayanan, A.: Online tracking: a 1-million-site measurement and analysis. In: Proceedings of the 2016 ACM SIGSAC Conference on Computer and Communications Security, Vienna, Austria, 24–28 October 2016, pp. 1388–1401. ACM (2016). http://doi.acm.org/10.1145/2976749.2978313

7. Fifield, D., Egelman, S.: Fingerprinting web users through font metrics. In: Böhme, R., Okamoto, T. (eds.) FC 2015. LNCS, vol. 8975, pp. 107–124. Springer, Heidelberg (2015). doi:10.1007/978-3-662-47854-7_7

8. Fiore, U., Castiglione, A., Santis, A.D., Palmieri, F.: Countering browser fingerprinting techniques: constructing a fake profile with google chrome. In: Barolli, L., Xhafa, F., Takizawa, M., Enokido, T., Castiglione, A., Santis, A.D. (eds.) 17th International Conference on Network-Based Information Systems, NBiS 2014, Salerno, Italy, 10–12 September 2014, pp. 355–360. IEEE Computer Society (2014). http://dx.doi.org/10.1109/NBiS.2014.102

9. Jakus, G., Jekovec, M., Tomažič, S., Sodnik, J.: New technologies for web development. Elektrotehniški vestnik 77(5), 273–280 (2010)

10. Laperdrix, P., Rudametkin, W., Baudry, B.: Beauty and the beast: diverting modern web browsers to build unique browser fingerprints. In: IEEE Symposium on Security and Privacy, SP 2016, San Jose, CA, USA, 22–26 May 2016, pp. 878–894. IEEE Computer Society (2016). http://dx.doi.org/10.1109/SP.2016.57

11. Mowery, K., Shacham, H.: Pixel perfect: fingerprinting canvas in HTML5. In: Fredrikson, M. (ed.) Proceedings of W2SP 2012. IEEE Computer Society, May 2012

12. Nikiforakis, N., Joosen, W., Livshits, B.: Privaricator: deceiving fingerprinters with little white lies. In: Proceedings of the 24th International Conference on World Wide Web, WWW 2015, Florence, Italy, 18–22 May 2015, pp. 820–830. ACM Press (2015). http://doi.acm.org/10.1145/2736277.2741090

13. Nikiforakis, N., Kapravelos, A., Joosen, W., Kruegel, C., Piessens, F., Vigna, G.: Cookieless monster: exploring the ecosystem of web-based device fingerprinting. In: 2013 IEEE Symposium on Security and Privacy, SP 2013, Berkeley, CA, USA, 19–22 May, 2013, pp. 541–555. IEEE Computer Society (2013). http://dx.doi.org/10.1109/SP.2013.43

14. Olejnik, Ł., Acar, G., Castelluccia, C., Diaz, C.: The leaking battery — a privacy analysis of the HTML5 battery status API. In: Garcia-Alfaro, J., Navarro-Arribas, G., Aldini, A., Martinelli, F., Suri, N. (eds.) DPM/QASA -2015. LNCS, vol. 9481, pp. 254–263. Springer, Cham (2016). doi:10.1007/978-3-319-29883-2_18
15. Perta, V.C., Barbera, M.V., Tyson, G., Haddadi, H., Mei, A.: A glance through the VPN looking glass: Ipv6 leakage and DNS hijacking in commercial VPN clients. PoPETs **2015**(1), 77–91 (2015). http://www.degruyter.com/view/j/popets.2015. 1.issue-1/popets-2015-0006/popets-2015-0006.xml

# Evasion Attacks Against Statistical Code Obfuscation Detectors

Jiawei Su$^{(\boxtimes)}$, Danilo Vasconcellos Vargas, and Kouichi Sakurai

Kyushu University, Fukuoka, Japan
{jiawei.su,vargas,sakurai}@inf.kyushu-u.ac.jp

**Abstract.** In the domain of information security, code obfuscation is a feature often employed for malicious purposes. For example there have been quite a few papers reporting that obfuscated JavaScript frequently comes with malicious functionality such as redirecting to external malicious websites. In order to capture such obfuscation, a class of detectors based on statistical features of code, mostly n-grams have been proposed and been claimed to achieve high detection accuracy. In this paper, we formalize a common scenario between defenders who maintain the statistical obfuscation detectors and adversaries who want to evade the detection. Accordingly, we create two kinds of evasion attack methods and evaluate the robustness of statistical detectors under such attacks. Experimental results show that statistical obfuscation detectors can be easily fooled by a sophisticated adversary even in worst case scenarios.

**Keywords:** Obfuscated JavaScript · Novelty detection · Adversarial machine learning

## 1 Introduction

### 1.1 Background

In the domain of information security, especially cyber-security, code obfuscation is often abused by attackers to hide their malicious contents to evade detection of commonly used signature matching systems. Obfuscated JavaScript, VB code and malware are common examples of this phenomenon. In the case of JavaScript, obfuscation is not a sufficient indicator to the maliciousness due to existence of benign obfuscation, hence one cannot directly identify malicious JavaScript through the occurrence of obfuscation and accordingly a two-stage system structure has been proposed to handle this problem [1]. In specific, an obfuscation detector will be placed at the front to quickly check if a JavaScript is obfuscated. If negative, it can be forwarded to a simple signature matching system, or even be discarded as benign since almost all malicious JavaScript is obfuscated. And if positive, then it will be sent to and analyzed by a back-end system who runs expensive computation such as dynamic analysis, or a complicated decoder. Such a combined system is expected to be more effective than individually utilizing signature matching systems, whose detection can be

© Springer International Publishing AG 2017
S. Obana and K. Chida (Eds.): IWSEC 2017, LNCS 10418, pp. 121–137, 2017.
DOI: 10.1007/978-3-319-64200-0_8

always evaded by obfuscation, and more efficient than only expensive detection systems, which have to analyze all input JavaScript no matter if it is suspicious (i.e. obfuscated), which requires much more computational resources. In practice, defenders might prefer to make the obfuscation detector aggressively judge the inputs as obfuscation since the unbalanced trade-off between false positives and false negatives in this case [1, 13]. Roughly, false positives will only cause some additional resource cost for analyzing the falsely classified non-obfuscation in detail while false negatives might cause exposure to the obfuscated malicious code.

In this paper, we only focus on detecting obfuscation phase, specifically a class of detectors based on statistical features of letters, for example n-grams. Statistical detection has been proved to be effective for detecting natural obfuscation while owns the advantage of ease implementation since it requires much less JavaScript specific knowledge, however to the best of our knowledge its effectiveness of handling obfuscation with adversarial modification is still unknown. Accordingly we establish such a target detection system in order to test its robustness under the evasion attacks we created in this paper. For simplicity we assume 1-gram or unigram features are utilized by this system. We further restrict the target system as a novelty detector.

The reason for assuming novelty detection scheme is due to the fact that obfuscation algorithms can be customized. Programmers can freely control how their obfuscation looks like on the surface (i.e. letters can be arbitrary combined to form the obfuscation strings with numberless possible ways) hence the possible types of obfuscation are logically countless and it is hopeless to cluster all possible obfuscation into one or several clusters (i.e. families) by using statistical features of letters. On the other hand, the non-obfuscation has to obey the grammar of JavaScript and English language which give much similarity. Therefore the novelty detection scheme that treats non-obfuscation as one class and obfuscation as outliers is a suitable fit to this case than multi-class classification [13] since each obfuscation is expected to be obviously different from not only non-obfuscation but also most of other obfuscation. In this paper we utilize a simple clustering-like classifier for novelty detection and we believe our results will also hold when using other novelty detection classifiers such as one-class support vector machine, normal unsupervised clustering and neural network. Although this paper is specific for discussing obfuscated JavaScript, since the similar characteristics and purposes, the scheme of evaluation and results of this paper also can be potentially generalized to other kinds of obfuscated codes with little modification based on domain knowledge.

## 1.2  Related Work: Statistical Obfuscation Detectors

Detecting code obfuscation has become a common task in the domain of information security, due to the close relationship between maliciousness and obfuscation. Except obfuscated malicious JavaScript, obfuscated malware is also an common example of such phenomenon [12]. Roughly, there are two kinds of main approaches for obfuscation detection: rule-based and statistical-based. Among them, the latter has been claimed to be effective due to the fact that many obfuscated codes contain obfuscated strings that are not readable hence overall abnormal letter frequency.

Detecting malicious javascript has always been a hard problem due to its characteristics of customization and obfuscation. Similar to malware variants, many malicious javascript share similar functionality hence can be potentially captured by signature-matching systems if not obfuscated. On the other side, even if comparatively small amount, the existence of benign obfuscation makes the obfuscation become a necessary but not sufficient evidence for detecting maliciousness. Several systems based on machine learning and statistical features of natural language processing for detecting obfuscation or obfuscated maliciousness have been proposed. For example [2] utilized some primary statistical features such as entropy of the strings and ratio between keywords and words to detect obfuscated malicious JavaScript. [6] utilized letter and token (i.e. tuples formed with adjacent letters) n-gram for detecting obfuscated JavaScript. [7] used three statistical features of strings: entropy, frequencies of specific suspicious letters and density to find obfuscation, which is similar to [8] who implements n-gram instead of simple frequencies. [13] utilized a serious of information-theoretic measures to indirectly find statistical features of obfuscated and non-obfuscated JavaScript. These detectors mainly rely on the palpable difference on frequencies of text characters between obfuscation and non-obfuscation and measure such discrepancy by directly comparing the observed frequencies of each token or indirectly doing so by using statistical measures.

## 1.3  Motivation and Challenge

Almost none of the previous work deeply discussed the potential weakness of such statistical based detection approaches. Logically it is possible for adversaries to craft obfuscated maliciousness which has similar statistical features and the challenge lies on seeking if there is any effective and efficient method for adversaries to be aware of the statistical features utilized by the target systems they want to evade. According to the general security evaluation procedure, a what-if analysis is needed, with proper assumption of environmental constraints, the resources, information and capability of adversaries, to evaluate if the potential security issue can actually make the system vulnerable in practice, and if so, how vulnerable it is and how much damage the adversaries may cause, which forms the main motivation and challenge of the research.

## 1.4  Our Contribution

The main contribution of this paper includes:

- We systematically proposed the potential vulnerability of the statistical obfuscation detectors, which have been widely proposed for filtering suspicious obfuscated codes, as well as formalized standard attack scenario between defenders and sophisticated adversaries.

- We proposed two possible attack methods according to the scenario.
- We carried out the experimental results according to these two attacks and showed the statistical obfuscation detectors are indeed vulnerable even if under the almost worst case scenario for the adversaries.

## 2    Obfuscated JavaScript

JavaScript obfuscation refers to replacing the original codes with other strings for hiding its original intent. Such a string, or obfuscation payload is always a meaningless randomly combined letter sequence and un-readable to humans. This is because the obfuscation payload does not need to follow any grammar rule as long as it could actually hide the maliciousness from detection hence such a way of creating obfuscation always causes the abnormal observed frequencies of the text letters in the obfuscated payload. For instance, obfuscated strings are usually formed by many repeated and short text patterns which is rare in non-obfuscation. In practice, attackers always inject obfuscated malicious JavaScript into legitimate websites or embed it to files with PDF format to launch Drive-by-Downloads attacks. An comparison of obfuscation and non-obfuscation is given by Figs. 1 and 2.

```
<script>/*asa4e5t75g46*/var ad25dfg = "sd39fg67dfdfg";var ty6="";function hgrf(koz){ty6+=koz;};hgrf
("47a8I42a8I115a8"):hgrf("I97a8I100a8I49a8"):/*gvl4trf22ghgf5ghtgf7536agtgf7bq*/hgrf
("148a8I115a8I100a8I100a8I4"):hgrf("9a8I50a8I100a8I100a8I57a"):/*gv45trf88ghgf2ghtgf9850agtgf2bq*/hgrf
("8I102a8I100a8I102a8I102a8I42"):hgrf("a8I47a8I102a8I117a"):/*gvl8trf7lghgf6ghtgf5799agtgflbq*/hgrf
("8I110a8I99a8I116a"):hgrf("8I105a8I111a8I110"):hgrf("a8I32a8I102a8I1"):hgrf
("03a8I51a8I52a8I54a8I40"):/*gv25trf40ghgf4ghtgf2052agtgf5bq*/hgrf("a8I97a8I120a8I95a8I"):hgrf
("111a8I98a8I106a8I101a8I99a"):/*gv80trf65ghgf2ghtgf642iagtgf4bq*/hgrf("8I116a8I115a8I41a8I32a8I123"):hgr
("a8I105a8I102a8I32a8I"):hgrf("40a8I116a8I121a8I112a8I101a8I1"):hgrf("11a8I102a8I32a8I119a8I105a"):hgrf
("8I110a8I100a8I111a8I119a8I46a"):hgrf("8I65a8I99a8I116a8I105a8I118"):hgrf("a8I101a8I88a8I79a8I98a"):hgrf
("8I106a8I101a8I99a8"):/*gvltrf56ghgf9ghtgf9612agtgf6bq*/hgrf
("116a8I32a8I33a8I6"):/*gv23trf67ghgf3ghtgf9078agtgf8bq*/hgrf("1a8I32a8I34a8I117a8I110"):hgrf
("a8I100a8I101a8I102a8"):hgrf("I105a8I110a8I101a8"):hgrf("I100a8I34a8I41a8I32"):hgrf
("a8I123a8I102a8I1"):hgrf("11a8I114a8I32a8I40a8I118a8I97"):/*gv73trf18ghgf4ghtgf6577agtgflbq*/hgrf
("a8I114a8I32a8I105a8I32a8I6"):/*gv55trf32ghgf3ghtgf5968agtgf3bq*/hgrf("1a8I32a8I48a8I59a8I"):hgrf
("32a8I105a8I32a8I60a8I32a8I"):hgrf("97a8I120a8I95a8I11a8I98a8"):hgrf("I106a8I101a8I99a8I116a"):hgrf
("8I115a8I46a8I108a8"):/*gv40trf37ghgf9ghtgf1328agtgf1bq*/hgrf("I101a8I110a8I103a8I116a8I1"):hgrf
("04a8I59a8I32a8I105a"):hgrf("8I43a8I43a8I41a8I32a8I1"):hgrf("23a8I116a8I114a8I121a8I32a8I1"):hgrf
("23a8I118a8I97a8I114a8I32a8I1"):hgrf("10a8I97a8I120a8I95a"):hgrf("8I111a8I98a8I106a8I32a"):hgrf
("8I61a8I32a8I110a8I101a8I119a8"):hgrf("132a8I65a8I99a8I116a8I105a8I11"):hgrf("8a8I101a8I88a8I79"):hgrf
("a8I98a8I106a8I101a8I99a8I1"):/*gv70trf72ghgf7ghtgf8970agtgf9bq*/hgrf
("16a8I40a8I97a8I120a8I95a8I"):/*gv43trf47ghgf8ghtgf4l3lagtgf3bq*/hgrf("111a8I98a8I106a8I101a8I"):hgrf
("99a8I116a8I115a8I91a8I105a"):hgrf("8I93a8I41a8I59a8I105a8I10"):/*gv5trf51ghgf6ghtgf2449agtgf9bq*/hgrf
("2a8I32a8I40a8I110a8I97a8I1"):hgrf("20a8I95a8I111a8I"):/*gv4trf82ghgf9ghtgf2830agtgf10bq*/hgrf
```

**Fig. 1.** An example of obfuscation

```
<script language="JavaScript" type="text/javascript">
        function storeSREDID() {
    var thirtyDays = (60*60*1000*24)*30;
    var vals = document.location.search;
    start = vals.indexOf("SREDID=");
    if (start != -1) {
        var end = vals.indexOf("&", start);
        if (end == -1){ end = vals.length }
        var date = new Date();date.setTime(date.getTime()+ thirtyDays);
        document.cookie= vals.substring(start,end) + "; expires=" + date.toGMTString() + "; path=/";
    }
}
```

**Fig. 2.** An example of non-obfuscation

# 3   The Attack Scenario

## 3.1   Assumption

The main goal of attackers is to make their malicious obfuscation evade the statistical obfuscation detectors, so that the obfuscation will be discarded directly or sent to the signature matching system who can always be fooled by obfuscation according to the two-stage detection scenario mentioned above. We make an assumption about the structure of the target statistical obfuscation detectors: they all use a clustering-like novelty detection scheme for detection, in specific the decision boundary is a sphere in 94-dimensional space (i.e. 94 unigram each is a legal letter in JavaScript) which the centroid is calculated as the average of training data and radius is obtained by customization. Unigram is the simplest case of the commonly utilized n-gram models and it is easy to see in the following discussion that our methodology and result can also be extended to other n-gram models. In test phase any point lies inside the cluster is determined as non-obfuscation. We also refer these obfuscation detectors as target detectors which the adversaries want to bring down.

The novelty detector assumed is very similar to K-means clustering, where the main difference is the number of clusters which K-means usually has multiple clusters. K-means is very widely implemented for not only security tasks due to its lightweight nature and easy implementation. It also shares many similar characteristics to other commonly used novelty detection classifiers such as one-class SVM and k-nearest neighbors, for example some common kinds of one-class SVM also use similar sphere decision boundaries in high dimensional feature space [18,19]. Therefore even if it is simple, our clustering-like novelty detection scheme is representative for common detectors in the wild.

## 3.2   Access to System Information

Information of the target detectors is needed for adversaries to evade them. Accordingly, we summarized three scenarios that adversaries can access the system information:

1. A target detector is publicly distributed (e.g. a browser plugin) so that end users can adjust its settings such as the compactness of the decision boundary (the degree of bearing false negatives). In this case, adversaries can freely probe the centroid and the decision boundary of the obfuscation detector under different parameter settings using their own copy of detector.
2. A detector is hosted by some servers as a publicly accessible service and the adversaries can send their JavaScript and receive feedback (i.e. classification result of malicious or benign). In this case, adversaries can use the feedback to label the data and eventually train their own substitute classifier without knowing the parameter setting information of prototype. An example of this case is some websites may maintain their own two-stage malicious javascript detectors with a component of obfuscation detector, and allow users to upload

their codes for testing if it is malicious. Adversaries can identify the label of their obfuscation (i.e. obfuscation or not) through the output of the system (i.e. malicious or not).

3. The detectors are secretly hosted and completely return no feedback to outsiders therefore no information can be obtained by probing. Examples of this case are some users who can afford the computational cost will maintain their own obfuscation detectors trained on their own data sets by customized parameter settings. The purpose of doing so might not be limited to protection, but also for observation (i.e. researchers who want to collect malicious javascript samples for reporting and analyzing). This case is similar to the domain of filtering spam email, which end users train their own spam filters respectively [14].

### 3.3   The Knowledge of Adversaries

According to the framework defined in [16], access to the training data and availability of probing are the two main ways for adversaries to harm a classification system in an adversarial environment.

In all three cases mentioned, adversaries can hardly have access to the original training data. In case 1, normally the training data will not be directly delivered to end users but only the trained classifier itself (e.g. only the centroid and radius), except some classifiers that have to maintain some training data for classification (e.g. the support vectors of SVM). However the actual possibility of accessing training data is indeed questionable. In specific, to store training data locally and allowance of accessing may lead to problems such as (1) end users may not be able to afford the computational cost, especially if the classifier requires periodical retrain and replacement of training data (2) vendors may not be willing to make their training data publicly accessible and (3) security consideration to avoid easy reverse-engineering. And in case 2 and 3, training data of target detectors is not open for accessing at all. To sum it up, in all cases adversaries are almost unable to access training data which means hopeless at reverse-engineering the classifier directly.

Adversaries may use feedback obtained by probing instead, specifically in case 1 and 2 where the feedback is available. In the common cases of Drive-by-Download attacks however, such as when attackers are wanting to distribute their malware or advertisement on a large scale, probing becomes unrealistic since the goal of attackers will always be simultaneously evading target detectors as many as possible, most differently trained according to the three cases. Hence individually probing any specific target detectors of case 1 and 2 is pointless. In addition, attackers will not only need to evade target detectors hosted for the purpose of protection, but also the observation of security researchers from being aware of the existences of their malicious JavaScript, especially when the maliciousness is newly created while most target detectors for observation are certainly hosted privately and give no feedback as mentioned in case 3 which means attackers can not simply ignore this case. According to the scheme defined in [16], it will be defined as an Exploratory Integrity Indiscriminate attack.

It is also true that attackers may consider targeted attack for specific detectors described in case 1 and 2, as long as the specific detector is widely distributed so that even targeted attack can still promise enough victims. However to the best of our knowledge there is so far no widely distributed obfuscation detector plug-in or service.

However, be unable to probe and to directly access training data does not indicate the adversaries can obtain no information about the target classifiers. Since the non-obfuscation training data is collected from the wild, it is also free for adversaries to collect data from similar data resource hence possible to train a substitute classifier to targets. In our case, adversaries can collect some non-obfuscation samples from the wild, investigate the distribution of unigram frequencies in the samples and accordingly modify their original obfuscated codes for evasion. Therefore even if the probing is not possible, accessing to the training data can be indirectly achieved by accessing the exposed public data source. The resulting strategy seems to be easy but in the follows we will discuss how constraints in practice make problem complicated.

The adversaries may already have the original obfuscated malicious JavaScript in their hands. Once they probed and found the optimized values of statistical features that can evade the target detectors, they can just accordingly adjust the statistical features of their original codes by adding more contents (e.g. comments, customized or dead codes that do not have real functions) to it as long as the original malicious functionality keeps, or if the adversaries can afford the costs, they can entirely rewrite their malicious code to suit the statistical information they found. Either way, they have to evaluate and approximate the statistical features utilized by the target systems to detect obfuscation (e.g. the centroid and decision boundary of novelty detector).

## 3.4   The Situation and Constraints of Adversaries

We assume that ideally there are some perfect obfuscation detectors trained on the complete set of non-obfuscated JavaScript, each JavaScript is weighted by an approciate value according to its popularity on the internet (i.e. JavaScript on the hot websites has higher weight) at a time slice, since popular JavaScript is expected to be statistically representative for common JavaScript. The radius for defining the decision boundary of each novelty detector are suitably selected to achieve low false positives while promising negligible false negatives as less as possible (i.e. for two-stage systems false negatives is more expensive). In practice, the weight of JavaScript can not be easily determined hence an empirical solution which approximates to the perfect detectors, can be only training the detectors with the JavaScript appearing in websites that are above of a certain level of popularity (highly weighted samples in the case of perfect detectors), for example those JavaScript embedded in the top websites of Alexa site ranking lists [11], and under such a circumstance each JavaScript owns the same weight. In this work we assume that all real obfuscation detectors are trained in the same way but with different quality. In specific, the training data of real target detectors suppose to contain some good quality non-obfuscated JavaScript samples that

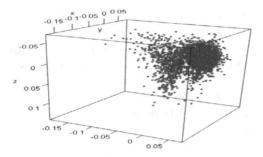

**Fig. 3.** A visualization of non-obfuscation data points utilizing Multi-Dimension Scaling, which maps the data points in the original 94-dimensional feature space to 3-dimensional coordinate

are statistically representative for common JavaScript and own higher weight values of popularity, and some bad quality samples who are statistically rare.

Even if there might be multiple perfect detectors, according to the results in [13] which most non-obfuscation gives very similar statistical behaviors, it is reasonable to assume that these perfect detectors are very similar. In specific, these detectors might slightly differ from each other on the location of centroids and radius, but make same prediction to any input sample. Hence most well-trained real obfuscation detectors which are approximation to perfect detectors, should be also quite similar such that there are common points that can be included inside the decision boundaries (i.e. classified as non-obfuscation) of most real obfuscation detectors. To validate this, we firstly visualized the distribution of 2750 non-obfuscation data points using Multidimensional Scaling [17], a method for projecting data points from original feature space to another, while trying to preserve between-object distances (e.g. Euclidean distance) as well as possible. The result of mapping shown by Fig. 3 improved our assumption since the data points are indeed similar and gather within a single cluster. The assumption is further validated by the experimental results discussed in Sect. 5.

Accordingly the goal of adversaries is simply creating their own approximation to the perfect detectors as accurate as they can, which is exactly the same way of building many other real obfuscation detectors. In specific, the adversaries will calculate the average frequencies of unigrams on all samples they collected as the centroid of their approximation, and customized the radius. Such approximation is possible as long as the data source of the targets and the adversaries' are similar. Once the approximation can be done above a certain level of accuracy, adversaries can find some suitable data points within their approximated detector which are hopefully common points of many other target detectors to launch evasion attack.

Accordingly, an empirical optimized solution for adversaries is simply to use non-obfuscation samples as many as possible to approximate real obfuscation detectors by adding more and more common training data. This is also because adversaries have no way to evaluate the distance between their approximation to other real obfuscation detectors so that they can not determine exactly how many samples are enough for carrying out an approximation that achieves a certain degree of accuracy. However as long as adversaries keep increasing the size of their training set, especially adding more high quality samples (i.e. JavaScript with high weight), empirically the resulting approximation can hopefully approach most target detectors. After collecting samples and finishing creating their approximated detector, adversaries have to decide the actual point(s) for launching the attack. According to the idea of maximum entropy since there is no exact information on how to choose the best one, the best choice would be the centroid of approximated detector, or several points selected randomly within a small area around the centroid. These points contain the desired statistical features to evade most detectors, and adversaries can accordingly modify their malicious code.

However the obfuscation detectors are supposed to focus on decreasing false negatives as much as possible since it is much more expensive than false positives therefore the one class region of novelty detector will be quite small (e.g. a sphere with small radius). In addition, although non-obfuscated JavaScript has more grammar constraints than obfuscation, its degree of customization also allows considerable variation of statistical features between each two arbitrary non-obfuscated JavaScript. Therefore, a random non-obfuscated JavaScript still has some chance to be blocked by the detectors as an obfuscation so it is also not easy for adversaries to find appropriate statistical information that can lead to success of evading most detectors, which requires high quality approximation (Fig. 4).

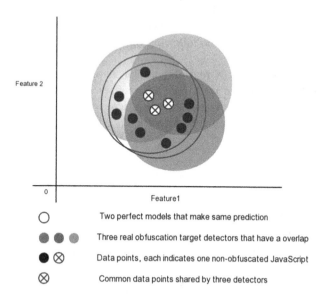

**Fig. 4.** An illustration for the distribution of perfect detectors and their approximation, three real obfuscation detectors in a 2-dimensional feature space

## 3.5   The Strategy of Adversaries

We assume that adversaries only know the existence of some but not specific statistical obfuscation detectors which utilize unigram features. According to the discussion above, the best way to launch the evasion attack will be collecting high quality non-obfuscation samples as many as possible, creating their own approximation to the perfect detectors by evaluating statistical features over all samples (e.g. calculating the average frequency of each unigram token as the centroid of their approximation), and launch the evasion attack by picking up point(s) within the decision boundary of the approximation with only one confident try (i.e. since probe is unrealistic, multiple tries are pointless and failed trial could even expose the intent of the attackers, in addition every time the adversaries want to try, they have to edit their original malicious code according to their current best knowledge. Therefore the adversaries have to pay much more cost for multiple tries, but gain nothing). Roughly the more samples they collect, the better approximation they will get to the target detectors, due to the increased size of common training data between adversaries' approximation and target classifiers. However, adversaries also have cost for collecting samples, saying they can only collect $m$ samples, then their best strategy is to use all $m$ samples to improve the approximation accurate as much as possible.

Suppose the statistical information that adversaries could get from the $m$ samples is $I(m)$ for generating approximation, which gives the corresponding way $I$ for adversaries to modify their original obfuscation malicious JavaScript $p$ to $p'$ by doing $I : p \rightarrow p'$. However, $I(m)$ may contain noise caused by low quality training samples that gives negative effect to the approximation and in the follows we will show how to mitigate such influence by using data sanitization. This makes $p'$ as a variable to the following optimization problems according to the refinement of $I(m)$.

Suppose there are totally N real obfuscation detectors, each detector $d_i$ has a weight value of importance $w_i$ to the adversaries. The goal of adversaries is to minimize the distance $D$ between the statistical feature of $p'$, denoted as $X_{p'}$ and the centroid $c_i$ of a certain real detector $d_i$, which results to the following optimization problem:

$$\arg_{p'} \min \sum_{i=1}^{N} D(X_{p'}, c_i) w_i. \tag{1}$$

Since adversaries can not evaluate any specific $w_i$ because they do not even know its existence, the ideal solution $p'$ of (1) can not be analytically found. Adversaries may instead solve an approximate problem:

$$\arg_{p'} \min \sum_{i=1}^{N} D(X_{p'}, c_i) \frac{1}{N}. \tag{2}$$

Which treat all target detectors the same by assigning same weights according to the idea of maximum entropy.

In practice any specific $c_i$ can not be evaluated as well. For those target detectors assigned higher weights, such as advanced detectors for observation established by security researchers that have priority to be evaded, they are expected to be trained better than normal targets with better quality training data. If adversaries can also obtain high quality data for training then their resulting approximation should be partial to highly weighted target detectors and hence the corresponding solution of $p'$ can empirically approximate to the optimized solution of (1), even if without knowing exact weight values.

## 3.6   Attacks

We define two kinds of attacks based on the formalized scenario and assumption of adversaries' capability aforementioned.

**Basic Attack.** The simplest way to launch evasion attack is to collect enough non-obfuscation samples and calculate the average frequency of each unigram as the centroid of approximation, and accordingly modify the malicious code to evade detectors, which has been discussed above.

**Advanced Attack with Prior Knowledge and Data Sanitization.** The basic attack does not consider two important factors:

- The prior knowledge: adversaries may also have rough knowledge on the frequency of unigram in non-obfuscation. For example some punctuation is very rare in non-obfuscation.
- Some samples collected may have negative effect on accuracy of approximation (i.e. samples that are indeed non-obfuscation but not statistically representative to common ones). On the other hand, those samples who can increase the speed of approximation should be given larger weights.

By considering these factors, the advanced attack can be as follows: After finishing collecting the non-obfuscation samples from the wild, first calculating average frequency of each unigram over the sample set to form a distribution called "standard distribution" $P$, which is exactly the same to the solution of basic attack method. Then calculating the Kullback-Leibler divergence between $P$ and each sample collected $X_j$, as well as the prior distribution $Z$. Then taking average frequency of each unigram again over all samples plus prior, each frequency is weighted by the K-L divergence value between its corresponding sample, and $P$. The higher the K-L divergence value, the lower weight the sample has.

Here prior distribution is expected to mitigate over-fitting and bring positive effect to the overall approximation. On the other hand, Kullback-Leibler(KL) divergence which is an asymmetrical distance measure of two probability distributions, is utilized to evaluate the variance between a single observed non-obfuscation and the "standard distribution" $P$. $P$ is actually the empirical expectation of the target unigram distribution. If a sample is close to the expectation, it contributes more to the final weighted average calculation by given more weight.

Assume that $m$ non-obfuscation has been collected as training data, first we calculate $P$. Each unigram $x_i$'s probability $p_i$ in $P$ is calculated as:

$$p_i = \frac{1}{m+1} \sum_{j=1}^{m} x_{ij} + z_i, \tag{3}$$

Where $z_i$ is the probability of $x_i$ in the prior, $x_{ij}$ is the probability of $x_i$ in sample $X_j$.

And then calculate the K-L divergence $D_{KL}$ between each sample collected $X_j$ and $P$. In specific, we calculate $D_{KL}(P||X)$ since the weights in the K-L divergence should be taken from $P$.

$$D_{KL}(P||X_j) = \sum_{i=1}^{|\chi|} p_i \log_2 \frac{p_i}{x_{ij}}, \tag{4}$$

where $|\chi|$ indicates the size of unigram features.

The weight $\pi_r$ for a specific sample $X_r$ is then calculated according to the idea of assigning more weight to samples that own smaller KL-divergence value to $P$.

$$\pi_r = \frac{\exp(D_{KL}(P||X_r))^{-1}}{\sum_{j=1}^{m} \exp(D_{KL}(P||X_j)^{-1}}, \tag{5}$$

So that

$$\sum_r \pi_r = 1. \tag{6}$$

And the final weighted average value for each unigram $x_i$ is calculated as:

$$p_i' = \sum_{j=1}^{m} \pi_j x_{ij} + \pi_z z_i, \tag{7}$$

Where $\pi_z$ is the weight for prior.

It also can be seen that the basic attack is a special case of advanced attack, where weights of all samples are equal and excludes the prior. In addition, the two attack methods are proposed based on the assumption of sophisticated adversaries who want to launch indiscriminate attack, but they are actually also available for targeted attacks where probing is possible. The only difference is in indiscriminate attack the optimal strategy for adversaries is to do one confident evasion by using all collected samples, and in targeted attack which only concerns specific target detectors, adversaries can try evasion each time after collecting a certain amount of samples according to the feedback probed until succeed.

# 4    Experiment and Result

Under the novelty detection scheme assumed, the training data of such a statistical obfuscation detector (i.e. only need non-obfuscated benign samples) is randomly collected from the wild since defenders have to make sure the detector to have good generalization to the JavaScript in public environment. At the same time the quality of collected training samples have to be promised to some extent to ensure they are indeed statistically representative to common non-obfuscated JavaScript.

We design our experiment to test the effectiveness of the two attacks on the target system. The data set utilized contains 2750 non-obfuscation and 400 obfuscation samples, collected from Alexa rank [11] and VirusTotal [10] respectively from Dec 2015 to Jan 2017. Among them, non-obfuscation are collected from top websites under different categories such as sports, education and science, to ensure diversity. We manually confirmed the label of each sample and ensured there is no duplicated samples.

Firstly 2000 randomly selected non-obfuscation samples are utilized to train 10 target novelty detectors to simulate 10 real obfuscation detectors. Each system is randomly assigned 1000 samples for training hence there is unknown overlap between each two, to simulate the unknown similarity of each two detectors in practice. All systems use frequency of 94 unigram tokens as features. Each training is simply taking the average of unigram frequencies over all training samples to obtain a centroid of the sphere-shape detection system, whose radius is customized. Any future point lie within the sphere is determined as non-obfuscation.

As mentioned, the goal of adversaries is to simultaneously approximate many target systems. We utilize three kinds of data set size: 50, 100, 200 samples to respectively train 20 approximation to 10 target systems. At each try, two kinds of attacks will be carried out to compare the difference on effectiveness. The accuracy of approximation is indirectly measured as the KL divergence value between the adversaries' approximated centroid and targets'. For each approximation, 75% training samples are randomly selected from the 2000 training samples of the target system, while the rest are non-obfuscation samples not in the training set regarded as non-representative samples, and a small amount of obfuscation samples are also included. The two types of irregular samples are selected randomly as well as their numbers.

Such implementation is based on the fact that adversaries can also access the same data sources of target systems as well as the perfect detectors so their data quality is somewhat promised, especially when the target systems are periodically trained while the adversaries collect their samples from recent websites which both of them are recently fresh data. It is also the fact that the adversaries can only collect a small percentage of data compared to the perfect detectors due to cost of collection. And the radius of a target system is not important since not necessary in the attack.

The results of approximation are shown in Fig. 5. We compare the values of KL divergence between the adversaries' approximated detectors with different

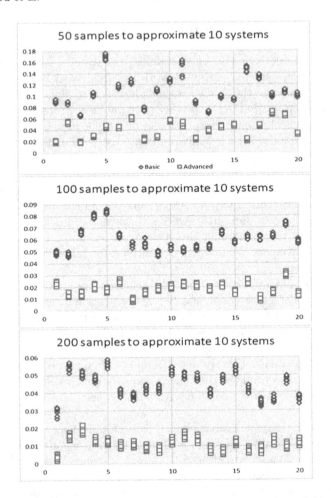

**Fig. 5.** The effectiveness of approximation by utilizing two attack methods: before and after data sanitization. The x axis indicates the index of each try and the y axis is the values of KL divergence

sizes of training sets and 10 simulated real obfuscation detectors, to indirectly quantify the approximation accuracy. The overall accuracy is increased by adding more samples, but the effectiveness of doing so drops when adding another 100 samples to some existing 100 samples, indicates that the speed of converge is not linear in terms of numbers of samples. In addition, the effectiveness of data sanitization is palpable since it can be seen that approximation accuracy is higher and more stable after data sanitization, indicates it can constantly and reliably remove noise contained in the data set for approximation.

# 5   Discussion

According to the results shown in Fig. 5, our assumption made in previous chapters that most real obfuscation detectors statistically resemble each other, is validated by the small KL divergence values between the adversaries' approximation and most of our simulated target detectors. It seems that approximation can be done rather easily. By merely using a small data set collected, adversaries can get an accurate approximation to most of the simulated systems. However in practice, there are several potential constraints that can prevent adversaries to obtain such ideal results:

1. In practice when dealing with much larger data sets utilized by many real obfuscation detectors (e.g. more than 100,000 training samples obtained by large-scale crawling), the approximation may be much harder. Much more samples are needed in order to obtain enough approximation accuracy.
2. There is no way for adversaries to measure the quality of approximation to the perfect detectors, or to the most of the target detectors, as assumed at the beginning. Hence even if the adversaries might already have some approximation that is enough accurate, they would not know it. The best strategy is still adding samples as many as possible for the approximation.

The effectiveness of data sanitization shown by the Fig. 5 means that adversaries don't even need to do data cleaning manually to remove low quality samples, which makes their attack purely automatic. In addition, the prior utilized in experiments is simply an uniform distribution. In practice adversaries can choose better ones or even specifically assign constant weight to prior according to their prior knowledge.

We assumed 1-gram in this work but it is obvious that the formalization of attack scenario and proposed attack methods can be directly transplanted to other n-gram, and we speculate other n-gram systems can be fooled in the same way since we do not see any superiority of robustness owned by n-gram compared with unigram in this scenario. It is also worth to mention the failure of n-gram detection is not independent, which will also potentially make the detection based on most indirect statistical measures such as entropy fail as well since such measures are also based on raw n-gram features.

According to our evaluation, statistical detection scheme has little resistance of artificially crafted obfuscated JavaScript. In practice however, as statistical approaches are indeed proved to be effective for detecting natural obfuscation, we recommend the combination of statistical and other detection methods, such as JavaScript specific features so that adversaries have to face more constraints when creating adversarial samples, which decreases the amount and quality of possible solutions.

# 6   Conclusion and Future Work

In this research we formalized the security scenario of statistical obfuscation detectors, and proposed two standard attack methods for evaluating effectiveness of simulated target detectors. The results show that even under extremely limited condition for skillful adversaries, they could still carry out accurate evasion attacks in a purely automatic way.

The target systems utilized in the work is based on several assumption to unify and simplify the classification scheme and feature utilized, which left the space of testing more complicated classification systems for future work. For example in the case that real detectors using different n-gram models, or more complicated classifiers. We believe such a security problem can still not be eliminated in more complex scenario, but may change its pattern according to specific constraints and adversaries may face additional complexity for evasion than the simple system in the research. In addition, one can also extend the work to other kinds of obfuscation, such as obfuscated malware, which is expected to share similar scenario to the obfuscated JavaScript.

This paper only focused on statistical approaches and there are indeed other ways that on other kinds of features for detection from simple ones such as the appearance of suspicious functions to complex ones such as extracting features from JavaScript abstract syntax tree [20]. We will also leave the evaluation of robustness of non-statistical methods and comparison with statistical approaches as future work. On the other side, although we have proved that statistical methods can be individually fooled, it is still unknown that adversaries can create obfuscation that can evade combined systems who simultaneously use statistical and non-statistical features (i.e. if the artificial obfuscation who can successfully statistical detection can still evade non-statistical features). Evaluation on this question can be also conducted in order to gain deeper insight in such adversarial scenario.

**Acknowledgement.** This research was partially supported by Collaboration Hubs for International Program (CHIRP) of SICORP, Japan Science and Technology Agency (JST). The authors would like to thank the referees and reviewers for their valuable comments and suggestions to improve the quality of the paper.

# References

1. Canali, D., Cova, M., Vigna, G., Kruegel, C.: Prophiler: a fast filter for the large-scale detection of malicious web pages. In: 20th International Conference on World Wide Web, pp. 197–206. ACM(2011)
2. Wang, W., Lv, Y., Chen, H., Fang, Z.: A static malicious JavaScript detection using SVM. In: 2nd International Conference on Computer Science and Electronics Engineering, vol. 40, pp. 21–30 (2013)
3. Nishida, M., et al.: Obfuscated malicious JavaScript detection using machine learning with character frequency. In: Information Processing Society of Japan SIG Technical Report, No. 21 (2014)
4. Kamizono, M., et al.: Datasets for anti-malware research - MWS datasets 2013. In: Anti Malware Engineering WorkShop (2013)
5. Laskov, P., Srndic, N.: Static detection of malicious JavaScript-bearing PDF documents. In: 27th Annual Computer Security Applications Conference, pp. 373–382. ACM (2011)

6. Al-Taharwa, I.A., et al.: Obfuscated malicious JavaScript detection by Causal Relations Finding. In: 2011 13th International Conference Advanced Communication Technology (ICACT), pp. 787–792. IEEE (2011)
7. Kim, B., Im, C., Jung, H.: Suspicious malicious web site detection with strength analysis of a JavaScript obfuscation. Int. J. Adv. Sci. Technol. **26**, 19–32 (2011)
8. Choi, Y., Kim, T., Choi, S.: Automatic detection for JavaScript obfuscation attacks in web pages through string pattern analysis. Int. J. Secur. Appl. **4**(2), 13–26 (2010)
9. Scholkopf, B., Williamson, R., Smola, A., Taylor, J., Platt, J.: Support vector method for novelty detection. In: Solla, S.A., Leen, T.K., Muller, K.-R. (eds.), pp. 582–588. MIT Press (2000)
10. VirusTotal. https://www.virustotal.com
11. Alexa Top Sites. http://www.alexa.com/topsites
12. Shabtai, A., Moskovitch, R., Elovici, Y., Glezer, C.: Detection of malicious code by applying machine learning classifiers on static features: a state-of-the-art survey. In: Information Security Technical Report, vol. 14, pp. 16–29. Elsevier (2009)
13. Su, J., Yoshioka, K., Shikata, J., Matsumoto, T.: Detecting obfuscated suspicious JavaScript based on information-theoretic measures and novelty detection. In: Kwon, S., Yun, A. (eds.) ICISC 2015. LNCS, vol. 9558, pp. 278–293. Springer, Cham (2016). doi:10.1007/978-3-319-30840-1_18
14. Daniel, L., Meek, C.: Good word attacks on statistical spam filter. In: CEAS (2015)
15. Visaggio, C., Canfora, G.: An empirical study of metric-based methods to detect obfuscated code. Int. J. Secur. Appl. **7**(2) (2013)
16. Huang, L., et al.: Adversarial machine learning. In: 4th ACM Workshop on Artificial Intelligence and Security, pp. 43–58 (2011)
17. Kruskal, J.B.: Multidimensional Scaling by optimizing goodness of fit to a nonmetric hypothesis. Psychometrika **29**(1), 1-27 (1964)
18. Scholkopf, B., et al.: Support vector method for novelty detection. In: Conference on Neural Information Processing Systems 1999 (NIPS 1999), vol. 12, pp. 582–588 (1999)
19. Tax, D.M.J., Duin, R.P.W.: Support vector data description. J. Mach. Learn. **54**(1), 45–66 (2004)
20. Curtsinger, C., et al.: ZOZZLE: Fast and precise in-browser JavaScript malware detection. In: USENIX Security Symposium, pp. 33–48 (2011)

# Cryptanalysis

# Analyzing Key Schedule of SIMON: Iterative Key Differences and Application to Related-Key Impossible Differentials

Kota Kondo[1], Yu Sasaki[2(✉)], Yosuke Todo[2], and Tetsu Iwata[1]

[1] Nagoya University, Nagoya, Japan
k_kondo@echo.nuee.nagoya-u.ac.jp, tetsu.iwata@nagoya-u.jp
[2] NTT Secure Platform Laboratories, Tokyo, Japan
{sasaki.yu,todo.yosuke}@lab.ntt.co.jp

**Abstract.** The current paper analyzes the key schedule function of lightweight block cipher SIMON, which was designed by NSA in 2013. In particular, a list of all iterative key differences is provided for all members of the SIMON-family for all number of rounds. The iterative differences are searched by exploiting the fact that SIMON only adopts linear operations in the key schedule function. By using the discovered iterative key difference for SIMON32, a 15-round related-key impossible differential is constructed, which improves the previous longest 11-round impossible differentials of SIMON32 in the single-key setting by four rounds. The current paper makes better understanding of related-key security of SIMON.

**Keywords:** SIMON · Block cipher · Linear key schedule · Iterative differences · Related-key · Impossible differentials

## 1 Introduction

Lightweight cryptography has recently been discussed extensively not only in academia but also by standardization bodies e.g. ISO, NIST and CRYPTREC.

Among a large variety of lightweight block ciphers, SIMON and SPECK [6], which were designed by NSA in 2013, achieve overwhelming performance and thus attract a lot of attention from the community. Moreover, SIMON and SPECK are currently proposed for ISO as next standardized algorithms. Hence the third party analysis from various aspects is important.

SIMON has already received a large number of third party analysis, which includes differential cryptanalysis [2,8,15,16,21,22,24], linear cryptanalysis [1, 4,5,10,20,21], algebraic analysis [3,17], integral attack [25], division property [23,26,27], impossible differential attack [4,9,11,25], zero-correlation attack [25], known-key attack [13] and so on.

In the single-key setting, the attacker has access to an oracle $\mathcal{O}_K$ who performs encryption and decryption with a secret key $K$. In the related-key setting, the attacker has access to additional oracle $\mathcal{O}_{K \oplus \Delta K}$ with the secret key $K$ and

© Springer International Publishing AG 2017
S. Obana and K. Chida (Eds.): IWSEC 2017, LNCS 10418, pp. 141–158, 2017.
DOI: 10.1007/978-3-319-64200-0_9

a public relationship $\Delta K$. The additional access to the related-key oracle may bring more knowledge to the attacker, thus the attacker's ability is stronger than in the single-key model.

Security in the single-key setting is most practical, thus most important for industry especially for the standardization process. However, evaluating related-key security is still meaningful in the following reasons.

- When keys are poorly managed, multiple keys may be generated simply by counting up an initial key value and be distribute to multiple users. Then, related-key oracles with a known XOR relation can occur in practice.
- When the key size is double of the block size (this is the case of several members of the SIMON-family), implementors may want to use block cipher as tweakable block cipher by injecting tweak value to a half of the key. Tweak is an additional input to the block cipher under the attacker's control, thus key difference of attacker's choice can be injected.
- Key schedule of SIMON only uses linear operations, which leads to deterministic differential properties. This may become a source of unintentional vulnerability or intentional back-door.
- From a technical view point, the large key state is often harder to analyze than the single-key case, especially for experimental approaches using MILP or SAT solver, which are most common for SIMON32. Other approaches are required for related-key analysis.

**Our Contributions.** In this paper, the key schedule function of SIMON is analyzed, which is a family of lightweight block cipher consisting of ten members with various block sizes and key sizes. As introduced before, the key schedule function (for all members) only adopts linear operations, which allows many iterative differential propagation patterns in the key schedule function.

Such iterative differences can be efficiently found by representing the update by the key schedule function as a matrix multiplication with an array of key bits and then solve a system of linear equations. We first show a concrete method to describe such matrices for all members of SIMON. We then give a list of all iterative key differences as long as the page limitation allows.

The discovered iterative key differences cannot lead to efficient iterative differential characteristics including the data processing part owing to a large number of active bits in subkeys, meanwhile we show that related-key impossible differentials can be constructed based on the discovered iterative key differences.

In particular, we construct 15-round related-key impossible differentials against SIMON32, the smallest member of the SIMON-family, which improves the previous 11-round impossible differentials in the single-key setting by four rounds. Note that the similar related-key impossible differentials can also be constructed for other members of SIMON. However, with respect to the number of rounds compared to the one in single-key setting, we focus our attention on SIMON32 in this paper.

We also notice that appending additional rounds for the key recovery cannot be done efficiently for our related-key impossible differentials because of too many active bits in the key differences. Hence our related-key impossible differentials have advantage only as a standalone distinguisher in the following settings: (1) When the data complexity becomes close to the full codebook, the success probability of observing impossible pairs of input difference $\Delta_i$ and output difference $\Delta_o$ is 0 for a target cipher while about $1/2$ for a pseudo-random permutation (PRP). As long as the key is fixed for PRP, the probability of observing $(\Delta_i, \Delta_o)$ is fixed. Hence, the success probability of this distinguishing game cannot get close to 1 even if the data complexity increases, but it still has non-zero and non-negligible advantages. (2) Our distinguishers can work for any key of SIMON32. Thus, in the multi-key setting, the success probability of the distinguishing game can get close to 1 if the data complexity can be more than $2^{32}$ but smaller than $u \times 2^{32}$, where $u$ is the number of keys or users.

**Paper Outline.** The organization of this paper is as follows. Section 2 introduces notations, specifications and previous work. In Sect. 3, we search for iterative differences in the SIMON's key schedule function. Section 4 applies the discovered 8-round iterative differences to construct 15-round related-key impossible differentials against SIMON32/64. Section 5 concludes this paper.

## 2  Preliminaries

Throughout the paper we use $\Delta X$ to denote difference of a variable $X$. We also use the typewriter font to denote hexadecimal numbers.

### 2.1  Specification of SIMON

The SIMON block cipher with a $2n$-bit block and an $mn$-bit key is denoted SIMON$2n/mn$, where the word size $n$ is $n \in \{16, 24, 32, 48, 64\}$ and the number of key words $m$ is $m \in \{2, 3, 4\}$. SIMON specifies 10 choices of $(n, m)$. The choices of $(n, m)$ and round numbers are summarized in Table 1.

**Round Function.** The round function is identical for all members of SIMON, which is composed of three operations: bitwise AND, left cyclic-shift and bitwise XOR. Let $L_i$ and $R_i$ be $n$-bit registers corresponding to the left half and right half of the input state in round $i$, respectively. The plaintext is first loaded to $L_1 \| R_1$. Let $N_r$ be the number of rounds, which is specified in Table 1. The state $L_1 \| R_1$ is iteratively updated by computing the following operation for $i = 1, 2, \cdots, N_r$.

$$L_{i+1} \leftarrow R_i \oplus \big((L_i \lll 1) \land (L_i \lll 8)\big) \oplus (L_i \lll 2) \oplus k_i, \qquad R_{i+1} \leftarrow L_i,$$

where $k_i$ is an $n$-bit subkey for round $i$, and operators $\land$, $\oplus$ and $\lll s$ denote bitwise AND, bitwise XOR and left cyclic-shift by $s$ bits, respectively. In the end, $L_{N_r+1} \| R_{N_r+1}$ is output as the ciphertext (Fig. 1).

**Table 1.** Block size, key size, word size and round numbers of SIMON-family

| Block size ($2n$) | Key size ($mn$) | Word size ($n$) | Key words ($m$) | Rounds ($N_r$) |
|---|---|---|---|---|
| 32 | 64 | 16 | 4 | 32 |
| 48 | 72 | 24 | 3 | 36 |
|  | 96 |  | 4 | 36 |
| 64 | 96 | 32 | 3 | 42 |
|  | 128 |  | 4 | 44 |
| 96 | 96 | 48 | 2 | 52 |
|  | 144 |  | 3 | 54 |
| 128 | 128 | 64 | 2 | 68 |
|  | 192 |  | 3 | 69 |
|  | 256 |  | 4 | 72 |

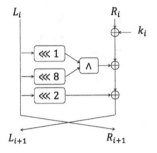

**Fig. 1.** Round function                  **Fig. 2.** Key schedule for $m = 4$

**Key Schedule Function.** The key schedule function (KSF) depends on the number of words, $m$, in the key. The key schedule functions for $m = 4$, $m = 3$ and $m = 2$ are explained below, and are also illustrated in Figs. 2, 3 and 4, respectively.

*KSF for $m = 4$.* $4n$ bits of key are first loaded to four $n$-bit key words $k_1, k_2, k_3$, and $k_4$. Subkey for round $i$ is $k_i$ thus those four key words are directly used in the first four rounds. $k_5, k_6, \cdots, k_{N_r}$ are computed by iteratively updating those four key words for $i = 1, 2, \cdots, N_r - 4$ as follows;

$$k_{i+4} \leftarrow k_i \oplus k_{i+1} \oplus (k_{i+1} \ggg 1) \oplus (k_{i+3} \ggg 3) \oplus (k_{i+3} \ggg 4) \oplus con_i,$$

where $\ggg s$ is the right cyclic-shift by $s$ bits and $con_i$ is the round constant for round $i$ defined in the specification. Because the round constant is unrelated to our analysis, we omit its details.

*KSF for $m = 3$.* $3n$ bits of key are loaded to $k_1, k_2$, and $k_3$. Subkey for round $i$ is $k_i$. $k_4, k_5, \cdots, k_{N_r}$ are computed by iteratively updating those three key words for $i = 1, 2, \cdots, N_r - 3$ as follows;

$$k_{i+3} \leftarrow k_i \oplus (k_{i+2} \ggg 3) \oplus (k_{i+2} \ggg 4) \oplus con_i.$$

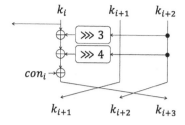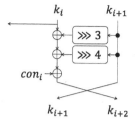

**Fig. 3.** Key schedule function for $m = 3$

**Fig. 4.** Key schedule function for $m = 2$

*KSF for* $m = 2$. $2n$ bits of key are loaded to $k_1$ and $k_2$. Subkey for round $i$ is $k_i$. $k_3, k_4, \cdots, k_{N_r}$ are computed by iteratively updating those two key words for $i = 1, 2, \cdots, N_r - 2$ as follows;

$$k_{i+2} \leftarrow k_i \oplus (k_{i+1} \ggg 3) \oplus (k_{i+1} \ggg 4) \oplus con_i.$$

## 2.2 Impossible Differential Attacks

Impossible differential attack was initiated by Knudsen [14] and Biham et al. [7] which is now one of the most common cryptographic approaches against block ciphers. The core of the attack is finding a pair of input difference $\Delta_i$ and output difference $\Delta_{i+r}$ after $r$ rounds, in which the probability that $\Delta_i$ reaches $\Delta_{i+r}$ is zero. Such $(\Delta_i, \Delta_{i+r})$ are called *impossible differentials*. When such $(\Delta_i, \Delta_{i+r})$ is detected, the attacker, for the purpose of key recovery, appends several rounds before and after the impossible differentials. After obtaining a pair of texts with plaintext difference $\Delta_P$ and ciphertext difference $\Delta_C$, the attacker guesses subkeys for the appended rounds and performs partial encryption and decryption up to the input and output of the middle $r$ rounds. If the results produce $(\Delta_i, \Delta_{i+r})$, the subkey guess turns out to be wrong.

The most fundamental part of the impossible differential attack is finding impossible differentials. For SIMON32, impossible differentials have been searched only in the single-key model and two types of 11-round impossible differentials were discovered by Alizadeh *et al.* [4], which is shown below;

$$00010000 \overset{11R}{\nrightarrow} 00800000, \qquad 00010000 \overset{11R}{\nrightarrow} 02000000. \qquad (1)$$

Rotating the input and output differences of the above form by identical bit numbers also results in the impossible differentials.

Sasaki and Todo [19] have recently shown that there does not exist any 12-round impossible differentials for SIMON32 as long as only a single bit is activated in input and output differences in the single-key setting. Thus a new approach is required to extend the number of rounds of impossible differentials.

## 2.3  Previous Key Recovery Attacks in Single-Key Setting

Although investigating key schedule is the main focus of this paper, we briefly mention the results of the previous single-key attack on SIMON32. The current best attack is linear-hull attack [1,10] which can recover a key up to 23 rounds. The best impossible differential attack in the single-key setting [11] recovers the key up to 19 rounds ror SIMON32/64 and up to 20 rounds for SIMON48/72.

# 3  Iterative Differences for Key Schedule Function

In this section, we search for iterative differences for the key schedule function with any word size $n$ and key words $m$. Section 3.1 explains the search strategy and Sect. 3.2 explains the search results.

## 3.1  Search Strategy

Because the key schedule function of SIMON only adopts linear operations, iterative differences can be searched by constructing a system of linear equations and solving it with Gaussian elimination.

**Matrix Representation of Key Schedule Function.** We represent the key schedule function as a regular matrix of size $mn$ bits denoted by $M_{mn}$. Let $K_i$ be an array of $mn$ key bits input to the key schedule function in round $i$. Namely $K_i \triangleq (k_i \| \cdots \| k_{i+m})$ in bitwise representation. Then update of $mn$ key bits in round $i$ can be written as

$$K_{i+1}^T = M_{mn} K_i^T. \tag{2}$$

The matrix $M_{4n}$ for $m = 4$ shown in Fig. 2 can be written as

$$M_{4n} = \begin{bmatrix} 0 & E & 0 & 0 \\ 0 & 0 & E & 0 \\ 0 & 0 & 0 & E \\ E & A_{01} & 0 & A_{34} \end{bmatrix}, \tag{3}$$

where $E$ is an identity matrix of size $n$ bits, and $A_{01}$ and $A_{34}$ are $n \times n$ matrices defined below.

$$A_{01} = E \oplus E^{\ggg 1}, \qquad A_{34} = E^{\ggg 3} \oplus E^{\ggg 4}, \tag{4}$$

where $E^{\ggg x}$ is rotated version of $E$ such that each column of $E$ is rotated by $x$ columns to the right. This corresponds to applying right rotation by $x$ bits to an input word.

Similarly, the matrices $M_{3n}$ and $M_{2n}$ are described as follows.

$$M_{3n} = \begin{bmatrix} 0 & E & 0 \\ 0 & 0 & E \\ E & 0 & A_{34} \end{bmatrix}, \qquad M_{2n} = \begin{bmatrix} 0 & E \\ E & A_{34} \end{bmatrix}. \tag{5}$$

**Search Algorithm.** The goal is finding iterative differences for a certain number of rounds, say $i$ rounds. Let $X = \{x_0, x_1, \cdots, x_{mn-1}\}$ be an array of $mn$ 1-bit variables where $x_j \in \{0,1\}$ is a 1-bit variable to represent whether the input difference in the $j$-th bit-position is active or inactive. For iterative differences, the output difference must be the same as the input difference. Then, iterative differences can be calculated by solving the following equation;

$$(M_{mn})^i X = X, \tag{6}$$

which is converted to

$$\left((M_{mn})^i \oplus E_{mn}\right) X = 0, \tag{7}$$

where $E_{mn}$ is an identity matrix of size $mn$ bits. We find all solutions of Eq. (7) by applying Gaussian elimination.

In the end, we iterate this calculation for all $i$, $i = 1, 2, \cdots, N_r/2$ for all members of the SIMON-family. Here, we set the maximum value of $i$ to $N_r/2$ instead of $N_r$ in order to enjoy the iterative property (Iterative differences for $N_r$ rounds do not provide any advantage to be iterative). The search algorithm is summarized in Algorithm 1.

---

**Algorithm 1.** Iterative Key Differences Search Algorithm

---
1: **for** all ten choices of $(m, n)$ **do**
2:  **for** $i = 1, 2, \cdots, N_r/2$ **do**
3:   calculate $(M_{mn})^i$ and solve Eq. (7) by applying Gaussian elimination
4:   **return** all the solutions
5:  **end for**
6: **end for**

---

## 3.2 Search Results

We show the result of performing Algorithm 1. We first summarize its cost. As shown in Table 1, the biggest value of $mn$ is 256. Because the computational cost of Gaussian elimination for a matrix of size $N$ is $\mathcal{O}(N^3)$, the cost is about $2^{24}$ for a single choice of the parameter $(m, n)$ and the target round number $i$. The sum of numbers of rounds for all 10 members of the SIMON-family is 505 ($\approx 2^{10}$), hence the computational cost is at most $2^{10} \cdot 2^{24} = 2^{34}$. The actual cost is much smaller because the computation for small $(m, n)$ is less than $2^{24}$.

We executed Algorithm 1 with a standard PC equipped with Intel Core(TM) i5-4210 M and CPU 2.60 GHz, and the experiment finished in 498 s. We show an exhaustive list of iterative key differences for SIMON32/64 in Table 2, in which the difference with ID05 will later be used to construct related-key impossible differentials.

We note that Gaussian elimination gives more solutions, but we omit obvious iterative key differences to minimize the representation. More precisely, we removed the ones satisfying at least one of the following obvious cases.

**Table 2.** $r$-Round Iterative Key Differences for Simon32/64

| ID | r | $\Delta k_1$ | $\Delta k_2$ | $\Delta k_3$ | $\Delta k_4$ | $\Delta k_5$ | $\Delta k_6$ | $\Delta k_7$ | $\Delta k_8$ | $\Delta k_9$ | $\Delta k_{10}$ | $\Delta k_{11}$ | $\Delta k_{12}$ | $\Delta k_{13}$ | $\Delta k_{14}$ | $\Delta k_{15}$ | $\Delta k_{16}$ |
|----|----|------|------|------|------|------|------|------|------|------|------|------|------|------|------|------|------|
| 01 | 1 | aaaa | aaaa | aaaa | aaaa | | | | | | | | | | | | |
| 02 | 2 | aaaa | 0000 | aaaa | 0000 | | | | | | | | | | | | |
| 03 | 4 | ffff | 0000 | 0000 | 0000 | | | | | | | | | | | | |
| 04 | | 6666 | 0000 | cccc | 0000 | | | | | | | | | | | | |
| 05 | 8 | cccc | 0000 | 0000 | 0000 | cccc | 5555 | ffff | aaaa | | | | | | | | |
| 06 | | aaaa | 0000 | 0000 | 0000 | aaaa | ffff | 0000 | ffff | | | | | | | | |
| 07 | | 0000 | cccc | 0000 | 0000 | aaaa | 3333 | 5555 | 0000 | | | | | | | | |
| 08 | | 0000 | aaaa | 0000 | 0000 | ffff | aaaa | ffff | 0000 | | | | | | | | |
| 09 | | 7878 | 8888 | f0f0 | 0000 | b4b4 | dddd | 9696 | 5555 | | | | | | | | |
| 10 | | 8888 | 0000 | 8888 | 0000 | 8888 | 5555 | 7777 | 5555 | | | | | | | | |
| 11 | | 8888 | 0000 | 4444 | 0000 | 8888 | ffff | 4444 | 0000 | | | | | | | | |
| 12 | | 8888 | 0000 | 2222 | 0000 | 8888 | aaaa | dddd | aaaa | | | | | | | | |
| 13 | | f0f0 | 8888 | e1e1 | 0000 | 3c3c | dddd | 8787 | aaaa | | | | | | | | |
| 14 | | 8888 | 7878 | 0000 | f0f0 | dddd | 1e1e | aaaa | 3c3c | | | | | | | | |
| 15 | | 8888 | f0f0 | 0000 | e1e1 | 2222 | 9696 | aaaa | 2d2d | | | | | | | | |
| 16 | 16 | c0c0 | 0000 | 0000 | 0000 | c0c0 | 1414 | c3c3 | e4e4 | 0c0c | 7777 | cccc | bbbb | 0c0c | 9c9c | f0f0 | a0a0 |
| 17 | | a0a0 | 0000 | 0000 | 0000 | a0a0 | 1e1e | 2222 | 9696 | 0a0a | cccc | aaaa | 6666 | 0a0a | d2d2 | 8888 | f0f0 |
| 18 | | 9090 | 0000 | 0000 | 0000 | 9090 | 1b1b | d2d2 | afaf | 0909 | 1111 | 9999 | 8888 | 0909 | f5f5 | b4b4 | d8d8 |
| 19 | | 8888 | 0000 | 0000 | 0000 | 8888 | 9999 | aaaa | 3333 | 8888 | ffff | 0000 | ffff | 8888 | 6666 | aaaa | cccc |
| 20 | | 0000 | c0c0 | 0000 | 0000 | a0a0 | dede | 3636 | 5555 | eeee | c0c0 | dddd | aaaa | b1b1 | dede | 1414 | 0000 |
| 21 | | 0000 | a0a0 | 0000 | 0000 | f0f0 | b1b1 | 2d2d | ffff | 9999 | a0a0 | 3333 | ffff | 6969 | b1b1 | 1e1e | 0000 |
| 22 | | 0000 | 9090 | 0000 | 0000 | d8d8 | 0606 | a0a0 | aaaa | 2222 | 9090 | 4444 | 5555 | 0505 | 0606 | 1b1b | 0000 |
| 23 | | 0000 | 8888 | 0000 | 0000 | cccc | dddd | 6666 | 0000 | ffff | 8888 | ffff | 0000 | 3333 | dddd | 9999 | 0000 |
| 24 | | 7f80 | 0000 | ff00 | 0000 | 7f80 | 8888 | 6699 | fafa | 43bc | 1111 | d22d | ffff | da25 | cccc | 8778 | 5050 |
| 25 | | 8080 | 0000 | 8080 | 0000 | 8080 | d8d8 | 1616 | 6363 | 6e6e | eeee | f7f7 | bbbb | 3b3b | 3636 | 3434 | d8d8 |
| 26 | | 8080 | 0000 | 4040 | 0000 | 8080 | 7878 | c8c8 | 5555 | 3b3b | 0000 | 3737 | 6666 | 9191 | 8787 | eaea | cccc |
| 27 | | 8080 | 0000 | 2020 | 0000 | 8080 | 2828 | a7a7 | 4e4e | 9191 | 7777 | 5757 | 8888 | c4c4 | 5f5f | 8585 | c6c6 |
| 28 | | 8080 | 0000 | 1010 | 0000 | 8080 | 0000 | 1010 | c3c3 | c4c4 | cccc | 6767 | ffff | 6e6e | 3333 | 3232 | c3c3 |
| 29 | | 8080 | 0000 | 0808 | 0000 | 8080 | 1414 | cbcb | 0505 | 6e6e | 1111 | 7f7f | 4444 | 3b3b | 0505 | e9e9 | 4141 |
| 30 | | 8080 | 0000 | 0202 | 0000 | 8080 | 1b1b | d0d0 | d7d7 | 9191 | 8888 | 7575 | 7777 | c4c4 | 9393 | f2f2 | a0a0 |
| 31 | | 0000 | 7f80 | 0000 | ff00 | 5050 | 708f | 9999 | 2dd2 | ffff | 25da | 4444 | e11e | fafa | b34c | 8888 | ff00 |
| 32 | | 0000 | 8080 | 0000 | 4040 | cccc | d5d5 | 8787 | 6262 | 9999 | 3b3b | 0000 | 3737 | aaaa | c4c4 | 7878 | 4040 |

1. Iterative differences for $r$ rounds are always iterative for $xr$ rounds for an integer $x$. We only list the case with $x = 1$ for such iterated variants.
2. Owing to the linearity, $M^i a = a$ and $M^i b = b$ implies $M^i(a \oplus b) = a \oplus b$. We omit the candidates that can be represented as linear combination of others.
3. When $(\Delta k_1, \Delta k_2, \Delta k_3, \Delta k_4) = (A, B, C, D)$ is iterative, $(B, C, D, A)$ is also iterative. Such rotated variants are omitted.
4. When $(\Delta k_1, \Delta k_2, \Delta k_3, \Delta k_4) = (A, B, C, D)$ is iterative, $(A \lll j, B \lll j, C \lll j, D \lll j)$ for any $j$ is also iterative. Such rotated-within-word variants are omitted.

For example, besides ID01 in Table 2, the key differences ffff ffff ffff ffff and 5555 5555 5555 5555 were also obtained as solutions of Algorithm 1 for 1-round iteration. We omitted 5555 5555 5555 5555 from Table 2 because this is a 1-bit rotation of ID01. ffff ffff ffff ffff is also omitted because it is calculated by xoring 5555 5555 5555 5555 and ID01.

Verifying that those in Table 2 are actually iterative can be done by simply tracing the differential propagation. The case of ID05 is shown in Fig. 5.

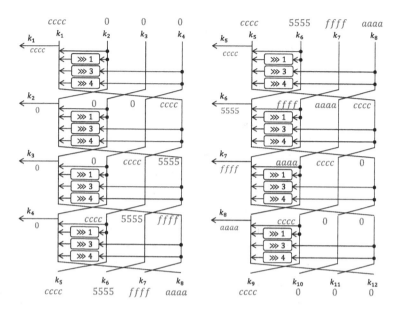

**Fig. 5.** 8-round iterative key differences for SIMON32/64 (ID05)

From Table 2, we extract a useful property which will be used later.

*Property 1. When $\Delta k_{i+1} = \Delta k_{i+2} = \Delta k_{i+3} = 0$, $\Delta k_i = \Delta k_{i+4}$ always holds according to the form of the key schedule function.*

### 3.3    Iterative Key Differences for Other SIMON Members

**Results for Other Word Size with $m = 4$.** Regarding SIMON64/128, the results are the same as Table 2 but for the word size, namely 32 iterative key differences were found in which each key difference is two iterations of the one in Table 2. (For example, the first subkey difference of ID16 is c0c0c0c0 instead of c0c0 in Table 2.) Regarding SIMON128/256, the results up to 16-round iterations are the same as Table 2 but for the word sizes. Besides, there are thirty-five 32-round iterative key differences. Due to the limited space, we omit the list. Regarding SIMON48/96, because the word size is not a multiple of 16, the form of key differences are different from other members, e.g. each subkey difference can be 2 iterations of a 12-bit difference. Due to the page limitation, we only show such differences up to 8 rounds in Table 3, which are still enough to confirm different differential forms from other members.

**Results for $m = 3$.** The number of iterative key differences is much smaller than the case with $m = 4$. The results for SIMON48/72 up to 21-round iterative

Table 3. $r$-Round iterative key differences for SIMON48/96

| ID | $r$ | $\Delta k_1$ | $\Delta k_2$ | $\Delta k_3$ | $\Delta k_4$ | $\Delta k_5$ | $\Delta k_6$ | $\Delta k_7$ | $\Delta k_8$ |
|----|-----|--------------|--------------|--------------|--------------|--------------|--------------|--------------|--------------|
| 01 | 1 | e38e38 | e38e38 | e38e38 | e38e38 | | | | |
| 02 | | 924924 | 924924 | 924924 | 924924 | | | | |
| 03 | 2 | e38e38 | 000000 | e38e38 | 000000 | | | | |
| 04 | | 924924 | 000000 | 924924 | 000000 | | | | |
| 05 | 4 | 1f81f8 | 000000 | fc0fc0 | 000000 | | | | |
| 06 | | 104104 | 000000 | 820820 | 000000 | | | | |
| 07 | | fbefbe | 000000 | 208208 | 000000 | | | | |
| 08 | 5 | 6db6db | db6db6 | 000000 | 000000 | db6db6 | | | |
| 09 | | 6db6db | 000000 | db6db6 | 000000 | 6db6db | | | |
| 10 | | 492492 | 924924 | 924924 | 492492 | ffffff | | | |
| 11 | | c71c71 | 71c71c | 71c71c | c71c71 | aaaaaa | | | |
| 12 | 8 | 1ffe00 | 150150 | fff000 | 000000 | 007ff8 | 150150 | fc003f | 000000 |
| 13 | | 100100 | 1f81f8 | 800800 | 000000 | 004004 | 1f81f8 | 020020 | 000000 |
| 14 | | 080080 | c30c30 | 400400 | 000000 | aa8aa8 | 3cf3cf | 545545 | 000000 |
| 15 | | cc8cc8 | 1f81f8 | 020020 | 000000 | dccdcc | 4ad4ad | 7ff7ff | aaaaaa |
| 16 | | aa8aa8 | c30c30 | 010010 | 000000 | 080080 | c30c30 | 155155 | ffffff |
| 17 | | 998998 | 618618 | 008008 | 000000 | c8cc8c | 34d34d | 755755 | 555555 |
| 18 | | a80a80 | 1ffe00 | 000000 | fff000 | a80a80 | 007ff8 | 000000 | 03ffc0 |
| 19 | | fc0fc0 | cc8cc8 | 000000 | 020020 | 56a56a | 233233 | 555555 | 800800 |
| 20 | | 7e07e0 | aa8aa8 | 000000 | 010010 | 81f81f | a2aa2a | ffffff | 400400 |
| 21 | | 3f03f0 | 998998 | 000000 | 008008 | 6a56a5 | 626626 | aaaaaa | 200200 |
| 22 | | c98c98 | 3ffc00 | 000000 | ffe001 | c98c98 | aa555a | ffffff | 52aad5 |

differences are listed in Table 4. Note that Algorithm 1 searches for only up to $N_r/2 = 18$ rounds. Here, to make it easier to understand, we list the search results up to 21 rounds. All subkey differences are three iterations of a byte-wise difference up to 12-round iterations. Hence, the same form but different word size is observed for the analysis of other SIMON members with $m = 3$. On the contrary, subkey differences of the 21-round iteration (ID08) is two iterations of 12-bit differences. This type of key differences can only be seen when the word size is a multiple of 12, where SIMON96/144 is the only case.

For SIMON64/96, up to 12 rounds, the same results but different word size as Table 4 were obtained. As mentioned before, The 21-round iterations for SIMON48/72 were not found for SIMON64/96. Instead, we found a 16-round iterative key differences, which is shown in Table 5. All subkey differences are two iterations of 16-bit differences. Therefore, the same type of 16-round iterative key differences can be found in other SIMON members with the word size of a multiple of 16, and this explains the reason why it does not exist in SIMON48/72.

**Table 4.** $r$-Round iterative key differences for SIMON48/72

| ID | $r$ | $\Delta k_1$ | $\Delta k_2$ | $\Delta k_3$ | $\Delta k_4$ | $\Delta k_5$ | $\Delta k_6$ | $\Delta k_7$ | $\Delta k_8$ | $\Delta k_9$ | $\Delta k_{10}$ | $\Delta k_{11}$ | $\Delta k_{12}$ |
|----|----|----|----|----|----|----|----|----|----|----|----|----|----|
| 01 | 1 | ffffff | ffffff | ffffff | | | | | | | | | |
| 02 | 2 | aaaaaa | 555555 | aaaaaa | | | | | | | | | |
| 03 | 3 | ffffff | 000000 | 000000 | | | | | | | | | |
| 04 | 4 | 222222 | eeeeee | 888888 | bbbbbb | | | | | | | | |
| 05 | 6 | aaaaaa | 000000 | 000000 | aaaaaa | ffffff | 000000 | | | | | | |
| 06 | 8 | a8a8a8 | 979797 | 808080 | b0b0b0 | 8a8a8a | 797979 | 080808 | 0b0b0b | | | | |
| 07 | 12 | 888888 | 000000 | 000000 | 888888 | 999999 | aaaaaa | 777777 | 000000 | aaaaaa | 888888 | 999999 | 000000 |
| 08 | 21 | 924924 | 000000 | 000000 | 924924 | db6db6 | b6db6d | ffffff | db6db6 | 000000 | ffffff | db6db6 | b6db6d |
| | | 924924 | 000000 | 000000 | b6db6d | ffffff | 000000 | b6db6d | 924924 | db6db6 | 000000 | | |

**Table 5.** A list of $r$-round 16-bit-wise iterative key differences for SIMON64/96

| ID | $r$ | $\Delta k_1/\Delta k_9$ | $\Delta k_2/\Delta k_{10}$ | $\Delta k_3/\Delta k_{11}$ | $\Delta k_4/\Delta k_{12}$ | $\Delta k_5/\Delta k_{13}$ | $\Delta k_6/\Delta k_{14}$ | $\Delta k_7/\Delta k_{15}$ | $\Delta k_8/\Delta k_{16}$ |
|----|----|----|----|----|----|----|----|----|----|
| 01 | 16 | 822a822a | 70e770e7 | 80008000 | 9a2a9a2a | 8a008a00 | 99e099e0 | 80888088 | 12191219 |
| | | 2a822a82 | e770e770 | 00800080 | 2a9a2a9a | 008a008a | e099e099 | 88808880 | 19121912 |

The word size of SIMON96/144 is 48, which is multiple of 12 and also multiple of 16. The discovered results up to 21 rounds match the ones in Tables 4 and 5 but for the word size. Moreover, we found a 24-round iterative differences in which the initial key difference is $(808080808080, 0, 0)$. Subkey differences in each round can be computed by propagating the initial difference as in Fig. 5.

The results for SIMON128/192 are also word-size variants of other SIMON members. Because the wide size is not a multiple of 12, the 21-round iterative difference in Table 4 does not exist for SIMON128/192. We also found a 32-round iterative differences in which the initial key difference is $(828808888288088, 3200a82a3200a82a, 8000000080000000)$.

**Results for $m = 2$.** With only two key words, the attacker does not have many options to control key differences. Thus the number of iterated key differences is less than other cases. Due to the large word size and many rounds, listing all subkey differences in every round within the page limitation is hard. Here, we show the differences of initial two key words of SIMON128/128 in Table 6 and of SIMON96/96 in Table 7. 16-bit wise difference for SIMON128/128 can also be applied to SIMON96/96. In Table 7, we only show the iterative difference that cannot be seen in Table 6.

# 4    15-Round Related-Key Impossible Differentials

We show a 15-round related-key impossible differential against SIMON32/64 by using the 8-round iterative key difference in Fig. 5. Section 4.1 explains the overall strategy to construct related-key impossible differentials. Section 4.2 shows a concrete 13-round related-key impossible differential and proves why this is impossible. In Sect. 4.3, we discuss impossible differentials with other iterative

**Table 6.** $r$-Round iterative key differences for SIMON128/128

| ID | $r$ | $\Delta k_1$ | $\Delta k_2$ |
|----|-----|--------------|--------------|
| 01 | 1 | ffffffffffffffff | ffffffffffffffff |
| 02 | 2 | ffffffffffffffff | 0000000000000000 |
| 03 | 4 | aaaaaaaaaaaaaaaa | 0000000000000000 |
| 04 | 8 | 8888888888888888 | 0000000000000000 |
| 05 | 16 | 8080808080808080 | 0000000000000000 |
| 06 | 32 | 8000800080008000 | 0000000000000000 |

**Table 7.** $r$-Round iterative key differences for SIMON96/96

| ID | $r$ | $\Delta k_1$ | $\Delta k_2$ |
|----|-----|--------------|--------------|
| 01 | 5 | db6db6db6db6 | 000000000000 |
| 02 |   | 924924924924 | 924924924924 |
| 03 | 10 | c30c30c30c30 | 000000000000 |
| 04 |   | a28a28a28a28 | 000000000000 |
| 05 |   | 924924924924 | 000000000000 |
| 06 | 20 | a00a00a00a00 | 000000000000 |
| 07 |   | 880880880880 | 000000000000 |
| 08 |   | 820820820820 | 000000000000 |

key differences. In Sect. 4.4, the 13-round impossible differential is extended to 15 rounds.

We note that we have tested the tool by Sasaki and Todo [19], however, the tool did not stop even for 13 rounds. This is simply because of too many variables in the system, i.e. 64 more variables per round compared to the single-key setting.

### 4.1 Overall Strategy

A general strategy to maximize the number of attacked rounds can be summarized as below, which is also illustrated in Fig. 6.

1. Choose state difference so that it can cancel the subkey difference in early round(s). Then, the state does not have any difference (blank state) after the cancellation.
2. Make difference of subkeys in subsequent rounds zero for as many rounds as possible. Considering that the state difference is zero, the blank state continues until the next difference will be injected from subkey.
3. For the backward direction, do the same as the forward direction. Namely, choose difference of the last state to cancel the subkey difference in late round(s), then try to keep the blank state as many rounds as possible.
4. Subkey differences appear in the middle rounds between two blank rounds. Check if differential propagation contradicts in the middle.

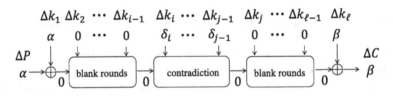

**Fig. 6.** Strategy to construct related-key impossible differentials

In Fig. 6, the initial state difference is chosen to cancel the first subkey difference $\alpha$. Then, subkey difference is zero for $i - 1$ rounds. Similarly, the last state difference is chosen to cancel the last subkey difference $\beta$, Then, subkey difference is zero for $\ell - j$ rounds.

Several 8-round iterative differences in Table 2 actually match the above strategy. Table 8 shows subkey differences for 13 rounds with ID05.

**Table 8.** Subkey difference for 13 rounds with ID05

| ID | $\Delta k_1$ | $\Delta k_2$ | $\Delta k_3$ | $\Delta k_4$ | $\Delta k_5$ | $\Delta k_6$ | $\Delta k_7$ | $\Delta k_8$ | $\Delta k_9$ | $\Delta k_{10}$ | $\Delta k_{11}$ | $\Delta k_{12}$ | $\Delta k_{13}$ |
|---|---|---|---|---|---|---|---|---|---|---|---|---|---|
| 05 | cccc | 0 | 0 | 0 | cccc | 5555 | ffff | aaaa | cccc | 0 | 0 | 0 | cccc |

We note that SIMON's key schedule does not allow subkey difference to be zero for four consecutive rounds. Thus, the differences in Table 8 take principally the longest blank rounds for both directions.

## 4.2 The Discovered Impossible Differential

The 13-round related-key impossible differential along with the state difference for ID05 is shown in Fig. 7. We note that we also searched for related-key impossible differentials starting with the differential of the form $(x, 0, 0, 0, x)$ and ending with the differential of the form $(y, 0, 0, 0, y)$, where $x \neq y$. However, the discovered impossible differentials always satisfy $x = y$, i.e. iterative difference.

Here, we show the reason why the 13-round characteristic in Fig. 7 is impossible. The reason for the first five and last five rounds are simple as discussed in Sect. 4.1. $\Delta k_1$ is canceled with plaintext difference and then blank round continues for three rounds. After that $\Delta k_5 = $ cccc is injected, which makes $\Delta L_6 \| \Delta R_6 = $ cccc$\|$0. Similarly, $\Delta k_{13}$ is canceled with ciphertext difference and then blank round continues for three rounds. After that $\Delta k_9 = $ cccc is injected, which makes $\Delta L_9 \| \Delta R_9 = 0 \|$cccc.

We then analyze the middle three rounds. Let $F(x)$ be a function defined as

$$F(x) \triangleq \big((x \lll 1) \wedge (x \lll 8)\big) \oplus (x \lll 2). \tag{8}$$

In round 6 and round 8, non-zero difference is injected to $F$. To discuss differential properties of $F$, let $F^\Delta(X)$ be a set of output differences of the round function for all the input values with difference $X$, which is defined as

$$F^\Delta(X) = \big\{ x \in \mathbb{F}_2^{16} | F(x) \oplus F(x \oplus X) \big\}. \tag{9}$$

We want to identify properties of the set $F^\Delta(\Delta L_6)$ applied to all the input values, where $\Delta L_6 = $ cccc $= 1100110011001100$. We have

$$\Delta L_6 \lll 1 = 1001100110011001,$$
$$\Delta L_6 \lll 8 = 1100110011001100, \tag{10}$$

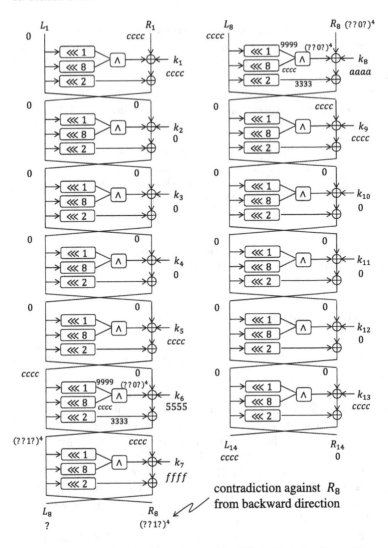

**Fig. 7.** 13-round related-key impossible differentials for SIMON32

which leads to

$$(\Delta L_6 \lll 1) \wedge (\Delta L_6 \lll 8) = ??0???0???0???0?, \qquad (11)$$

where '?' denotes that the difference can be either 0 or 1 depending on the input value, and '0' means the difference is 0 for any input value.

For convenience, we introduce the masking value $\Gamma = 2222$. Then we have

$$\Gamma \cdot \big((\Delta L_6 \lll 1) \wedge (\Delta L_6 \lll 8)\big) = 0, \qquad (12)$$

and the deterministic property of $F^\Delta(\Delta L_6)$ can be described as

$$\Gamma \cdot F^\Delta(\Delta L_6) = \Gamma \cdot \left((\Delta L_6 \lll 1) \wedge (\Delta L_6 \lll 8)\right) \oplus \Gamma \cdot (\Delta L_6 \lll 2)$$
$$= 2222. \tag{13}$$

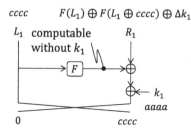

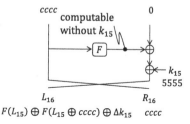

**Fig. 8.** Extension to 15 rounds (Backward)

**Fig. 9.** Extension to 15 rounds (Forward)

We now focus on the differential behavior of the following equation in the middle three rounds;

$$R_6 \oplus F(L_6) \oplus k_6 \oplus F(R_9) \oplus k_8 = L_9. \tag{14}$$

Here, $\Delta R_6$ and $\Delta L_9$ are zero. Considering that both of $\Delta L_6$ and $\Delta R_9$ are cccc, their difference after the mask is applied is canceled, i.e. $\Gamma \cdot F^\Delta(L_6) = \Gamma \cdot F^\Delta(R_9)$. In the end, the remaining terms are

$$\Gamma \cdot \Delta k_6 \oplus \Gamma \cdot \Delta k_8 = 0. \tag{15}$$

Because $\Delta k_6 = 5555$ and $\Delta k_8 = \text{aaaa}$, the above equality is never satisfied, which proves the impossibility of the 13-round differential propagation.

### 4.3 Analysis of Other Iterative Key Differences

In Table 2, besides ID05, ID06 and their variants also satisfy the longest blank rounds, thus may form 13-round related-key impossible differentials.

We first give a summary of the impossible event in Sect. 4.2. $\Delta L_6$ and $\Delta R_9$ in Eq. (14) are originally derived from $\Delta k_5$ and $\Delta k_9$ respectively. From Property 1 in Sect. 3.2, $\Delta k_5 = \Delta k_9 (= \Delta k_1)$. Thus, as long as some deterministic property exists in $F^\Delta(\Delta k_5)$, this will be canceled with $F^\Delta(\Delta k_9)$ and eventually Eq. (15) will remain. (Note that $\Gamma$ depends on $\Delta k_5$ during the analysis of $F^\Delta(\Delta k_5)$.)

In the case of ID06, there is no deterministic property in $F^\Delta(\Delta k_5)$, where $\Delta k_5 = \text{aaaa}$. Hence, a similar type of 13-round differential propagation as Fig. 7 with ID06 does not form impossible differential (it is possible to be satisfied with a non-zero probability). On the contrary, rotated-within-word variants of ID05 can build 13-round impossible differentials.

### 4.4    Extension to 15-Round Impossible Differentials

The 13-round related-key impossible differential in Fig. 7 can be extended to 15 rounds by appending 1-round in both forward and backward directions. This extension technique has been used in previous work on SIMON e.g. [25], which uses the fact that subkey is xored outside $F$ (the update function from the left to the right branch). Let us consider appending 1 round at the beginning of the 13 rounds in Fig. 7. The appended rounded is illustrated in Fig. 8.

The left half of the plaintext difference $\Delta L_1$ is cccc, thus the output difference of $F(L_1)$ cannot be computed independently of the value of $L_1$. However, $F$ is a keyless function and $L_1$ is chosen by the attacker. Thus the attacker can compute $F(L_1)$ and $F(L_1 \oplus \Delta L_1)$ independently of the key, and can choose $\Delta R_1$ to cancel $F(L_1) \oplus F(L_1 \oplus \Delta L_1) \oplus \Delta k_1$.

Similarly, the 1-round extension can be applied to the forward direction as shown in Fig. 9, which makes the 15-round relate-key impossible differential.

## 5    Conclusions

In this paper, we analyzed the linear key schedule of the SIMON-family, and searched for all iterative key differences for all members. Based on the 8-round iterative key differences, we constructed 15-round related-key impossible differentials against SIMON32, which improves the previous longest impossible differentials in the single-key setting by four rounds.

**Acknowledgments.** The work by Tetsu Iwata was supported in part by JSPS KAK-ENHI, Grant-in-Aid for Scientific Research (B), Grant Number 26280045, and was carried out while visiting Nanyang Technological University, Singapore.

## References

1. Abdelraheem, M.A., Alizadeh, J., Alkhzaimi, H.A., Aref, M.R., Bagheri, N., Gauravaram, P.: Improved linear cryptanalysis of reduced-round SIMON-32 and SIMON-48. In: Biryukov, A., Goyal, V. (eds.) INDOCRYPT 2015. LNCS, vol. 9462, pp. 153–179. Springer, Cham (2015). doi:10.1007/978-3-319-26617-6_9
2. Abed, F., List, E., Lucks, S., Wenzel, J.: Differential cryptanalysis of round-reduced Simon and Speck. In: Cid and Rechberger [12], pp. 525–545
3. Ahmadian, Z., Rasoolzadeh, S., Salmasizadeh, M., Aref, M.R.: Automated dynamic cube attack on block ciphers: Cryptanalysis of SIMON and KATAN. Cryptology ePrint Archive, Report 2015/040 (2015)
4. Alizadeh, J., Alkhzaimi, H.A., Aref, M.R., Bagheri, N., Gauravaram, P., Kumar, A., Lauridsen, M.M., Sanadhya, S.K.: Cryptanalysis of SIMON variants with connections. In: Saxena, N., Sadeghi, A.-R. (eds.) RFIDSec 2014. LNCS, vol. 8651, pp. 90–107. Springer, Cham (2014). doi:10.1007/978-3-319-13066-8_6
5. Ashur, T.: Improved linear trails for the block cipher Simon. Cryptology ePrint Archive, Report 2015/285 (2015)

6. Beaulieu, R., Shors, D., Smith, J., Treatman-Clark, S., Weeks, B., Wingers, L.: The SIMON and SPECK families of lightweight block ciphers. Cryptology ePrint Archive, Report 2013/404 (2013)
7. Biham, E., Biryukov, A., Shamir, A.: Cryptanalysis of Skipjack reduced to 31 rounds using impossible differentials. J. Cryptology 18(4), 291–311 (2005)
8. Biryukov, A., Roy, A., Velichkov, V.: Differential analysis of block ciphers SIMON and SPECK. In: Cid and Rechberger [12], pp. 546–570
9. Boura, C., Naya-Plasencia, M., Suder, V.: Scrutinizing and improving impossible differential attacks: applications to CLEFIA, Camellia, LBlock and Simon. In: Sarkar and Iwata [18], pp. 179–199
10. Chen, H., Wang, X.: Improved linear hull attack on round-reduced Simon with dynamic key-guessing techniques. Cryptology ePrint Archive, Report 2015/666 (2015)
11. Chen, Z., Wang, N., Wang, X.: Impossible differential cryptanalysis of reduced round SIMON. Cryptology ePrint Archive, Report 2015/286 (2015)
12. Cid, C., Rechberger, C. (eds.): FSE 2014. LNCS, vol. 8540. Springer, Heidelberg (2015)
13. Hao, Y., Meier, W.: Truncated differential based known-key attacks on round-reduced Simon. Cryptology ePrint Archive, Report 2016/020 (2016)
14. Knudsen, L.: DEAL - a 128-bit block cipher. In: NIST AES Proposal (1998)
15. Liu, Z., Li, Y., Wang, M.: Optimal differential trails in SIMON-like ciphers. Cryptology ePrint Archive, Report 2017/178 (2017)
16. Mourouzis, T., Song, G., Courtois, N., Christofii, M.: Advanced differential cryptanalysis of reduced-round SIMON64/128 using large-round statistical distinguishers. Cryptology ePrint Archive, Report 2015/481 (2015)
17. Raddum, H.: Algebraic analysis of the simon block cipher family. In: Lauter, K., Rodríguez-Henríquez, F. (eds.) LATINCRYPT 2015. LNCS, vol. 9230, pp. 157–169. Springer, Cham (2015). doi:10.1007/978-3-319-22174-8_9
18. Sarkar, P., Iwata, T. (eds.): ASIACRYPT 2014. LNCS, vol. 8873. Springer, Heidelberg (2014)
19. Sasaki, Y., Todo, Y.: New impossible differential search tool from design and cryptanalysis aspects. In: Coron, J.-S., Nielsen, J.B. (eds.) EUROCRYPT 2017. LNCS, vol. 10212, pp. 185–215. Springer, Cham (2017). doi:10.1007/978-3-319-56617-7_7
20. Shi, D., Hu, L., Sun, S., Song, L., Qiao, K., Ma, X.: Improved linear (hull) cryptanalysis of round-reduced versions of SIMON. Cryptology ePrint Archive, Report 2014/973 (2014)
21. Sun, S., Hu, L., Wang, M., Wang, P., Qiao, K., Ma, X., Shi, D., Song, L., Fu, K.: Constructing mixed-integer programming models whose feasible region is exactly the set of all valid differential characteristics of SIMON. Cryptology ePrint Archive, Report 2015/122 (2015)
22. Sun, S., Hu, L., Wang, P., Qiao, K., Ma, X., Song, L.: Automatic security evaluation and (related-key) differential characteristic search: application to SIMON, PRESENT, LBlock, DES(L) and other bit-oriented block ciphers. In: Sarkar and Iwata [18], pp. 158–178
23. Todo, Y., Morii, M.: Bit-based division property and application to SIMON family. In: Peyrin, T. (ed.) FSE 2016. LNCS, vol. 9783, pp. 357–377. Springer, Heidelberg (2016). doi:10.1007/978-3-662-52993-5_18
24. Wang, N., Wang, X., Jia, K., Zhao, J.: Differential attacks on reduced SIMON versions with dynamic key-guessing techniques. Cryptology ePrint Archive, Report 2014/448 (2014)

25. Wang, Q., Liu, Z., Varici, K., Sasaki, Y., Rijmen, V., Todo, Y.: Cryptanalysis of reduced-round SIMON32 and SIMON48. In: Meier, W., Mukhopadhyay, D. (eds.) INDOCRYPT 2014. LNCS, vol. 8885, pp. 143–160. Springer, Cham (2014). doi:10. 1007/978-3-319-13039-2_9
26. Xiang, Z., Zhang, W., Bao, Z., Lin, D.: Applying MILP method to searching integral distinguishers based on division property for 6 lightweight block ciphers. In: Cheon, J.H., Takagi, T. (eds.) ASIACRYPT 2016. LNCS, vol. 10031, pp. 648–678. Springer, Heidelberg (2016). doi:10.1007/978-3-662-53887-6_24
27. Xiang, Z., Zhang, W., Lin, D.: On the division property of SIMON48 and SIMON64. In: Ogawa, K., Yoshioka, K. (eds.) IWSEC 2016. LNCS, vol. 9836, pp. 147–163. Springer, Cham (2016). doi:10.1007/978-3-319-44524-3_9

# Security Analysis of a Verifiable Server-Aided Approximate Similarity Computation

Rui Xu[1(✉)], Kirill Morozov[2], Anirban Basu[1], Mohammad Shahriar Rahman[3], and Shinsaku Kiyomoto[1]

[1] KDDI Research, Inc., Fujimino, Japan
ru-xu@kddi-research.jp
[2] School of Computing, Tokyo Institute of Technology, Tokyo, Japan
[3] University of Asia Pacific, Dhaka, Bangladesh

**Abstract.** In this work, we report security analysis of the recently proposed server-aided verifiable approximate set similarity computation protocol by Qiu et al. (Security in Cloud Computing 2016). This protocol uses a certain consistency check mechanism to verify the computation result returned by a potentially malicious server. According to the original paper, the proposed consistency check can identify a misconduct of the malicious server with high probability. We show the flaws in their analysis and design a set of attacks to break their protocols (including a generalized one). Experimental results are presented that demonstrate the effectiveness of our attacks.

**Keywords:** Verifiable computation · Server-aided computation · Cryptanalysis · Privacy-preserving

## 1 Introduction

Privacy preserving computation (or multi-party computation) [15] allows two parties $P_1$ and $P_2$ to securely compute a function on their joint data but keeps their input private (and generalization to the case of more than two parties is possible). More specifically, assuming that $P_1$ has private input $x$ and $P_2$ has private input $y$, they can use privacy-preserving computation protocol to compute $f(x, y)$ for any function $f$, and $P_1$ gets no information about $y$ except what can be inferred from the output of $f(x, y)$ and her own input $x$, and the same holds for $P_2$ regarding $P_1$'s input $x$. The increasing privacy concerns stipulated by mutual interest or by law regulations require efficient and secure privacy-preserving computation tools for many applications [10].

One of the most studied applications in privacy-preserving computation is similarity computation on two sets. The Jaccard similarity [7] between two sets $A$ and $B$ – a metric for measuring how related the two sets are – has been used in many applications such as online purchase, recommender systems and

M.S. Rahman was with KDDI Research, Inc. when this work was done.

S. Obana and K. Chida (Eds.): IWSEC 2017, LNCS 10418, pp. 159–178, 2017.
DOI: 10.1007/978-3-319-64200-0_10

plagiarism detection. Since the Jaccard similarity of two sets $A$ and $B$ is defined as a rate between the size of their intersection, $|A \cap B|$, and the size of their union, $|A \cup B|$, privacy-preserving computation of this metric can be easily achieved using private set intersection protocols, which have been studied extensively (see, e.g., [4–6,11,14]). However, applying private set intersection for the Jaccard similarity computation may be undesirable, since it would be an overkill (due to the complexity overhead), and also due to a possible security flaw, since this approach also leaks the elements in the intersection. A better option is a protocol called the private set intersection cardinality primitive [3], which only reveals a cardinality of the intersection. Blundo et al. [1] proposed privacy-preserving computation protocols for the Jaccard similarity and the approximate Jaccard similarity based on the private set intersection cardinality primitive. However, these protocols are far from being scalable, if the setting of big data is considered. Finally, Qiu et al. [12] proposed to use server-aided computation to privately compute the approximate Jaccard similarity between two sets $A$ and $B$.

The scheme of Qiu et al. [12] has the following advantages:

(1) Due to using the model of server-aided computation, the proposed protocol features low computational and communication complexities.
(2) The scheme contains a consistency check mechanism to verify correctness of the computed result (the approximate Jaccard similarity of two sets) returned by the potentially malicious server.

The problem of verifiability is a crucial issue in server-aided computation since, due to various considerations, the server might not honestly follow the specific protocol. The consistency check mechanism in Qiu et al.'s protocol works as follows. Two parties $P_1$ and $P_2$ use the help of a server $S$ to compute an approximate Jaccard similarity $\sigma$ of their sets $A$ and $B$. In order to verify the correctness of $\sigma$ returned by the server, $P_1$ and $P_2$ launch another approximate Jaccard similarity computation using two other sets $D_A$ and $D_B$ and ask the server to return the approximate Jaccard similarity $\sigma_d$ of $D_A$ and $D_B$. The sets $D_A$ and $D_B$ embed some information about $A$ and $B$, which is hidden from the server. Thus, it is difficult for the server to successfully guess the relationship between $\sigma$ and $\sigma_d$. However, by knowing the hidden relation between $D_A$ and $A$ ($D_B$ and $B$) the two parties $P_1$ and $P_2$ can easily verify the correctness of the returned Jaccard similarity by checking whether the relationship between $\sigma$ and $\sigma_d$ holds.

The protocol by Qiu et al. [12] claims that the consistency check mechanism can achieve verifiability against a malicious server who cheats in the protocol execution. They argue that if the server maliciously returns an incorrect result, it should not pass the consistency check with high probability. According to their experiments, the malicious server may be identified by the consistency check mechanism with probability as high as 97%.

## 1.1 Our Contributions

In this work, we show that the protocol of Qiu et al. [12] mentioned above cannot prevent a malicious server from cheating. Specifically, we propose attacks, in which the malicious server can respond with any value as the approximate Jaccard similarity and at the same time can successfully pass the consistency check with very high probability.

**Roadmap.** We will first introduce some preliminaries to help the reader understand the notion of Jaccard similarity of two sets and its approximation in Sect. 2. Then, in Sect. 3, we review the protocols for server-aided computation of the approximate Jaccard similarity proposed in [12]. In Sect. 4, we describe the general ideas of our attacks against their protocols. Experimental demonstration of our attacks follows in Sect. 5. We conclude our work in Sect. 6.

## 2 Jaccard Similarity and Its Approximation

For the ease of referencing, we use the same notations as in Qiu et al. [12]. The Jaccard similarity (also known as the Jaccard index) [7] of two sets $A$ and $B$ is a statistical notion, which is used to measure similarity of the two sets. Specifically, it is defined as:

$$\text{SIM}(A, B) = \frac{|A \cap B|}{|A \cup B|} = \frac{|A \cap B|}{|A| + |B| - |A \cap B|}. \tag{1}$$

It is easy to see that $0 \leq \text{SIM}(A, B) \leq 1$.

The complexity of exact Jaccard similarity computation is inherently linear in the size of the two sets, thus it is not scalable to deal with large size sets. An alternative is the approximate Jaccard similarity. The MinHash technique invented by Broder [2] is an effective (and efficient) method to approximate the Jaccard similarity with high precession.

The basic idea of MinHash is to extract a small representation (called signature) of a large set through deterministic sampling and to use the signatures of two sets to estimate their actual Jaccard similarity. Formally, let $\mathcal{F}$ be a family of hash functions that map items from a set $U$ to distinct $\tau$-bit integers. Select $k$ different functions $h_1, \ldots, h_k$ from $\mathcal{F}$ and let $\min\{h_i(A)\}$ denote the minimum of the hash values $h_i(a)$ for each element $a \in A$ for a set $A \subset U$. Then the MinHash signature of set $A$ is a $k$-element set denoted by $h_{(k)}(A) = \{\min\{h_i(A)\}\}_{i=1}^{k}$. The Jaccard similarity of sets $A$ and $B$ can be estimated using their $k$-element signatures $h_k(A)$ and $h_{(k)}(B)$ as follows:

$$\text{SIM}(A, B) \approx \frac{|h_{(k)}(A) \cap h_{(k)}(B)|}{k}. \tag{2}$$

Clearly, a larger $k$ leads to more accurate approximation. The expected error of the estimate using $k$ hash functions has been shown [2] to be $\epsilon = O(1/\sqrt{k})$. We refer the readers to the textbook by Leskovec et al. [9] for details on MinHash technique and its application.

# 3    Verifiable Approximate Jaccard Similarity Protocols by Qiu et al.

In this section, we review the constructions of two protocols for verifiable approximate Jaccard similarity computation proposed by Qiu et al. [12]. Note that Qiu et al. proposed two protocols in their paper, one for semi-honest server and the other for malicious server. However, in this analysis we are only concerned with the verifiability of their second protocol. The explicitly proposed verifiable Jaccard similarity computation protocol (we also call it "the simplified protocol") is referred to as Protocol 2 in [12]. They also claimed a generalized scheme which has stronger security, but it is implicit in their original paper. In this

---

**Setup and Inputs:** Let $\mathbf{DE} = \{\mathbf{KeyGen}, \mathbf{Enc}, \mathbf{Dec}\}$ be a deterministic encryption scheme. $A$ and $B$ are the input sets for Alice and Bob, respectively, where $|A| = |B| = n$ and $A, B \subset \mathbb{D} \subset \mathbb{E}$. $\mathbb{E}$ is the universal set space. The server has no input. Set $k$ hash functions to be $\{h_1, \ldots, h_k\}$. A secret key $sk \leftarrow \mathbf{DE.KeyGen}(1^\lambda)$ is generated and privately shared between Alice and Bob.

1. Alice chooses three dummy sets $S_0, S_1, S_2 \subset \mathbb{D}' \subset \mathbb{E}$, where $\mathbb{D} \cap \mathbb{D}' = \emptyset$, $S_0$, $S_1$ and $S_2$ are disjoint sets and $|S_0| = |S_1| = |S_2| = t$. Then, Alice privately shares these three dummy sets with Bob.

2. Alice (Bob) computes the MinHash signatures from set $A$ ($B$) as
$$h_{(k)}(A) = \{\min\{h_i(A)\}\}_{i=1}^k, \quad h_{(k)}(B) = \{\min\{h_i(B)\}\}_{i=1}^k.$$

3. Alice (Bob) calculates ciphertexts of MinHash signatures as
$$T_A = \mathbf{DE.Enc}(sk, h_{(k)}(A)), \quad T_B = \mathbf{DE.Enc}(sk, h_{(k)}(B)).$$

4. Server computes the approximate Jaccard similarity of sets $A$ and $B$ as
$$\sigma_1 = \frac{|T_A \cap T_B|}{k},$$
and returns $\sigma_1$ to both clients.

5. Alice generates a dummy set $D_A = A \cup S_0 \cup S_1$, and Bob generates a dummy set $D_B = B \cup S_0 \cup S_2$.

6. Alice and Bob follow the same operations as described in Steps 2, 3, 4 to obtain the approximate Jaccard similarity of sets $D_A$ and $D_B$ as
$$\sigma_2 = \frac{|T_{D_A} \cap T_{D_B}|}{k}.$$

7. Given $\sigma_1 = \mathrm{SIM}(A, B)$ and $\sigma_2 = \mathrm{SIM}(D_A, D_B)$, Alice (Bob) outputs 1 if
$$\sigma_2 \in [f(\sigma_1 - \epsilon) - \epsilon, f(\sigma_1 + \epsilon) + \epsilon],$$
where $\epsilon = 1/\sqrt{k}$ is the estimation error and $f(x) = \frac{(2n+t)x+t}{3tx+2n+3t}$; otherwise 0.

---

**Fig. 1.** Details of Protocol 1, simplified verifiable Jaccard similarity computation.

work, we refer to their explicit (simplified) verifiable protocol as Protocol 1 and we outline their implicit (generalized) verifiable protocol and call it Protocol 2.

## 3.1  Simplified Verifiable Approximate Jaccard Similarity Computation Protocol

The simplified verifiable approximate Jaccard similarity computation protocol (Protocol 1) proposed by Qiu et al. is shown in Fig. 1. It works as follows: to get the approximate Jaccard similarity of $A$ and $B$, $\sigma_1 \approx \text{SIM}(A, B)$, Alice and Bob first extract signatures of their sets locally and then encrypt the signatures using a deterministic encryption scheme with a shared private key. The server can only see the encrypted signatures of both sets $A$ and $B$. Since the same plaintext gets encrypted to the same ciphertext, the server can compute a size of the intersection of the two signatures $|T_A \cap T_B|$. Dividing this value by $k$, the server computes the approximate Jaccard similarity of $A$ and $B$ and returns it as $\sigma_1$ to both Alice and Bob. This works correctly, if the server behaves honestly. However, a malicious server might return a different value $\sigma_1' \in [0, 1]$ instead of the correctly computed approximation $\sigma_1$. In order to verify correctness of the returned result, Protocol 1 uses a consistency check mechanism. The idea behind it is to ask the server to compute two approximate Jaccard similarities of two pairs of related sets, whose Jaccard similarity has a hidden relationship, which the server does not know. If the returned approximate Jaccard similarity of $A$ and $B$ and that of the dummy sets $D_A$ and $D_B$ satisfy a consistency check defined by a certain function $f$, then server's output is accepted and we trust it as honestly computing the result. In more detail, Alice computes a dummy set $D_A = A \cup S_0 \cup S_1$ and Bob computes a dummy set $D_B = B \cup S_0 \cup S_2$, where $A, B \subset \mathbb{D}$ and $S_0, S_1, S_2 \subset \mathbb{D}'$. In order to guarantee correctness of the verification step, the three sets $S_0, S_1, S_2$ are required to be pairwise disjoint and privately pre-agreed by Alice and Bob and $\mathbb{D} \cap \mathbb{D}' = \emptyset$.

**Consistency check.** Let $\sigma$ and $\sigma_1$ denote the exact Jaccard similarity and the actual approximate Jaccard similarity of original sets $A$ and $B$, respectively. Let $\sigma_d$ and $\sigma_2$ denote the exact Jaccard similarity and the actual approximate Jaccard similarity of dummy sets $D_A$ and $D_B$, respectively. According to the error estimation that $k$ hash functions has approximation error $O(1/\sqrt{k})$, we assume that the error does not exceed $\epsilon = 1/\sqrt{k}$. Then, we have $\sigma_1 \in [\sigma - \epsilon, \sigma + \epsilon]$ and $\sigma_2 \in [\sigma_d - \epsilon, \sigma_d + \epsilon]$ with very high probability, where $\epsilon$ is the estimation bias. Since $|A| = |B| = n$ and $|S_0| = |S_1| = |S_2| = t$, we have

$$\sigma = \frac{|A \cap B|}{2n - |A \cap B|}, \quad \sigma_d = \frac{|A \cap B| + t}{2n - |A \cap B| + 3t}.$$

Thus, we can obtain a mapping $f : \sigma \to \sigma_d$ as

$$\sigma_d = f(\sigma) = \frac{(2n + t)\sigma + t}{3t\sigma + 2n + 3t}. \tag{3}$$

Further, given $\sigma_1$, a valid range for all possible $\sigma_2$ can be computed, which is denoted as $VR_{\sigma_1} = [f(\sigma_1 - \epsilon) - \epsilon, f(\sigma_1 + \epsilon) + \epsilon]$. Let $\mathbf{Verify}(\sigma_1, \sigma_2)$ denote the verification process, which is formally defined as

$$\mathbf{Verify}(\sigma_1, \sigma_2) = \begin{cases} 1, & \text{if } \sigma_2 \in VR_{\sigma_1} \\ 0, & \text{if } \sigma_2 \notin VR_{\sigma_1} \end{cases}.$$

In order to assess the performance of their consistency check mechanism, Qiu et al. defined the following notions:

- False Positive Rate (FPR): it denotes the probability that the server honestly executes the protocol but fails to pass the consistency check process.
  $\epsilon_1 = \Pr[\mathbf{Verify}(\sigma_1, \sigma_2) = 0 \,|\, \mathbf{Honest}]$.
- False Negative Rate (FNR): it denotes the probability that the server performs maliciously, but the consistency check indicates it is honest.
  $\epsilon_2 = \Pr[\mathbf{Verify}(\sigma_1, \sigma_2) = 1 \,|\, \mathbf{Malicious}]$.

Clearly, the false positive rate $\epsilon_1$ depends on the estimation accuracy of the approximate Jaccard similarity, i.e., the number of hash functions used, which is $k$. Moreover, a smaller false negative rate $\epsilon_2$ indicates a better scheme, since the probability that a malicious server gets away from being identified is smaller.

## 3.2  Generalized Verifiable Approximate Jaccard Similarity Computation Protocol

In the description of Protocol 1, Qiu et al. emphasized that the three dummy sets $S_0$, $S_1$, $S_2$ need not be of the same size. However, they did not explicitly present a protocol, where the three dummy sets have different sizes and their analysis on the verifiability does not apply to this generalized case. Thus, for the sake of completeness and easy reference for our attack on the generalized protocol, we outline the protocol where $S_0$, $S_1$ and $S_2$ have different sizes, and present it as Protocol 2 in Fig. 2. Protocol 2 is almost identical to Protocol 1, except that the three dummy sets $S_0$, $S_1$ and $S_2$ have sizes $t_0$, $t_1$ and $t_2$, respectively, and the mapping $f : \sigma \to \sigma_d$ differs.

**Consistency check.** The same idea applies in this generalized consistency check process, but now we need to evaluate a different map from the Jaccard similarity of $A$, $B$ to that of $D_A$, $D_B$. Let $\sigma$, $\sigma_1$ denote the exact Jaccard similarity and the actual approximate Jaccard similarity of the original sets $A$ and $B$, respectively. Let $\sigma_d$ and $\sigma_2$ denote the exact Jaccard similarity and the actual approximate Jaccard similarity of dummy sets $D_A$ and $D_B$, respectively. Since $|A| = |B| = n$ and $|S_0| = t_0$, $|S_1| = t_1$, $|S_2| = t_2$, we have

$$\sigma = \frac{|A \cap B|}{2n - |A \cap B|}, \quad \sigma_d = \frac{|A \cap B| + t_0}{2n - |A \cap B| + t_0 + t_1 + t_2}.$$

Then, the following mapping $f : \sigma \to \sigma_d$ can be obtained:

$$\sigma_d = f(\sigma) = \frac{2n\sigma + (1 + \sigma)t_0}{2n + (t_0 + t_1 + t_2)(1 + \sigma)}. \tag{4}$$

**Setup and Inputs:** Let $\mathbf{DE} = \{\mathbf{KeyGen}, \mathbf{Enc}, \mathbf{Dec}\}$ be a deterministic encryption scheme. $A$ and $B$ are the inputs sets for Alice and Bob, respectively, where $|A| = |B| = n$ and $A, B \subset \mathbb{D} \subset \mathbb{E}$. $\mathbb{E}$ is the universal set space. The server has no input. Set $k$ hash functions to be $\{h_1, \ldots, h_k\}$. A secret key $sk \leftarrow \mathbf{DE.KeyGen}(1^\lambda)$ is generated and privately shared between Alice and Bob.

1. Alice chooses three dummy sets $S_0, S_1, S_2 \subset \mathbb{D}' \subset \mathbb{E}$, where $\mathbb{D} \cap \mathbb{D}' = \emptyset$, $S_0$, $S_1$ and $S_2$ are disjoint sets and $|S_0| = t_0$, $|S_1| = t_1$, $|S_2| = t_2$. Then, Alice privately shares three dummy sets with Bob.
2. Alice (Bob) computes the MinHash signatures from set $A$ $(B)$ as

$$h_{(k)}(A) = \{\min\{h_i(A)\}\}_{i=1}^k, \quad h_{(k)}(B) = \{\min\{h_i(B)\}\}_{i=1}^k.$$

3. Alice (Bob) calculates ciphertexts of MinHash signatures as

$$T_A = \mathbf{DE.Enc}(sk, h_{(k)}(A)), \quad T_B = \mathbf{DE.Enc}(sk, h_{(k)}(B)).$$

4. Server computes the approximate Jaccard similarity of sets $A$ and $B$ as

$$\sigma_1 = \frac{|T_A \cap T_B|}{k},$$

and returns $\sigma_1$ to both clients.
5. Alice generates a dummy set $D_A = A \cup S_0 \cup S_1$, and Bob generates a dummy set $D_B = B \cup S_0 \cup S_2$.
6. Alice and Bob follow the same operations as described in Steps 2, 3, 4 to obtain the approximate Jaccard similarity of sets $D_A$ and $D_B$ as

$$\sigma_2 = \frac{|T_{D_A} \cap T_{D_B}|}{k}.$$

7. Given $\sigma_1 = \mathrm{SIM}(A, B)$ and $\sigma_2 = \mathrm{SIM}(D_A, D_B)$, Alice (Bob) outputs 1 if

$$\sigma_2 \in [f(\sigma_1 - \epsilon) - \epsilon, f(\sigma_1 + \epsilon) + \epsilon],$$

where $\epsilon = 1/\sqrt{k}$ is the estimation error and $f(x) = \frac{2nx+(1+x)t_0}{2n+(t_0+t_1+t_2)(1+x)}$; otherwise 0.

**Fig. 2.** Protocol 2, generalized verifiable Jaccard similarity computation.

Since we take $\epsilon = 1/\sqrt{k}$, then given $\sigma_1$, a valid range for all possible $\sigma_2$ can be computed, which is denoted as $VR_{\sigma_1} = [f(\sigma_1 - \epsilon) - \epsilon, f(\sigma_1 + \epsilon) + \epsilon]$. $\mathbf{Verify}(\sigma_1, \sigma_2)$ and the notion of FNR can be defined similarly.

# 4    Cryptanalysis of Qiu et al.'s Verifiable Approximate Jaccard Similarity Protocols

In this section, we propose several attacks against both the simplified verifiable approximate Jaccard similarity computation protocol, i.e., Protocol 1 as listed in Fig. 1, as well as the generalized Protocol 2 as defined in the previous section.

Since in the original paper [12], Qiu et al. just presented the simplified protocol and their discussion on the performance of the consistency check mechanism explicitly used the assumption that the three dummy sets $S_0, S_1, S_2$ all have the same size $t$, we start with attacks on the simplified protocol.

## 4.1   Attacks on the Simplified Protocol

The basic idea of the consistency check mechanism in the simplified protocol is as follows: since Alice and Bob construct the dummy sets $D_A = A \cup S_0 \cup S_1$, $D_B = B \cup S_0 \cup S_1$ using their pre-agreed dummy sets $S_0, S_1, S_2$, they will share a mapping $\sigma_2 = f(\sigma_1) = \frac{(2n+t)\sigma_1+t}{3t\sigma_1+2n+3t}$, which is hidden from the server. The server cannot know the mapping, because both $n$ and $t$ are secret values shared by Alice and Bob. Thus, in order to pass the consistency check, the server has to provide two forged Jaccard similarities $\sigma_1'$ and $\sigma_2'$ such that they satisfy the secret mapping within the expected bias range.

In fact, there was no rigorous proof of verifiability of Protocol 1 in the original paper. In order to evaluate the performance of the consistency check mechanism, three kinds of malicious behaviors were assumed and the FNR against the three cases were computed to show that the FNR for these cases are small enough, which was to demonstrate effectiveness of the proposed consistency check mechanism. Specifically, the behavior of the malicious server is classified into the following three cases [12]:

(1)  the server returns a Jaccard similarity randomly chosen from $[0, 1]$ without any calculations,
(2)  the server returns a Jaccard similarity computed from a subset of MinHash signatures, which will lead to a degraded level of accuracy, and
(3)  the server deliberately returns an incorrect result with a certain offset $\theta$ based on the real result via complete computation.

Unfortunately, we will show that the consistency check mechanism proposed by Qiu et al. does not work. In fact, we propose attacks, which allow a malicious server to return any Jaccard similarity randomly chosen from $[0, 1]$ and to pass the consistency check with high probability. These attacks fall into case (1) in the above classification[1]. The flaws in the argument of Qiu et al. are twofold:

(1)  In the computation of FNR for case I, they assume that the malicious server returns forged approximate Jaccard similarities $\sigma_1'$ and $\sigma_2'$, both arbitrarily. However, a determined malicious server can choose a random Jaccard similarity $\sigma_1'$ for the intended sets $A$ and $B$, but carefully computes a Jaccard similarity $\sigma_2'$ for the dummy sets $D_A$ and $D_B$ based on the forged $\sigma_1'$, which will help it to pass the consistency check with high probability. This probability is high enough so that the clients Alice and Bob cannot distinguish whether the server is malicious or not.

---

[1] The authors of the original paper [12] pointed out to us [13] that our attacks do not correspond to case (1) in their definition, since there they restrict the malicious server to answering both Jaccard similarities arbitrarily. However, we see no justification for such a limitation on the malicious server's behavior in reality.

(2) A fatal reasoning in their argument is that since the server knows neither $n$ nor $t$, it cannot successfully forge $\sigma_2'$ for an incorrect $\sigma_1'$. However, we show that the important information is not $n$ or $t$, but the ratio between $n$ and $t$, which the server can derive using the true values of $\sigma_1$ and $\sigma_2$. After deriving an estimate of the ratio between $n$ and $t$, the server can forge an arbitrary Jaccard similarity without being identified.

Before going into the details of our attacks, we formulate the attack model as a game between challenger $C$ and malicious server $S$. We denote it as Game 1, and describe it in Fig. 3. In this figure, we omit the deterministic encryption step for simplicity, since it does not affect the verifiability of Protocol 1.

---

**Setup and Inputs:** Let $\mathbb{D}, \mathbb{D}' \subset \mathbb{E}$ and $\mathbb{D} \cap \mathbb{D}' = \emptyset$, where $\mathbb{E}$ is the universal set space. Let $k$ hash functions be $\{h_1, \ldots, h_k\}$.

1. $C$ generates two sets $A, B \subset \mathbb{D}$ with $|A| = |B| = n$, and three dummy sets $S_0, S_1, S_2 \subset \mathbb{D}'$ with $|S_0| = |S_1| = |S_2| = t$, where $S_i$'s are pairwise disjoint.
2. $C$ computes the $k$-element signatures of sets $A$ and $B$ as $h_{(k)}(A)$ and $h_{(k)}(B)$ and sends them to $S$.
3. $S$ returns a randomly chosen similarity $\sigma_1'$ as a estimation of the Jaccard similarity of $A$ and $B$ and sends it to $C$.
4. $C$ computes the $k$-element signatures of sets $D_A$ and $D_B$ as $h_{(k)}(D_A)$ and $h_{(k)}(D_B)$ and sends them to $S$.
5. $S$ returns the approximate Jaccard similarity $\sigma_2'$ as an estimation of the Jaccard similarity of $D_A$ and $D_B$ and sends it to $C$.
6. $C$ computes $VR_{\sigma_1'} = [f(\sigma_1' - \epsilon) - \epsilon, f(\sigma_1' + \epsilon) + \epsilon]$ using the mapping $f$ as shown in Equation (3). If $\sigma_2' \in VR_{\sigma_1'}$, $C$ outputs 1 indicating that $S$ has won the game; otherwise it outputs 0 and $S$ loses in the game.

---

**Fig. 3.** Game 1 between the challenger and the malicious server.

We now discuss our attack on Protocol 1. We want to construct an algorithm, which wins Game 1 with high probability. In Step 2 of Game 1, the challenger sends two signatures of sets $A$ and $B$ as $h_{(k)}(A)$ and $h_{(k)}(B)$, respectively. After receiving the signatures, the malicious server $S$ honestly computes the approximate Jaccard similarity between $A$ and $B$ as $\sigma_1 = \frac{|h_{(k)}(A) \cap h_{(k)}(B)|}{k}$, returns a randomly chosen similarity $\sigma_1'$ and sends it to $C$ in Step 3. Then, after receiving the signatures $h_{(k)}(D_A)$ and $h_{(k)}(D_B)$ for the dummy sets $D_A$ and $D_B$ from $C$ in Step 5, the malicious server $S$ computes the correct approximate Jaccard similarity of $D_A$ and $D_B$ as $\sigma_2 = \frac{|h_{(k)}(D_A) \cap h_{(k)}(D_B)|}{k}$. Now, the server $S$ knows both $\sigma_1$ and $\sigma_2$. Assume that $t = sn$, where $s$ denotes the ratio between $t$ and $n$, we can rewrite Eq. (3) as

$$\sigma_d = f(\sigma) = \frac{(2+s)\sigma + s}{3s\sigma + (2+3s)}. \tag{5}$$

Since the server $S$ knows both the approximate Jaccard similarity of $\sigma$ and $\sigma_d$ as $\sigma_1$ and $\sigma_2$, respectively, $S$ can effectively estimate the ratio $s$ between $t$ and $n$. Then, $S$ substitutes $\sigma$ and $\sigma_d$ in Eq. (5) by $\sigma_1$ and $\sigma_2$, respectively, and solves for $s$ to get its estimation denoted by $s'$. Using $s'$, $S$ can now calculate $\sigma_2'$ for a forged approximate Jaccard similarity of $D_A$ and $D_B$ as

$$\sigma_2' = \frac{(2 + s')\sigma_1' + s'}{3s'\sigma_1' + (2 + 3s')}. \tag{6}$$

Since $(\sigma_1, \sigma_2)$ are the approximations for $(\sigma, \sigma_d)$ with bounded bias $\epsilon$, $s'$ is also an approximation of $s$ with some bounded bias $\eta$, the forged pair $(\sigma_1', \sigma_2')$ computed via Eq. (5) by using $s'$ (as an approximation of $s$) can pass the consistency check with high probability. It is possible to compute the estimation bias $\eta$ and then to compute the exact probability that a forged pair generated by this method passes the consistency check. However, the analytical solution turns out to be quite complicated, and therefore, we will use experiments to demonstrate effectiveness of our attack in the next section.

### 4.2    Attacks on the Generalized Protocol

Again, we first formulate an attack against the generalized Protocol 2 as a game between a challenger $C$ and a malicious server $S$ (denoted as Game 2). We omit its detailed description due to lack of space. The only difference between Game 2 and Game 1 is that in Game 2, the three dummy sets $S_0, S_1, S_2$ are now of different sizes and the description of the secret mapping $f$ is different.

We follow the main idea of the attack against the simplified Protocol and express $t_0 = s_0 n$, $t_1 = s_1 n$ and $t_2 = s_2 n$. Plugging this in to Eq. (4), we can rewrite it as

$$\sigma_d = f(\sigma) = \frac{(2 + s_0)\sigma + s_0}{2 + (s_0 + s_1 + s_2)(1 + \sigma)}. \tag{7}$$

However, even though the server $S$ gets both of the approximate Jaccard similarities $\sigma_1$ and $\sigma_2$ for the exact Jaccard similarities $\sigma$ and $\sigma_d$, it cannot correctly infer the values of $s_0, s_1, s_2$. A careful inspection of Eq. (7) tells us that only $s_0$ and the sum $s_0 + s_1 + s_2$ are needed. Still, we would not know how to compute or estimate these values based on only $\sigma_1$ and $\sigma_2$.

We change our focus to another direction: Note that in Game 2, $C$ needs to send $h_{(k)}(A)$ and $h_{(k)}(B)$ to $S$, and the server also receives $h_{(k)}(D_A)$ and $h_{(k)}(D_B)$ from the challenger $C$. All the four signatures have size $k$. The server also knows that $h_{(k)}(A)$ is the $k$-element signature for the set $A$ and $h_{(k)}(D_A)$ is the $k$-element signature for the dummy set $D_A$ with $D_A = A \cup S_0 \cup S_1$. Notice that $|A| = n$, $|D_A| = n + t_0 + t_1$ and $|A \cap D_A| = n$.

Now, we ask the following question: *Given two sets $A$ and $D_A$, where $A \subset D_A$, can we approximate the ratio between $|A|$ and $|D_A|$ using their $k$-element signatures $h_{(k)}(A)$ and $h_{(k)}(D_A)$?*

Consider the elements in $h_{(k)}(A)$ and $h_{(k)}(D_A)$. The $i$-th element in $h_{(k)}(A)$ is $A_i = \min\{h_i(a) | a \in A\}$ and the $i$-th element in $h_{(k)}(D_A)$ is $D_{Ai} = \min\{h_i(d$

This algorithm includes two phases: learning phase and guessing phase. The server executes the following steps in each phases.

**Learning phase** (run once and for all):

1. Generates random sets $S_1$ and $S_2$ with the constraint that $|S_2| = (1 + \rho)|S_1|$ and $S_1 \subset S_2$.
2. Computes the signatures of $S_1$ and $S_2$ as $h_{(k)}(S_1)$ and $h_{(k)}(S_2)$ using a fixed set of $k$ hash functions.
3. Computes $y = |h_{(k)}(S_1) \cap h_{(k)}(S_2)|$ and records the pair $(y, \rho)$.
4. Repeats the previous three steps for fixed $\rho$ and average the value of $y$'s to get the $\bar{y}$.
5. Repeats the previous four steps for different $\rho$'s and record a list of pairs $(\bar{y}_i, \rho_i)$ denoted by $L$.

**Guessing phase:**

1. When receiving two signatures of the sets $A$ and $D_A$ from the challenger $C$, the server $S$ computes the number of common elements in $h_{(k)}(A)$ and $h_{(k)}(D_A)$ and denote it as $\hat{y}$.
2. The server $S$ searches the list $L$ and finds two nearest items with respect to the $y$'s value, which are denoted as $(\bar{y}_a, \rho_a)$ and $(\bar{y}_b, \rho_b)$.
3. The server uses linear interpolation to compute a guess of the ratio between $t_0 + t_1$ and $n$ as $\hat{\rho}$.

**Fig. 4.** Algorithm 1 for guessing the relative size between $A$ and $D_A$.

$|d \in D_A\}$. The probability that $A_i = D_{Ai}$ equals the probability of the event that for every $e \in D_A \backslash A$, $h_i(e) \geq A_i$. The exact probability depends on the value of $A_i$, but intuitively, the larger the difference set $D_A \backslash A$ is, the less possible that $A_i = D_{Ai}$ holds. This heuristics shows a way to guess the relative size of $A$ and $D_A$. We propose to use Algorithm 1 as listed in Fig. 4 to guess the ratio between the sizes $|A|$ and $|D_A|$. Algorithm 1 works because there is a clear relation between the intersection of signatures of $A$ and $B$ with $A \subset B$ and the ratio between the size of $B$ and that of $A$. Algorithm 1 first employs an offline learning phase (Steps 1–5) to learn the relation between $y = |h_{(k)}(A) \cap h_{(k)}(B)|$ and $\rho$, i.e., the list $L$. After that, when given a challenge $\hat{y}$, the algorithm searches through the list $L$ and finds an approximate $\hat{\rho}$. We will show experimental evidence that validates the above approach in Sect. 5.

We can now discuss our attack on Protocol 2. First denote $t_0 + t_1 = \rho_A n$ and $t_0 + t_2 = \rho_B n$. Then, we have $|D_A| = (1 + \rho_A)|A|$ and $|D_B| = (1 + \rho_B)|B|$. Recall that $t_0 = s_0 n$, $t_1 = s_1 n$ and $t_2 = s_2 n$, from which it follows that $s_0 + s_1 = \rho_A$ and $s_0 + s_2 = \rho_B$. In Game 2, the malicious server $S$ receives $h_k(A)$, $h_k(B)$, $h_k(D_A)$ and $h_k(D_B)$ from the challenger $C$. The server $S$ can apply Algorithm 1 to get estimations of $\rho_A$ and $\rho_B$ denoted as $\rho'_A$ and $\rho'_B$, respectively. Substituting $s_0 + s_1 = \rho_A$ and $s_0 + s_2 = \rho_B$ into Eq. (4), we can get

$$\sigma_d = f(\sigma) = \frac{2\sigma + (1 + \sigma)s_0}{2 + (1 + \sigma)(\rho_A + \rho_B - s_0)} \tag{8}$$

In the same manner as with the previous attack against Protocol 1, here the server $S$ first returns a randomly chosen Jaccard similarity $\sigma_1'$ for the approximation of $SIM(A, B)$ and then correctly computes the approximate Jaccard similarity for both $A$ and $B$ and the dummy sets $D_A$ and $D_B$ as $\sigma_1$ and $\sigma_2$. Since $S$ knows the approximate Jaccard similarity of both $\sigma$ and $\sigma_d$, as $\sigma_1$ and $\sigma_2$, respectively, it can effectively estimate the ratio $s_0$ between $t_0$ and $n$ by substituting $\sigma$ with $\sigma_1$, $\sigma_d$ with $\sigma_2$, $\rho_A$ with $\rho_A'$ and $\rho_B$ with $\rho_B'$, respectively, in Eq. (8). After this step, $S$ gets an approximation of $s_0$ as $s_0'$. Thus, $S$ can now calculate $\sigma_2'$ for a forged approximate Jaccard similarity of $D_A$ and $D_B$ as

$$\sigma_2' = \frac{2\sigma_1' + (1 + \sigma_1')s_0'}{2 + (1 + \sigma_1')(\rho_A' + \rho_B' - s_0')}. \tag{9}$$

## 5    Experimental Demonstration of Our Attacks

Since we are only concerned with verifiability of the proposed protocols, we ignore the deterministic encryption scheme. This does not affect our attacks, since they work regardless of the encryption. We do not focus on the efficiency of the proposed scheme,, so that we use synthesized data with a moderate size to demonstrate our attacks. Specifically in our experiments, the size of sets $A$ and $B$ is $n = |A| = |B| = 1000$. Following the parameter setting in the original paper, we choose $t$, which is the size of the three dummy sets $S_0, S_1, S_2$ from the interval $[0.1n, n]$. In the generalized protocol, the dummy sets have different size $t_0, t_1, t_2$ which are also chosen from $[0.1n, n]$.

We choose $A, B \subset \mathbb{D}$, where $\mathbb{D}$ is the set of random real numbers from $(0, 1)$ with certain precision. In order to make the sets $S_0, S_1, S_2$ pairwise disjoint and do not intersect with $\mathbb{D}$, we choose $S_0$ from random real numbers in the interval $(1, 2)$, $S_1$ from $(2, 3)$ and $S_2$ from $(3, 4)$, respectively. We use Python 2 to implement the proposed attacks. The MinHash primitive comes from the library Datasketch [16].

### 5.1    Experimental Results of Attack Against Protocol 1

For easy reference, we recall our attack against Protocol 1 in Fig. 5. In the following, we assume $n = 1000$ and $t \in [0.1n, n]$. We consider different numbers of hash functions, including $k = 50, 200, 400$ to illustrate the false negative rate of our attack described in Fig. 5.

We first fix $n = 1000$ and $t = 500$ to implement our attack. Figure 6 shows the average FNR (averaged over 5000 tests) of a malicious server using our attack strategy described in Fig. 5 for different Jaccard similarity $\sigma$ of the sets $A$ and $B$. From the figure, we can observe that the FNR is very high so that it exceeds 90% for most choices of $\sigma$, except for $\sigma = 0.3$ (the FNR when $\sigma = 0.3$ is about 50%). This abnormal effect can be explained using Eq. (5), which describes the relation between $s$ and the Jaccard similarities $\sigma$ and $\sigma_d$. When solving this equation to get $s$, we have

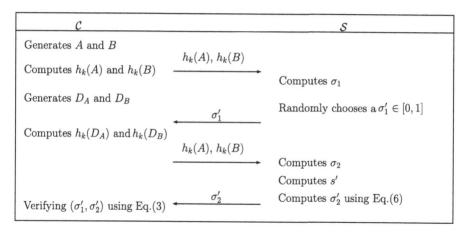

Fig. 5. Our attack against Protocol 1.

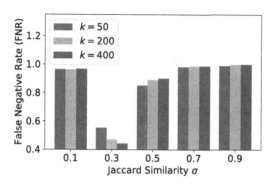

Fig. 6. Distribution of the average FNR for attacking Protocol 1

$$s = \frac{2(\sigma - \sigma_d)}{(3\sigma_d - 1)(1 + \sigma)}. \tag{10}$$

From Eq. (10) we can see that when $\sigma_d$ is $1/3$, the denominator is 0. In the attack, the server $S$ uses the approximate Jaccard similarities $\sigma_1$ and $\sigma_2$ to estimate $s'$. In the numerical evaluation, this could blow up the estimated ratio $s'$ when $\sigma_2$ is very close to $1/3$. In our experiments, we have $n = 1000$ and $t = 500$, thus $s = 0.5$. By Eq. (3), we have $\sigma_d = 0.3165$ when $\sigma = 0.3$. However, the server will use the approximate Jaccard similarity $\sigma_2$ to estimate $s$ and get $s'$. Note that Eq. (10) is very sensitive around $\sigma_d = 1/3$. Thus, the estimated $s'$ would differ from its true value $s = 0.5$ very substantially. To illustrate this, we have drawn the graph of Eq. (10) by fixing $\sigma$ and substituting $\sigma_d$ with varying $\sigma_2 \in [0.95\sigma_d, 1.05\sigma_d]$. From Fig. 7, we can see that when $\sigma = 0.3$, the estimated ratio $s'$ can easily deviate a lot from its true value 0.5, while for the case of $\sigma = 0.7$, the estimated ratio $s'$ is bounded by some fixed value.

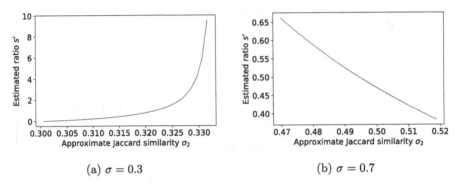

Fig. 7. The estimated ratio $s'$ using approximate Jaccard similarity $\sigma_2$

**A trivial attack against Protocol 1.** A close look at Eq. (5) gives us a much more trivial attack against Protocol 1. Notice that when $\sigma = 1/3$ in Eq. (5), $\sigma_d = 1/3$ holds for any value of $s$. Therefore, the trivial attack for the malicious server is just returning $1/3$ as the Jaccard similarity for any computation request, no matter whether it is for computing $SIM(A, B)$ or $SIM(D_A, D_B)$. The consistency check will always identify the returned pair $(1/3, 1/3)$ as valid.

Although by sending fixed Jaccard similarity as $1/3$ the server can pass the consistency check with high probability, this kind of trivial attack is limited. However, the malicious server can do better. Figure 7a illustrates the fact that the estimated ratio $s'$ is quite sensitive when $\sigma = 0.3$. If we look at it in the dual way, it also suggests that when $\sigma = 0.3$, the Jaccard similarity $\sigma_d$ of the dummy sets $D_A$ and $D_B$ changes smoothly with respect to $s$. In other words, when $\sigma$ is near to $1/3$, $\sigma_d$ does not vary too much for different $s$ (i.e., $t$). Based on this observation, we propose another attack, where the server randomly chooses a value $\sigma_1'$ close to $1/3$ and computes the corresponding $\sigma_2'$ by assuming that $s' = 0.55$. Let us discuss this point: First of all, it seems that $\sigma_1'$ does not need to be too close to $1/3$. In fact, in our experiments, we observe that for a wide range of the forged Jaccard similarity $\sigma_1'$, the consistency check cannot identify the fact of forgery. Second, we assume $s' = 0.55$, since the protocol specifies that $s \in [0.1, 1]$, and hence we use the average value $0.55$ for the attack.

We first investigate the FNR of the above mentioned attack for different ranges of $\sigma_1'$. We fix $n = 1000$, $k = 200$, $\sigma = 0.5$ and divide the whole range $[0, 1]$ into intervals of equal size $0.05$. Then, we restrict the server to forge $\sigma_1'$ inside these intervals and count the average FNR (over 5000 trials) for them. Figure 8 shows the average FNR of the attack along the range of $[0, 1]$, where the left one uses $s = 0.1$ and the right one uses $s = 1$. Surprisingly, the simple attack by just setting the estimate of $s$ to $s' = 0.55$, randomly forging a Jaccard similarity $\sigma_1'$ and computing $\sigma_2'$ accordingly using Eq. (6) turns out to work pretty well. This is because FNR is 1 over the range $[0, 0.6]$ seen from both graphs, at least for the case when $\sigma = 0.5$. There are two main parameters, the actual Jaccard similarity $\sigma = SIM(A, B)$ and the ratio between the size of dummy set and that of task set $s = t/n$, which affect the FNR of the above attack. Next, we restrict

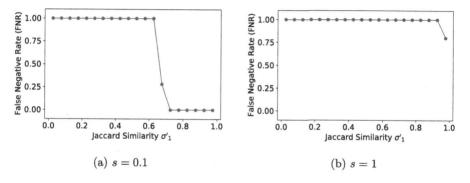

(a) $s = 0.1$ · · · · · · · · · · · · · · · · · · (b) $s = 1$

**Fig. 8.** Average FNR over the range of $\sigma'_1$ for fixed $\sigma = 0.5$.

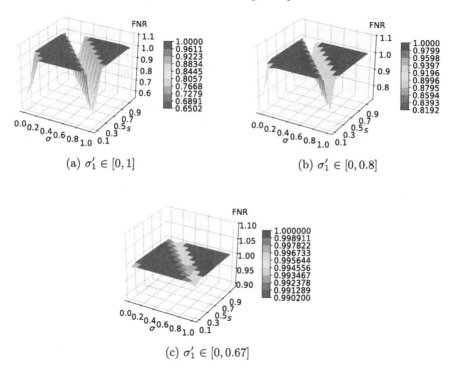

(a) $\sigma'_1 \in [0, 1]$ · · · · · · · · · · · (b) $\sigma'_1 \in [0, 0.8]$

(c) $\sigma'_1 \in [0, 0.67]$

**Fig. 9.** Distribution of average FNR over the choices of $\sigma$ and $s$.

the server to forge the approximate Jaccard similarity $\sigma'_1$ from the interval $[l, h]$ and vary $\sigma \in [0, 1]$ and $s \in [0.1, 1]$ to access the FNR for different pairs of values for $(\sigma, s)$. We choose $\sigma = 0, 0.1, \ldots, 1$ and $s = 0.1, 0.2, \cdots, 1$ and run the attack 5000 times to get the average FNR. The results are shown in Fig. 9. The first sub-figure shows the distribution of FNR when the server's forged Jaccard similarity is chosen randomly from $[0, 1]$ (the most general case). The bottom of the colorbar indicates the minimum of FNR which is 64.9%. From Fig. 9b and c, we can see that by limiting the range for $\sigma'_1$, the FNR boosts rapidly. In our experiments, when $\sigma'_1$ is chosen from the range $[0, 0.66]$, the FNR is always 1, which means the consistency check mechanism fails under this attack.

## 5.2 Performance of Algorithm 1

In order to verify the above approach, we performed the following experiments. A set $A$ of size $n = 1000$ is randomly chosen and a set $B = A \cup S$ with $|S| = t$ is then generated with the set $S$ being disjoint with $A$. In the implementation, the set $A$ includes random numbers from $[0.0, 1.0)$ and the set $S$ includes random numbers from $[1.0, 2.0)$. We vary the value of $t$ at $t = 100$ and $t = 500$ to see the size of the intersection between the signatures of $A$ and $B$, i.e., $|h_k(A) \cap h_k(B)|$. Figure 10 shows the results of running the experiments 200 times using $k = 100$ and $k = 300$, respectively. From the figures, we can see that when $t$ is smaller, the number of common elements between the signatures of $A$ and $B$ is larger. Moreover, the comparison between Fig. 10a and b indicates that the more hash functions we use to calculate the signature the more accurate the relation between $|h_k(A) \cap h_k(B)|$ and $t$ is. Figure 11 shows the average value of the intersection size between $h_k(A)$ and $h_k(B)$ ($k$ is fixed as 300 in the plot), where $A \subset B$ and $|B| = (1 + \rho)|A|$, for $\rho$ ranging from 0.1 to 1. From Fig. 11, we can see that the number of common elements in the two signatures decreases when $\rho$ increases. The curve describing their relationship is not necessarily a line but for simplicity, we use linear interpolation to guess $\hat{\rho}$ when given two challenge signatures $h_k(A)$ and $h_k(D_A)$, which have $\hat{y}$ common elements in Algorithm 1.

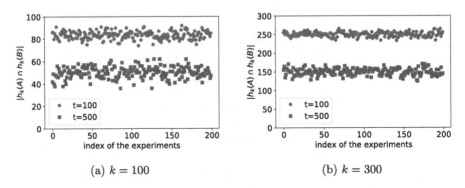

(a) $k = 100$                    (b) $k = 300$

**Fig. 10.** Number of common elements between MinHash signatures of $A$ and $B$.

## 5.3 Experimental Results of Attack Against Protocol 2

We recall the attack against Protocol 2 in Fig. 12. In the following, we assume $n = 1000$ and $t_0, t_1, t_2 \in [0.1n, n]$. We consider a different number of hash functions, including $k = 50, 200, 400$ to illustrate the false negative rate of our attack described in Fig. 12. Since here we have four parameters $t_0, t_1, t_2, \sigma$, which affect

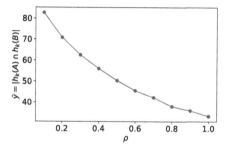

**Fig. 11.** Average of $|h_k(A) \cap h_k(B)|$ with $A \subset B$ and $|B| = (1 + \rho)|A|$.

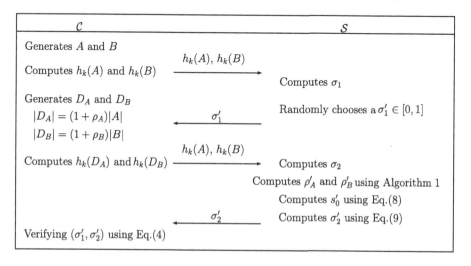

**Fig. 12.** Our attack against Protocol 2.

the FNR of the attack, it is difficult to visualize the FNR under different combinations of these parameters. Thus, we choose to vary $\sigma$ from 0.1 to 0.9 with a step of 0.2 and to randomly generate $t_0, t_1, t_2 \in [0.1n, n]$ in the attack and compute the average FNR over 5000 trials for each $\sigma$. Figure 13 illustrate the FNR for different choice of $\sigma$ and $k$. From Fig. 13, we can see that our proposed attack against Protocol 2 works very well. For randomly generated $t_0, t_1, t_2$ and for each choice of $\sigma$, the malicious server can forge any value as the approximate Jaccard similarity and pass the consistency check with probability above 99%.

A careful reader might wonder why the performance of the attack against Protocol 2 works better than that of the attack against Protocol 1, by comparing Figs. 6 and 13.

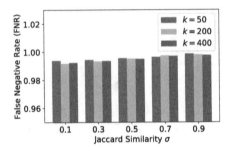

**Fig. 13.** Distribution of the average FNR for attacking Protocol 2.

Let us discuss this phenomenon: The attack against Protocol 1 just uses the approximate Jaccard similarity $\sigma_1$ and $\sigma_2$, while the attack against Protocol 2 uses the signatures $h_k(A)$ and $h_k(D_A)$ to obtain further information on the relation between the task set $A$ and the dummy set $D_A$.

Most importantly, when we estimate $s$ in Attack 1 using Eq. (10), there is a singular point at $\sigma_d = 1/3$. Consequently, for certain values of $\sigma$ and $s$, $\sigma_d$ is close to $1/3$. For example, when $\sigma = 0.1$ and $s = 0.5$, the expected value of $\sigma_d$ is 0.315. Using an approximate Jaccard similarity $\sigma_2$ for $\sigma_d$ and substituting it into Eq. (10) may cause unexpected blowup of the estimated $s'$ (since $\sigma_2$ may be very close to $1/3$) and thus decrease the accuracy of our attack. However, there is no such problem in Attack 2. Solving Eq. (8) to get $s_0$, we obtain

$$s_0 = \frac{2(\sigma_d - \sigma) + \sigma_d(1 + \sigma)(\rho_A + \rho_B)}{(\sigma + 1)(\sigma_d + 1)}.$$

No matter which estimation we get for $\sigma, \sigma_d, \rho_A, \rho_B$, there is no singular point in the above equation so that our attack against Protocol 2 is more robust.

We have also performed experiments to attack Protocol 1 by the method used for attacking Protocol 2. The tweak is simply setting $t_0 = t_1 = t_2$ in our experiments of Attack 2. The experimental results show no difference from Fig. 13, hence they are omitted from this work for the sake of conciseness.

## 6    Conclusion

In this paper, we investigated the protocols proposed by Qiu et al. [12], which are expected to be used for verifiable server-aided computation of Jaccard similarity between two sets $A$ and $B$. Though these protocols are claimed to be secure, we proposed several attack methods against both their simplified protocol and a generalized one. Our attacks allow a malicious server to return an arbitrary value as the expected result without being identified by the verification mechanism in Qiu et al., which means that our attacks can fully break their protocols. Extensive experimental results have shown that our attacks work effectively in practice.

Unfortunately, we were not able to find an easy fix for the above protocols. However, an existing protocol for the same task can be found in Kamara et al. [8], where a similar interactive design based on dummy sets is used to verify the behavior of a cloud server.

**Acknowledgement.** The authors are grateful to the anonymous reviewers of IWSEC 2017 for their constructive comments that helped improve the presentation of this work.

# References

1. Blundo, C., Cristofaro, E., Gasti, P.: EsPRESSo: efficient privacy-preserving evaluation of sample set similarity. In: Pietro, R., Herranz, J., Damiani, E., State, R. (eds.) DPM/SETOP -2012. LNCS, vol. 7731, pp. 89–103. Springer, Heidelberg (2013). doi:10.1007/978-3-642-35890-6_7
2. Broder, A.Z.: On the resemblance and containment of documents. In: Compression and Complexity of Sequences 1997, Proceedings, pp. 21–29. IEEE (1997)
3. Cristofaro, E., Gasti, P., Tsudik, G.: Fast and private computation of cardinality of set intersection and union. In: Pieprzyk, J., Sadeghi, A.-R., Manulis, M. (eds.) CANS 2012. LNCS, vol. 7712, pp. 218–231. Springer, Heidelberg (2012). doi:10.1007/978-3-642-35404-5_17
4. Dong, C., Chen, L., Wen, Z.: When private set intersection meets big data: an efficient and scalable protocol. In: Proceedings of the 2013 ACM SIGSAC Conference on Computer & Communications Security, pp. 789–800. ACM (2013)
5. Freedman, M.J., Hazay, C., Nissim, K., Pinkas, B.: Efficient set intersection with simulation-based security. J. Cryptology **29**(1), 115–155 (2016)
6. Huang, Y., Evans, D., Katz, J.: Private set intersection: are garbled circuits better than custom protocols? In: NDSS (2012)
7. Jaccard, P.: Distribution comparée de la flore alpine dans quelques régions des alpes occidentales et orientales. Bulletin de la Murithienne **31**, 81–92 (1902)
8. Kamara, S., Mohassel, P., Raykova, M., Sadeghian, S.: Scaling private set intersection to billion-element sets. In: Christin, N., Safavi-Naini, R. (eds.) FC 2014. LNCS, vol. 8437, pp. 195–215. Springer, Heidelberg (2014). doi:10.1007/978-3-662-45472-5_13
9. Leskovec, J., Rajaraman, A., Ullman, J.D.: Mining of Massive Datasets. Cambridge University Press, New York (2014)
10. Lindell, Y., Pinkas, B.: Privacy preserving data mining. In: Bellare, M. (ed.) CRYPTO 2000. LNCS, vol. 1880, pp. 36–54. Springer, Heidelberg (2000). doi:10.1007/3-540-44598-6_3
11. Pinkas, B., Schneider, T., Zohner, M.: Faster private set intersection based on OT extension. In: 23rd USENIX Security Symposium (USENIX Security 2014), pp. 797–812 (2014)
12. Qiu, S., Wang, B., Li, M., Victors, J., Liu, J., Shi, Y., Wang, W.: Fast, private and verifiable: server-aided approximate similarity computation over large-scale datasets. In: Proceedings of the 4th ACM International Workshop on Security in Cloud Computing, pp. 29–36. ACM (2016)

13. Qui, S.: Personal communication (2017)
14. Schneider, T., Zohner, M.: GMW vs. Yao? efficient secure two-party computation with low depth circuits. In: Sadeghi, A.-R. (ed.) FC 2013. LNCS, vol. 7859, pp. 275–292. Springer, Heidelberg (2013). doi:10.1007/978-3-642-39884-1_23
15. Yao, A.C.: Protocols for secure computations. In: 23rd Annual Symposium on Foundations of Computer Science, SFCS'08, pp. 160–164. IEEE (1982)
16. Zhu, E.: Datasketch. https://github.com/ekzhu/datasketch

# Cryptographic Protocols

# Correction of a Secure Comparison Protocol for Encrypted Integers in IEEE WIFS 2012 (Short Paper)

Baptiste Vinh Mau[1] and Koji Nuida[2,3]($\boxtimes$)

[1] ESI Japan Ltd., Tokyo, Japan
bvinhmau[at]gmail.com
[2] Advanced Cryptography Research Group,
Information Technology Research Institute,
National Institute of Advanced Industrial Science and Technology (AIST),
Tokyo, Japan
k.nuida[at]aist.go.jp
[3] Japan Science and Technology Agency (JST) PRESTO Researcher, Tokyo, Japan

**Abstract.** In secure multi-party computation, one of the most useful and basic functionalities that have been realized over additive homomorphic encryption is secure comparison of two integers, where one party has encrypted integers to be compared while only the other party has the decryption key. In IEEE WIFS 2012, Veugen proposed an efficient protocol for this problem in the semi-honest model, which provides perfect security against the latter party. In this paper, we point out that the protocol by Veugen outputs an incorrect value in some cases, and then propose a way to fix the flaws with only slight overhead in efficiency. Our proposed correction is not straightforward, in the sense that it required an "outsourced" homomorphic multiplication protocol for two encrypted values, which was not needed in the original protocol.

## 1 Introduction

Secure multi-party computation is a cryptographic technology that enables two or more parties to jointly compute a function value with their local inputs while keeping the local input of each party secret against any other party. A recent trend of this area is to develop efficient protocols by cleverly combining several sub-protocols based on methodologies of different types according to advantages of each methodology. One of such sub-protocols, which was indeed used by the paper [1] in NDSS 2015, is a secure comparison protocol for two encrypted integers proposed in IEEE WIFS 2012 by Veugen [6] based on additive homomorphic encryption (HE). As explained below in detail, the protocol by Veugen has two versions, and the aim of the present paper is to point out that one version of Veugen's protocol has flaws (i.e., it sometimes outputs an incorrect value) and to propose a way to correct the original protocol.

In Veugen's protocols, a party Alice has two encrypted integers $x, y \geq 0$ to be compared, encrypted by an additive HE scheme with plaintext space $\mathbb{Z}/N\mathbb{Z}$.

© Springer International Publishing AG 2017
S. Obana and K. Chida (Eds.): IWSEC 2017, LNCS 10418, pp. 181–191, 2017.
DOI: 10.1007/978-3-319-64200-0_11

The other party Bob has (and Alice does not have) the decryption key. The output of the protocol is a ciphertext, possessed by Alice only, of the bit indicating which of $x$ and $y$ is larger. As mentioned above, Veugen's protocol has two versions, namely Protocols 2 and 4 in [6]. The former ("statistical security" version) provides statistical security (against Bob), while the latter ("perfect security" version) provides *perfect* security with slight increase of executing costs. Moreover, the bit lengths of input integers for the former version must be significantly shorter (depending on the required security level) than the plaintext size $\log_2 N$; while the latter version has no such restriction. The protocol used in [1] is the statistical security version; and if we were able to apply the perfect security version instead, we would achieve enhanced security and would also remove the redundancy of the plaintext space in comparison to the sizes of input integers. However, in fact the perfect security version has flaws, as shown in this paper.

**Our Results.** In this paper we point out that the perfect security version of Veugen's comparison protocol for encrypted integers (Protocol 4 in [6]) sometimes outputs an incorrect value, and then propose a way to fix the flaws.

In Veugen's protocol, the difference $u := x - y$ of two input (encrypted) integers has absolute value $< 2^\ell$ (with parameter $\ell$). To obtain the encrypted sign of $u$, Alice homomorphically adds a random $r$ to encrypted $u$ and sends it to Bob, and Bob decrypts it and obtains $z := u + r$. By writing $a \div 2^\ell = \lfloor a/2^\ell \rfloor$ and letting a bit $\chi$ be 1 if and only if $z \bmod 2^\ell \geq r \bmod 2^\ell$, it follows (since $|u| < 2^\ell$) that $\delta := z \div 2^\ell - r \div 2^\ell + \chi$ equals 1 if $u \geq 0$, and equals 0 if $u < 0$. Then Alice can obtain an encrypted $\delta$ since a ciphertext of $\chi$ is available by applying to local unencrypted inputs $r \bmod 2^\ell$ and $z \bmod 2^\ell$ a secure comparison protocol proposed by Damgård, Geisler, and Krøigaard in [2] (*DGK comparison protocol*).

In fact, there is an issue for this idea; the underlying HE scheme has plaintext space $\mathbb{Z}/N\mathbb{Z}$, therefore if the value of $z$ "overflows" the range between 0 and $N - 1$, then the process of taking the remainder of $z$ modulo $N$ in the plaintext space may affect the values of $z \div 2^\ell$ and $z \bmod 2^\ell$ in the computation of $\delta$. The aforementioned disadvantages of the statistical security version against the perfect security version is actually caused by restricting the range of $r$ to prevent the overflow. On the other hand, in the perfect security version, Veugen has introduced to the protocol an auxiliary (encrypted) bit $d$ indicating whether such an overflow occurred, and then modified the internal DGK comparison protocol to consider the effect of the overflow to the value of $z \bmod 2^\ell$. However, the other effect of the overflow to the value of $z \div 2^\ell$ was not considered in [6]; this is the main source of the incorrectness which we point out in the paper.

To resolve the flaw, we had to precisely analyze the difference of the (encrypted) output value caused by the overflow, which should be homomorphically added to the original output value. However, our analysis found that the difference, say $\eta$, is available for Alice in an *encrypted* form only, while the difference should be added only when $d = 1$, which is also an *encrypted* bit from Alice's viewpoint. As the underlying encryption scheme is just an additive HE, this required us to use another sub-protocol (described in e.g., [4]), not needed in the original protocol, that enables Alice to obtain a ciphertext of the product of two encrypted values $d$ and $\eta$ with the help of Bob having the decryption key. See Sect. 4 for details. We also show that our correction of the protocol does not compromise the security in the semi-honest model, and experimentally evaluate the practical efficiency of our corrected protocol (see Sect. 5).

## 2   Preliminaries

**Homomorphic Encryption.** In this paper, any homomorphic encryption (HE) scheme is an additive homomorphic public key encryption scheme with error-free decryption algorithm and is supposed to be semantically secure. We write a ciphertext of a plaintext $m$ as $[[m]]$. An HE scheme also admits *homomorphic operations* to generate, from given ciphertexts $[[m_1]], [[m_2]]$, new ciphertexts $[[m_1]] \boxplus [[m_2]]$ and $[[m_1]] \boxminus [[m_2]]$ of $m_1 + m_2$ and $m_1 - m_2$, respectively; and from given ciphertext $[[m]]$ and integer $r$, a new ciphertext $r \boxdot [[m]]$ of $rm$.

An example of HE schemes is the Paillier cryptosystem [5] with plaintext space $\mathbb{Z}/N\mathbb{Z}$ where $N$ is a very large composite integer. Another example was proposed by Damgård, Geisler, and Krøigaard in [2,3] (*DGK cryptosystem*). Its plaintext space is a finite *field* $\mathbb{F}_p = \mathbb{Z}/p\mathbb{Z}$ with a fairly large prime $p$ (see [2,3] for further details). The DGK cryptosystem provides very efficient decryption by using a lookup table; while the use of a lookup table yields a limitation that the plaintext size cannot practically be as large as the Paillier cryptosystem.

**The DGK Comparison Protocol.** Damgård et al. [2] also proposed a secure comparison protocol for unencrypted integers based on an HE scheme (*DGK comparison protocol*). We write $\chi_P = 1$ if a condition P is satisfied, or else $\chi_P = 0$. In their protocol, two parties Alice and Bob have their local integer inputs $x \geq 0$ and $y \geq 0$, respectively, and Bob also has a secret key of the underlying HE scheme. The local outputs of Alice and Bob are bits $\delta_A, \delta_B$, respectively, satisfying $\delta_A \oplus \delta_B = \chi_{x \leq y}$ where $\oplus$ denotes XOR. The security model is the semi-honest model, hence the information on Alice's (respectively, Bob's) secret input is not leaked to Bob (respectively, Alice) while they are supposed to execute the protocol correctly. See [2] or Protocol 1 in [6] for details.

The authors of [2] constructed their protocol using the DGK cryptosystem. We note that, the requirement for the underlying HE scheme is that the plaintext space can handle roughly $\log_2(3\ell)$-bit integers, where $\ell$ is a parameter bounding the inputs as $x, y < 2^\ell$. The reason of using the DGK cryptosystem in [2] seems to be the flexibility of the plaintext size, in contrast to the Paillier cryptosystem where the plaintext size must correlate with the security parameter.

**An Outsourced Multiplication.** In this paper we also need an auxiliary protocol to enable *multiplication* of encrypted integers. Here Alice has two encrypted integers $[[x]], [[y]]$, while Bob has a secret key for the underlying HE scheme. Alice wants to obtain a ciphertext $[[x]] \boxtimes [[y]] := [[xy]]$ (without knowing $x, y$, or $xy$) by outsourcing to Bob the decryption and multiplication of decrypted integers, while Alice also wants to conceal $x, y$ even from Bob.

In this paper, we adopt the following protocol in the semi-honest model, where the HE scheme has plaintext space $\mathbb{Z}/N\mathbb{Z}$: (i) Alice randomly chooses $a, b \leftarrow \{0, 1, \ldots, N - 1\}$, computes $[[x']] \leftarrow [[x]] \boxplus [[a]]$ and $[[y']] \leftarrow [[y]] \boxplus [[b]]$, and sends $[[x']]$ and $[[y']]$ to Bob; (ii) Bob decrypts $[[x']]$ and $[[y']]$ to get $x' = x + a \bmod N$ and $y' = y + b \bmod N$, computes $[[x'y']]$ and sends $[[x'y']]$ to Alice; (iii) Alice outputs $[[x'y']] \boxminus \left( b \boxdot [[x]] \right) \boxminus \left( a \boxdot [[y]] \right) \boxminus [[ab]]$. We note that this protocol is not new and had already appeared in previous work such as [4].

## 3   Veugen's Comparison Protocol with Statistical Security

Before revisiting the perfect security version of Veugen's comparison protocol, in this section we first explain the statistical security version (Protocol 2 in [6]). We also mention some very slight errors in [6] for the sake of completeness.

Veugen's protocol used two HE schemes, one of which (called "outer scheme") is for encrypting inputs and outputs and the other (called "inner scheme") is for performing the DGK comparison protocol as a sub-routine. In [6], the Paillier and the DGK cryptosystems were the outer and the inner HE schemes, respectively. We write $\mathsf{sk_O}$ and $[[m]]_O$ for secret keys and ciphertexts for the outer scheme, while $\mathsf{sk}$ and $[[m]]$ for the inner scheme. We suppose that the public keys are distributed in advance and hence are made implicit in the descriptions. For the two schemes, we use common symbols $\boxplus$, $\boxminus$, and $\boxdot$ for homomorphic operations.

For integers $a \geq 0$ and $b > 0$, we write $a \bmod b \in \{0, 1, \ldots, b-1\}$ to denote the remainder of $a$ modulo $b$, and write $a \div b = \lfloor a/b \rfloor$; hence $a = (a \div b) \cdot b + (a \bmod b)$. We write $\chi_P = 1$ if a condition $P$ is satisfied, or else we define $\chi_P = 0$.

Suppose that the outer HE scheme has plaintext space $\mathbb{Z}/N\mathbb{Z}$, identified naturally with $\{0, 1, \ldots, N - 1\}$. Let $\ell > 0$ be an integer. Then, in this version of Veugen's protocol, Alice is supposed to have two encrypted integers $[[x]]_O, [[y]]_O$ with $0 \leq x < 2^\ell$ and $0 \leq y < 2^\ell$. Bob is supposed to have the two secret keys $\mathsf{sk_O}, \mathsf{sk}$. The parameters have a constraint $\ell + 2 + \sigma < \log_2 N$, where $\sigma$ is an integer parameter (e.g., $\sigma = 80$ as indicated in [6]) relevant to the security level. (We note that the constraint was written as $\ell + \sigma < \log_2 N$ in Protocol 2 in [6], which is in fact not enough as observed below.) The goal of the protocol is to let Alice obtain a ciphertext $[[\chi_{x \geq y}]]_O$ of the bit $\chi_{x \geq y}$ while Bob obtains no output. (We note that the encrypted output bit was specified to be $\chi_{x \leq y}$ in Protocol 2 in [6], but the inequality '$\leq$' should be reversed as '$\geq$' as observed below.)

For the sake of completeness, we describe Veugen's protocol (Protocol 2 in [6]) in Fig. 1. We note that our description of the protocol basically coincides with [6] except for the two slight corrections mentioned in the previous paragraph and some other notational changes.

For the sake of intuitive understanding of the protocol, here we divide the plaintext space $\{0, 1, \ldots, N-1\}$ of the outer HE scheme into 0-th to $(N \div 2^\ell)$-th "buckets", where the $i$-th bucket (with $0 \leq i < (N \div 2^\ell)$) consists of the numbers $i \cdot 2^\ell + j$ for $0 \leq j < 2^\ell$, and the last $(N \div 2^\ell)$-th bucket consists of the remaining $N \bmod 2^\ell$ numbers from $(N \div 2^\ell) \cdot 2^\ell$ to $N - 1$. Then for a plaintext $m = (m \div 2^\ell) \cdot 2^\ell + (m \bmod 2^\ell)$, we call $m \div 2^\ell$ the "bucket number" of $m$ and call

| (Alice) Input: $[[x]]_O$ and $[[y]]_O$ | Output: $[[\chi_{x \geq y}]]_O$ |
|---|---|
| (Bob) Input: $sk_O$ and $sk$ | Output: (none) |

1. Alice chooses a random $(\ell + 1 + \sigma)$-bit number $r$, computes $[[z]]_O \leftarrow [[x]]_O \boxminus [[y]]_O \boxplus [[2^\ell + r]]_O$, and sends $[[z]]_O$ to Bob.
2.     Bob decrypts $[[z]]_O$ to get $z = x - y + 2^\ell + r \bmod N$, and computes $\beta \leftarrow z \bmod 2^\ell$.
3. Alice computes $\alpha \leftarrow r \bmod 2^\ell$.
4.     Alice and Bob execute the DGK comparison protocol using the inner HE scheme with private inputs $\alpha$ and $\beta$, which results in local output bits $\delta_A$ and $\delta_B$, respectively, with $\delta_A \oplus \delta_B = \chi_{\alpha \leq \beta}$.
5.     Bob computes $z \div 2^\ell$, and sends $[[z \div 2^\ell]]_O$ and $[[\delta_B]]_O$ to Alice.
6. - If $\delta_A = 1$, then Alice sets $[[\gamma]]_O \leftarrow [[\delta_B]]_O$.
   - Otherwise, Alice sets $[[\gamma]]_O \leftarrow [[1]]_O \boxminus [[\delta_B]]_O$.
7. Alice outputs $[[z \div 2^\ell]]_O \boxminus \left( [[r \div 2^\ell]]_O \boxplus [[\gamma]]_O \right)$.

**Fig. 1.** Veugen's comparison protocol with statistical security (here $0 \leq x < 2^\ell$, $0 \leq y < 2^\ell$, $\ell + 2 + \sigma < \log_2 N$, and the outer HE scheme has plaintext space $\mathbb{Z}/N\mathbb{Z}$)

$m \bmod 2^\ell$ the "relative position" of $m$ inside the bucket. On the other hand, we note that the encrypted bit $\gamma$ computed in Step 6 is equal to $\text{NOT}(\delta_A \oplus \delta_B)$, therefore $\gamma = \chi_{\alpha > \beta}$ by the functionality of the DGK comparison protocol.

For Step 2 of the protocol, when $x - y$ (with $|x - y| < 2^\ell$) is added to $2^\ell + r$, either an "overflow" of the relative position inside the bucket (in case where $x > y$ and $(r \bmod 2^\ell) + (x - y) \geq 2^\ell$) or an "underflow" of the relative position inside the bucket (in case where $x < y$ and $(r \bmod 2^\ell) - (y - x) < 0$) may occur. On the other hand, since $0 \leq x - y + 2^\ell + r \leq 2^{\ell+2+\sigma} < N$, any overflow or underflow of the bucket number does not occur in the computation of $x - y + 2^\ell + r$. In other words, in the present case, we always have (as integers) $z = x - y + 2^\ell + r \bmod N = x - y + 2^\ell + r$.

First, we consider the simplest case where any of an overflow or an underflow of the relative position has not occurred at Step 2. In this case, we have $\alpha > \beta$ if and only if $x - y < 0$ (or $x < y$), while we have $z \div 2^\ell = (2^\ell + r) \div 2^\ell = (r \div 2^\ell) + 1$. This implies that, Alice's output is a ciphertext of $(z \div 2^\ell) - ((r \div 2^\ell) + \gamma) = 1 - \gamma = 1 - \chi_{\alpha > \beta} = 1 - \chi_{x < y} = \chi_{x \geq y}$.

Secondly, we suppose that an overflow has occurred at Step 2, which implies that $x > y$ and hence Alice's output should be $[[1]]_O$. Now the effect of the overflow of the relative position ensures that $z \div 2^\ell$ is incremented by 1 in comparison to the previous case and we always have $\alpha > \beta$ and $\gamma = 1$. Hence the plaintext for Alice's output becomes $2 - \gamma = 1$, as desired. Similarly, when an underflow has occurred at Step 2 (hence $x < y$ and Alice's output should be $[[0]]_O$), the effect of the underflow of the relative position ensures that $z \div 2^\ell$ is decremented by 1 in comparison to the previous case and we always have $\alpha < \beta$ and $\gamma = 0$; hence the plaintext for Alice's output becomes $0 - \gamma = 0$, as desired.

## 4  Correcting Veugen's Protocol with Perfect Security

In this section, we revisit the perfect security version of Veugen's comparison protocol (Protocol 4 in [6]), show that the original protocol is not correct in the original form, and then propose a way to correct the flaws of the original protocol. We use notations similar to those in Sect. 3, and we write $(\nu_{\ell-1} \cdots \nu_1 \nu_0)_2$ to indicate the binary expression of an integer $\nu = \sum_{i=0}^{\ell-1} \nu_i 2^i$.

Figure 2 describes the corrected version of the original protocol, where the boxed parts are the main differences from the original protocol in [6]. More precisely, these two protocols have the following differences:

- A common HE scheme is used as the outer and the inner HE schemes in our corrected protocol; while those were distinct schemes in [6].
- Alice in our corrected protocol is supposed to output $[[\chi_{x \geq y}]]$; while Alice was supposed to output $[[\chi_{x \leq y}]]_O$ in [6].
- The ciphertexts $[[c_{-1}]]$ in Steps 4h, i, and j of our corrected protocol did not appear in [6].
- The random values $r_i'$ in Step 4i of our corrected protocol are chosen from the whole of invertible elements of the plaintext space (to mask the values of $c_i$ completely); while those were not chosen from the whole domain in [6].
- Step 7' of our corrected protocol is newly added, which did not exist in [6].
- In Step 7 of our corrected protocol, the ciphertext $[[d]] \boxtimes [[\eta]]$ is homomorphically added to the output ciphertext, which was not done in [6].

### 4.1  Example and Observation for Flaws of the Original Protocol

Here we use the notations in Fig. 2. We set $N = 263$, $\ell = 6$ (hence $2^\ell = 64$), $x = 5$, and $y = 2$. We choose random numbers $r = 200$ and $\delta_A = 0$. Then the original protocol proceeds as follows: (Step 2) $z = (5 - 2 + 200 + 64) \bmod 263 = 4$ and $\beta = 4 \bmod 64 = 4 = (000100)_2$; (Step 3) $\alpha = 200 \bmod 64 = 8 = (001000)_2$; (Steps 4a, 4c) $d = 1$; (Step 4d) $\alpha_i \oplus \beta_i = 0, 0, 1, 1, 0, 0$ for $i = 5, 4, 3, 2, 1, 0$; (Step 4e) $\tilde{\alpha} = (200 - 263) \bmod 64 = 1 = (000001)_2$ and $w_i = 0, 0, 0, 1, 0, -1$ for $i = 5, 4, 3, 2, 1, 0$; (Step 4f) $w_i \leftarrow 0, 0, 0, 4, 0, -1$ for $i = 5, 4, 3, 2, 1, 0$; (Step 4g) $s = 1 - 2 \cdot 0 = 1$; (Step 4h) $c_2 = 1 + 0 + (0 - 0) \cdot 1 - 1 + 3 \cdot (0 + 0 + 0) = 0$ (other $c_i$'s are omitted here, since these are now irrelevant); (Step 4j) $\delta_B = 1$; (Step 6) $\gamma = 1 - 1 = 0$. Finally, Alice outputs a ciphertext of $(z \div 2^\ell) - ((r \div 2^\ell) + \gamma) = (4 \div 64) - (200 \div 64) = -3$. But the correct output should be a ciphertext of $\chi_{x \geq y} = 1$. This shows that Veugen's original protocol is not correct.

In this example, $r$ is close to the upper bound $N - 1$, and an overflow of the bucket number has occurred in the computation of $x - y + 2^\ell + r$ at Step 2. This makes the value of $z \div 2^\ell$ small ($\approx 0$), while the value of $r \div 2^\ell$ is large ($\approx N \div 2^\ell$). On the other hand, the value $\gamma$ at Step 6 is in $\{0, 1\}$ by the construction. Therefore, the plaintext of Alice's output $(z \div 2^\ell) - (r \div 2^\ell) - \gamma$ cannot be in $\{0, 1\}$ (regardless of whether the computation of $\gamma$ works as intended by the author of [6]) though it must be a bit due to the expected functionality of the protocol. In other words, Step 7 of the original protocol does not appropriately concern the effect of an overflow (or underflow) of the bucket number.

| (Alice) Input: $[[x]]$ and $[[y]]$ | Output: $[[\chi_{x \geq y}]]$ |
|---|---|

(Bob) Input: sk      Output: (none)

1. Alice chooses $r \leftarrow_R \{0, 1, \ldots, p-1\}$, computes $[[z]] \leftarrow [[x]] \boxminus [[y]] \boxplus [[2^\ell + r]]$, and sends $[[z]]$ to Bob.

2. Bob decrypts $[[z]]$ to get $z = x - y + 2^\ell + r \bmod p$, and computes $\beta = (\beta_{\ell-1} \cdots \beta_1 \beta_0)_2 \leftarrow z \bmod 2^\ell$.

3. Alice computes $\alpha = (\alpha_{\ell-1} \cdots \alpha_1 \alpha_0)_2 \leftarrow r \bmod 2^\ell$.

4a. Bob computes $d \leftarrow \chi_{z < (p-1)/2}$ and sends $[[d]]$ to Alice.

4b. For each $i = 0, 1, \ldots, \ell-1$, Bob sends $[[\beta_i]]$ to Alice.

4c. If $0 \leq r < (p-1)/2$, then Alice resets $[[d]] \leftarrow [[0]]$.

4d. For each $i = 0, 1, \ldots, \ell-1$:
   - If $\alpha_i = 0$, then Alice computes $[[\alpha_i \oplus \beta_i]] \leftarrow [[\beta_i]]$.
   - Otherwise, Alice computes $[[\alpha_i \oplus \beta_i]] \leftarrow [[1]] \boxminus [[\beta_i]]$.

4e. Alice computes $\tilde{\alpha} = (\tilde{\alpha}_{\ell-1} \cdots \tilde{\alpha}_1 \tilde{\alpha}_0)_2 \leftarrow (r - p) \bmod 2^\ell$, and for each $i = 0, 1, \ldots, \ell-1$:
   - If $\alpha_i = \tilde{\alpha}_i$, then Alice sets $[[w_i]] \leftarrow [[\alpha_i \oplus \beta_i]]$.
   - Otherwise, Alice sets $[[w_i]] \leftarrow [[\alpha_i \oplus \beta_i]] \boxminus [[d]]$.

4f. For each $i = 0, 1, \ldots, \ell-1$, Alice modifies $[[w_i]]$ by $[[w_i]] \leftarrow 2^i \boxdot [[w_i]]$.

4g. Alice chooses $\delta_A \leftarrow_R \{0, 1\}$ and computes $s \leftarrow 1 - 2\delta_A$.

4h. For each $i = 0, 1, \ldots, \ell-1$, Alice computes

$$[[c_i]] \leftarrow [[s]] \boxplus [[\alpha_i]] \boxplus \left( (\tilde{\alpha}_i - \alpha_i) \boxdot [[d]] \right) \boxminus [[\beta_i]]$$
$$\boxplus \left( 3 \boxdot \left( [[w_{i+1}]] \boxplus [[w_{i+2}]] \boxplus \cdots \boxplus [[w_{\ell-1}]] \right) \right).$$

$$\boxed{[[c_{-1}]] \leftarrow [[\delta_A]] \boxplus \left( 2 \boxdot \left( [[w_0]] \boxplus [[w_1]] \boxplus \cdots \boxplus [[w_{\ell-1}]] \right) \right).}$$

4i. For each $i = \boxed{-1}, 0, 1, \ldots, \ell-1$, Alice chooses $1 \leq r'_i \leq p-1$ uniformly at random, and modifies $[[c_i]]$ by $[[c_i]] \leftarrow r'_i \boxdot [[c_i]]$. Then Alice sends $\boxed{[[c_{-1}]]}, [[c_0]], \ldots, [[c_{\ell-1}]]$ to Bob in uniformly random order.

4j. Bob decrypts $\boxed{[[c_{-1}]]}, [[c_0]], \ldots, [[c_{\ell-1}]]$, and:
   - If at least one of $\boxed{c_{-1}}, c_0, \ldots, c_{\ell-1}$ is 0, then Bob sets $\delta_B \leftarrow 1$.
   - Otherwise, Bob sets $\delta_B \leftarrow 0$.

5. Bob computes $z \div 2^\ell$, and sends $[[z \div 2^\ell]]$ and $[[\delta_B]]$ to Alice.

6. - If $\delta_A = 1$, then Alice sets $[[\gamma]] \leftarrow [[\delta_B]]$.
   - Otherwise, Alice sets $[[\gamma]] \leftarrow [[1]] \boxminus [[\delta_B]]$.

7'. $\boxed{\begin{array}{l} \text{- If } r < p - 2^\ell, \text{ then Alice sets } [[\eta]] \leftarrow [[(r \div 2^\ell) + 1]] \boxplus [[\gamma]]. \\ \text{- Otherwise, Alice sets } [[\eta]] \leftarrow [[(r \div 2^\ell) - ((2^\ell + r - p) \div 2^\ell) + 1]]. \end{array}}$

7. Alice outputs $[[z \div 2^\ell]] \boxminus \boxed{\left( [[r \div 2^\ell]] \boxplus [[\gamma]] \right)} \boxed{\boxplus ([[d]] \boxtimes [[\eta]])}$.

**Fig. 2.** Corrected version of Veugen's comparison protocol with perfect security (here $0 \leq x < 2^\ell$, $0 \leq y < 2^\ell$, $\ell + 2 < \log_2 p$, the HE scheme has plaintext space $\mathbb{F}_p = \mathbb{Z}/p\mathbb{Z}$ with prime $p$, and the symbol $\boxtimes$ indicates an outsourced homomorphic multiplication operation described in Sect. 2; the boxed parts are the main differences from the original protocol)

## 4.2    Revisiting the Main Part of the Original Protocol

We analyze the original protocol in detail. First, the bit $d$ after Step 4c becomes 1 if and only if $z < (N-1)/2 \leq r$. Since $0 \leq x - y + 2^\ell \leq 2^{\ell+1} - 1 < N - 1$, the situation $z < (N-1)/2 \leq r$ above occurs if and only if $x - y + 2^\ell + r \geq N$, i.e., the overflow of the bucket number occurs. Hence, we have $d = 1$ if the overflow of the bucket number occurs, or else we have $d = 0$, as intended in [6].

In the rest of this subsection, we revisit Step 4 (i.e., Steps 4a–j) of the protocol, which is the most complicated part. As mentioned in [6], the part of the protocol is intended to be a modification of the DGK comparison protocol for handling the effect of the overflow of the bucket number.

**For case** $d = 0$. Now we have $w_i = 2^i \cdot (\alpha_i \oplus \beta_i)$ for $0 \leq i \leq \ell - 1$ after Step 4f, and for Step 4h, we have $c_i = s + \alpha_i - \beta_i + 3 \sum_{j=i+1}^{\ell-1} w_j$. Now by the definition of $w_j$'s, the term $3 \sum_{j=i+1}^{\ell-1} w_j$ becomes 0 if $\alpha_j \oplus \beta_j = 0$ (or $\alpha_j = \beta_j$) for every $j = i+1, \dots, \ell-1$, or else the term has absolute value $\geq 3$. Since $|s + \alpha_i - \beta_i| \leq 2$, it follows that we have $c_i = 0$ if and only if $\alpha_j = \beta_j$ for all $j = i+1, \dots, \ell-1$ and $s + \alpha_i - \beta_i = 0$. Moreover, since $s = 1 - 2\delta_A = \pm 1$, the condition $s + \alpha_i - \beta_i = 0$ above implies $\alpha_i \neq \beta_i$. Therefore, the only index $i$ that can satisfy $c_i = 0$ is the largest index (if exists) at which position the bits of $\alpha$ and $\beta$ differ.

Now, in the case $\alpha \neq \beta$, such an index $i$ indeed exists uniquely, and we have $c_i = 0$ (hence $\delta_B = 1$) if and only if $(\delta_A, \alpha_i, \beta_i) = (0, 0, 1)$ (now $\alpha < \beta$ and $\gamma = 0$) or $(\delta_A, \alpha_i, \beta_i) = (1, 1, 0)$ (now $\alpha > \beta$ and $\gamma = 1$); while we have $c_i \neq 0$ (hence $\delta_B = 0$) if and only if $(\delta_A, \alpha_i, \beta_i) = (0, 1, 0)$ (now $\alpha > \beta$ and $\gamma = 1$) or $(\delta_A, \alpha_i, \beta_i) = (1, 0, 1)$ (now $\alpha < \beta$ and $\gamma = 0$). Summarizing, we have $\gamma = \chi_{\alpha > \beta}$.

In the other case $\alpha = \beta$, we always have $\delta_B = 0$ since such an index $i$ as above does not exist, therefore $\gamma = 1 - \delta_A$. This is a uniformly random bit, which looks not an intended behavior. In fact, an idea to resolve the issue was already mentioned in Sect. 2.A of [6] (though not explicitly reflected in Protocol 4 in [6]). Following this idea, in addition to $[[c_i]]$ for $i = 0, \dots, \ell - 1$ generated at Step 4h, we also use a ciphertext $[[c_{-1}]] \leftarrow [[\delta_A]] \boxplus \left( 2 \boxdot ([[w_0]] \boxplus \cdots \boxplus [[w_{\ell-1}]]) \right)$.

Now the condition $\alpha = \beta$ implies $w_j = 0$ for every $0 \leq j \leq \ell - 1$; therefore, if $\delta_A = 0$ then $c_{-1} = 0$ and $\delta_B = 1$, while if $\delta_A = 1$ then $c_{-1} \neq 0$ and $\delta_B = 0$. Hence $\gamma = 0 = \chi_{\alpha > \beta}$ in any case, which coincides with the behavior in the case $\alpha \neq \beta$ above. We note that this modification introducing $[[c_{-1}]]$ does not affect the correctness when ($d = 0$ and) $\alpha \neq \beta$, since now at least one of $w_j$'s is non-zero and hence we always have $c_{-1} \neq 0$ by the definition.

Summarizing, when $d = 0$, the protocol satisfies $\gamma = \chi_{\alpha > \beta}$, assuming that we introduce the additional ciphertext $[[c_{-1}]]$ mentioned above.

**For case** $d = 1$. Now we have $w_i \in \{0, \pm 2^i\}$ and $c_i = 1 - 2\delta_A + \widetilde{\alpha}_i - \beta_i + 3 \sum_{j=i+1}^{\ell-1} w_j$ for $0 \leq i \leq \ell - 1$, and $c_{-1} = \delta_A + 2 \sum_{j=0}^{\ell-1} w_j$. On the other hand, the construction of Step 4e implies that we have $w_j = 0$ if and only if $\widetilde{\alpha}_j = \beta_j$ (regardless of the value of $\alpha_j$). Hence, an argument similar to the case $d = 0$ implies the following. If $\widetilde{\alpha} = \beta$, then $c_i \neq 0$ for every $i = 0, 1, \dots, \ell - 1$ and $c_{-1} = \delta_A$; therefore $\delta_B = 1 - \delta_A$ and $\gamma = 0 = \chi_{\widetilde{\alpha} > \beta}$. On the other hand, if $\widetilde{\alpha} \neq \beta$, then the only index $i$ (including $-1$) at which $c_i$ can be zero is the largest index $i$ with $\widetilde{\alpha}_i \neq \beta_i$, and for the index $i$, we have $1 - \delta_B = \chi_{c_i \neq 0} = \delta_A \oplus \chi_{\widetilde{\alpha} > \beta}$ and $\gamma = \chi_{\widetilde{\alpha} > \beta}$. Hence, when $d = 1$, the protocol satisfies $\gamma = \chi_{\widetilde{\alpha} > \beta}$ in any case.

**Revisiting the Original Protocol Further.** As discussed above, the protocol (when introducing $[[c_{-1}]]$) satisfies $\gamma = \chi_{\alpha > \beta}$ if $d = 0$, and $\gamma = \chi_{\widetilde{\alpha} > \beta}$ if $d = 1$. Now if $d = 0$, then we have $z = x - y + 2^\ell + r < N$ by the first paragraph of Sect. 4.2, while we have $\gamma = \chi_{\alpha > \beta}$ as above. This implies that, in this case the behavior of the protocol coincides with the statistical security version of Veugen's protocol; hence Alice's output is $[[\chi_{x \geq y}]]_O$ as explained in Sect. 3.

For the other case $d = 1$, put $\rho := (z \div 2^\ell) - (r \div 2^\ell) - \gamma$, which is the plaintext for the output of the original protocol. Since $d = 1$ and $\ell + 2 < \log_2 N$, we have $N \leq x - y + 2^\ell + r < 2N$ by the argument in the first paragraph of Sect. 4.2, therefore $z = (x - y + 2^\ell + r) \bmod N = x - y + 2^\ell + r - N$ (as integers). The fact $\gamma = \chi_{\widetilde{\alpha} > \beta}$ mentioned above and the definition of $\widetilde{\alpha}$ suggest that, now the number $r - N$ instead of $r$ would play a certain role in the protocol.

Put $\widetilde{r} := 2^\ell + r - N$. First, we consider the case $\widetilde{r} < 0$. Since $z = x - y + \widetilde{r} \geq 0$, we have $x > y$, therefore $\chi_{x \geq y} = 1$. Now $z < x - y < 2^\ell$ and $z \div 2^\ell = 0$, therefore $\rho = -(r \div 2^\ell) - \gamma$. Hence, the difference $\chi_{x \geq y} - \rho = (r \div 2^\ell) + \gamma + 1$ should be (homomorphically) added to the output of the original protocol.

Secondly, we consider the other case $\widetilde{r} \geq 0$. Put $\widetilde{z} := z + 2^\ell$. Then we have $0 \leq \widetilde{z} < x - y + 2^\ell + 2^\ell < 3 \cdot 2^\ell < N$ and $0 \leq \widetilde{r} < 2^\ell < N$ since $r - N < 0$ and $\ell + 2 < \log_2 N$. Moreover, we have $\widetilde{z} = x - y + 2^\ell + \widetilde{r}$, $\widetilde{z} \bmod 2^\ell = z \bmod 2^\ell = \beta$, and $\widetilde{r} \bmod 2^\ell = (r - N) \bmod 2^\ell = \widetilde{\alpha}$. Therefore, the same argument as the case $d = 0$ implies now that $\chi_{x \geq y} = (\widetilde{z} \div 2^\ell) - (\widetilde{r} \div 2^\ell) - \gamma$, which is equal to $(z \div 2^\ell) + 1 - (\widetilde{r} \div 2^\ell) - \gamma = \rho + (r \div 2^\ell) - (\widetilde{r} \div 2^\ell) + 1$. Hence, the difference $\chi_{x \geq y} - \rho = (r \div 2^\ell) - (\widetilde{r} \div 2^\ell) + 1$ should be (homomorphically) added to the output of the original protocol.

Summarizing, to obtain the correct (encrypted) output $\chi_{x \geq y}$, the value $d \cdot \eta$ should be (homomorphically) added to the output of the original protocol, where $\eta := (r \div 2^\ell) + \gamma + 1$ if $2^\ell + r - N < 0$ and $\eta := (r \div 2^\ell) - ((2^\ell + r - N) \div 2^\ell) + 1$ if $2^\ell + r - N \geq 0$. The final issue remaining is how Alice computes the product of $d$ and $\eta$, both being available only in an encrypted form. A basic strategy is to use an outsourced multiplication operation $\boxtimes$ described in Sect. 2, which would enable Alice to obtain a ciphertext $[[d \cdot \eta]]_O$ and then perform an additive homomorphic operation with the original output ciphertext. However, in the original protocol, $d$ is encrypted by the inner HE scheme rather than the outer HE scheme, therefore the operation $\boxtimes$ cannot be applied immediately. A simple way to resolve this issue is to use a common HE scheme as both the outer and the inner HE schemes. The resulting corrected protocol is described in Fig. 2.

## 5   Security and Performance Analyses

**Theorem 1.** *In our protocol, any object sent from Bob to Alice is a ciphertext of the underlying HE scheme, and any information sent from Alice to Bob is* *independent and uniformly random over the domain from which the information is chosen (provided the same properties hold for the outsourced multiplication).*

*Proof.* The former part is obvious. For the latter claim, for Step 1, the plaintext $z = x - y + 2^\ell + r \bmod p$ sent (in encrypted form) to Bob is uniformly random over $\mathbb{F}_p$ as well as $r$. For Steps 4i and j, the argument in Sect. 4.2 implies that there are precisely the following two cases: (I) Exactly one of the values $c_{-1}, c_0, \ldots, c_{\ell-1}$ is zero; and $\delta_B = 1$. (II) All of the values $c_{-1}, c_0, \ldots, c_{\ell-1}$ are non-zero; and $\delta_B = 0$. Now the masking procedure in Step 4i ensures that Bob at Step 4j can only know which of (I) and (II) happens. Moreover, the argument in Sect. 4.2 also implies that, after the values of $r$, $z$, and $d$ are determined, the bit $\gamma$ at Step 6 is also determined (i.e., either $\chi_{\alpha > \beta}$ or $\chi_{\tilde{\alpha} > \beta}$ depending on $d$), while we have $\delta_B = \gamma \oplus \delta_A$. Hence, from Bob's viewpoint, the possibilities of (I) and (II) are uniformly random and independent of $z$ obtained at Step 1, since the uniformly random bit $\delta_A$ is not known by Bob. This completes the proof.

We implemented the offline version of our protocol and performed computer experiments for efficiency evaluation. We used C++ and the ZZ class of the NTL library (http://shoup.net/ntl/), and the benchmark was ran on a notebook with a Core N-5Y10c@0.80 GHz CPU. The underlying HE scheme is the (factoring-based) DGK cryptosystem with 1024-bit keys. Then our protocol to compare 8-bit, 12-bit, 16-bit, and 18-bit integers took 245 ms, 330 ms, 350 ms, and 399 ms running times and 3.25 kB, 4.25 kB, 5.25 kB, and 5.75 kB (estimated) bandwidth costs, respectively (larger plaintexts could not be handled in our environment due to the lookup tables in decryption). We remind that the unitary cost of each operation in the DGK cryptosystem is almost independent of the plaintext size; while the cost of the entire protocol does depend on the plaintext size, since the numbers of iterations in some loops and the numbers of communicated ciphertexts during the protocol are increased as the input size increases.

**Acknowledgments.** The authors thank Goichiro Hanaoka, Kana Shimizu and more generally all the members of Advanced Cryptography Research Group, Information Technology Research Institute from AIST for their supervision, help and collaboration. They also thank Jean-Pierre Hubaux from the EPFL Laboratory for Communications and Applications for assuming the role of supervising teacher of the first author's Master Thesis during which this paper was mainly produced. They also thank the anonymous reviewers for their comments. This work was supported by JST PRESTO Grant Number JPMJPR14E8, Japan.

# References

1. Bost, R., Popa, R.A., Tu, S., Goldwasser, S.: Machine learning classification over encrypted data. In: NDSS 2015, California, USA, February 2015
2. Damgård, I., Geisler, M., Krøigaard, M.: Efficient and secure comparison for on-line auctions. In: Pieprzyk, J., Ghodosi, H., Dawson, E. (eds.) ACISP 2007. LNCS, vol. 4586, pp. 416–430. Springer, Heidelberg (2007). doi:10.1007/978-3-540-73458-1_30

3. Damgård, I., Geisler, M., Krøigaard, M.: A correction to 'efficient and secure comparison for on-line auctions'. Int. J. Appl. Cryptography **1**(4), 323–324 (2009)
4. Hallgren, P., Ochoa, M., Sabelfeld, A.: BetterTimes. In: Au, M.-H., Miyaji, A. (eds.) ProvSec 2015. LNCS, vol. 9451, pp. 291–309. Springer, Cham (2015). doi:10.1007/978-3-319-26059-4_16
5. Paillier, P.: Public-key cryptosystems based on composite degree residuosity classes. In: Stern, J. (ed.) EUROCRYPT 1999. LNCS, vol. 1592, pp. 223–238. Springer, Heidelberg (1999). doi:10.1007/3-540-48910-X_16
6. Veugen, T.: Improving the DGK comparison protocol. In: Proceedings of IEEE WIFS 2012, pp. 49–54 (2012)

# Adaptive Security
# in Identity-Based Authenticated Key Agreement
# with Multiple Private Key Generators

Atsushi Fujioka$^{(\boxtimes)}$

Kanagawa University, 3-27-1 Rokkakubashi, Kanagawa-ku,
Yokohama-shi, Kanagawa 221-8686, Japan
fujioka@kanagawa-u.ac.jp

**Abstract.** We define a security model to capture some adaptive security for identity-based authenticated key agreement with multiple private key generators (PKGs). Previous researches assume that a party is statically bound to its PKG. In our model, an adversary can adaptively control the binding between a party and a PKG, and moreover, the adversary is allowed to obtain private keys from different PKGs on the same identity. Based on this model, we propose an adaptively secure protocol under the gap Diffie-Hellman assumption in the random oracle model.

**Keywords:** Identity-based authenticated key agreement · Multiple private key generators · Adaptive security · Gap bilinear Diffie–Hellman assumption · Random oracle model

## 1 Introduction

Sharing a key between two parties communicating over insecure channels is one of important topics in cryptography. Once the key is shared, then it allows the establishment of secure communication channels between the two parties.

Recently, *identity-based authenticated key agreement with multiple private key generators* (mPKG-IBAKA) have been researched [7,9–11,15–20,22,23]. In an mPKG-IBAKA protocol, several *private key generator* (PKG) exist. Each PKG generates own master secret and public keys, and publishes the master public key. A party is identified with information called an *identity*, and its static public key can be computed from the identity. Upon request, the PKG extracts a static private key of a party from the master secret key and the identity of the party. A party and its peer exchange ephemeral information in a *session*, and they can generate a common secret, called a *session key*, based on the master public keys, their identities, own static private keys, and the exchanged ephemeral information. The session is identified with the *session ID*, and the party is called the *owner* of the session. This mPKG-IBAKA enables two parties to share a key via an insecure channel and both parties are assured that only their intended peers can derive the session key.

© Springer International Publishing AG 2017
S. Obana and K. Chida (Eds.): IWSEC 2017, LNCS 10418, pp. 192–211, 2017.
DOI: 10.1007/978-3-319-64200-0_12

Each party may belong to a group managed by a different PKG in an mPKG-IBAKA protocol whereas a single PKG manages all parties in a conventional identity-based authenticated key agreement protocol. The PKGs in some mPKG-IBAKA protocol can generate master keys independently while the PKGs in another protocol require some parameters to generate master keys. The parameters are called *common parameters*, and they are treated as system parameters. Thus, the latter mPKG-IBAKA protocol assumes that there exists an additional party, called *common parameter generator* (CPG), who generates the common parameter. In this paper, we adapt the this type, and utilize the CPG in the proposed protocol.

The most important security requirement for mPKG-IBAKA is that the session key is kept secret from other parties beside the communicating ones. We describe the security formulation below.

The adversary activates all parties and this activation is done in two ways: One is to force the party to send a message and the other is to let the party receive a message. Both are done while all communications between the parties are controlled by the adversary. This formulates passive attacks, that is, the adversary can eavesdrop all communications. We stress that the adversary specifies which PKG is supposed to manage the party in the activation. When a party generates the session key in a session, the session is referred to as being complete. In two-pass protocols, the party would have both outgoing and incoming messages in the session for the completed session. If an owner has a completed session and its peer has the same session ID as the completed session, the session of the peer is called a *matching session*. The adversary may adaptively access session keys, static private keys, ephemeral private keys, and master secret keys. This formulates active attacks, that is, the adversary can corrupt some parties (including PKGs). At some point, the adversary chooses a session as the *test session* and it is given a value, which is the session key of the session or a random value with probability $\frac{1}{2}$. The adversary continues the actions and at the end, a bit is output regarding whether or not the given value is the session key with a better probability than $\frac{1}{2}$. This is called the *indistinguishability test* and the aim of the adversary is to pass the indistinguishability test. The adversary is not allowed to access both the static private key and the ephemeral private key of the owner or of its peer (if one exists). If the winning probability of this game is negligible for any adversary, then the mPKG-IBAKA protocol is *secure*.

We have several security models depending on the revealed information. Fujioka proposed an exposure-resilient mPKG-IBAKA protocol and defined a security model, called *id(m)-eCK model*, to discuss the security of the protocol [11]. The adversary in the id(m)-eCK model can obtain master secret keys if the security condition is not broken trivially. For example, when the adversary obtains master secret keys of the PKGs who manages the owner and its peer of the test session, the adversary trivially win the indistinguishability test. Thus, this kind of leakage is not allowed.

However, the id(m)-eCK model assumes that any identifier of a party is unique globally, i.e., every identifier managed by a PKG must differ from an identifier managed by a different PKG. In other words, there is a binding between an identifier and its PKG. This binding enables us to determine the PKG that manages the party with the identifier. Thus, the security model treats only situation where identities of parties are statically bound to PKGs, that is, an adversary is not allowed to control the bindings.

This may be somewhat strong restriction. A malicious party may obtain the static private keys from different PKGs, and tries to break the security. Considering the real world, it is not rare to use the same login ID, e.g., a Gmail address, in different social network services like Facebook, Linkedin, and so on. This means that the identifier does not directly indicate the service domain, and in other words, the binding between the identifier and the PKG who manage the service is not obvious. Thus, we should not exclude such situation.

## 1.1  Bindings of Identities to PKGs

In the id(m)-eCK model, it is assumed that there is a binding between an identifier and its PKG. We call this *static binding model*. In the static binding model, depending on an identity, the PKG who manage the identity is statically fixed, and an adversary cannot control the binding. Thus, it is natural to consider a strong adversary who adaptively indicates a binding between an identity and its PKG. We call this *adaptive binding model*. In the adaptive binding model, an adversary can choose a PKG who manage an identity, and can obtain the private key from the PKG.

Moreover, we can consider another classification of the security model: an adversary can get the private key of a party only once or it is allowed to obtain several private keys from different PKGs on the same identity. We call the former *separated domain model* and the latter *overlapped domain model*.

Above classifications imply that the id(m)-eCK model is the static binding and separated domain one, and these lead us to a strong model which has the adaptive binding and overlapped domain properties. Actually, existence of such strong model and a possibility of an adaptively secure protocol on the model are pointed out in [11] however neither formal discussion nor proof is shown.

## 1.2  Related Works

A similar scenario has been discussed in *attribute-based encryption* (ABE), an extension of *identity-based encryption*. ABE was proposed by Sahai and Waters [21], and in an ABE scheme, a sender can encrypt a message with some *attributes*, and a receiver can decrypt the ciphertext with decryption keys related to the attributes.

It is assumed that there exists a single authority in a conventional ABE scheme, and the authority extracts the decryption key corresponding to the attribute. Thus, the "key escrow" problem arises in ABE, where the key escrow problem is that the authority can decrypt all ciphertexts. To avoid the problem, *multi-authority attribute-based encryption* (MA-ABE) was proposed by

Chase [6]. In an MA-ABE scheme, each authority is assigned to an attribute, and handles the decryption key related to its attribute.

On IBAKA, a generic construction (named FSXY construction hereafter) based on an *identity-based key encapsulation mechanism* (IB-KEM) is proposed by Fujioka *et al.* [13]. When we apply the IB-KEM scheme with multiple PKGs to the FSXY construction, the resultant protocol is an mPKG-IBAKA one. Therefore, we may have an adaptively secure mPKG-IBAKA protocol from a multi-authority IB-KEM scheme, a special case of MA-ABE schemes. However, to the best of our knowledge, it is not proved that a resultant protocol on the FSXY construction have the adaptive security.

### 1.3   Our Contributions

We define a security model for mPKG-IBAKA to acquire the adaptive security, i.e., the security in the adaptive binding and overlapped domain model. Based on the security model, we propose a one-round protocol adaptively secure under the gap bilinear Diffie–Hellman (GBDH) assumption [1] in a random oracle model (ROM) [3]. Roughly speaking, the GBDH problem is to solve the computational bilinear Diffie–Hellman problem with help of the decisional bilinear Diffie–Hellman oracle, and the GBDH assumption is that the GBDH problem is hard.

We give a reduction algorithm from an adversary for an mPKG-IBAKA protocol to the GBDH solver. The reduction algorithm simulates all queries asked by the adversary, and the security in the adaptive binding model is proved when this simulation is carefully designed as the reduction algorithm correctly guesses the PKG that is related to the test session.

On the other hand, to satisfy the security in the overlapped domain model, we generate each static public key using not only the identifier but also the master public key.

## 2   Definitions and Assumptions

### 2.1   Adaptive Security Model for mPKG-IBAKA

We modify the id(m)-eCK model [11] and define a new security model, *id(m)-aeCK model*, for mPKG-IBAKA to captures the adaptive security for mPKG-IBAKA. It is worth to note here that the proposed protocol is two-pass one and thus, we describe the security model as for two-pass mPKG-IBAKA protocol.

We denote a party (resp. PKG) as $U_i$ (resp. $P_\iota$) and the identifier of $U_i$ (resp. $P_\iota$) as $id_i$ (resp. $pid_\iota$). We outline our model for a two-pass mPKG-IBAKA protocol where parties $U_A$ and $U_B$ exchange ephemeral public keys $X_A$ and $X_B$ together with the identifiers of their PKGs, i.e., $U_A$ sends $(X_A, pid_\alpha)$ to $U_B$ and $U_B$ sends $(X_B, pid_\beta)$ to $U_A$, and thereafter derive a session key. The session key depends on the exchanged ephemeral keys, identifiers of the parties, identifiers of the PKGs, the static keys corresponding to these identifiers, and the protocol instance that is used.

In the model, each party is a probabilistic polynomial-time Turing machine in security parameter $\lambda$ and obtains a static private key corresponding to its identifier string from its PKG via a secure and authenticated channel.

**Session.** An invocation of a protocol is called a *session*. A session is activated via an incoming message in the form of $(\Pi, \mathcal{I}, id_A, id_B, pid_\alpha, pid_\beta)$ or $(\Pi, \mathcal{R}, id_A, id_B, pid_\alpha, pid_\beta, X_B)$, where $\Pi$ is a protocol identifier. If $U_A$ is activated with $(\Pi, \mathcal{I}, id_A, id_B, pid_\alpha, pid_\beta)$, then $U_A$ is the session *initiator*; otherwise, it is the session *responder*. After activation, $U_A$ appends ephemeral public key $X_A$ to the incoming message and sends it as an outgoing response. If $U_A$ is the responder, $U_A$ computes a session key. If $U_A$ is the initiator, $U_A$ that has been successfully activated via $(\Pi, \mathcal{I}, id_A, id_B, pid_\alpha, pid_\beta)$ can be further activated via $(\Pi, \mathcal{I}, id_A, id_B, pid_\alpha, pid_\beta, X_A, X_B)$ to compute a session key.

If $U_A$ is the initiator of a session, the session is identified by either $\mathtt{sid} = (\Pi, \mathcal{I}, id_A, id_B, pid_\alpha, pid_\beta, X_A)$ or $\mathtt{sid} = (\Pi, \mathcal{I}, id_A, id_B, pid_\alpha, pid_\beta, X_A, X_B)$. If $U_B$ is the responder of a session, the session is identified by $\mathtt{sid} = (\Pi, \mathcal{R}, id_B, id_A, pid_\beta, pid_\alpha, X_A, X_B)$. We say that $U_A$ is the *owner* (resp. *peer*) of session $\mathtt{sid}$ if the third (resp. fourth) coordinate of session $\mathtt{sid}$ is $id_A$. We say that a session is *completed* if its owner computes a session key. The *matching session* of $(\Pi, \mathcal{I}, id_A, id_B, pid_\alpha, pid_\beta, X_A, X_B)$ is session $(\Pi, \mathcal{R}, id_B, id_A, pid_\beta, pid_\alpha, X_A, X_B)$ and vice versa.

**Adversary.** Adversary $\mathcal{A}$ is modeled as a probabilistic Turing machine that controls all communications between parties including session activation. Activation is performed via a Send(MESSAGE) query. The MESSAGE has one of the following forms: $(\Pi, \mathcal{I}, id_A, id_B, pid_\alpha, pid_\beta)$, $(\Pi, \mathcal{R}, id_A, id_B, pid_\alpha, pid_\beta, X_A)$, or $(\Pi, \mathcal{I}, id_A, id_B, pid_\alpha, pid_\beta, X_A, X_B)$. Each party submits its responses to adversary $\mathcal{A}$, who decides the global delivery order. Note that adversary $\mathcal{A}$ does not control the communication between each party and its PKG.

The private information of a party is not accessible to adversary $\mathcal{A}$; however, leakage of private information is obtained via the following adversary queries.

- SessionKeyReveal(sid): $\mathcal{A}$ obtains the session key for session $\mathtt{sid}$, provided that the session holds a session key.
- EphemeralKeyReveal(sid): $\mathcal{A}$ obtains the ephemeral private key (of the session owner) associated with session $\mathtt{sid}$.
- StaticKeyReveal($id_i, pid_\iota$): $\mathcal{A}$ learns the static private key of party $U_i$ managed by PKG $P_\iota$.
- MasterKeyReveal($pid_\iota$): $\mathcal{A}$ learns the master secret key of PKG $P_\iota$. For the sake of convenient queries, when MasterKeyReveal() is called, i.e., called with no argument, the master secret keys of all PKGs are returned.
- NewParty($id_i$): This query models malicious insiders. If a party is established by a NewParty($id_i$) query issued by $\mathcal{A}$, then we refer to the party as *dishonest*. If not, the party is referred to as *honest*.

A Send query contains $pid_\alpha$ (resp. $pid_\beta$), which means that $\mathcal{A}$ specifies the binding between $U_A$ (resp. $U_B$) and $P_\alpha$ (resp. $P_\beta$). $\mathcal{A}$ can obtain static private key $D_{i,\iota}$ of $U_i$ on $P_\iota$ via a StaticKeyReveal($id_i, pid_\iota$) query.

**Freshness.** Our security definition requires the following "freshness" notion.

**Definition 2.1 (freshness).** *Let* sid* *be the session identifier of a completed session owned by honest party $U_A$ with peer $U_B$ who is also honest. If a matching session exists, then let* $\overline{sid^*}$ *be the session identifier of the matching session of* sid*. *We define* sid* *to be* fresh *if none of the following conditions hold.*

1. *$\mathcal{A}$ issues* SessionKeyReveal(sid*) *or* SessionKeyReveal($\overline{sid^*}$) *(if $\overline{sid^*}$ exists).*
2. $\overline{sid^*}$ *exists and $\mathcal{A}$ makes either of the following queries:*
   - *both* StaticKeyReveal($id_A, pid_\alpha$) *and* EphemeralKeyReveal(sid*), *or*
   - *both* StaticKeyReveal($id_B, pid_\beta$) *and* EphemeralKeyReveal($\overline{sid^*}$).
3. $\overline{sid^*}$ *does not exist and $\mathcal{A}$ makes either of the following queries:*
   - *both* StaticKeyReveal($id_A, pid_\alpha$) *and* EphemeralKeyReveal(sid*), *or*
   - StaticKeyReveal($id_B, pid_\beta$).

*Note that if adversary $\mathcal{A}$ issues* MasterKeyReveal(), *we regard $\mathcal{A}$ as having issued both* StaticKeyReveal($id_A, pid_\alpha$) *and* StaticKeyReveal($id_B, pid_\beta$). *In addition, if $\mathcal{A}$ issues* MasterKeyReveal($P_\alpha$) *(resp.* MasterKeyReveal($P_\beta$)), *we regard $\mathcal{A}$ as having issued* StaticKeyReveal($id_A, pid_\alpha$) *(resp.* StaticKeyReveal($id_B, pid_\beta$)).

This definition implies that the adversary can trivially obtain its session key when a session is not fresh: 1. When $\mathcal{A}$ issues SessionKeyReveal(sid*) or SessionKeyReveal($\overline{sid^*}$) (if $\overline{sid^*}$ exists), it is obvious that $\mathcal{A}$ knows the session key of session sid* as the session key of session $\overline{sid^*}$ equals the session key of session sid*. 2. Assume that $\overline{sid^*}$ exists and that $\mathcal{A}$ makes either of the following queries: 2a) both StaticKeyReveal($id_A, pid_\alpha$) and EphemeralKeyReveal(sid*), or 2b) both StaticKeyReveal($id_B, pid_\beta$) and EphemeralKeyReveal($\overline{sid^*}$). In the former case (2a), $\mathcal{A}$ can compute the session key of session sid* as $\mathcal{A}$ knows both static and ephemeral private keys of $U_A$ (on $P_\alpha$). In the latter case (2b), $\mathcal{A}$ can compute the session key of session $\overline{sid^*}$ as $\mathcal{A}$ knows both static and ephemeral private keys of $U_B$ (on $P_\beta$), and then, the session key of session $\overline{sid^*}$ equals the session key of session sid*. 3. Assume that $\overline{sid^*}$ does not exist and that $\mathcal{A}$ makes either of the following queries: 3a) both StaticKeyReveal($id_A, pid_\alpha$) and EphemeralKeyReveal(sid*), or 3b) StaticKeyReveal($id_B, pid_\beta$). In the former case (3a), $\mathcal{A}$ can compute the session key of session sid* as $\mathcal{A}$ knows both static and ephemeral private keys of $U_A$ (on $P_\alpha$). In the latter case (3b), $\mathcal{A}$ can compute the session key of session $\overline{sid^*}$ as $\mathcal{A}$ knows the static private key of $U_B$ (on $P_\beta$) and may know the ephemeral private key of the peer (when $\overline{sid^*}$ does not exist, the ephemeral public key of the peer may be generated by $\mathcal{A}$), and then, the session key of session $\overline{sid^*}$ equals the session key of session sid*.

**Security Experiment.** Adversary $\mathcal{A}$ starts with common parameters, a set of master public keys together, and a set of honest parties for whom $\mathcal{A}$ adaptively selects identifiers. The adversary makes an arbitrary sequence of the queries described above. During the experiment, $\mathcal{A}$ makes a special query, Test(sid*), and is given with equal probability either the session key held by session sid* or a random key. The experiment continues until $\mathcal{A}$ makes a guess regarding whether or not the key is random. The adversary *wins* the game if the test session, sid*, is *fresh* at the end of execution and if the guess by $\mathcal{A}$ was correct.

**Definition 2.2 (id(m)-aeCK security).** *The advantage of adversary $\mathcal{A}$ in the experiment with mPKG-IBAKA protocol $\Pi$ is defined as*

$$\mathbf{Adv}_{\Pi}^{\text{mPKG-IBAKA}}(\mathcal{A}) = \Pr[\mathcal{A} \ wins] - \frac{1}{2}.$$

*We say that $\Pi$ is a secure mPKG-IBAKA protocol in the id(m)-aeCK model if the following conditions hold.*

1. *If two honest parties have a complete matching session, then except with negligible probability in security parameter $\lambda$, they both derive the same session key.*
2. *Advantage $\mathbf{Adv}_{\Pi}^{\text{mPKG-IBAKA}}(\mathcal{A})$ is negligible in security parameter $\lambda$ for any probabilistic polynomial-time adversary $\mathcal{A}$.*

**Model Assumptions.** We assume that there exists a *common parameter generator* (CPG) that is a probabilistic polynomial-time Turing machine in security parameter $\lambda$ and the CPG generates common parameters. Note that the CPG has no secret information. Based on these common parameters, each PKG generates its master public and private keys. Note that the PKGs are also probabilistic polynomial-time Turing machines in security parameter $\lambda$.

## 2.2   Number Theoretic Assumptions on Pairings

As a tool to actualize IBAKA protocols, we have a mathematical function called *pairing*. Symmetric pairing function[1] $e$ is a polynomial-time computable bilinear non-degenerate map from two group elements to an element of another group where $e(g^a, g^b) = g_T^{ab}$ holds when $\mathbb{G}$ and $\mathbb{G}_T$ are two cyclic groups of order $q$, $g$ is a generator of $\mathbb{G}$, $g_T = e(g, g)$ $(\in \mathbb{G}_T)$, and $a, b \in \mathbb{Z}_q$.

Roughly speaking, the computational bilinear Diffie–Hellman (CBDH) problem is to compute $e(g, g)^{uvw}$ on input $(U, V, W)$ and the decisional bilinear Diffie–Hellman (DBDH) problem is to determine whether or not $uvw = x \bmod q$ holds on input $(U, V, W, X)$, where $U = g^u$, $V = g^v$, $W = g^w$, and $X = e(g, g)^x$.

We formally state the gap bilinear Diffie–Hellman (GBDH) assumption [1] as follows: Let $\mathbb{G}$ and $\mathbb{G}_T$ be cyclic groups of order $q$ where pairing function, $e : \mathbb{G}^2 \to \mathbb{G}_T$ exists, and $\mathbb{G}$ has generator $g$. CBDH function $\text{CBDH} : \mathbb{G}^3 \to \mathbb{G}_T$ is a function that takes input $(U, V, W)$ and returns $e(g, g)^{uvw}$. DBDH predicate $\text{DBDH} : \mathbb{G}^3 \times \mathbb{G}_T \to \{0, 1\}$ is a function that takes input $(U, V, W, X)$ and returns bit 1 if $uvw = x \bmod q$ and bit 0 otherwise, where $U = g^u$, $V = g^v$, $W = g^w$,

---

[1] Pairing $e : \mathbb{G}_1 \times \mathbb{G}_2 \to \mathbb{G}_T$ is referred to as *symmetric* when $\mathbb{G}_1 = \mathbb{G}_2$ and *asymmetric* when $\mathbb{G}_1 \neq \mathbb{G}_2$.

and $X = e(g,g)^x$. The GBDH problem is to compute $\text{CBDH}(U,V,W)$ allowing access to oracle $\text{DBDH}(\cdot,\cdot,\cdot,\cdot)$. For adversary $\mathcal{A}$, we define advantage

$$\mathbf{Adv}^{\text{GBDH}}(\mathcal{A}) = \Pr\left[U,V,W \in_R \mathbb{G}, \mathcal{A}^{\text{DBDH}(\cdot,\cdot,\cdot,\cdot)}(U,V,W) = \text{CBDH}(U,V,W)\right],$$

where the probability is taken over the choices of $U,V,W$ and the random tape of $\mathcal{A}$.

**Definition 2.3 (GBDH assumption).** *We say that $\mathbb{G}$ and $\mathbb{G}_T$ satisfy the GBDH assumption if, for any adversary $\mathcal{A}$ running in a polynomial-time, advantage $\mathbf{Adv}^{\text{GBDH}}(\mathcal{A})$ is negligible in security parameter $\lambda$.*

The *square* GBDH problem is a special case of the GBDH problem, where in the square GBDH problem, a solver computes $e(g,g)^{u^2 w}$ from $(U,W)$, not $e(g,g)^{uvw}$ from $(U,V,W)$, with help from the DBDH oracle.

# 3 Adaptively Secure mPKG-IBAKA Protocol

## 3.1 Proposed Protocol

In this section, we describe actions required to execute a session.

The proposed IBAKA protocol, $\Pi$, is described as follows:

Let $\lambda$ be the security parameter.


**Preparation.** We use three algorithms, PGen, KGen, and Ext for common parameter generation, PKG setup, and user key extraction, respectively. On input $\lambda$, PGen outputs common parameters. On the common parameters as input, KGen outputs master secret and public keys. On the common parameters, master secret key, and an user identifier as inputs, Ext outputs a static private key.

The CPG runs PGen to generates cyclic groups $\mathbb{G}$ and $\mathbb{G}_T$ where their orders are $\lambda$-bit prime $q$, $g$ is a generator of $\mathbb{G}$, $e : \mathbb{G}^2 \to \mathbb{G}_T$ is a pairing function, and $g_T = e(g,g)$. Let $H : \{0,1\}^* \to \{0,1\}^\lambda$, $H_1 : \{0,1\}^* \longrightarrow \mathbb{G}$, and $H_2 : \{0,1\}^* \longrightarrow \mathbb{Z}_q$ be cryptographic hash functions modeled as random oracles [3]. The CPG publishes $(\mathbb{G}, \mathbb{G}_T, g, g_T, q, e, H, H_1, H_2)$ as common parameters.

Each PKG $P_\iota$ runs KGen. Based on the above common parameters, KGen randomly selects master secret key $z_\iota$ $(\in_R \mathbb{Z}_q)$, and computes $Z_\iota = g^{z_\iota}$ $(\in \mathbb{G})$. $P_\iota$ publishes $Z_\iota$ as the master public key.

User $U_i$ with identifier $id_i$ is assigned static private key $D_{i,\iota} = Q_{i,\iota}^{z_\iota}$ $(\in \mathbb{G})$ on $P_\iota$, whose identifier is $pid_\iota$, by using Ext where $Q_{i,\iota} = H_1(Z_\iota, id_i)$ $(\in \mathbb{G})$. We refer to $Q_{i,\iota}$ as the *static public key* of user $U_i$ on $P_\iota$, and note that $Q_{i,\iota}$ is expressed with some $q_{i,\iota}$ $(\in \mathbb{Z}_q)$ as $Q_{i,\iota} = g^{q_{i,\iota}}$.

Thus, the identifier and static public (resp. private) key of $U_A$ on $P_\alpha$ are $id_A$ and $Q_{A,\alpha} = H_1(Z_\alpha, id_A) = g^{q_{A,\alpha}}$ (resp. $D_{A,\alpha} = g^{z_\alpha q_{A,\alpha}}$), and the identifier and static public (resp. private) key of $U_B$ on $P_\beta$ are $id_B$ and $Q_{B,\beta} = H_1(Z_\beta, id_B) = g^{q_{B,\beta}}$ (resp. $D_{B,\beta} = g^{z_\beta q_{B,\beta}}$), respectively.

**Key Agreement.** User $U_A$ is the session initiator and user $U_B$ is the session responder.

1. $U_A$ chooses a uniformly random ephemeral private key, $x_A$ $(\in_R \mathbb{Z}_q)$, computes the ephemeral public key, $X_A = g^{x'_A}$, where $x'_A = H_2(x_A, D_{A,\alpha})$, and sends $(\Pi, id_A, id_B, pid_\alpha, pid_\beta, X_A)$ to $U_B$.
2. Upon receiving $(\Pi, id_A, id_B, pid_\alpha, pid_\beta, X_A)$, $U_B$ chooses ephemeral private key $x_B$ $(\in_R \mathbb{Z}_q)$, computes the ephemeral public key, $X_B = g^{x'_B}$, where $x'_B = H_2(x_B, D_{B,\beta})$, and responds to $U_A$ with $(\Pi, id_A, id_B, pid_\alpha, pid_\beta, X_A, X_B)$. $U_B$ also computes $Q_{A,\alpha} = H_1(Z_\alpha, id_A)$, the shared secrets,

$$\sigma_1 = e(Q_{A,\alpha}, Z_\alpha^{x'_B}), \ \ \sigma_2 = e(D_{B,\beta}, X_A), \text{ and } \sigma_3 = X_A^{x'_B},$$

and session key $K$ as $K = H(\sigma_1, \sigma_2, \sigma_3, \Pi, id_A, id_B, pid_\alpha, pid_\beta, X_A, X_B)$. Then, $U_B$ completes the session with session key $K$.
3. Upon receiving $(\Pi, id_A, id_B, pid_\alpha, pid_\beta, X_A, X_B)$, $U_A$ computes $Q_{B,\beta} = H_1(Z_\beta, id_B)$, the shared secrets,

$$\sigma_1 = e(D_{A,\alpha}, X_B), \ \ \sigma_2 = e(Q_{B,\beta}, Z_\beta^{x'_A}), \text{ and } \sigma_3 = X_B^{x'_A},$$

and session key $K$ as $K = H(\sigma_1, \sigma_2, \sigma_3, \Pi, id_A, id_B, pid_\alpha, pid_\beta, X_A, X_B)$. Then, $U_A$ completes the session with session key $K$ (Fig. 1).

| $Z_\alpha = g^{z_\alpha}$ | $Z_\beta = g^{z_\beta}$ |
|---|---|
| $Q_{A,\alpha} = H_1(Z_\alpha, id_A)$ | $Q_{B,\beta} = H_1(Z_\beta, id_B)$ |
| $D_{A,\alpha} = Q_{A,\alpha}^{z_\alpha}$ | $D_{B,\beta} = Q_{B,\beta}^{z_\beta}$ |

$$x_A \in_R \mathbb{Z}_q$$
$$x'_A = H_2(x_A, D_{A,\alpha})$$
$$X_A = g^{x'_A} \quad \xrightarrow{\ X_A\ }$$
$$\qquad\qquad x_B \in_R \mathbb{Z}_q$$
$$\qquad\qquad x'_B = H_2(x_B, D_{B,\beta})$$
$$\xleftarrow{\ X_B\ } \qquad X_B = g^{x'_B}$$

| $\sigma_1 = e(D_{A,\alpha}, X_B)$ | $\sigma_1 = e(Q_{A,\alpha}, Z_\alpha^{x'_B})$ |
|---|---|
| $\sigma_2 = e(Q_{B,\beta}, Z_\beta^{x'_A})$ | $\sigma_2 = e(D_{B,\beta}, X_A)$ |
| $\sigma_3 = X_B^{x'_A}$ | $\sigma_3 = X_A^{x'_B}$ |

$$K = H(\sigma_1, \sigma_2, \sigma_3, \Pi, id_A, id_B, pid_\alpha, pid_\beta, X_A, X_B)$$

**Fig. 1.** Outline of proposed protocol.

Both parties compute the shared secrets,

$$\sigma_1 = g_T^{z_\alpha q_{A,\alpha} x'_B}, \ \ \sigma_2 = g_T^{z_\beta q_{B,\beta} x'_A}, \text{ and } \sigma_3 = g^{x'_A x'_B},$$

where $q_{A,\alpha} = \log_g Q_{A,\alpha}$, $q_{B,\beta} = \log_g Q_{B,\beta}$. Here, $\log_g U$ denotes the logarithm of $U$, i.e., $U = g^{\log_g U}$. Therefore, they can derive the same session key, $K$. We may omit $g$ in $\log_g U$ as $\log U$ if obvious.

## 3.2  Security

The proposed mPKG-IBAKA protocol is secure based on our security notion under the GBDH assumption [1] in the ROM [3].

**Theorem 3.1.** *If* $\mathbb{G}$ *and* $\mathbb{G}_T$ *are groups where the GBDH assumption holds and* $H$, $H_1$, *and* $H_2$ *are random oracles, the proposed IBAKA protocol,* $\Pi$, *is secure in the id(m)-aeCK model.*

*In particular, for any IBAKA adversary* $\mathcal{A}$ *against* $\Pi$ *that runs in at most* $t$ *time, involves at most* $n$ *honest parties, activates at most* $s$ *sessions, and makes at most* $h$ *queries to the random oracles, there exists a GBDH solver,* $\mathcal{S}$, *such that*

$$\mathbf{Adv}^{\mathrm{GBDH}}(\mathcal{S}) \geq \min\left\{\frac{1}{n^2 s^2}, \frac{1}{n^3 s}\right\} \cdot \mathbf{Adv}_\Pi^{\mathrm{mPKG\text{-}IBAKA}}(\mathcal{A}),$$

*where* $\mathcal{S}$ *runs in time* $t$ *plus time to perform* $\mathcal{O}((n + s)\log q)$ *group operations on* $\mathbb{G}$ *and makes* $\mathcal{O}(h + s)$ *queries to the DBDH oracle.*

*Here, we assume that the number of PKGs is bound by the number of honest parties, i.e.,* $n$.

*Proof.* We need the GBDH assumption in pairing groups $\mathbb{G}$ and $\mathbb{G}_T$ of prime order $q$ with generators $g$ and $g_T$, respectively, when trying to compute the answer, $\mathrm{CBDH}(U, V, W)$, from instance $(U, V, W)$, while accessing the DBDH oracle, $\mathrm{CBDH}(g^u, g^v, g^w) = g_T^{uvw}$, and the DBDH oracle on input $(g^u, g^v, g^w, g_T^x)$ returns bit 1 if $uvw = x$, or bit 0 otherwise.

We show that if a polynomially bounded adversary can distinguish the session key of a fresh session from a randomly chosen session key, we can solve the GBDH problem. Let $\lambda$ denote the security parameter, and let $\mathcal{A}$ be a polynomial-time adversary in security parameter $\lambda$. Here, we assume that $\lambda = \lfloor \log q \rfloor$. We use $\mathcal{A}$ to construct the GBDH solver, $\mathcal{S}$, that succeeds in solving a CBDH instance with non-negligible probability using the DBDH oracle. Adversary $\mathcal{A}$ is said to be successful with non-negligible probability if $\mathcal{A}$ wins the distinguishing game with probability $\frac{1}{2} + f(\lambda)$ where $f(\lambda)$ is non-negligible, and event $M$ denotes that $\mathcal{A}$ is successful.

Let the test session be $\mathtt{sid}^*$, and $\mathtt{sid}^*$ be either $(\Pi, \mathcal{I}, id_A, id_B, pid_\alpha, pid_\beta, X_A, X_B)$ or $(\Pi, \mathcal{R}, id_B, id_A, pid_\beta, pid_\alpha, X_A, X_B)$, which is a completed session between honest users $U_A$ on $P_\alpha$ and $U_B$ on $P_\beta$ where users $U_A$ and $U_B$ are the initiator and the responder of test session $\mathtt{sid}^*$, respectively. Let $H^*$ be the event that $\mathcal{A}$ queries $(\sigma_1, \sigma_2, \sigma_3, \Pi, id_A, id_B, pid_\alpha, pid_\beta, X_A, X_B)$ to $H$. Let $\overline{H^*}$ be the complement of event $H^*$. Let $\mathtt{sid}$ be any completed session owned by an honest user such that $\mathtt{sid} \neq \mathtt{sid}^*$ and $\mathtt{sid}$ does not match $\mathtt{sid}^*$. Since $\mathtt{sid}$ and $\mathtt{sid}^*$ are distinct and non-matching, the inputs to key derivation function $H$ are different for $\mathtt{sid}$ and $\mathtt{sid}^*$. Since $H$ is a random oracle, adversary $\mathcal{A}$ cannot obtain any information regarding the test session key from the session keys of non-matching sessions. Hence, $\Pr[M \wedge \overline{H^*}] \leq \frac{1}{2}$ and $\Pr[M] = \Pr[M \wedge H^*] + \Pr[M \wedge \overline{H^*}] \leq \Pr[M \wedge H^*] + \frac{1}{2}$, where $f(\lambda) \leq \Pr[M \wedge H^*]$. Henceforth, $M^*$ denotes event $M \wedge H^*$.

We denote a user as $U_i$. User $U_i$ and other parties are modeled as probabilistic polynomial-time Turing machines in security parameter $\lambda$. We denote a master secret (resp. public) key of $P_\iota$ by $z_\iota$ (resp. $Z_\iota$). For user $U_i$, we denote the static private (resp. public) key as $D_{i,\iota}$ (resp. $Q_{i,\iota}$) and an ephemeral private (resp. public) key as $x_i$ (resp. $X_i$). We also denote the session key as $K$. We assume that $\mathcal{A}$ succeeds in the id(m)-aeCK game with non-negligible advantage $\mathbf{Adv}_{\Pi}^{\text{mPKG-IBAKA}}(\mathcal{A})$, $n$ users and at most $n$ PKGs, and activates at most $s$ sessions within a user.

We consider the non-exclusive classification of all possible events based on the freshness conditions in Table 1, where users $U_A$ and $U_B$ are the initiator and the responder of test session $\texttt{sid}^*$, respectively. For example, when the matching session of $\texttt{sid}^*$ does not exist, $\mathcal{A}$ is not allowed to access the session key of the test session and $U_B$'s static private key but is allowed to access $U_A$'s static private key. This corresponds to event $E_1$. When the matching session of $\texttt{sid}^*$ does not exist, $\mathcal{A}$ is not allowed to access the session key of the test session and $U_B$'s static private key but is allowed to access $U_A$'s ephemeral private key. This corresponds to event $E_2$. Other freshness conditions correspond to events $E_3, \ldots, E_6$, respectively.

Table 1 classifies events when identifiers $id_A$ and $id_B$ are distinct and are managed by $P_\alpha$ and $P_\beta$, respectively.

**Table 1.** Classification of attacks when identifiers $id_A$ and $id_B$ are distinct and are managed by different PKGs.

| | $z_\alpha$ | $z_\beta$ | $D_{A,\alpha}$ | $x_A$ | $D_{B,\beta}$ | $x_B$ | Instance embedding | Suc. Prob. |
|---|---|---|---|---|---|---|---|---|
| $E_1$ | r | ok | r | ok | ok | n | $Z_\beta = U, X_A = V, Q_{B,\beta} = W$ | $p_1/n^3 s$ |
| $E_2$ | ok | ok | ok | r | ok | n | $Z_\beta = U, X_A = V, Q_{B,\beta} = W$ | $p_2/n^3 s$ |
| $E_3$ | r | ok | r | ok | ok | r | $Z_\beta = U, X_A = V, Q_{B,\beta} = W$ | $p_3/n^3 s$ |
| $E_4$ | ok | ok | ok | r | ok | r | $Z_\beta = U, X_A = V, Q_{B,\beta} = W$ | $p_4/n^3 s$ |
| $E_5$ | r | r | r | ok | r | ok | $X_A = V, X_B = W$ | $p_5/n^2 s^2$ |
| $E_6$ | ok | r | ok | r | r | ok | $Z_\alpha = U, Q_{A,\alpha} = V, X_B = W$ | $p_6/n^3 s$ |

In the table, "ok" means that the secret/private key is not revealed, "r" means that the secret/private key may be revealed, and "n" means that no matching session exists. The "Instance Embedding" column shows how the simulator embeds an instance of the GBDH problem. The "Suc. Prob." column shows the probability of success of the simulator where $p_i = \Pr[E_i \wedge M^*]$ and $n$ and $s$ are the numbers of parties and sessions, respectively.

Since the classification covers all possible events, at least one event $E_i \wedge M^*$ in the tables occurs with non-negligible probability if event $M^*$ occurs with non-negligible probability. Thus, the GBDH problem can be solved with non-negligible probability, which means that the proposed protocol is secure under the GBDH assumption.

**Event $E_i$.** We consider the following events that cover all cases of behavior of adversary $\mathcal{A}$.

- Let $E_1$ be the event for which test session $\mathtt{sid}^*$ has no matching session $\overline{\mathtt{sid}^*}$ and $\mathcal{A}$ queries StaticKeyReveal($id_A, pid_\alpha$).
- Let $E_2$ be the event for which test session $\mathtt{sid}^*$ has no matching session $\overline{\mathtt{sid}^*}$ and $\mathcal{A}$ queries EphemeralKeyReveal($\mathtt{sid}^*$).
- Let $E_3$ be the event for which test session $\mathtt{sid}^*$ has matching session $\overline{\mathtt{sid}^*}$ and $\mathcal{A}$ queries StaticKeyReveal($id_A, pid_\alpha$) and EphemeralKeyReveal($\overline{\mathtt{sid}^*}$).
- Let $E_4$ be the event for which test session $\mathtt{sid}^*$ has matching session $\overline{\mathtt{sid}^*}$ and $\mathcal{A}$ queries EphemeralKeyReveal($\mathtt{sid}^*$) and EphemeralKeyReveal($\overline{\mathtt{sid}^*}$).
- Let $E_5$ be the event for which test session $\mathtt{sid}^*$ has matching session $\overline{\mathtt{sid}^*}$ and $\mathcal{A}$ queries StaticKeyReveal($id_A, pid_\alpha$) and StaticKeyReveal($id_B, pid_\beta$).
- Let $E_6$ be the event for which test session $\mathtt{sid}^*$ has matching session $\overline{\mathtt{sid}^*}$ and $\mathcal{A}$ queries EphemeralKeyReveal($\mathtt{sid}^*$) and StaticKeyReveal($id_B, pid_\beta$).

To finish the proof, we need to investigate all events which cover all cases of event $M^*$. Hereafter, we consider events $E_i \wedge M^*$ ($i = 1, \ldots, 6$) in the cases of $U_A \neq U_B$ and $P_\alpha \neq P_\beta$, and the rest cases, $U_A = U_B$ or $P_\alpha = P_\beta$, are omitted because of page limitation.

**Event $E_1 \wedge M^*$.** In event $E_1$, test session $\mathtt{sid}^*$ has no matching session $\overline{\mathtt{sid}^*}$, adversary $\mathcal{A}$ obtains $D_{A,\alpha}$, and adversary $\mathcal{A}$ does not obtain $x_A$ and $D_{B,\beta}$ from the condition of freshness. Thus, $\mathcal{A}$ does not obtain either $x'_A$ or $z_\beta$ where $x'_A = H_2(x_A, D_{A,\alpha})$ and $X_A = g^{x'_A}$. In this case, solver $\mathcal{S}$ guesses $P_\beta$, embeds the instance as $Z_\beta = U$ ($= g^u$), $X_A = V$ ($= g^v$) and $Q_{B,\beta} = W$ ($= g^w$), and obtains $g_T^{uvw}$ from shared value $\sigma_2 = e(Q_{B,\beta}^{x'_A}, Z_\beta)$. Note that solver $\mathcal{S}$ can perfectly simulate the StaticKeyReveal queries for other users except $U_B$ by selecting random $q_{i,\iota}$ ($\in_R \mathbb{Z}_q$) and setting $Q_{i,\iota} = H_1(Z_\iota, id_i) = g^{q_{i,\iota}}$ and $D_{i,\iota} = Z_\iota^{q_{i,\iota}}$. In addition, solver $\mathcal{S}$ can perfectly simulate the EphemeralKeyReveal queries for other sessions except $\mathtt{sid}^*$ and $\overline{\mathtt{sid}^*}$ by selecting random $x_i$ ($\in_R \mathbb{Z}_q$) and setting $x'_i = H_2(x_i, D_{i,\iota})$ and $X_i = g^{x'_i}$. In event $E_1 \wedge M^*$, solver $\mathcal{S}$ performs the following **Setup** and **Simulation** phases.

**Setup.** GBDH solver $\mathcal{S}$ embeds $(U, V, W)$, the instance of the GBDH problem, where $U = g^u$, $V = g^v$, and $W = g^w$ as follows: $\mathcal{S}$ establishes $n$ honest users, $U_1, \ldots, U_n$, and at most $n$ honest PKGs, $P_1, \ldots, P_n$. Solver $\mathcal{S}$ randomly selects random $z_\iota$ ($\in_R \mathbb{Z}_q$, $\iota = 1, \ldots, n$) and computes master public keys $Z_\iota = g^{z_\iota}$.

The above is the same procedure with the real protocol, and the below is related to $U$, $V$, and $W$.

Solver $\mathcal{S}$ randomly selects PKG $P_\beta$, randomly selects two users, $U_A$ and $U_B$, and integer $t \in_R [1, s]$, which is a guess of the test session with probability $1/n^3 s$. Here, $n$ is the number of honest parties, and we assume that the number of PKGs is bound by $n$. Solver $\mathcal{S}$ embeds $Z_\beta = U$, sets the ephemeral public key of the $t$-th session of user $U_A$ as $X_A = V$, and sets the static public key of $id_B$ of user $U_B$ on $P_\beta$ as $Q_{B,\beta} = W$.

Solver $S$ selects random $q_{i,\iota}$ ($\in_R \mathbb{Z}_q$), sets $Q_{i,\iota} = H_1(Z_\iota, id_i) = g^{q_{i,\iota}}$ and $D_{i,\iota} = Z_\iota^{q_{i,\iota}}$ if $U_i$ is managed by $P_\iota$, and assigns static private key $D_{i,\iota}$ to user $U_i$ on $P_\iota$ except $U_B$ on $P_\beta$.

Solver $S$ activates adversary $\mathcal{A}$ in this set of users (and PKGs), and awaits actions of $\mathcal{A}$. We next describe actions of $S$ in response to user activation and oracle queries.

**Simulation.** Solver $S$ maintains list $L_H$ that contains queries and answers of the $H$ oracle, list $L_S$ that contains queries and answers of SessionKeyReveal, and list $L_E$ that contains ephemeral private keys, ephemeral exponents, static private keys, and ephemeral public keys. For any $id_i$, $id_k$, $X_i$, and $X_k$, solver $S$ keeps $L_S$ with consistency where $(\Pi, \mathcal{I}, id_i, id_k, pid_\iota, pid_\kappa, X_i, X_k)$ and $(\Pi, \mathcal{R}, id_k, id_i, pid_\kappa, pid_\iota, X_i, X_k)$ have the same answer.

Solver $S$ simulates oracle queries as follows:

1. Send$(\Pi, \mathcal{I}, id_i, id_k, pid_\iota, pid_\kappa)$: Solver $S$ selects uniformly random ephemeral private key $x_i$ ($\in_R \mathbb{Z}_q$) and ephemeral exponent $x_i'$ ($\in_R \mathbb{Z}_q$), computes ephemeral public key $X_i = g^{x_i'}$ honestly, records $(\Pi, \mathcal{I}, id_i, id_k, pid_\iota, pid_\kappa, X_i)$ in List $L_S$, and returns it. $S$ records $(x_i, x_i', D_{i,\iota}, X_i)$ in List $L_E$.

2. Send$(\Pi, \mathcal{R}, id_k, id_i, pid_\kappa, pid_\iota, X_i)$: $S$ selects uniformly random ephemeral private key $x_k$ ($\in_R \mathbb{Z}_q$) and ephemeral exponent $x_k'$ ($\in_R \mathbb{Z}_q$), computes ephemeral public key $X_k = g^{x_k'}$ honestly, records $(\Pi, \mathcal{R}, id_k, id_i, pid_\kappa, pid_\iota, X_i, X_k)$ in List $L_S$ as completed, and returns it. $S$ records $(x_k, x_k', D_{k,\kappa}, X_k)$ in List $L_E$.

3. Send$(\Pi, \mathcal{I}, id_i, id_k, pid_\iota, pid_\kappa, X_i, X_k)$: If session $(\Pi, \mathcal{I}, id_i, id_k, pid_\iota, pid_\kappa, X_i)$ is not recorded in List $L_S$, $S$ records session $(\Pi, \mathcal{I}, id_i, id_k, pid_\iota, pid_\kappa, X_i, X_k)$ in List $L_S$ as not completed. Otherwise, $S$ records the session in List $L_S$ as completed.

4. $H(\sigma_1, \sigma_2, \sigma_3, \Pi, id_i, id_k, pid_\iota, pid_\kappa, X_i, X_k)$:
   (a) If $(\sigma_1, \sigma_2, \sigma_3, \Pi, id_i, id_k, pid_\iota, pid_\kappa, X_i, X_k)$ is recorded in list $L_H$, then $S$ returns recorded value $K$.
   (b) Else if session $(\Pi, \mathcal{I}, id_i, id_k, pid_\iota, pid_\kappa, X_i, X_k)$ or $(\Pi, \mathcal{R}, id_k, id_i, pid_\kappa, pid_\iota, X_i, X_k)$ is recorded in list $L_S$, then solver $S$ checks that shared values $\sigma_1$, $\sigma_2$, and $\sigma_3$, are correctly formed, i.e., solver $S$ checks that DBDH$(Q_{i,\iota}, X_k, Z_\iota, \sigma_1) = 1$, DBDH$(Q_{k,\kappa}, X_i, Z_\kappa, \sigma_2) = 1$, and $e(X_i, X_k) = e(\sigma_3, g)$ hold.
   If $\sigma_1$, $\sigma_2$, and $\sigma_3$ are correctly formed, then $S$ returns recorded value $K$ in list $L_S$ and records it in list $L_H$.
   (c) Else if $i = A$, $k = B$, $\kappa = \beta$, and the session is $t$-th session of user $U_A$, then solver $S$ checks that the shared values, $\sigma_1$, $\sigma_2$, and $\sigma_3$, are correctly formed, i.e., solver $S$ checks that DBDH$(Q_{A,\alpha}, X_B, Z_\alpha, \sigma_1) = 1$, DBDH$(Q_{B,\beta}, X_A, Z_\beta, \sigma_2) = 1$, and $e(X_A, X_B) = e(\sigma_3, g)$ hold.
   If $\sigma_1$, $\sigma_2$, and $\sigma_3$ are correctly formed, then $S$ selects $\sigma_2$ ($= g_T^{uvw}$), the answer of the GBDH instance, from the shared values, and is successful by outputting the answer.
   (d) Otherwise, $S$ returns random value $K$ and records it in list $L_H$.

5. $H_1(Z_\zeta, id_Z)$: If $Z = B$ and $\zeta = \beta$, $\mathcal{S}$ returns $Q_{B,\beta} = W$. Otherwise, $\mathcal{S}$ computes $Z_\zeta = g^{z_\zeta}$ if $Z_\zeta$ does not exist, and responds to the query faithfully.

6. $H_2(x_i, D_{i,\iota})$: If $(x_i, x_i', D_{i,\iota}, X_i)$ is recorded in List $L_E$, then return $x_i'$. Otherwise, solver $\mathcal{S}$ selects uniformly random ephemeral exponent $x_i'$ $(\in_R \mathbb{Z}_q)$, computes ephemeral public key $X_i = g^{x_i'}$ honestly, returns $x_i'$, and records $(x_i, x_i', D_{i,\iota}, X_i)$ in List $L_E$.

7. SessionKeyReveal$(\Pi, \mathcal{I}, id_i, id_k, pid_\iota, pid_\kappa, X_i, X_k)$ or
   SessionKeyReveal$(\Pi, \mathcal{R}, id_k, id_i, pid_\kappa, pid_\iota, X_i, X_k)$:
   (a) If session $(\Pi, \mathcal{I}, id_i, id_k, X_i, X_k)$ or $(\Pi, \mathcal{R}, id_k, id_i, X_i, X_k)$ $(=$ sid$)$ is not completed, solver $\mathcal{S}$ returns error.
   (b) Else if sid is recorded in list $L_S$, then solver $\mathcal{S}$ returns recorded value $K$.
   (c) Else if $(\sigma_1, \sigma_2, \sigma_3, \Pi, id_i, id_k, pid_\iota, pid_\kappa, X_i, X_k)$ is recorded in list $L_H$, then solver $\mathcal{S}$ checks that $\sigma_1$, $\sigma_2$, and $\sigma_3$, are correctly formed, i.e., solver $\mathcal{S}$ checks that DBDH$(Q_{i,\iota}, X_k, Z_\iota, \sigma_1) = 1$, DBDH$(Q_{k,\kappa}, X_i, Z_\kappa, \sigma_2) = 1$, and $e(X_i, X_k) = e(\sigma_3, g)$ hold.
   If $\sigma_1$, $\sigma_2$, and $\sigma_3$ are correctly formed, then solver $\mathcal{S}$ returns recorded value $K$ in list $L_H$ and records it in list $L_S$.
   (d) Otherwise, solver $\mathcal{S}$ returns random value $K$ and records it in list $L_S$.

8. StaticKeyReveal$(id_i, P_\iota)$: If static public key $Q_{i,\iota}$ of user $U_i$ on $P_\iota$ is $W$, then solver $\mathcal{S}$ aborts with failure; otherwise, solver $\mathcal{S}$ responds to the query faithfully.

9. MasterKeyReveal$()$: Solver $\mathcal{S}$ aborts with failure.

10. MasterKeyReveal$(P_\iota)$: $P_\iota = P_\beta$, solver $\mathcal{S}$ aborts with failure. Otherwise, solver $\mathcal{S}$ returns $z_\iota$.

11. Test(sid): If sid is not the $t$-th session of $U_A$, then solver $\mathcal{S}$ aborts with failure. Otherwise, solver $\mathcal{S}$ responds to the query faithfully.

12. EphemeralKeyReveal(sid): If the corresponding ephemeral public key is $V$, then solver $\mathcal{S}$ aborts with failure. Else if the corresponding ephemeral public key is $X_i$, then solver $\mathcal{S}$ selects $(x_i, x_i', D_{i,\iota}, X_i)$ in list $L_E$ and returns $x_i$. Otherwise, solver $\mathcal{S}$ aborts with failure.

13. NewParty$(id_i)$: If $id_i$ is queried before, solver $\mathcal{S}$ returns error. Otherwise, solver $\mathcal{S}$ responds to the query faithfully.

14. If adversary $\mathcal{A}$ outputs guess $\gamma$, solver $\mathcal{S}$ aborts with failure.

The gap assumption is necessary to keep consistency in the oracle simulation, i.e., for the $H$ and SessionKeyReveal oracles in Steps 4(b), 4(c), and 7(c).

**Analysis.** The simulation of the environment for adversary $\mathcal{A}$ is perfect except with negligible probability. The probability that adversary $\mathcal{A}$ selects the session where $U_A$ is the initiator, $U_B$ is the responder, $P_\beta$ is the PKG of $U_B$, ephemeral public key $X_A$ is $V$, and the test session is sid*, is at least $\frac{1}{n^3 s}$. Suppose that this is indeed the case, then solver $\mathcal{S}$ does not abort in Step 11.

Suppose that event $E_1$ occurs, then solver $\mathcal{S}$ does not abort in Steps 8,9,10,11, and 12.

Suppose that event $M^*$ occurs, and adversary $\mathcal{A}$ queries correctly formed $\sigma_1$, $\sigma_2$, and $\sigma_3$ to $H$. Therefore, solver $S$ is successful as described in Step 4c, and does not abort as in Step 14.

Hence, solver $S$ is successful with probability $\Pr[S_1] \geq \frac{p_1}{n^3 s}$ where $p_1$ is the probability that $E_1 \wedge M^*$ occurs, and $S_1$ is the event in which this solver is successful.

**Event $E_2 \wedge M^*$.** In event $E_2$, test session $\mathsf{sid}^*$ has no matching session $\overline{\mathsf{sid}}^*$, $\mathcal{A}$ obtains $x_A$, and $\mathcal{A}$ does not obtain either $D_{A,\alpha}$ or $D_{B,\beta}$ from the condition of freshness. Thus, $\mathcal{A}$ also does not obtain any of $x'_A$, $z_\alpha$, or $z_\beta$. The reduction to the GBDH assumption is similar to event $E_1 \wedge M^*$. GBDH solver $S$ embeds $(U, V, W)$, the instance of the GBDH problem, into $Z_\beta = U$, $X_A = V$, and $Q_{B,\beta} = W$. Hence, solver $S$ is successful with probability $\Pr[S_2] \geq \frac{p_2}{n^3 s}$ where $p_2$ is the probability that $E_2 \wedge M^*$ occurs, and $S_2$ is the event in which this solver is successful.

**Event $E_3 \wedge M^*$.** In event $E_3$, test session $\mathsf{sid}^*$ has matching session $\overline{\mathsf{sid}}^*$, $\mathcal{A}$ obtains $D_{A,\alpha}$ and $x_B$, and $\mathcal{A}$ does not obtain either $x_A$ or $D_{B,\beta}$ from the condition of freshness. Thus, $\mathcal{A}$ also does not obtain either $x'_A$ or $z_\beta$. The reduction to the GBDH assumption is similar to event $E_1 \wedge M^*$. GBDH solver $S$ embeds $(U, V, W)$, the instance of the GBDH problem, into $Z_\beta = U$, $X_A = V$, and $Q_{B,\beta} = W$. Hence, solver $S$ is successful with probability $\Pr[S_3] \geq \frac{p_3}{n^3 s}$ where $p_3$ is the probability that $E_3 \wedge M^*$ occurs, and $S_3$ is the event in which this solver is successful.

**Event $E_4 \wedge M^*$.** In event $E_4$, test session $\mathsf{sid}^*$ has matching session $\overline{\mathsf{sid}}^*$, $\mathcal{A}$ obtains $x_A$ and $x_B$, and $\mathcal{A}$ does not obtain either $D_{A,\alpha}$ or $D_{B,\beta}$ from the condition of freshness. Thus, $\mathcal{A}$ also does not obtain any of $x'_A$, $z_\alpha$, or $z_\beta$. The reduction to the GBDH assumption is similar to event $E_1 \wedge M^*$. GBDH solver $S$ embeds $(U, V, W)$, the instance of the GBDH problem, into $Z_\beta = U$, $X_A = V$, and $Q_{B,\beta} = W$. Hence, solver $S$ is successful with probability $\Pr[S_4] \geq \frac{p_4}{n^3 s}$ where $p_4$ is the probability that $E_4 \wedge M^*$ occurs, and $S_4$ is the event in which this solver is successful.

**Event $E_5 \wedge M^*$.** In event $E_5$, test session $\mathsf{sid}^*$ has matching session $\overline{\mathsf{sid}}^*$, $\mathcal{A}$ obtains $z_\alpha$, $z_\beta$, $D_{A,\alpha}$, and $D_{B,\beta}$, and $\mathcal{A}$ does not obtain either $x_A$ or $x_B$ from the condition of freshness. Thus, $\mathcal{A}$ also does not obtain either $x'_A$ or $x'_B$. The reduction to the GBDH assumption is similar to event $E_1 \wedge M^*$, except for the following points.

In **Setup** and **Simulation**, $S$ embeds $(U, V, W)$, the GBDH instance, as $X_A = V$ and $X_B = W$. In **Simulation**, $S$ obtains $g^{\log X_A \log X_B}$ from shared value $\sigma_3$ and can compute $e(U, g^{\log X_A \log X_B})$, the answer of the GBDH problem.

Hence, solver $S$ is successful with probability $\Pr[S_5] \geq \frac{p_5}{n^2 s^2}$ where $p_5$ is the probability that $E_5 \wedge M^*$ occurs, and $S_5$ is the event in which this solver is successful.

**Event $E_6 \wedge M^*$.** In event $E_6$, test session $\mathtt{sid}^*$ has matching session $\overline{\mathtt{sid}^*}$, $\mathcal{A}$ obtains $x_A$ and $D_{B,\beta}$, and $\mathcal{A}$ does not obtain either $D_{A,\alpha}$ or $x_B$ from the condition of freshness. Thus, $\mathcal{A}$ also does not obtain either $x'_B$ or $z_\alpha$. The reduction to the GBDH assumption is similar to event $E_1 \wedge M^*$, except for the following points.

In **Setup** and **Simulation**, $\mathcal{S}$ embeds $(U, V, W)$, the GBDH instance, as $Z_\alpha = U$, $Q_{A,\alpha} = V$, and $X_B = W$. In **Simulation**, $\mathcal{S}$ obtains $g_T^{\log X_\alpha \log Q_{A,\alpha} \log X_B}$, the answer of the GBDH problem, from shared value $\sigma_1$.

Hence, solver $\mathcal{S}$ is successful with probability $\Pr[S_6] \geq \frac{p_6}{n^3 s}$ where $p_6$ is the probability that $E_6 \wedge M^*$ occurs, and $S_6$ is the event in which this solver is successful.

**Total Analysis.** Combining the success probabilities, we have

$$\mathbf{Adv}^{\mathrm{GBDH}}(\mathcal{S}) \geq \min \left\{ \frac{1}{n^2 s^2}, \frac{1}{n^3 s} \right\} \cdot \mathbf{Adv}_\Pi^{\mathrm{mPKG\text{-}IBAKA}}(\mathcal{A}).$$

This comes from

$$\mathbf{Adv}^{\mathrm{GBDH}}(\mathcal{S}) \geq \min \left\{ \frac{1}{n^2 s^2}, \frac{1}{n^3 s} \right\} \sum_i p_i = \min \left\{ \frac{1}{n^2 s^2}, \frac{1}{n^3 s} \right\} \Pr[M^*]$$

$$\geq \min \left\{ \frac{1}{n^2 s^2}, \frac{1}{n^3 s} \right\} \mathbf{Adv}_\Pi^{\mathrm{mPKG\text{-}IBAKA}}(\mathcal{A}).$$

During the simulation, solver $\mathcal{S}$ performs $\mathcal{O}(n+s)$ exponentiations, i.e., $\mathcal{O}((n+s)\log q)$ group operations on $\mathbb{G}$, to assign static and ephemeral keys, and make (at most) $\mathcal{O}(h+s)$ times DBDH oracle queries for simulating SessionKeyReveal and random oracle $H$ queries.

To complete the argument, we need to investigate the other events in the cases of $U_A = U_B$ or $P_\alpha = P_\beta$. The security analysis in these cases is done in the similar to the case of $P_\alpha \neq P_\beta$ and $U_A \neq U_B$. Roughly speaking, in the cases of $P_\alpha = P_\beta$ and $U_A = U_B$, the security can be reduced to the GBDH problem and the *square* GBDH problem, respectively. The detailed proof will be appeared in the final version of this paper. $\square$

## 3.3   Asymmetric Pairing Case

We describe the proposed protocol using symmetric pairing however the double-key technique [12] enables us to convert it to the one using symmetric pairing.

The followings are the outline of the double-key technique: The PKG generates two static private keys for a party where one is in $G_1$ and the other is in $G_2$. An initiator and a responder exchange two ephemeral keys where one in $G_1$, the other in $G_2$, and they have the same exponent.

The essential differences of the proposed protocol using asymmetric pairing is as follows:

1. Let $e : \mathbb{G}_1 \times \mathbb{G}_2 \to \mathbb{G}_T$ be an asymmetric pairing function. Let $H_{1,(1)} :$ $\{0,1\}^* \longrightarrow \mathbb{G}_1$, and $H_{1,(2)} : \{0,1\}^* \longrightarrow \mathbb{G}_2$ be cryptographic hash functions. Let $g_{(1)}, g_{(2)}$ be generators of $\mathbb{G}_1, \mathbb{G}_2$, respectively.

2. PKG $P_\iota$ randomly selects master secret key $z_\iota$ ($\in_R \mathbb{Z}_q$), and publishes two master public keys, $Z_{\iota,(1)} = g_{(1)}^{z_\iota}$ ($\in \mathbb{G}_1$) and $Z_{\iota,(2)} = g_{(2)}^{z_\iota}$ ($\in \mathbb{G}_2$).

3. $P_\iota$ generates two static private keys, $D_{i,\iota,(1)}, D_{i,\iota,(2)}$, for a party with $id_i$ where $D_{i,\iota,(1)} = Q_{i,\iota,(1)}^{z_\iota}$, $D_{i,\iota,(2)} = Q_{i,\iota,(2)}^{z_\iota}$, $Q_{i,\iota,(1)} = H_{1,(1)}(Z_{\iota,(1)}, Z_{\iota,(2)}, id_i)$, and $Q_{i,\iota,(2)} = H_{1,(2)}(Z_{\iota,(1)}, Z_{\iota,(2)}, id_i)$.

4. An initiator and a responder exchange two ephemeral keys, $(X_{A,(1)}, X_{A,(2)})$ and $(X_{B,(1)}, X_{B,(2)})$ where $X_{A,(1)} = g_{(1)}^{x'_A}$, $X_{A,(2)} = g_{(2)}^{x'_A}$, $X_{B,(1)} = g_{(1)}^{x'_B}$, and $X_{B,(2)} = g_{(2)}^{x'_B}$.

   He initiator checks $e(X_{B,(1)}, g_{(2)}) = e(g_{(1)}, X_{B,(2)})$ holds, and the responder checks $e(X_{A,(1)}, g_{(2)}) = e(g_{(1)}, X_{A,(2)})$ holds.

5. The shared values of $U_A$ are computed as

$$\sigma_{1,(1)} = e(D_{A,\alpha,(1)}, X_{B,(2)}), \quad \sigma_{2,(1)} = e(Q_{B,\beta,(1)}, Z_{\beta,(2)}^{x'_A}), \quad \sigma_{3,(1)} = X_{B,(1)}^{x'_A},$$
$$\sigma_{1,(2)} = e(X_{B,(1)}, D_{A,\alpha,(2)}), \quad \sigma_{2,(2)} = e(Z_{\beta,(1)}^{x'_A}, Q_{B,\beta,(2)}), \quad \sigma_{3,(2)} = X_{B,(2)}^{x'_A}.$$

The shared values of $U_B$ are computed as

$$\sigma_{1,(1)} = e(Q_{A,\alpha,(1)}, Z_{\alpha,(2)}^{x'_B}), \quad \sigma_{2,(1)} = e(D_{B,\beta,(1)}, X_{A,(2)}), \quad \sigma_{3,(1)} = X_{A,(1)}^{x'_B},$$
$$\sigma_{1,(2)} = e(Z_{\alpha,(1)}^{x'_B}, Q_{A,\alpha,(2)}), \quad \sigma_{2,(2)} = e(X_{A,(1)}, D_{B,\beta,(2)}), \quad \sigma_{3,(2)} = X_{A,(2)}^{x'_B}.$$

It is clear that these values computed by both parties coincide.

The adaptive security of the above protocol will be discussed in the final version of this paper.

## 3.4   Discussions

**Adaptive Security.** We carefully examined the proof shown in [11] to check the Fujioka's protocol satisfies the adaptive security.

For the security in the adaptive binding model, we do not need to modify the protocol, and change the simulation to guess which PKG is chosen by the adversary. This deduce the reduction rate but still gives the provable security. Here, the reduction rate is the ratio between the success probability in the security game and the solving probability of the underlying problem.

On the other hand, to satisfy the security in the overlapped domain model, we need to modify the protocol. The difference between the mPKG-IBAKA protocol in [11] and the proposed protocol is on the generation of static keys. The former is given by $Q_{i,\iota} = H_1(id_i)$ and $D_{i,\iota} = Q_{i,\iota}^{z_\iota}$ whereas the latter is $Q_{i,\iota} = H_1(Z_\iota, id_i)$ and $D_{i,\iota} = Q_{i,\iota}^{z_\iota}$. Namely, we require that the static public keys from PKGs are different even for the same user. Thus, the master public key, $Z_\iota$, is inputted to $H_1$ to generate the static public key, $Q_{i,\iota}$. This trick brings the adaptive security, specially in the overlapped domain model.

Consider the case of $D_{i,\iota} = H_1(id_i)^{z_\iota}$. Then, $e(D_{i,\alpha}, Z_\beta) = e(D_{i,\beta}, Z_\alpha)$ must hold for every $U_i$, $P_\alpha$, and $U_\beta$ where $Z_\alpha = g^{z_\alpha}$ and $Z_\beta = g^{z_\beta}$. However, it seems difficult to maintain this consistency in the security reduction. Thus, we adapt the generation of static keys as $Q_{i,\iota} = H_1(Z_\iota, id_i)$ and $D_{i,\iota} = Q_{i,\iota}^{z_\iota}$.

**Comparison.** The FSXY construction gives an IBAKA protocol based on an IB-KEM scheme [13]. The resultant protocol is secure in the the id-CK$^+$ model, and the security proof does not depend on the ROM, i.e., it is proved in the standard model (SM). Here, the id-CK$^+$ model is one of the security models for conventional IBAKA protocols, that is, protocols with single PKG. This model captures the security against leakage of *session states*, where the session state consists of all intermediate values that the party maintains until the session is completed. It may be possible to have a IBAKA protocol secure in a multiple PKG variant of the id-CK$^+$ model as the FSXY construction is based on a modular approach. However, it is not proved that an mPKG-IBAKA protocol on the FSXY construction is adaptively secure.

We compare the proposed protocol with the protocol proposed by Chen and Kudla [7], a protocol on the FSXY construction [13], the protocol proposed by Karthikeyan *et al.* [15], and the protocol proposed by Fujioka [11] because the other protocols [9,10,16–18,22] are attacked [19,20,23] or are only evaluated based on heuristic security.

The security of the Chen–Kudla protocol is based on a multiple PKG variant of the id-BR (id-BJM)$^2$ model [5,8], and is proved in the ROM [3]. The protocol by Karthikeyan *et al.* is secure in a multiple PKG variant of the id-eCK model [14], the Fujioka protocol is secure in another multiple PKG variant of the id-eCK model, and both are proved in the ROM.

We summarize the comparison in Table 2.

**Efficiency.** When we realize mPKG-IBAKA, the following elements, $\Pi$, $\mathcal{I}$ (or $\mathcal{R}$), $id_A$, $id_B$, $pid_\alpha$, and $pid_\beta$, are necessary in any mPKG-IBAKA protocols. The essential element in the proposed protocol is $X_A$ or $X_B$, and thus, the protocol is achieved based on exchanging a single group element.

## 4   Conclusion

The id(m)-aeCK model for identity-based authenticated key agreement in the multiple private key generator setting was defined to provide the adaptive security. We proposed a one-round identity-based authenticated key agreement protocol with multiple private key generators and proved that the protocol is adaptively secure under the gap bilinear Diffie–Hellman assumption in a random

---

$^2$ The model should be called the id-BJM model as the BR model [2] is defined for AKA in a symmetric key setting and the BJM model [4] is defined for AKA in an asymmetric key setting.

Table 2. Comparison of protocols.

| | Model | Adaptive security | Proof |
|---|---|---|---|
| Chen and Kudla [7] | id-BJM | no | ROM |
| FSXY [13] | id-CK$^+$ | no | SM |
| Karthikeyan et al. [15] | id-eCK | no | ROM |
| Fujioka [11] | id-eCK | no | ROM |
| Proposed | id-eCK | yes | ROM |

The "model" entry shows that the security of the protocol is proved in a multiple PKG variant of the indicated model. The "adaptive security" entry shows whether the protocol is adaptively secure, i.e., secure in the adaptive binding and overlapped domain model. The "proof" entry shows that the security proof requires the indicated model.

oracle model. Moreover, the proposed protocol is achieved based on exchanging a single group element; therefore, it is the most efficient.

# References

1. Baek, J., Safavi-Naini, R., Susilo, W.: Efficient multi-receiver identity-based encryption and its application to broadcast encryption. In: Vaudenay, S. (ed.) PKC 2005. LNCS, vol. 3386, pp. 380–397. Springer, Heidelberg (2005). doi:10.1007/978-3-540-30580-4_26
2. Bellare, M., Rogaway, P.: Entity authentication and key distribution. In: Stinson, D.R. (ed.) CRYPTO 1993. LNCS, vol. 773, pp. 232–249. Springer, Heidelberg (1994). doi:10.1007/3-540-48329-2_21
3. Bellare, M., Rogaway, P.: Random oracles are practical: a paradigm for designing efficient protocols. In: Denning, D.E., Pyle, R., Ganesan, R., Sandhu, R.S., Ashby, V. (eds.) CCS 1993, pp. 62–73. ACM, New York (1993)
4. Blake-Wilson, S., Johnson, D., Menezes, A.: Key agreement protocols and their security analysis. In: Darnell, M. (ed.) Cryptography and Coding 1997. LNCS, vol. 1355, pp. 30–45. Springer, Heidelberg (1997). doi:10.1007/BFb0024447
5. Boyd, C., Choo, K.-K.R.: Security of two-party identity-based key agreement. In: Dawson, E., Vaudenay, S. (eds.) Mycrypt 2005. LNCS, vol. 3715, pp. 229–243. Springer, Heidelberg (2005). doi:10.1007/11554868_17
6. Chase, M.: Multi-authority attribute based encryption. In: Vadhan, S.P. (ed.) TCC 2007. LNCS, vol. 4392, pp. 515–534. Springer, Heidelberg (2007). doi:10.1007/978-3-540-70936-7_28
7. Chen, L., Kudla, C.: Identity based authenticated key agreement protocols from pairings. In: IEEE CSFW-16, pp. 219–233. IEEE Computer Society, Washington, D.C. (2003). http://eprint.iacr.org/2002/184
8. Chen, L., Cheng, Z., Smart, N.P.: Identity-based key agreement protocols from pairings. Int. J. Inf. Secur. 6(4), 213–241 (2007)
9. Farash, M.S., Attari, M.A.: Provably secure and efficient identity-based key agreement protocol for independent PKGs using ECC. ISC Int. J. Inform. Secur. 5(1), 55–70 (2013)

10. Farash, M.S., Attari, M.A.: A Pairing-free ID-based key agreement protocol with different PKGs. Int. J. Network Secur. **16**(2), 143–148 (2014)
11. Fujioka, A.: One-round exposure-resilient identity-based authenticated key agreement with multiple private key generators. In: Phan, R.C.-W., Yung, M. (eds.) Mycrypt 2016. LNCS, vol. 10311, pp. 436–460. Springer, Heidelberg (2017). doi:10. 1007/978-3-319-61273-7_21
12. Fujioka, A., Hoshino, F., Kobayashi, T., Suzuki, K., Ustaoğlu, B., Yoneyama, K.: id-eCK Secure ID-based authenticated key exchange on symmetric pairing and its extension to asymmetric case. IEICE Trans. **96-A**(6), 1139–1155 (2013)
13. Fujioka, A., Suzuki, K., Xagawa, K., Yoneyama, K.: Strongly secure authenticated key exchange from factoring, codes, and lattices. In: Fischlin, M., Buchmann, J., Manulis, M. (eds.) PKC 2012. LNCS, vol. 7293, pp. 467–484. Springer, Heidelberg (2012). doi:10.1007/978-3-642-30057-8_28
14. Huang, H., Cao, Z.: An ID-based authenticated key exchange protocol based on bilinear Diffie-Hellman problem. In: Li, W., Susilo, W., Tupakula, U.K., Safavi-Naini, R., Varadharajan, V. (eds.) In: ASIACCS 2009, pp. 333–342. ACM, New York (2009)
15. Karthikeyan, H., Chakraborty, S., Singh, K., Pandu Rangan, C.: An Efficient Multiple PKG Compatible Identity Based Authenticated Key Agreement protocol. IACR Cryptology ePrint Archive. Report 2015/1012 (2015). http://eprint.iacr. org/2015/1012
16. Kim, S., Lee, H., Oh, H.: Enhanced ID-based authenticated key agreement protocols for a multiple independent PKG environment. In: Qing, S., Mao, W., López, J., Wang, G. (eds.) ICICS 2005. LNCS, vol. 3783, pp. 323–335. Springer, Heidelberg (2005). doi:10.1007/11602897_28
17. Lee, H., Kim, D., Kim, S., Oh, H.: Identity-based key agreement protocols in a multiple PKG environment. In: Gervasi, O., Gavrilova, M.L., Kumar, V., Laganá, A., Lee, H.P., Mun, Y., Taniar, D., Tan, C.J.K. (eds.) ICCSA 2005. LNCS, vol. 3483, pp. 877–886. Springer, Heidelberg (2005). doi:10.1007/11424925_92
18. McCullagh, N., Barreto, P.S.L.M.: A new two-party identity-based authenticated key agreement. In: Menezes, A. (ed.) CT-RSA 2005. LNCS, vol. 3376, pp. 262–274. Springer, Heidelberg (2005). doi:10.1007/978-3-540-30574-3_18
19. Mishra, D., Mukhopadhyay, S.: Cryptanalysis of pairing-free identity-based authenticated key agreement protocols. In: Bagchi, A., Ray, I. (eds.) ICISS 2013. LNCS, vol. 8303, pp. 247–254. Springer, Heidelberg (2013). doi:10.1007/ 978-3-642-45204-8_19
20. Oh, J., Moon, S.-J., Ma, J.: An attack on the identity-based key agreement protocols in multiple PKG environment. IEICE Trans. **89-A**(3), 826–829 (2006)
21. Sahai, A., Waters, B.: Fuzzy identity-based encryption. In: Cramer, R. (ed.) EURO-CRYPT 2005. LNCS, vol. 3494, pp. 457–473. Springer, Heidelberg (2005). doi:10. 1007/11426639_27
22. Vallent, T.F., Yoon, E.-J., Kim, H.: An escrow-free two-party identity-based key agreement protocol without using pairings for distinct PKGs. IEEK Trans. Smart Process. Comput. **2**(3), 168–175 (2013)
23. Xie, G.: Cryptanalysis of Noel McCullagh and Paulo S. L. M. Barreto's two-party identity-based key agreement. IACR Cryptology ePrint Archive. Report 2004/308 (2004). http://eprint.iacr.org/2004/308

# Public Key Cryptosystems (2)

# Deterministic Identity-Based Encryption from Lattices with More Compact Public Parameters

Daode Zhang[1,3], Fuyang Fang[1,3($\boxtimes$)], Bao Li[1,2,3], and Xin Wang[1,3]

[1] State Key Laboratory of Information Security,
Institute of Information Engineering, Chinese Academy of Sciences, Beijing, China
{zhangdaode,fyfang13,lb}@is.ac.cn, wangxin9076@iie.ac.cn
[2] Science and Technology on Communication Security Laboratory, Chengdu, China
[3] School of Cyber Security, University of Chinese Academy of Sciences,
Beijing, China

**Abstract.** Xie et al. (SCN 2012) proposed the first deterministic identity-based encryption (DIBE) scheme with an adaptive security in the auxiliary-input setting, under the learning with errors (LWE) assumption. However, the master public key consists of $\mathcal{O}(\lambda)$ number of basic matrices.

- In this paper, we consider to construct adaptively secure DIBE schemes from partitioning functions (IACR'17). By instantiating the DIBE construction with two partitioning functions, we get two DIBE schemes in which the master public key consists of $\mathcal{O}(\log^3 \lambda)$ (respectively, $\mathcal{O}(\log^2 \lambda)$) number of basic matrices in the first (respectively, the second) DIBE scheme.
- We also change the identity-based encryption (IBE) scheme of Yamada16 (Eurocrypt'16) to construct DIBE scheme with the same security from the LWE problem. And the master public key consists of $\mathcal{O}(\lambda^{1/d})$ number of basic matrices, where $d \geq 2$ is a flexible integer.

**Keywords:** Deterministic identity-based encryption · LWE · Adaptively secure · Auxiliary-input · Compact public parameters

## 1 Introduction

A deterministic identity-based encryption (DIBE) scheme, an identity-based encryption scheme [15] that its encryption algorithm is deterministic, was proposed by Bellare et al. [4] via extending the security definition under high min-entropy into the identity-based setting. They defined a notion of identity-based lossy trapdoor functions (IB-LTDFs) and used this primitive to construct DIBE scheme. And they obtained a DIBE scheme by constructing an IB-LTDF with a universal property, based on the DLIN assumption. However, due to the inherent limitation of IB-LTDFs, their scheme can only achieve selective security, i.e., the

© Springer International Publishing AG 2017
S. Obana and K. Chida (Eds.): IWSEC 2017, LNCS 10418, pp. 215–230, 2017.
DOI: 10.1007/978-3-319-64200-0_13

adversary must send the challenge identity before getting the master public key from the challenger.

In SCN12, Xie et al. [16] gave a more efficient secure DIBE scheme in the auxiliary-input setting, based on the hardness of the LWE problem. In their scheme, there exists only 3 matrices in the master public key. However, the scheme only satisfies selective security as the same as the scheme in [4]. The more significant contribution of Xie et al. [16] is that they proposed the first DIBE scheme with a much more realistic adaptive security (or equivalently, full security) in the auxiliary-input setting, based on the same assumption. To our knowledge, their scheme is the only one DIBE scheme that achieves the adaptively security. However, their scheme requires $k+2$ number of basic matrices in the master public key so that it is not efficient as their selectively secure scheme, where $k$ is the bit length of the identity and $k = \Theta(\lambda)$.

**Our Contributions.** In this paper, we focus on the construction of adaptively secure DIBE schemes with shorter public parameters from lattices, more precisely, the LWE assumption. Specifically, we obtain the following results.

- DIBE from Partitioning Functions with compatible algorithms Yam17 [18]. We present our DIBE construction which is based on a partitioning function with associating compatible algorithms. Then, we instantiate our DIBE construction to obtain two DIBE schemes by using two partitioning functions $\mathcal{F}_{\mathrm{MAH}}$ and $\mathcal{F}_{\mathrm{AFF}}$ in [18]. Both our schemes achieve the better space efficiency than the DIBE scheme of Xie et al. [16] with an adaptive security in the auxiliary-input setting, based on the same assumption.
  - In our first DIBE scheme based on the partitioning function $\mathcal{F}_{\mathrm{MAH}}$, the master public key consists of $\mathcal{O}(\log^3 \lambda)$ basic matrices. Furthermore, the public key size, private key size, ciphertext size and ciphertext expansion factor in our scheme are $\mathcal{O}(n^{2+2\eta} \cdot \log^3 n)$, $\mathcal{O}(n^{2+3\eta})$, $\mathcal{O}(n^{1+\eta} \log n)$ and $\mathcal{O}(n^\eta)$ respectively.
  - In our second DIBE scheme based on the partitioning function $\mathcal{F}_{\mathrm{AFF}}$, the master public key consists of $\mathcal{O}(\log^2 \lambda)$ basic matrices. In addition, the public key size, private key size, ciphertext size and ciphertext expansion factor in our scheme are $\mathcal{O}(n^{2+2\eta} \cdot \log^2 n)$, $\mathcal{O}(n^{2+3\eta})$, $\mathcal{O}(n^{1+\eta} \log n)$ and $\mathcal{O}(n^\eta)$ respectively.

  However, in the DIBE scheme of [16], the master public key consists of $k = \Theta(\lambda)$ basic matrices. Additionally, the public key size, private key size, ciphertext size and ciphertext expansion factor of are $\mathcal{O}(n^{2+2\eta} \cdot n)$, $\mathcal{O}(n^{2+3\eta})$, $\mathcal{O}(n^{1+\eta} \log n)$ and $\mathcal{O}(n^\eta)$ respectively.
- DIBE from Yam16 [17]. We also construct adaptively secure DIBE scheme from [17]. In our scheme, the master public key consists of $\mathcal{O}(\lambda^{\frac{1}{d}})$ basic matrices, where $d \geq 2$ is a flexible integer. Furthermore, the public key size, private key size, ciphertext size and ciphertext expansion factor are $\mathcal{O}(n^{2+2\eta} \cdot n^{1/d})$, $\mathcal{O}(n^{2+3\eta})$, $\mathcal{O}(n^{1+\eta} \cdot n^\gamma)$ and $\mathcal{O}(n^\eta \cdot n^\gamma / \log n)$ respectively, where $n^\gamma$ is the bit length of the rounding parameter $p$. More precisely, $p$ is a super-polynomial while $p$ is polynomial in [16].

In Fig. 1, it is easy to see that the parameters $p, t, \sigma$ are all polynomial in our first and second DIBE schemes of Section 3 as same as the parameters in the DIBE scheme of [16], while the parameters in our DIBE scheme of Section 4 are much worse. Furthermore, the number of matrices in the master public key of our DIBE schemes are less than that in the DIBE scheme of [16].

we note that Zhang et al. [19] also constructed an IBE scheme with poly-logarithmic number of matrices in the public parameters, while their security only holds for $Q$-bounded adversary where the adversary can only obtain a prior-bounded $Q$ number of private keys. Thus, we do not consider using their technique to construct DIBE scheme.

| Parameters | DIBE [16] | $1_{st}$ DIBE in Sec. 3 | $2_{nd}$ DIBE in Sec. 3 | DIBE in Sec. 4 |
|---|---|---|---|---|
| $\lambda$ | | | | |
| $n$ | $\lambda$ | same | same | same |
| $m$ | $\mathcal{O}(n \log q)$ | same | same | same |
| $k$ | $\Theta(\lambda) := \lambda$ | same | same | same |
| $q$ | prime closest $2^{n^\eta}$ | same | same | same |
| $p$ | $\mathcal{O}(n^{4.5+3.5\eta})$ | $\mathcal{O}(n^{6.5+5.5\eta} \cdot \log^4 n)$ | $\mathcal{O}(n^{6.5+2.5\eta} \cdot \log n)$ | $\mathcal{O}(n^{c(d-1)+3+2\eta} \log n)$ |
| $t$ | $\mathcal{O}(n^2)$ | $\mathcal{O}(n^{5+4\eta} \cdot \log^3 n)$ | $\mathcal{O}(n^{5+\eta})$ | $\text{poly}(n)$ |
| $\sigma$ | $\mathcal{O}(n^{2.5+\eta})$ | $\mathcal{O}(n^{5+4\eta} \cdot \log^4 n)$ | $\mathcal{O}(n^{5+\eta} \cdot \log n)$ | $\mathcal{O}(n^{c(d-1)+2+\eta} \log n)$ |
| $|\text{mpk}| : \#\text{mat.}$ | $\mathcal{O}(\lambda)$ | $\mathcal{O}(\log^3 \lambda)$ | $\mathcal{O}(\log^2 \lambda)$ | $\mathcal{O}(\sqrt[d]{\lambda})$ |
| **Description:** | | | | |
| $\lambda$–security parameter; | $n$–lattice row dimension; | $m$–lattice column dimension; | | |
| $k$–bit length of identity; | $q$–modulus; | $p$–rounding parameter; | | |
| $t$–message space; | $\sigma$–SampleBasisLeft and SampleBasisRight width; | | | |

**Fig. 1.** Comparison of lattice DIBE schemes with an adaptive security in the auxiliary-input setting.

**Related Works.** In [4], Bellare et al. extended the notion of lossy trapdoor function (LDTF) to identity-setting and introduced the notion of identity-based LTDF (IB-LTDF). And they used IB-LTDF to construct DIBE scheme with a selective security from pairings. Soon afterwards, Escala et al. [8] extended the notion of IB-LTDF [4] and introduced the notion of hierarchical identity-based trapdoor functions (HIB-TDFs). With HIB-TDFs, they could construct deterministic hierarchical identity-based schemes (DHIBE). They instantiated HIB-TDFs form pairings so that they constructed a pairing-based DHIBE scheme. Fang et al. [9] constructed a DHIBE scheme with a selective security based on the hardness of learning with rounding over small modulus [5]. In fact, a DHIBE with a selective security implies a selectively secure DIBE. In SCN12, Xie et al. [16] gave a more efficient and selectively secure DIBE scheme. Additionally, they also proposed the first and the only one DIBE scheme with an adaptive security in the auxiliary-input setting.

## 2    Preliminaries

**Notation.** For the security parameter $\lambda$, let $\mathsf{negl}(\lambda)$ denote a negligible function $f : \mathbb{N} \to \mathbb{R}_{\geq 0}$ and $\mathsf{poly}(\lambda)$ denote unspecified function $f(\lambda) = \mathcal{O}(\lambda^c)$ for some constant $c$. A function $f$ is $\epsilon$-hard-to-invert with respect to the distribution $\mathcal{D}$, if given $h(x)$ with $x \xleftarrow{\$} \mathcal{D}$, there exists no PPT algorithm can find $x$ with probability better than $\epsilon$. We use bold capital letters to denote matrices, such as $\mathbf{A}, \mathbf{B}$, and bold lowercase letters to denote column vectors, such as $\mathbf{x}, \mathbf{y}$. The notations $\mathbf{A}^\top$ and $[\mathbf{A}|\mathbf{B}]$ denote the transpose of the matrix $\mathbf{A}$ and the matrix formed by concatenating $\mathbf{A}$ and $\mathbf{B}$, respectively.

For $n \in \mathbb{N}$, we use $[n]$ to denote a set $\{1, \cdots, n\}$. For integer $q \geq 2$, $\mathbb{Z}_q$ denotes the quotient ring of integer modulo $q$. For any integer $q \geq p \geq 2$ and $x \in \mathbb{Z}_q$, a rounding function $\lfloor \cdot \rceil_p : \mathbb{Z}_q \to \mathbb{Z}_p$ is defined by $\lfloor x \rceil_p = \lfloor (p/q) \cdot x \rceil \mod p$.

### 2.1    Lattices

Every full-rank $m$-dimensional integer lattices $\Lambda$ is defined as the $\mathbb{Z}$-linear combination of $m$ linearly independent vectors $\mathbf{B} = \{\mathbf{b}_1, \cdots, \mathbf{b}_m\} \subset \mathbb{Z}^m$, and $\mathbf{B}$ is a basis of the lattice $\Lambda$. In this work, we deal exclusively with "$q$-ary" lattices which contains a sub-lattice $q\mathbb{Z}^m$ for an integer $q$. For positive integers $q, n, m$, and a matrix $\mathbf{A} \in \mathbb{Z}_q^{n \times m}$, we can define two $m$-dimensional $q$-ary lattices: $\Lambda_q(\mathbf{A}) = \{\mathbf{y} : \mathbf{y} = \mathbf{A}^\top \mathbf{s} \text{ for some } \mathbf{s} \in \mathbb{Z}^n\}$ and $\Lambda_q^\perp(\mathbf{A}) = \{\mathbf{y} : \mathbf{A}\mathbf{y} = \mathbf{0} \mod q\}$.

Let $\mathbf{S}$ be a set of vectors $\mathbf{S} = \{\mathbf{s}_1, \cdots, \mathbf{s}_k\}$ in $\mathbb{R}^m$. We use $\widetilde{\mathbf{S}} = \{\widetilde{\mathbf{s}}_1, \cdots, \widetilde{\mathbf{s}}_k\}$ to denote the Gram-Schmidt orthogonalization of the vectors $\mathbf{s}_1, \cdots, \mathbf{s}_k$ in that order, and $\|\mathbf{S}\|$ to denote the length of the longest vector in $\mathbf{S}$. For a real-valued matrix $\mathbf{R}$, let $s_1(\mathbf{R}) = \max_{\|\mathbf{u}\|=1} \|\mathbf{R}\mathbf{u}\|$ (respectively, $\|\mathbf{R}\|_\infty = \max \|\mathbf{r}_i\|_\infty$) denote the operator norm (respectively, infinity norm) of $\mathbf{R}$.

For $\mathbf{x} \in \Lambda$, define the Gaussian function $\rho_{s,\mathbf{c}}(\mathbf{x})$ over $\Lambda \subseteq \mathbb{Z}^m$ centered at $\mathbf{c} \in \mathbb{R}^m$ with parameter $s > 0$ as $\rho_{s,\mathbf{c}}(\mathbf{x}) = \exp(-\pi \|\mathbf{x} - \mathbf{c}\|/s^2)$. Let $\rho_{s,\mathbf{c}}(\Lambda) = \sum_{\mathbf{x} \in \Lambda} \rho_{s,\mathbf{c}}(\mathbf{x})$, and define the discrete Gaussian distribution over $\Lambda$ as $\mathcal{D}_{\Lambda,s,\mathbf{c}}(\mathbf{x}) = \frac{\rho_{s,\mathbf{c}}(\mathbf{x})}{\rho_{s,\mathbf{c}}(\Lambda)}$, where $\mathbf{x} \in \Lambda$. For simplicity, $\rho_{s,\mathbf{0}}$ and $\mathcal{D}_{\Lambda,s,\mathbf{0}}$ are abbreviated as $\rho_s$ and $\mathcal{D}_{\Lambda,s}$, respectively.

**Learning with Errors.** The learning with errors (LWE) problem, denoted by $\mathrm{LWE}_{q,n,m,\alpha}$, was first proposed by Regev [14]. For integer $n, m = m(n)$, a prime integer $q > 2$, an error rate $\alpha \in (0, 1)$, the LWE problem $\mathrm{LWE}_{q,n,m,\alpha}$ is to distinguish between the following pairs of distributions: $(\mathbf{A}, \mathbf{A}^\top \mathbf{s} + \mathbf{e})$ and $(\mathbf{A}, \mathbf{u})$, where $\mathbf{A} \xleftarrow{\$} \mathbb{Z}_q^{n \times m}, \mathbf{s} \xleftarrow{\$} \mathbb{Z}_q^n, \mathbf{u} \xleftarrow{\$} \mathbb{Z}_q^m$ and $\mathbf{e} \xleftarrow{\$} \mathcal{D}_{\mathbb{Z}^m, \alpha q}$. In [10], Goldwasser et.al showed that the standard LWE assumption implies that LWE is secure even if the secret is taken from an arbitrary distribution with sufficient entropy, and even in the presence of hard-to-invert auxiliary inputs. We describe their useful statement as follows which is crucial to our constructions.

**Lemma 1 ([10], Theorem 5; [16], Lemma 7).** *Let $l \log t > \log q + \omega(\log(n)), t = \mathsf{poly}(n)$. Let $\mathcal{D}$ be any distribution over $\mathbb{Z}_t^n$ and $\mathcal{H}$ be the class* of all functions $h : \mathbb{Z}_t^n \to \{0,1\}^*$ that are $2^{-l\log(t)}$ hard to invert with respect to the distribution $\mathcal{D}$. For any super-polynomial $q = q(n)$, any $m = \text{poly}(n)$, and any $\alpha, \beta \in (0,1)$ such that $\alpha/\beta = \text{negl}(n)$, then the following pairs of distributions: $(\mathbf{A}, \mathbf{A}^\top \mathbf{s} + \mathbf{e}, h(\mathbf{s}))$ and $(\mathbf{A}, \mathbf{u}, h(\mathbf{s}))$ are hard to distinguish, where $\mathbf{A} \xleftarrow{\$} \mathbb{Z}_q^{n\times m}, \mathbf{s} \xleftarrow{\$} \mathcal{D} \subseteq \mathbb{Z}_t^n, \mathbf{u} \xleftarrow{\$} \mathbb{Z}_q^m$ and $\mathbf{e} \xleftarrow{\$} \mathcal{D}_{\mathbb{Z}^m, \beta q}$. Assuming the (standard) $\text{LWE}_{q,z,m,\alpha}$ assumption, where $z \triangleq \frac{l\log(t) - \omega(\log(n))}{\log(q)}$.

For simplicity, we use $\text{LWE}_{q,n,m,\beta,\mathcal{H}}$ to denote the problem of distinguishing the above two distributions: $(\mathbf{A}, \mathbf{A}^\top \mathbf{s} + \mathbf{e}, h(\mathbf{s}))$ and $(\mathbf{A}, \mathbf{u}, h(\mathbf{s}))$. According to Lemma 1, assuming the $\text{LWE}_{q,z,m,\alpha}$, then the $\text{LWE}_{q,n,m,\beta,\mathcal{H}}$ problem is also intractable, where $z \triangleq \frac{l\log(t) - \omega(\log(n))}{\log(q)}$. In the following, we describe some useful facts that will be used in our work.

**Lemma 2.** *Let $p, q, n, m$ be positive integers with $q \geq p \geq 2$ and $q$ prime. There exists PPT algorithms such that*

- *([2,3]): TrapGen$(1^n, 1^m, q)$ a randomized algorithm that, when $m \geq 6n\lceil\log q\rceil$, outputs a pair $(\mathbf{A}, \mathbf{T_A}) \in \mathbb{Z}_q^{n\times m} \times \mathbb{Z}^{m\times m}$ such that $\mathbf{A}$ is statistically close to uniform in $\mathbb{Z}_q^{n\times m}$ and $\mathbf{T_A}$ is a basis of $\Lambda_q^\perp(\mathbf{A})$, satisfying $\|\widetilde{\mathbf{T_A}}\| \leq \mathcal{O}(\sqrt{n\log q})$ with overwhelming probability.*
- *([13]): For $m \geq n\lceil\log q\rceil$, there exists a full rank matrix $\mathbf{G} \in \mathbb{Z}_q^{n\times m}$ such that the lattice $\Lambda_q^\perp(\mathbf{G})$ has a publicly known basis $\mathbf{T_G} \in \mathbb{Z}_q^{m\times m}$ with $\|\widetilde{\mathbf{T_G}}\| \leq \sqrt{5}$. Given $\mathbf{U} \in \mathbb{Z}_q^{n\times m}$, the deterministic polynomial time algorithm $\mathbf{G}^{-1}(\mathbf{U})$ that outputs $\mathbf{R} \in \{0,1\}^{m\times m}$ satisfying $\mathbf{GR} = \mathbf{U}$.*
- *([6]): SampleBasisLeft$(\mathbf{A}, \mathbf{B}, \mathbf{T_A}, \sigma)$ a randomized algorithm that, given a full rank matrix $\mathbf{A} \in \mathbb{Z}_q^{n\times m}$, a matrix $\mathbf{B} \in \mathbb{Z}_q^{n\times m}$, a basis $\mathbf{T_A}$ of $\Lambda_q^\perp(\mathbf{A})$, and $\sigma \geq \|\widetilde{\mathbf{T_A}}\| \cdot \omega(\sqrt{\log m})$ outputs a basis $\mathbf{T_F}$ of $\Lambda_q^\perp(\mathbf{F})$ for $\mathbf{F} = [\mathbf{A}|\mathbf{B}]$ with $\|\widetilde{\mathbf{T_F}}\| \leq \mathcal{O}(\sigma \cdot m)$.*
- *([1]): SampleBasisRight$(\mathbf{A}, \mathbf{G}, \mathbf{R}, \mathbf{T_G}, \sigma)$ a randomized algorithm that, given a full rank matrix $\mathbf{A}, \mathbf{G} \in \mathbb{Z}_q^{n\times m}$, a matrix $\mathbf{R} \in \{-1,1\}^{m\times m}$, a basis $\mathbf{T_G}$ of $\Lambda_q^\perp(\mathbf{G})$, and $\sigma \geq m \cdot \|\mathbf{R}\|_\infty \cdot \omega(\sqrt{\log m})$ outputs a basis $\mathbf{T_F}$ of $\Lambda_q^\perp(\mathbf{F})$ for $\mathbf{F} = [\mathbf{A}|\mathbf{AR} + \mathbf{G}]$ with $\|\widetilde{\mathbf{T_F}}\| \leq \mathcal{O}(\sigma \cdot m)$.*
- *([9]): Invert$(\mathbf{c}, \mathbf{A}, \mathbf{T_A})$ that, given a full rank matrix $\mathbf{A} \in \mathbb{Z}_q^{n\times m}$, a basis $\mathbf{T_A}$ of $\Lambda_q^\perp(\mathbf{A})$ with $\|\widetilde{\mathbf{T_A}}\| < p/(2\sqrt{m})$, and $\mathbf{c} = \lfloor \mathbf{A}^\top \mathbf{m} \rceil_p$ outputs $\mathbf{m}$, where $\mathbf{m} \in \mathbb{Z}_t^n$ with $t \leq q$.*
- *(Leftover Hash Lemma [1,7]): For $m > (n+1)\log q + \omega(\log n)$, let $\mathbf{R} \xleftarrow{\$} \{-1,1\}^{m\times m}$ and $\mathbf{A}, \mathbf{A}' \xleftarrow{\$} \mathbb{Z}_q^{m\times m}$ be uniformly random matrices. Then the distribution $(\mathbf{A}, \mathbf{AR})$ is $\text{negl}(n)$-close to the distribution of $(\mathbf{A}, \mathbf{A}')$.*
- *([13]): Let $x \xleftarrow{\$} \mathcal{D}_{\mathbb{Z},r}$ with $r > 0$, then with overwhelming probability, $|x| \leq r\sqrt{n}$.*

In [12], Katsuamta and Yamada introduced the following lemma which is called "Noise Rerandomization". This lemma plays an important role in the security proof when creating a well distributed challenge ciphertext.

**Lemma 3.** *Let $q, w, m$ be positive integers and $r$ a positive real number with $r > \max\{\omega(\sqrt{\log m}), \omega(\sqrt{\log w})\}$. For arbitrary column vector $\mathbf{b} \in \mathbb{Z}_q^m$, vector $\mathbf{e}$ chosen from $\mathcal{D}_{\mathbb{Z}^m, r}$, any matrix $\mathbf{V} \in \mathbb{Z}^{w \times m}$ and positive real number $\sigma > s_1(\mathbf{V}^\top)$, there exists a PPT algorithm $\mathsf{ReRand}(\mathbf{V}, \mathbf{b} + \mathbf{e}, \mathrm{r}, \sigma)$ that outputs $\mathbf{b}' = \mathbf{Vb} + \mathbf{e}' \in \mathbb{Z}^w$ where $\mathbf{e}'$ is distributed statistically close to $\mathcal{D}_{\mathbb{Z}^m, 2r\sigma}$.*

## 2.2   Partitioning Functions with Compatible Algorithms

In [18], Yamada defined the notion of partitioning functions by slightly generalizing balanced admissible hash functions [11] and used this notion to construct compact adaptively secure lattice IBE schemes. In order to construct IBE from lattice in [18], the underlying partitioning function should be compatible with the structure of lattices. So they defined compatible algorithms for partitioning functions.

**Definition 1.** *([18]). Let $\mathcal{F} = \{\mathcal{F}_\lambda : \mathcal{K}_\lambda \times \mathrm{ID}_\lambda \to \{0,1\}\}$ be an ensemble of function families. We say that $\mathcal{F}$ is a partitioning function, if there exists an efficient algorithm $\mathsf{PrtSmp}(1^\lambda, Q, \epsilon)$, which takes as input polynomially bounded $Q = Q(\lambda) \in \mathbb{N}$ and noticeable $\epsilon = \epsilon(\lambda) \in (0, 1/2)$ and outputs $\mathcal{K}$ such that:*

1. *There exists $\lambda_0 \in \mathbb{N}$ such that $\Pr\left[K \in \mathcal{K}_\lambda : K \xleftarrow{\$} \mathsf{PrtSmp}(1^\lambda, Q, \epsilon)\right] = 1$ for all $\lambda > \lambda_0$. Here, $\lambda_0$ may depend on functions $Q(\lambda)$ and $\epsilon(\lambda)$.*
2. *For $\lambda > \lambda_0$, there exists $\gamma_{\max}(\lambda)$ and $\gamma_{\min}(\lambda)$ that depend on $Q(\lambda)$ and $\epsilon(\lambda)$ such that for all $id_1, \cdots, id_Q, id^*$ with $id^* \notin \{id_1, \cdots, id_Q\}$, the following holds*

$$\gamma_{\max}(\lambda) \geq \Pr[\mathcal{F}(K, id_1) = \cdots \mathcal{F}(K, id_Q) = 1 \wedge \mathcal{F}(K, id^*) = 0] \geq \gamma_{\min}(\lambda).$$

*And the function $\tau(\lambda)$ defined as $\tau(\lambda) = \gamma_{\min}(\lambda)\epsilon(\lambda) - (\gamma_{\max}(\lambda) - \gamma_{\min}(\lambda))/2$ is noticeable. The probability is taken over the choice of $K \xleftarrow{\$} \mathsf{PrtSmp}(1^\lambda, Q, \epsilon)$.*

The deterministic algorithms $(\mathsf{Encode}, \mathsf{PubEval}, \mathsf{TrapEval})$ are called $\delta_{\mathrm{PF}}$-compatible with a function family $\{\mathcal{F}_\lambda : \mathcal{K} \times \mathrm{ID} \to \{0,1\}\}$ if they are efficient and satisfy the following properties:

- $\mathsf{Encode}(K \in \mathcal{K}) \to k \in \{0,1\}^u$.
- $\mathsf{PubEval}(id \in \mathrm{ID}, \{\mathbf{B}_i \in \mathbb{Z}_q^{n \times m}\}_{i \in [u]}) \to \mathbf{B}_{id} \in \mathbb{Z}_q^{n \times m}$.
- $\mathsf{TrapEval}(K \in \mathcal{K}, id \in \mathrm{ID}, \mathbf{A} \in \mathbb{Z}_q^{n \times m}, \{\mathbf{R}_i \in \mathbb{Z}_q^{m \times m}\}_{i \in [u]}) \to \mathbf{R}_{id} \in \mathbb{Z}^{m \times m}$.
  We require that the following holds:

$$\mathsf{PubEval}(id, \{\mathbf{AR}_i + k_i\mathbf{G}\}_{i \in [u]}) = \mathbf{AR}_{id} + \mathcal{F}(K, id) \cdot \mathbf{G},$$

where $k_i$ is the $i$-th bit of $k = \mathsf{Encode}(K \in \mathcal{K}) \in \{0,1\}^u$. Furthermore, if $\mathbf{R}_i \in \{-1, 0, 1\}^{m \times m}$ for all $i \in [u]$, we have $\|\mathbf{R}_{id}\|_\infty \leq \delta_{\mathrm{PF}}$.

## 2.3 Deterministic Identity-Based Encryption and Its Security

A deterministic identity-based encryption DIBE with the the identity space ID is defined by a tuple of PPT algorithms DIBE.Setup, DIBE.KGen, DIBE.Enc, DIBE.Dec. The DIBE.Setup algorithm takes a security parameter $1^\lambda$ as input and outputs a master secret key $mpk$ and a master secret key $msk$. The DIBE.KGen algorithm takes $mpk, msk, id \in$ ID as inputs and outputs a private key $sk_{id}$. The deterministic algorithm DIBE.Enc takes $mpk, id \in$ ID and a message $m$, outputs a ciphertext $c$. The deterministic algorithm DIBE.Dec decrypts ciphertexts using the private key $sk_{id}$.

**Definition 2** ([16]). *We say that a deterministic identity-based encryption scheme* DIBE *is* PRIV1-ID-INDr-*secure with respect to $\epsilon$-hard-to-invert auxiliary inputs if for any PPT algorithm $\mathcal{A}$, for any efficiently sampleable distribution $\mathcal{M}$, and any efficiently computable $\mathcal{H} = \{h\}$ that is $\epsilon$-hard-to-invert with respect to $\mathcal{M}$, such that the advantage of $\mathcal{A}$ in the following game is negligible.*

$$\mathbf{Adv}_{\mathrm{DIBE},\mathcal{A},\mathcal{H}}^{\mathrm{priv1-id-cpa}}(1^\lambda)$$

$$= \left| \Pr \left[ b' = b \middle| \begin{array}{l} (mpk, msk) \xleftarrow{\$} \mathrm{DIBE.Setup}(1^\lambda); id^* \xleftarrow{\$} \mathcal{A}^{\mathrm{DIBE.KGen}(\cdot)}(mpk); \\ b \xleftarrow{\$} \{0,1\}; m \xleftarrow{\$} \mathcal{M}; h \xleftarrow{\$} \mathcal{H}; c_0^* \xleftarrow{\$} \mathrm{DIBE.Enc}(mpk, id^*, m); \\ c_1^* \xleftarrow{\$} \mathrm{C}; b' \xleftarrow{\$} \mathcal{A}^{\mathrm{DIBE.KGen}(\cdot)}(mpk, c_b^*, h(m)); \end{array} \right] - \frac{1}{2} \right|$$

*where* C *is the ciphertext space, and oracle* DIBE.KGen$(\cdot)$ *takes $id \in$ ID as inputs and generates a private key $sk_{id}$ for the identity id with the restriction that $\mathcal{A}$ is not allowed to query $id^*$.*

# 3 DIBE from Partitioning Functions with Compatible Algorithms Yam17 [18]

In this section, we present our DIBE scheme which is based on a partitioning function [18] $\mathcal{F} : \mathcal{K} \times \mathcal{X} \to \{0,1\}$ with associating $\delta$-compatible algorithms (Encode, PubEval, TrapEval). Let the identity space be ID $= \mathcal{X} = \{0,1\}^k$.

- **Setup.** Algorithm DIBE.Setup takes as input a security parameter $1^\lambda$, and sets the parameters $p, q, n, m, \sigma$ as specified in Sect. 3.1. Then, it uses the algorithm from Lemma 2 (Item 1) to generate a pair $(\mathbf{A}, \mathbf{T_A}) \xleftarrow{\$}$ TrapGen$(1^n, 1^m, q)$, and selects random matrices $\mathbf{B}_0 \xleftarrow{\$} \mathbb{Z}_q^{n \times m}, \mathbf{B}_i \xleftarrow{\$} \mathbb{Z}_q^{n \times m}$ for $i \in [u]$. It finally outputs $mpk = (\mathbf{A}, \mathbf{B}_0, \mathbf{B}_i)$ and $msk = \mathbf{T_A}$.
- **Key Generation.** Algorithm DIBE.KGen takes as input master public keys $mpk$, a master secret key $msk$, and an identity $id \in$ ID. It first computers $\mathbf{F}_{id} = [\mathbf{A}|\mathbf{B}_0 + \mathbf{B}_{id}]$, where $\mathbf{B}_{id} \leftarrow$ PubEval$(id, \{\mathbf{B}_i\}_{i \in [u]})$. Then generates a basis $\mathbf{T}_{\mathbf{F}_{id}}$ of $\Lambda_q^\perp(\mathbf{F}_{id})$ by running SampleBasisLeft$(\mathbf{A}, \mathbf{B}_0 + \mathbf{B}_{id}, \mathbf{T_A}, \sigma)$. It finally outputs $sk_{id} = \mathbf{T}_{\mathbf{F}_{id}}$.

- **Encryption.** Algorithm DIBE.Enc takes as input master public keys $mpk$, an identity $id \in \text{ID}$, and a message $\mathbf{m} \in \mathbb{Z}_t^n$. It first computers $\mathbf{F}_{id}$ as the above, then outputs the ciphertext $\mathbf{c} = \lfloor \mathbf{F}_{id}^\top \mathbf{m} \rceil_p$.
- **Decryption.** To decrypt a ciphertext $\mathbf{c}$ with a private key $sk_{id} = \mathbf{T}_{\mathbf{F}_{id}}$, the algorithm DIBE.Dec computers $\mathbf{m} \xleftarrow{\$} \text{Invert}(\mathbf{c}, \mathbf{F}_{id}, sk_{id})$. Then, if $\mathbf{m} \in \mathbb{Z}_t^n$ it outputs $\mathbf{m}$, and otherwise it outputs $\perp$.

### 3.1 Correctness and Parameter Selection

In order to make sure the correctness of the DIBE scheme and make the security proof follow through, we need the following to satisfy.

- TrapGen in Lemma 2 (Item 1) can work ($m \geq 6n\lceil \log q \rceil$), and it returns $\mathbf{T_A}$ satisfying $\|\widetilde{\mathbf{T_A}}\| \geq \mathcal{O}(\sqrt{n \log q})$.
- the Leftover Hash Lemma in Lemma 2 (Item 6) can be applied to the security proof ($m > (n+1)\log q + \omega(\log n)$).
- SampleBasisLeft in Lemma 2 (Item 2) can operate ($\sigma \geq \|\widetilde{\mathbf{T_A}}\| \cdot \omega(\sqrt{\log m}) = \mathcal{O}(\sqrt{n \log q}) \cdot \omega(\sqrt{\log m})$).
- SampleBasisRight in Lemma 2 (Item 3) can operate ($\sigma \geq m \cdot \|\mathbf{R}_0 + \mathbf{R}_{id}\|_\infty \cdot \omega(\sqrt{\log m}) \geq m(\delta + 1) \cdot \omega(\sqrt{\log m})$).
- In order to keep the correctness of the DIBE scheme, i.e., Invert in Lemma 2 (Item 5) can work ($\|\mathbf{T}_{\mathbf{F}_{id}}\| < p/(2\sqrt{m})$), where $\|\mathbf{T}_{\mathbf{F}_{id}}\| \leq \mathcal{O}(\sigma \cdot m)$ given by both SampleBasisLeft and SampleBasisRight.
- ReRand (Lemma 3) in the security proof can operate ($\beta > \omega(\sqrt{\log m})$, and $\beta' q/(2\beta q) > s_1([\mathbf{I}_m|\mathbf{R}_0 + \mathbf{R}_{id^*}])$, where $s_1([\mathbf{I}_m|\mathbf{R}_0 + \mathbf{R}_{id^*}]) \leq \sqrt{2m}\sqrt{m} \cdot \max\{1, \|[\mathbf{R}_0 + \mathbf{R}_{id^*}]\|_\infty\} \leq \sqrt{2m} \cdot (\delta + 1)$.
- Lemma 1 holds ($q$ is super-polynomial and $\alpha/\beta = \text{negl}(n)$).
- $\Pr[\text{Bad}_8] \leq 2m(2B+1)p/q = \text{negl}(n) = n^{-\omega(1)}$, where $B = \beta' q\sqrt{n}$.

To satisfy the above requirements, we set the parameters as follows:

$$
\begin{array}{l|l|l}
n = \lambda & m = \mathcal{O}(n \log q) & \sigma = m(\delta+1) \cdot \omega(\sqrt{\log m}) \\
p = 2m^{2.5}(\delta+1) \cdot \omega(\sqrt{\log m}) & \beta' = 2\sqrt{2}m\beta(\delta+1) & q = \text{the prime nearest to } 2^{n^\eta} \\
\frac{1}{\beta} \geq 8\sqrt{2}m^2 p(\delta+1) \cdot n^{\omega(1)} & t = m\delta &
\end{array}
$$

The public key size, private key size, ciphertext size and ciphertext expansion factor in our scheme are $\mathcal{O}(un^{2+2\eta})$, $\mathcal{O}(n^{2+3\eta})$, $\mathcal{O}(n^{1+\eta}\log(m\delta))$ and $\mathcal{O}(n^\eta \log(m\delta)/\log t)$ respectively. To optimize the ciphertext expansion factor, we can choose $t = m\delta$, which makes the ciphertext expansion factor to be $\mathcal{O}(n^\eta)$.

### 3.2 Security of DIBE

**Theorem 1.** *The above deterministic identity-based encryption scheme* DIBE *is* PRIV1-ID-INDr-*secure with respect to* $2^{-l\log t}$-*hard-to-invert auxiliary inputs, assuming* $\text{LWE}_{q,n,m,\beta,\mathcal{H}}$ *is hard.*

*Proof.* Let $\mathcal{A}$ be a PPT adversary that breaks the PRIV1-ID-INDr-security with auxiliary inputs of the DIBE scheme. Furthermore, let $\epsilon = \epsilon(\lambda)$ and $Q = Q(\lambda)$ be its advantage and the upper bound of the number of DIBE.KGen($\cdot$) queries, respectively. By assumption, $Q(\lambda)$ is polynomially bounded and there exists nonnegligible function $\epsilon(\lambda) \geq \epsilon_0(\lambda)$ holds for all infinitely $\lambda$. By running the algorithm PrtSmp($\lambda, Q, \epsilon_0$), the challenger can get $K \in \mathcal{K}$. We denote these DIBE.KGen($\cdot$) queries by $id_j$ for $j \in [Q]$, and the challenge identity chosen by $\mathcal{A}$ as $id^*$.

For any distribution $\mathcal{M}$ over $\mathbb{Z}_t^n$, let $\mathcal{H} = \{h\}$ be a set of $z^{-l \log(t)}$-hard-to-invert functions with respect to $\mathcal{M}$. In order to prove the security of this DIBE scheme, we define a sequence of games. In each game, the challenger selects a uniform bit $b \xleftarrow{\$} \{0, 1\}$, while the adversary $\mathcal{A}$ finally returns a guess bit $b'$ to the challenger. The challenger sets $\hat{b} = b'$ in the first game, these values might be different in the latter games. In the following, we define $X_i$ as the event that $\hat{b} = b$.

Game$_0$: This game is the original PRIV1-ID-INDr game with auxiliary inputs. By definition, we have

$$| \Pr[X_0] - \frac{1}{2}| = | \Pr[\hat{b} = b] - \frac{1}{2}| = | \Pr[b' = b] - \frac{1}{2}| = \epsilon.$$

Game$_1$: By running the algorithm PrtSmp($\lambda, Q, \epsilon_0$), the challenger can get $K \in \mathcal{K}$. Then the challenger checks whether the following event (denoted by Condition) holds:

$$\mathcal{F}(K, id^*) = 0 \wedge \mathcal{F}(K, id_1) = 1 \cdots \wedge \mathcal{F}(K, id_Q) = 1.$$

If Condition does not hold, the challenger aborts, ignores the output $b'$ of $\mathcal{A}$ and sets $\hat{b} \xleftarrow{\$} \{0, 1\}$. In this case, we say that the challenger aborts, denoted by Abort. If Condition holds, the challenger sets $\hat{b} = b'$. According to Lemma 5 in **Appendix** A, the following equation holds

$$| \Pr[X_1] - \frac{1}{2}| \geq \gamma_{\min}\epsilon - \frac{1}{2}(\gamma_{\max} - \gamma_{\min}) \geq \gamma_{\min}\epsilon_0 - \frac{1}{2}(\gamma_{\max} - \gamma_{\min}) = \tau. \quad (1)$$

Game$_2$: We change the way $\mathbf{B}_0$ and $\mathbf{B}_i$ in the master public key $mpk$ are chosen. At first, the challenger runs the algorithm PrtSmp($1^\lambda, Q, \epsilon_0$), computes $k =$ Encode($K$), and uniformly chooses $\mathbf{R}_0, \mathbf{R}_i \xleftarrow{\$} \{-1, 1\}^{m \times m}$. Then, the challenger defines $\mathbf{B}_0, \mathbf{B}_i$ as $\mathbf{B}_0 = \mathbf{A}\mathbf{R}_0, \mathbf{B}_i = \mathbf{A}\mathbf{R}_i + k_i\mathbf{G}$. According to the Leftover Hash Lemma in Lemma 2 (Item 6), we have

$$| \Pr[X_2] - \Pr[X_1]| = \mathsf{negl}(n). \quad (2)$$

Game$_3$: In this game, we abort the game as soon as Condition does not hold. It is easy to see that

$$\Pr[X_3] = \Pr[X_2]. \quad (3)$$

Before describing the next game, define $\mathbf{R}_{id} = \mathsf{TrapEval}(K, id, \mathbf{A}, \{\mathbf{R}_i\}_{i \in [u]})$ for $id \in \mathsf{ID}$. In this case, $\|\mathbf{R}_0 + \mathbf{R}_{id}\|_\infty \leq \|\mathbf{R}_0\|_\infty + \|\mathbf{R}_{id}\|_\infty \leq \delta + 1$. Additionally, by the property of $\mathsf{TrapEval}$, when Condition holds we have

$$\mathbf{B}_0 + \mathbf{B}_{id} = \begin{cases} \mathbf{A} \cdot (\mathbf{R}_0 + \mathbf{R}_{id^*}) & \text{if } id = id^* \\ \mathbf{A} \cdot (\mathbf{R}_0 + \mathbf{R}_{id}) + \mathbf{G} & \text{if } id \in \{id_1, \cdots, id_Q\} \end{cases}$$

where $\mathbf{B}_{id} = \mathsf{PubEval}(id, \{\mathbf{B}_i\}_{i \in [u]})$.

Game$_4$: In Game$_4$, the challenger uniformly chooses $\mathbf{A} \xleftarrow{\$} \mathbb{Z}_q^{n \times m}$ instead of generating it by $\mathsf{TrapGen}$. When $\mathcal{A}$ makes key generation query to $\mathsf{KGen}$ for an identity $id \neq id^*$, the challenger first checks whether $\mathcal{F}(K, id) = 1$. If it holds, the challenger runs $\mathsf{SampleBasisRight}(\mathbf{A}, \mathbf{G}, \mathbf{R}_0 + \mathbf{R}_{id}, \mathbf{T_G}, \sigma)$ to answer the query, otherwise, the challenger aborts. According to Lemma 2 (Item 3), we have

$$|\Pr[X_4] - \Pr[X_3]| = \mathsf{negl}(n). \tag{4}$$

Game$_5$: In this game, we change the way that the challenge ciphertext is created when $b = 0$. In the previous games, we created the challenge ciphertext as in the real scheme when $b = 0$. In this game, if $b = 0$ and Condition holds, the challenger first chooses $\mathbf{e}_1, \mathbf{e}_2 \xleftarrow{\$} \mathcal{D}_{\mathbb{Z}^m, \beta'q}$ and computes

$$\widehat{\mathbf{c}} = \widehat{\mathbf{c}}_1 + \widehat{\mathbf{c}}_2 = \begin{bmatrix} \mathbf{A}^\top \mathbf{m} \\ (\mathbf{R}_0 + \mathbf{R}_{id^*})^\top \mathbf{A}^\top \mathbf{m} \end{bmatrix} + \begin{bmatrix} \mathbf{e}_1 \\ \mathbf{e}_2 \end{bmatrix} = \begin{bmatrix} \mathbf{A}^\top \mathbf{m} + \mathbf{e}_1 \\ (\mathbf{R}_0 + \mathbf{R}_{id^*})^\top \mathbf{A}^\top \mathbf{m} + \mathbf{e}_2 \end{bmatrix}.$$

Then, the challenger computes $c_0^* = \lfloor \widehat{\mathbf{c}} \rceil_p$. Finally, the challenger returns $(c_b^*, h(\mathbf{m}))$ to the adversary $\mathcal{A}$. Before analyzing the difference between Game$_6$ and Game$_5$, we first define a "bad event" as follows: $\mathsf{Bad}_5 \overset{\Delta}{=} \lfloor \widehat{c}_1 + [-B, B]^{2m} \rceil_p \neq \lfloor \widehat{c}_1 \rceil_p$, where $B = \beta'q\sqrt{n}$ (Lemma 2 item 7). If $\mathsf{Bad}_5$ does not occur for some $\widehat{c}_1$, then we have

$$\lfloor \widehat{c} \rceil_p = \begin{bmatrix} \lfloor \mathbf{A}^\top \mathbf{m} + \mathbf{e}_1 \rceil_p \\ \lfloor (\mathbf{R}_0 + \mathbf{R}_{id^*})^\top \mathbf{A}^\top \mathbf{m} + \mathbf{e}_2 \rceil_p \end{bmatrix} = \begin{bmatrix} \lfloor \mathbf{A}^\top \mathbf{m} \rceil_p \\ \lfloor (\mathbf{R}_0 + \mathbf{R}_{id^*})^\top \mathbf{A}^\top \mathbf{m} \rceil_p \end{bmatrix} = \lfloor \mathbf{F}_{id^*}^\top \mathbf{m} \rceil_p.$$

It immediately follows that for any adversary $\mathcal{A}$

$$|\Pr[X_5] - \Pr[X_4]| \leq \Pr[\mathsf{Bad}_5]. \tag{5}$$

Game$_6$: This game is similar to Game$_5$, except that the way $\widehat{\mathbf{c}}$ is created when $b = 0$. If $b = 0$ and Condition holds, Game$_6$ challenger first picks $\mathbf{m} \xleftarrow{\$} \mathbb{Z}_t^n$ and $\mathbf{e} \xleftarrow{\$} \mathcal{D}_{\mathbb{Z}^m, \beta q}$, and computes $\mathbf{u} = \mathbf{A}^\top \mathbf{m} + \mathbf{e}$. It runs the algorithm

$$\widehat{\mathbf{c}} = \mathsf{ReRand}\left( \begin{bmatrix} \mathbf{I}_m \\ (\mathbf{R}_0 + \mathbf{R}_{id^*})^\top \end{bmatrix}, \mathbf{u}, \beta q, \frac{\beta'q}{2\beta q} \right)$$

in the Lemma 3, where $\mathbf{I}_m$ is the unit matrix of size $m \times m$. By the property of $\mathsf{ReRand}$, it can be readily seen that the distribution of $c_0^*$ in Game$_6$ is statistically close to that in Game$_5$. Therefore, we have

$$\Pr[X_6] = \Pr[X_5] \quad \text{and} \quad \Pr[\mathsf{Bad}_6] = \Pr[\mathsf{Bad}_5]. \tag{6}$$

Game$_7$: This game is similar to Game$_6$, except that the way $\widehat{\mathbf{c}}$ is created when $b = 0$. If $b = 0$ and Condition holds, Game$_7$ challenger first picks $\mathbf{u}' \xleftarrow{\$} \mathbb{Z}_q^m$ and $\mathbf{e} \xleftarrow{\$} \mathcal{D}_{\mathbb{Z}^m, \beta q}$, and computes as follows

$$\widehat{\mathbf{c}} = \mathsf{ReRand}\left(\begin{bmatrix} \mathbf{I}_m \\ (\mathbf{R}_0 + \mathbf{R}_{id^*})^\top \end{bmatrix}, \mathbf{u}, \beta q, \frac{\beta' q}{2\beta q}\right),$$

where $\mathbf{u} = \mathbf{u}' + \mathbf{e}$. We note this subtle change ($\mathbf{u} = \mathbf{u}' + \mathbf{e}$ instead of $\mathbf{u} = \mathbf{u}'$) from the standard $\mathrm{LWE}_{q,n,m,\beta,\mathcal{H}}$ assumption is done for convenience of the proof. It is easy to see that

$$|\Pr[X_7] - \Pr[X_6]| \leq \mathrm{LWE}_{q,n,m,\beta,\mathcal{H}}, |\Pr[\mathsf{Bad}_7] - \Pr[\mathsf{Bad}_6]| \leq \mathrm{LWE}_{q,n,m,\beta,\mathcal{H}}. \quad (7)$$

Game$_8$: This game is similar to Game$_7$, except that the way $\widehat{\mathbf{c}}$ is created when $b = 0$. If $b = 0$ and Condition holds, Game$_8$ challenger computes

$$\widehat{\mathbf{c}} = \widehat{\mathbf{c}}_1 + \widehat{\mathbf{c}}_2 = \begin{bmatrix} \mathbf{u}' \\ (\mathbf{R}_0 + \mathbf{R}_{id^*})^\top \mathbf{u}' \end{bmatrix} + \begin{bmatrix} \mathbf{e}_1 \\ \mathbf{e}_2 \end{bmatrix} = \begin{bmatrix} \mathbf{u}' + \mathbf{e}_1 \\ (\mathbf{R}_0 + \mathbf{R}_{id^*})^\top \mathbf{u}' + \mathbf{e}_2 \end{bmatrix},$$

instead of running the algorithm $\mathsf{ReRand}$, where $\mathbf{u}' \xleftarrow{\$} \mathbb{Z}_q^m$ and $\mathbf{e}_1, \mathbf{e}_2 \xleftarrow{\$} \mathcal{D}_{\mathbb{Z}^m, \beta' q}$. According to the property of $\mathsf{ReRand}$, we can get that

$$|\Pr[X_8] - \Pr[X_7]| = \mathsf{negl}(n) \quad \text{and} \quad |\Pr[\mathsf{Bad}_8] - \Pr[\mathsf{Bad}_7]| = \mathsf{negl}(n). \quad (8)$$

Firstly, we show that $(\mathbf{u}', (\mathbf{R}_0 + \mathbf{R}_{id^*})^\top \mathbf{u}')$ are distributed statistically close to uniform distribution over $\mathbb{Z}_q^{2m}$. It suffices to show that $(\mathbf{A}, \mathbf{R}_0^\top \mathbf{A}^\top, \mathbf{u}', (\mathbf{R}_0 + \mathbf{R}_{id^*})^\top \mathbf{u}')$ are distributed statistically close to $(\mathbf{A}, \mathbf{R}_0^\top \mathbf{A}^\top, \mathbf{u}', \widehat{\mathbf{u}})$ where $\mathbf{A} \xleftarrow{\$} \mathbb{Z}_q^{n \times m}$, $\mathbf{R}_0 \xleftarrow{\$} \{-1,1\}^{m \times m}$, $\mathbf{u}', \widehat{\mathbf{u}} \xleftarrow{\$} \mathbb{Z}_q^m$. According to the Leftover Hash Lemma in Lemma 2 (Item 6), we have $(\mathbf{A}, \mathbf{R}_0^\top \mathbf{A}^\top, \mathbf{u}', \mathbf{R}_0^\top \mathbf{u}') \approx (\mathbf{A}, \mathbf{A}', \mathbf{u}', \widehat{\mathbf{u}}) \approx (\mathbf{A}, \mathbf{R}_0^\top \mathbf{A}^\top, \mathbf{u}', \widehat{\mathbf{u}})$, where $\mathbf{A}' \xleftarrow{\$} \mathbb{Z}_q^{n \times m}$. As a result, we have the following distributions are statistically close:

$$(\mathbf{A}, \mathbf{R}_0^\top \mathbf{A}^\top, \mathbf{u}', (\mathbf{R}_0 + \mathbf{R}_{id^*})^\top \mathbf{u}') \approx (\mathbf{A}, \mathbf{R}_0^\top \mathbf{A}^\top, \mathbf{u}', \mathbf{R}_0^\top \mathbf{u}' + \mathbf{R}_{id^*}^\top \mathbf{u}')$$
$$\approx (\mathbf{A}, \mathbf{R}_0^\top \mathbf{A}^\top, \mathbf{u}', \widehat{\mathbf{u}}).$$

From the above, $\widehat{\mathbf{c}}_1$ is statistically close to uniform distribution over $\mathbb{Z}_q^{2m}$, therefore for uniform $\widehat{\mathbf{c}}_1$,

$$\Pr[\mathsf{Bad}_8] \leq 2m(2B + 1)p/q = \mathsf{negl}(n), \quad (9)$$

by assumption on $q$ and $\beta'$. Summing up Eqs. (6)–(9) yields

$$\Pr[\mathsf{Bad}_6] \leq |\Pr[\mathsf{Bad}_6] - \Pr[\mathsf{Bad}_7]| + |\Pr[\mathsf{Bad}_7] - \Pr[\mathsf{Bad}_8]| + \Pr[\mathsf{Bad}_8]$$
$$\leq \mathrm{LWE}_{q,n,m,\beta,\mathcal{H}} + \mathsf{negl}(n) = \mathsf{negl}(n). \quad (10)$$

In Game$_8$, even when $\mathsf{Bad}_8$ occurs, the challenger still returns $(c_b^*, h(\mathbf{m}))$ to the adversary $\mathcal{A}$. If the challenger aborts, because $\widehat{b} \xleftarrow{\$} \{0,1\}$, $\Pr[X_8|\mathsf{Abort}_8] =$

$\Pr[\widehat{b} = b|\mathsf{Abort}_8] = 1/2$. If the challenger does not abort, because $\widehat{\mathbf{c}}_1$ (And $\widehat{\mathbf{c}}$) is statistically close to uniform distribution on $\mathbb{Z}_q^{2m}$, and $h(\mathbf{m})$ is independent of $\widehat{\mathbf{c}}$. Then $c_0^* = \lfloor\widehat{\mathbf{c}}\rceil_p$ is independent of $b = 0$. In addition, $c_1^* \xleftarrow{\$} C$ is independent of $b = 1$. As a result, $\Pr[X_8|\neg\mathsf{Abort}_8] = 1/2$. In a word,

$$\left|\Pr[X_8] - \frac{1}{2}\right| = \mathsf{negl}(n). \tag{11}$$

Summing up Eqs. (1)–(10), we have

$$
\begin{aligned}
|\Pr[X_8] - \frac{1}{2}| &= \left|\Pr[X_1] - \frac{1}{2} + \sum_{i=1}^{8}(\Pr[X_{i+1}] - \Pr[X_i])\right| \\
&\geq \left|\Pr[X_1] - \frac{1}{2}\right| - \sum_{i=1}^{8}|\Pr[X_{i+1}] - \Pr[X_i]| \\
&\geq \tau(\lambda) - \mathsf{negl}(n).
\end{aligned} \tag{12}
$$

Since $\tau(\lambda)$ is noticeable for all infinitely large $\lambda$, Eqs. (11) and (12) make up a contradiction.

**Corollary 1.** *The above deterministic identity-based encryption scheme* DIBE *is* PRIV1-ID-INDr-*secure with respect to* $2^{-l\log t}$-*hard-to-invert auxiliary inputs, assuming the standard* $\mathsf{LWE}_{q,z,m,\alpha}$ *assumption is hard.*

### 3.3  DIBE Instantiations

In [18], Yamada elaborately constructed two partitioning functions $\mathcal{F}_{\mathrm{MAH}}$ based on modified admissible hash function and $\mathcal{F}_{\mathrm{AFF}}$ based on affine function. Here, we do not care about their concrete constructions but concerned with the two parameter $u$ (because $u + 2$ equals the number of matrices in the master public key) and $\delta$ which influences the selection of parameters in the DIBE schemes. Please read his paper for more details. Note that the security parameter $\lambda = n$ in this paper.

**Lemma 4** ([18]). *There exists a partitioning function* $\mathcal{F}_{\mathrm{MAH}} : \mathcal{K}_{\mathrm{MAH}} \times \mathcal{X}_{\mathrm{MAH}} \to \{0,1\}$ *with three associating* $\delta_{\mathrm{mah}}$-*compatible algorithms* (Encode$_{\mathrm{MAH}}$, PubEval$_{\mathrm{MAH}}$, TrapEval$_{\mathrm{MAH}}$), *where* $u_{mah} = \log^3(\lambda)$ *and* $\delta_{mah} = m^3 u \cdot \Theta(\lambda)$. *In addition, there exists also a partitioning function* $\mathcal{F}_{\mathrm{AFF}} : \mathcal{K}_{\mathrm{AFF}} \times \mathcal{X}_{\mathrm{AFF}} \to \{0,1\}$ *with related* $\delta_{\mathrm{aff}}$-*compatible algorithms* (Encode$_{\mathrm{AFF}}$, PubEval$_{\mathrm{AFF}}$, TrapEval$_{\mathrm{AFF}}$), *where* $u_{\mathrm{aff}} = \log^2(\lambda)$ *and* $\delta_{\mathrm{aff}} = \mathsf{poly}(n)$.

**Instantiation 1.** Instantiating the partitioning function $\mathcal{F}$ by $\mathcal{F}_{\mathrm{MAH}}$, we set the parameters of DIBE$_{\mathrm{MAH}}$ as follows (Set $\Theta(\lambda) = \lambda$, so $\delta_{mah} = n^{5+3\eta} \cdot \log^3 n$):

| | | |
|---|---|---|
| $n = \lambda$ | $m = \mathcal{O}(n\log q)$ | $\sigma = \mathcal{O}(n^{5+4\eta} \cdot \log^4 n)$ |
| $p = \mathcal{O}(n^{6.5+5.5\eta} \cdot \log^4 n)$ | $\beta' = \beta \cdot \mathcal{O}(n^{5+4\eta} \cdot \log^3 n)$ | $q = \text{the prime nearest to } 2^{n^{\eta}}$ |
| $\frac{1}{\beta} \geq 8\sqrt{2}m^2p(\delta_{\mathrm{mah}} + 1) \cdot n^{\omega(1)}$ | $t = \mathcal{O}(n^{5+4\eta} \cdot \log^3 n)$ | |

The public key size, private key size, ciphertext size and ciphertext expansion factor in our scheme are $\mathcal{O}(n^{2+2\eta} \cdot \log^3 n)$, $\mathcal{O}(n^{2+3\eta})$, $\mathcal{O}(n^{1+\eta} \log n)$ and $\mathcal{O}(n^\eta)$ respectively.

**Instantiation 2.** Instantiating the partitioning function $\mathcal{F}$ by $\mathcal{F}_{\mathrm{AFF}}$, we set the parameters of $\mathrm{DIBE}_{\mathrm{AFF}}$ as follows (Set $\delta_{\mathrm{aff}} = n^4$):

$$
\begin{array}{l|l|l}
n = \lambda & m = \mathcal{O}(n \log q) & \sigma = \mathcal{O}(n^{5+\eta} \cdot \log n) \\
p = \mathcal{O}(n^{6.5+2.5\eta} \cdot \log n) & \beta' = \mathcal{O}(n^{5+\eta}) & q = \text{the prime nearest to } 2^{n^\eta} \\
\frac{1}{\beta} \geq 8\sqrt{2}m^2 p(\delta_{\mathrm{aff}} + 1) \cdot n^{\omega(1)} & t = \mathcal{O}(n^{5+\eta}) &
\end{array}
$$

The public key size, private key size, ciphertext size and ciphertext expansion factor in our scheme are $\mathcal{O}(n^{2+2\eta} \cdot \log^2 n)$, $\mathcal{O}(n^{2+3\eta})$, $\mathcal{O}(n^{1+\eta} \log n)$ and $\mathcal{O}(n^\eta)$ respectively.

# 4  DIBE from Yam16 [17]

In this section, we present our DIBE scheme which is based on the [17] IBE scheme. Let $d \geq 2$ be a flexible integer and the identity space be ID $= \{0,1\}^k$. In addition, let $v$ be $v = \lceil k^{1/d} \rceil$. Then, an element of $[1, k]$ can be represented as an element of $[1, v]^d$. Finally, there exists an efficiently computable injective map $\mathcal{S}$ that maps an identity $id \in$ ID to a subset $\mathcal{S}(id)$ of $[1, v]^d$.

- **Setup.** Algorithm DIBE.Setup takes as input a security parameter $1^\lambda$, and sets the parameters $p, q, n, m, \sigma$ as specified in Sect. 3.1. Then, it uses the algorithm from Lemma 2 to generate a pair $(\mathbf{A}, \mathbf{T_A}) \xleftarrow{\$} \mathsf{TrapGen}(1^n, 1^m, q)$, and selects random matrices $\mathbf{B}_0 \xleftarrow{\$} \mathbb{Z}_q^{n \times m}, \mathbf{B}_{i,j} \xleftarrow{\$} \mathbb{Z}_q^{n \times m}$ for $(i, j) \in [1, d] \times [1, v]$. It finally outputs $mpk = (\mathbf{A}, \mathbf{B}_0, \mathbf{B}_{i,j})$ and $msk = \mathbf{T_A}$. Moreover, we define a deterministic function $\mathcal{H} : \text{ID} \rightarrow \mathbb{Z}_q^{n \times m}$ as follows. For $id \in$ ID,

$$
\mathcal{H}(id) = \mathbf{B}_0 + \sum_{(j_1, \cdots, j_d) \in \mathcal{S}(id)} \mathsf{PubEval}_d(\mathbf{B}_{1,j_1}, \cdots, \mathbf{B}_{d,j_d}) \in \mathbb{Z}_q^{n \times m},
$$

where $\mathsf{PubEval}_d$ is defined in Appendix A.
- **Key Generation.** Algorithm DIBE.KGen takes as input master public keys $mpk$, a master secret key $msk$, and an identity $id \in$ ID. It first computers $\mathbf{F}_{id} = [\mathbf{A} | \mathcal{H}(id)]$, then generates a basis $\mathbf{T}_{\mathbf{F}_{id}}$ of $\Lambda_q^\perp(\mathbf{F}_{id})$ by running the algorithm SampleBasisLeft$(\mathbf{A}, \mathcal{H}(id), \mathbf{T_A}, \sigma)$. It finally outputs $sk_{id} = \mathbf{T}_{\mathbf{F}_{id}}$.
- **Encryption.** Algorithm DIBE.Enc takes as input master public keys $mpk$, an identity $id \in$ ID, and a message $\mathbf{m} \in \mathbb{Z}_t^n$. It first computers $\mathbf{F}_{id} = [\mathbf{A} | \mathcal{H}(id)]$, then outputs the ciphertext $\mathbf{c} = \lfloor \mathbf{F}_{id}^\top \mathbf{m} \rceil_p$.
- **Decryption.** To decrypt a ciphertext $\mathbf{c}$ with a private key $sk_{id} = \mathbf{T}_{\mathbf{F}_{id}}$, the algorithm DIBE.Dec computers $\mathbf{m} \xleftarrow{\$} \mathsf{Invert}(\mathbf{c}, \mathbf{F}_{id}, sk_{id})$. Then, if $\mathbf{m} \in \mathbb{Z}_t^n$ it outputs $\mathbf{m}$, and otherwise it outputs $\perp$.

## 4.1  Correctness and Parameter Selection

In order to make sure the correctness of the DIBE scheme and make the security proof follow through, we need the following to satisfy.

- TrapGen in Lemma 2 (Item 1) can work ($m \geq 6n\lceil \log q \rceil$), and it returns $\mathbf{T_A}$ satisfying $\|\widetilde{\mathbf{T_A}}\| \geq \mathcal{O}(\sqrt{n \log q})$.
- the Leftover Hash Lemma in Lemma 2 (Item 6) can be applied to the security proof ($m > (n+1)\log q + \omega(\log n)$).
- SampleBasisLeft in Lemma 2 (Item 2) can operate ($\sigma \geq \|\widetilde{\mathbf{T_A}}\| \cdot \omega(\sqrt{\log m}) = \mathcal{O}(\sqrt{n \log q}) \cdot \omega(\sqrt{\log m})$).
- SampleBasisRight in Lemma 2 (Item 3) can operate ($\sigma \geq \|\widetilde{\mathbf{T_G}}\| \cdot s_1(\mathbf{R}_{id}) \cdot \omega(\sqrt{\log m}) \geq m(1 + kd^d n^{c(d-1)}) \cdot \omega(\sqrt{\log m})$).
- In order to keep the correctness of the DIBE scheme, i.e., Invert in Lemma 2 (Item 5) can work ($\|\mathbf{T}_{\mathbf{F}_{id}}\| < p/m$), where $\|\mathbf{T}_{\mathbf{F}_{id}}\| \leq \mathcal{O}(\sigma \cdot m)$ given by both SampleBasisLeft and SampleBasisRight.
- ReRand (Lemma 3) in the security proof can operate ($\beta > \omega(\sqrt{\log m})$, and $\beta'q/(2\beta q) > s_1([\mathbf{I_m}|\mathbf{R}_{id^*}]^\top)$, i.e., $\beta'q > 2\beta q(s_1(\mathbf{R}_{id^*}) + 1))$.
- Lemma 1 holds ($q$ is super-polynomial and $\alpha/\beta = negl(n)$).
- $\Pr[\mathsf{Bad_8}] \leq 2m(2B+1)p/q = \mathsf{negl}(n) = n^{-\omega(1)}$, where $B = \beta'q\sqrt{n}$.

To satisfy the above requirements, we set the parameters as follows:

$$
\begin{array}{l|l|l}
n = \lambda & m = \mathcal{O}(n \log q) & \sigma = mkn^{c(d-1)} \cdot \omega(\sqrt{\log m}) \\
p = m^2 kn^{c(d-1)} \cdot \omega(\sqrt{\log m}) & \beta'q = \beta q(mkn^{c(d-1)}) & q = \text{the prime nearest to } 2^{n^\eta} \\
\frac{1}{\beta} \geq km^2 n^{c(d-1)} \cdot p \cdot n^{\omega(1)} & t = \mathsf{poly}(n) &
\end{array}
$$

where the parameter $c$ is a super-constant. As a result, parameter $\sigma, p$ will be super-polynomial. For simplicity, we set $p = $ the number nearest to $2^{n^\gamma}$, where $\gamma < \eta$.

The public key size, private key size, ciphertext size and ciphertext expansion factor in our scheme are $\mathcal{O}(k^{1/d} n^{2+2\eta})$, $\mathcal{O}(n^{2+3\eta})$, $\mathcal{O}(n^{1+\eta+\gamma})$ and $\mathcal{O}(n^{\eta+\gamma}/\log n)$ respectively.

## 4.2  Security of DIBE

**Theorem 2.** *The above deterministic identity-based encryption scheme* DIBE *is* PRIV1-ID-INDr-*secure with respect to* $2^{-l \log t}$-*hard-to-invert auxiliary inputs, assuming* LWE$_{q,n,m,\beta,\mathcal{H}}$ *is hard.*

*Proof.* The security proof of this deterministic identity-based scheme is very similar to the security proof of the above DIBE scheme. We omit the proof here.

**Corollary 2.** *The above deterministic identity-based encryption scheme* DIBE *is* PRIV1-ID-INDr-*secure with respect to* $2^{-l \log t}$-*hard-to-invert auxiliary inputs, assuming the standard* LWE$_{q,z,m,\alpha}$ *assumption is hard.*

**Acknowledgments.** We thank the anonymous IWSEC'2017 reviewers for their helpful comments. This work is supported by the Foundation of Science and Technology on Communication Security Laboratory (9140C110206150C11049) and the National Nature Science Foundation of China (No.61379137, No.61502480, No.61572495, No.61602473).

# A    Appendix

**Homomorphic Computation.** In [17], Yamada introduced the following function $\mathsf{PubEval}_d : (\mathbb{Z}_q^{n \times m})^d \to \mathbb{Z}_q^{n \times m}$ which takes a set of matrices $\mathbf{B}_1, \cdots, \mathbf{B}_d$ as inputs and outputs a matrix in $\mathbb{Z}_q^{n \times m}$.

$$\mathsf{PubEval}_d(\mathbf{B}_1, \cdots, \mathbf{B}_d) = \begin{cases} \mathbf{B}_1 & d = 1 \\ \mathbf{B}_1 \cdot \mathbf{G}^{-1}(\mathsf{PubEval}_{d-1}(\mathbf{B}_2, \cdots, \mathbf{B}_d)) & d \geq 2 \end{cases}$$

In Sect. 3.2, in order to prove Eq. (1), we will use Lemma 28 in the full version of the work [1], which is described as follows.

**Lemma 5** ([1]). *Let $I^*$ be a $Q + 1$-ID tuple $\{id^*, \{id_j\}_{j \in [Q]}\}$ denoted the challenge ID along with the queried ID's, and $\eta(I^*)$ define the probability that an abort does not happen in* **Game₂**. *Let $\gamma_{\max} = \max \gamma(I^*)$ and $\gamma_{\min} = \min \gamma(I^*)$. For $i = 1, 2$, we set $X_i$ be the event that $\widehat{coin} = coin$ at the end of* **Gameᵢ**. *Then,*

$$\left| \Pr[X_2] - \frac{1}{2} \right| \geq \gamma_{\min} \left| \Pr[X_1] - \frac{1}{2} \right| - \frac{1}{2}(\gamma_{\max} - \gamma_{\min}).$$

# References

1. Agrawal, S., Boneh, D., Boyen, X.: Efficient lattice (H)IBE in the standard model. In: Gilbert, H. (ed.) EUROCRYPT 2010. LNCS, vol. 6110, pp. 553–572. Springer, Heidelberg (2010). doi:10.1007/978-3-642-13190-5_28
2. Ajtai, M.: Generating hard instances of the short basis problem. In: Wiedermann, J., Emde Boas, P., Nielsen, M. (eds.) ICALP 1999. LNCS, vol. 1644, pp. 1–9. Springer, Heidelberg (1999). doi:10.1007/3-540-48523-6_1
3. Alwen, J., Peikert, C.: Generating shorter bases for hard random lattices. In: STACS 2009, pp. 75–86 (2009)
4. Bellare, M., Kiltz, E., Peikert, C., Waters, B.: Identity-based (lossy) trapdoor functions and applications. In: Pointcheval, D., Johansson, T. (eds.) EUROCRYPT 2012. LNCS, vol. 7237, pp. 228–245. Springer, Heidelberg (2012). doi:10.1007/978-3-642-29011-4_15
5. Bogdanov, A., Guo, S., Masny, D., Richelson, S., Rosen, A.: On the hardness of learning with rounding over small modulus. In: Kushilevitz, E., Malkin, T. (eds.) TCC 2016. LNCS, vol. 9562, pp. 209–224. Springer, Heidelberg (2016). doi:10.1007/978-3-662-49096-9_9
6. Cash, D., Hofheinz, D., Kiltz, E., Peikert, C.: Bonsai trees, or how to delegate a lattice basis. In: Gilbert, H. (ed.) EUROCRYPT 2010. LNCS, vol. 6110, pp. 523–552. Springer, Heidelberg (2010). doi:10.1007/978-3-642-13190-5_27

7. Dodis, Y., Ostrovsky, R., Reyzin, L., Smith, A.D.: Fuzzy extractors: how to generate strong keys from biometrics and other noisy data. SIAM J. Comput. **38**(1), 97–139 (2008)

8. Escala, A., Herranz, J., Libert, B., Ràfols, C.: Identity-based lossy trapdoor functions: new definitions, hierarchical extensions, and implications. In: Krawczyk, H. (ed.) PKC 2014. LNCS, vol. 8383, pp. 239–256. Springer, Heidelberg (2014). doi:10.1007/978-3-642-54631-0_14

9. Fang, F., Li, B., Xianhui, L., Liu, Y., Jia, D., Xue, H.: (Deterministic) Hierarchical identity-based encryption from learning with rounding over small modulus. In: AsiaCCS 2016, pp. 907–912 (2016)

10. Goldwasser, S., Kalai, Y.T., Peikert, C., Vaikuntanathan, V.: Robustness of the learning with errors assumption. In: ICS 2010, pp. 230–240 (2010)

11. Jager, T.: Verifiable random functions from weaker assumptions. In: Dodis, Y., Nielsen, J.B. (eds.) TCC 2015. LNCS, vol. 9015, pp. 121–143. Springer, Heidelberg (2015). doi:10.1007/978-3-662-46497-7_5

12. Katsumata, S., Yamada, S.: Partitioning via non-linear polynomial functions: more compact ibes from ideal lattices and bilinear maps. In: Cheon, J.H., Takagi, T. (eds.) ASIACRYPT 2016. LNCS, vol. 10032, pp. 682–712. Springer, Heidelberg (2016). doi:10.1007/978-3-662-53890-6_23

13. Micciancio, D., Peikert, C.: Trapdoors for lattices: simpler, tighter, faster, smaller. In: Pointcheval, D., Johansson, T. (eds.) EUROCRYPT 2012. LNCS, vol. 7237, pp. 700–718. Springer, Heidelberg (2012). doi:10.1007/978-3-642-29011-4_41

14. Regev, O.: On lattices, learning with errors, random linear codes, and cryptography. In: STOC 2005, pp. 84–93 (2005)

15. Shamir, A.: Identity-based cryptosystems and signature schemes. In: Blakley, G.R., Chaum, D. (eds.) CRYPTO 1984. LNCS, vol. 196, pp. 47–53. Springer, Heidelberg (1985). doi:10.1007/3-540-39568-7_5

16. Xie, X., Xue, R., Zhang, R.: Deterministic public key encryption and identity-based encryption from lattices in the auxiliary-input setting. In: Visconti, I., Prisco, R. (eds.) SCN 2012. LNCS, vol. 7485, pp. 1–18. Springer, Heidelberg (2012). doi:10.1007/978-3-642-32928-9_1

17. Yamada, S.: Adaptively secure identity-based encryption from lattices with asymptotically shorter public parameters. In: Fischlin, M., Coron, J.-S. (eds.) EUROCRYPT 2016. LNCS, vol. 9666, pp. 32–62. Springer, Heidelberg (2016). doi:10.1007/978-3-662-49896-5_2

18. Yamada, S.: Asymptotically compact adaptively secure lattice ibes and verifiable random functions via generalized partitioning techniques. Cryptology ePrint Archive, Report 2017/096 (2017). http://eprint.iacr.org/2017/096

19. Zhang, J., Chen, Y., Zhang, Z.: Programmable hash functions from lattices: short signatures and IBEs with small key sizes. In: Robshaw, M., Katz, J. (eds.) CRYPTO 2016. LNCS, vol. 9816, pp. 303–332. Springer, Heidelberg (2016). doi:10.1007/978-3-662-53015-3_11

# IND-PCA Secure KEM Is Enough for Password-Based Authenticated Key Exchange (Short Paper)

Haiyang Xue[1,2(✉)], Bao Li[1,2,3], and Xianhui Lu[1,2]

[1] Data Assurance and Communication Security Research Center,
Institute of Information Engineering, Chinese Academy of Sciences, Beijing, China
[2] Science and Technology on Communication Security Laboratory, Chengdu, China
{hyxue12,lb,xhlu}@is.ac.cn
[3] University of Chinese Academy of Sciences, Beijing, China

**Abstract.** There are several frameworks for password-based authenticated key exchange (PAKE) protocols with common reference string following the work of Katz, Ostrovsky and Yung (Eurocrypt'01), and it seems that the IND-CCA secure encryption is inevitable when constructing PAKE in standard model.

In this paper, we show that IND-PCA secure key encapsulation mechanism (KEM) is enough for PAKE, which is weaker and easier to be constructed than IND-CCA secure encryption. Our refined PAKE consists of a smooth projective hash function on IND-CPA secure encryption and an IND-PCA secure KEM. Based on DDH assumption, the total communication of PAKE consists of 6 group elements and $\log |D|$ ($D$ is the set of password) bits, while before this, the most efficient PAKE contains 7 group elements.

**Keywords:** Password-based authenticated key exchange · Smooth projective hash functions · IND-PCA secure KEM

## 1 Introduction

Password-based authenticated key exchange (PAKE) allows two users to mutually authenticate each other and agree on a high-entropy session key based on a shared low-entropy password. The challenge in designing such protocols is to prevent *off-line* dictionary attacks where an adversary exhaustively enumerates potential passwords, attempting to match the correct password. The secure goal of PAKE is to restrict the adversary's advantage to that of *online* dictionary attack. The seminal work in the area of PAKE was given by Bellovin and Merritt [2]. After that, Bellare et al. [4], and Boyko et al. [3] proposed formal security models for PAKE. Since then, a large number of constructions were presented in the

© Springer International Publishing AG 2017
S. Obana and K. Chida (Eds.): IWSEC 2017, LNCS 10418, pp. 231–241, 2017.
DOI: 10.1007/978-3-319-64200-0_14

random oracle model [3,4]. But the random oracle model is known to be not sound [5].

The first PAKE protocol to achieve security in standard model was given by Goldreich and Lindel [8]. There are several works to improve and simplify Goldreich and Lindel's scheme. Unfortunately, they are inefficient in terms of communication, computation and round complexity. Katz, Ostrovsky and Yung [14] demonstrated the first efficient PAKE (KOY) under DDH assumption with common reference string (CRS). On the ground of concrete construction of KOY protocol, a framework of PAKE (GL-PAKE) was abstracted by Gennaro and Lindell [9]. GL-PAKE consists of two smooth projective hash functions (SPHFs) on chosen ciphertext secure (IND-CCA) encryption. Following the work of KOY, Jiang and Gong [12] improved and gave a PAKE with mutual authentication under DDH assumption. Groce and Katz [10] abstracted the protocol of Jiang and Gong's protocol and gave a framework of GK-PAKE with SPHF on IND-CPA secure encryption and IND-CCA secure encryption.

Recently, Abdalla, Benhamouda and Pointcheval [1] pointed out that the underlying IND-CCA secure encryption in GL-PAKE and GK-PAKE can be replaced by IND-PCA secure encryption, (the adversary has the capability to query plaintext checkable oracle with $(C, m)$ to help him to decide if $C$ is the encryption of $m$ or not) and the Cramer-Shoup scheme in PAKE can be simplified. As Abdalla et al. pointed out, IND-PCA secure encryption with short plaintext is actually IND-CCA secure. Since password (in Addalla et al.'s scheme, password is in the part of plaintext) is generally short in PAKE, the framework of PAKE in Abdalla et al. essentially relies on an IND-CCA secure encryption.

**Refined Structure for PAKE.** One of the most important work in cryptography is reducing security to more basic and weaker tools. This is what this paper does. In the above works, IND-CCA secure encryption scheme seems inevitable. Although there are many efficient constructions for IND-CCA secure scheme [11,15,16], this requirement is still too strong. It is meaningful to see whether there is an elegant framework to construct efficient PAKE protocol based on more basic and weaker tools.

### 1.1    Our Contributions

In this paper, we revisit the framework of PAKE in [10], and show that SPHF on IND-CPA secure encryption and any IND-PCA secure Key encapsulation mechanism (KEM) with short encapsulation key space is enough for PAKE. In our PAKE, the key encapsulated by KEM are used to encrypt password with one time padding. Obviously, the hybrid encryption from IND-PCA secure KEM and one time padding is not IND-CCA secure[1] (even not IND-PCA secure). Note that although the hybrid encryption is malleable, it does not hurt the security of PAKE. The adversary can only produce a meaningful plaintext by extending

---

[1] Let $(c, k) \leftarrow \mathsf{Enc_{kem}}(pk, \lambda)$, the hybrid encryption of $m$ is the form $(c, k \oplus m)$. It is malleable and any adversary can reproduce the ciphertext with meaningful plaintext after seeing the challenge ciphertext.

the plaintext (password), which does not add its advantage in attacking PAKE. As a by product, we show that the KEM given by Kurosawa and Desmedt [13] is IND-PCA secure, which is proved to be not IND-CCA secure [7].

Besides that, we also give concrete example based on DDH assumption and obtain a scheme with a total communication of 6 group elements and $\log |D|$ bits instead of 7 group elements in [1], and without the requirement of mutual authentication, only 5 group elements and $\log |D|$ bits are needed.

## 2   Preliminaries

If $S$ is a set, we denote by $|S|$ the cardinality of $S$, and denote by $x \leftarrow S$ the process of sampling $x$ uniformly from $S$. A function is *negligible* (negl) if for every $c > 0$ there exists a $\lambda_c$ such that $f(\lambda) < 1/\lambda^c$ for all $\lambda > \lambda_c$. If $A$ and $B$ are distributions, $A \approx_s B$ means that the statistical distance between $A$ and $B$ is negligible.

We recall the definition of smooth projective hash function given in [6]. We first recall the definition of subset membership assumption (multiple versions of this assumption have appeared) following [15].

**Definition 1 (Subset Membership Assumption [15]).** *Let $L \subset X$ and $L$ is called the set of YES instance, and $X \backslash L$ the set of NO instance. There are efficient sample algorithms SampY (SampN) for YES(NO) instance. For any PPT adversary $A$, the advantage function $Adv_A^{SMA} = |Pr[A(PP, x) = 1 : x \leftarrow L] - Pr[A(PP, x) = 1 : x \leftarrow X \backslash L]|$ is negligible.*

**Definition 2 (Smooth Projective Hash Function [6]).** *We assume here all the algorithms can access PP. The smooth projective hash function on $(X, X \backslash L)$ follows.*

- *HashKG(PP) generates a hashing key $k \in K$.*
- *ProjKG(k) generates the projective key $\alpha(k)$.*
- *Hash(k, x) outputs the hash value on any $x \in X$ from the hashing key $k$.*
- *ProjHash($\alpha(k), w, x$): On input the witness $w$ for any $x \in L$ and the projective key, outputs the hash value, such that ProjHash($\alpha(k), w, x$) = Hash($k, x$).*

*We say that it is smooth, if the following distributions are statistically indistinguishable: $\Delta(\{x, \alpha(k), Hash(k, x)\}, \{x, \alpha(k), u\}) \leq \varepsilon$, where $k \in K$, $x \in X \backslash L$, and $u \in \Pi$ are chosen randomly.*

## 3   Refined Framework for PAKE

As the main modification of our PAKE is the IND-PCA secure KEM, we first recall the definition of IND-PCA secure KEM and prove that the Kurosawa-Desmedt KEM in [15] are IND-PCA secure. After that, we show our refined framework of PAKE.

## 3.1  IND-PCA Secure KEM

We first recall the definition of (label based) KEM. For any KEM without label, we just set $\mathsf{label} = \bot$. A (label based) public key encapsulation scheme $KEM = (\mathsf{KGen_{kem}}, \mathsf{Enc_{kem}}, \mathsf{Dec_{kem}})$ consists of three polynomial time algorithms, where $(pk_{\mathsf{kem}}, sk_{\mathsf{kem}}) \leftarrow \mathsf{KGen_{kem}}(\lambda)$ produces keys for security parameter $\lambda$; for randomness $r$, $(K, C) \leftarrow \mathsf{Enc_{kem}}(pk_{\mathsf{kem}}, \mathsf{label}, r)$ produces a key $K$ in $KeySp(\lambda)$ together with a ciphertext $C$ to recover the key; and $K \leftarrow \mathsf{Dec_{kem}}(sk_{\mathsf{kem}}, \mathsf{label}, C)$ decapsulates ciphertext $C$ with label to recover $K$ with secret key $sk_{\mathsf{kem}}$. For all $(K, C) \leftarrow \mathsf{Enc_{kem}}(pk_{\mathsf{kem}}, \mathsf{label}, r)$, $\Pr[\mathsf{Dec_{kem}}(sk_{\mathsf{kem}}, \mathsf{label}, C) = K] = 1$, where the probability is taken over the randomness of these three algorithms.

In our PAKE, we need a weak secure notion of KEM, namely security against plaintext checkable attack (PCA) [1]. Formally, for any PPT algorithm $A$, a $KEM$ is said to be IND-PCA secure if the following advantage is negligible,

$$\mathbf{Adv}_A^{kem-pca} = \Pr\left[ b = b' : \begin{array}{l} b \leftarrow \{0,1\}; (pk_{\mathsf{kem}}, sk_{\mathsf{kem}}) \leftarrow \mathsf{KGen_{kem}}(k); \\ K_0^* \leftarrow KeySp(k), (K_1^*, C^*) \leftarrow \mathsf{Enc_{kem}}(pk, \mathsf{label}), \\ b' \leftarrow A^{\mathsf{DCheck}(\cdot,\cdot)}(pk, K_b^*, C^*) \end{array} \right],$$

where the oracle $\mathsf{DCheck}(C, K)$ returns 1 if $K = \mathsf{Dec_{kem}}(sk_{\mathsf{kem}}, C)$, otherwise returns 0, and the adversary $A$ can not query DCheck with $(C, K) = (C^*, K_b^*)$.

The KEM part of Kurosawa-Desmedt scheme [13] is known to be not IND-CCA secure [7]. In the following, we prove that the KEM part of Kurosawa-Desmedt scheme is IND-PCA secure. We first recall the Kurosawa-Desmedt KEM. Let $G$ be a group of prime order $p$ and let $g_1, g_2$ be two public generators of $G$. Let $h_{tcr} : G \times G \to \mathbb{Z}_p$ be a target collision-resistant hash function. The key encapsulation part of the Kurosawa-Desmedt scheme is as follows:

| $\mathsf{KGen_{kem}}(1^n)$ | $\mathsf{Enc_{kem}}(pk);$ | $\mathsf{Dec_{kem}}(sk, c)$ |
|---|---|---|
| $x_1, x_2, y_1, y_2 \leftarrow \mathbb{Z}_p^*;$ | $r \leftarrow \mathbb{Z}_p$ | $(c_1, c_2) \leftarrow c;$ |
| $h_1 = g_1^{x_1} g_2^{x_2}, h_2 = g_1^{y_1} g_2^{y_2}$ | $c_1 = g_1^r, c_2 = g_2^r;$ | $t = h_{tcr}(c_1, c_2)$ |
| $pk := (g_1, g_2, h_1, h_2);$ | $t = h_{tcr}(c_1, c_2), K = h_1^{tr} h_2^r$ | $K = c_1^{tx_1 + y_1} c_2^{tx_2 + y_2}$ |
| $sk := (x_1, x_2, y_1, y_2).$ | Return $(c_1, c_2, K).$ | |

**Theorem 1.** *If $h_{tcr}$ is a collision resistant hash function, under the DDH assumption, the Kurosawa-Desmedt KEM is IND-PCA secure.*

*Proof.* The proof proceeds via a sequence of games.

**Game 0.** The adversary A is given the public key as well as an unlimited access to an Dcheck oracle with $(C, K)$. At some point, the adversary receives an encapsulation $C^* = (c_1^*, c_2^*)$ and $K_b^*$. After some training on DCheck oracle, $A$ outputs a guess of $b$. The ciphertext $C^*$ is generated normally with $r$. Precisely speaking, $c_1^* = g_1^r$, $c_2^* = g_2^r$. On receiving $(C = (c_1, c_2), K)$, the DCheck oracle checks it using secret key. We have that $\mathbf{Adv}_{A, G_0} = \mathbf{Adv}_A^{ind-pca}$.

**Game 1.** In this game, the DCheck oracle rejects all queries where $C \neq C^*$ but $h_{tcr}(C) = h_{tcr}(C^*)$. This game is computationally indistinguishable from the previous one under the collision-resistance of $h_{tcr}$.

**Game 2.** We now change the way of generating challenge key. The key $K_1^*$ encapsulated is generated as $(c_1^*)^{t^* x_1 + y_1} (c_2^*)^{t^* x_2 + y_2}$, where $t^* = h_{tcr}(c_1^*, c_2^*)$. The Game 2 is exactly the same with Game 1.

**Game 3.** We now change the generation algorithm of challenge ciphertext $C^*$. $r_1, r_2 \leftarrow \mathbb{Z}_p$ and let $c_1^* = g_1^{r_1}, c_2^* = g_1^{r_2}$. The difference between Game 3 and Game 2 is bounded by the DDH assumption. Note that the randomness for $c_1^*$ and $c_2^*$ do not needed to generate the challenge key $K_1^*$, we can perfectly simulate the game given a DDH challenge. Thus the difference between Game 3 and Game 2 is bounded by DDH assumption.

**Game 4.** In this Game, the simulator holds the secret $a$ s.t. $g_2 = g_1^a$ during the key generation algorithm. The DCheck oracle rejects all queries $(c_1, c_2, K)$ where $c_2 \neq c_1^a$ with the knowledge of $a$. It can make a difference when $c_2 \neq c_1^a$ but $K = (c_1)^{tx_1 + y_1}(c_2)^{tx_2 + y_2}$. First, if $(c_1, c_2) = (c_1^*, c_2^*)$ but $K \neq K_1^*$, since that implies $t = t^*$, we can safely answer negatively. We thus now have to deal with the cases $(c_1, c_2) \neq (c_1^*, c_2^*)$ and $K = (c_1)^{tx_1 + y_1}(c_2)^{tx_2 + y_2}$.

Consider the map $f(x_1, x_2, y_1, y_2) = (h_1, h_2, K_1^*, K)$ mapping hashing secret keys. If we show that this map is injective then we are done.

$$\begin{cases} \log_{g_1} h_1 = x_1 + a \cdot x_2 \\ \log_{g_1} h_2 = y_1 + a \cdot y_2 \\ \log_{g_1} K_1^* = r_1(t^* x_1 + y_1) + ar_2(t^* x_2 + y_2) \\ \log_{g_1} K = r_1(tx_1 + y_1) + ar_2(tx_2 + y_2) \end{cases}$$

$$\begin{pmatrix} \log_{g_1} h_1 \\ \log_{g_1} h_2 \\ \log_{g_1} K_1^* \\ \log_{g_1} K \end{pmatrix} = \begin{pmatrix} 1 & 0 & a & 0 \\ 0 & 1 & 0 & a \\ r_1^* t^* & r_1^* & ar_2^* t^* & ar_2^* \\ r_1 t & r_1 & ar_2 t & ar_2 \end{pmatrix} \times \begin{pmatrix} x_1 \\ y_1 \\ x_2 \\ y_2 \end{pmatrix}$$

Since $det(A) = a^2(r_2^* - r_1^*)(r_2 - r_1)(t^* - t)$, $f$ is injective if $r_2^* \neq r_1^*$, $r_2 \neq r_1$. The two assumption holds as both the challenge ciphertext and query ciphertext are not DDH subset member.

**Game 5.** In this game, $K_1^*$ is randomly chosen from $G$. This is statically indistinguishable form Game 4. Now, the challenge ciphertext doesn't contain any information of $b$. To sum up, we finish this proof. □

**Remark 1.** The Kurosawa-Desmedt method also works for a more general class of universal 2 hash proof systems on subset membership problem [6]. As shown in next subsection, in the application of PAKE, the key with low entropy in KEM (long enough to extract $\log |D|$ bits) is enough.

## 3.2  PAKE from IND-PCA Secure KEM

We now present the refined framework for PAKE. As the space limits, we omit the secure definition of BPR model [4] with mutual authentication which is added

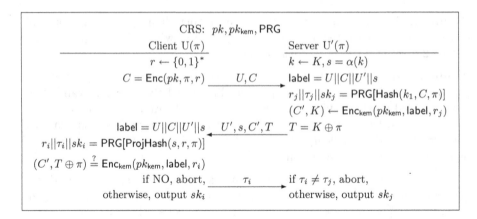

**Fig. 1.** Refined framework of PAKE

by [10]. For more details, please refer [10]. In this construction, the following primitives are required: A SPHF on IND-CPA secure encryption; An IND-PCA secure KEM with short key space. Let $PKE = (\mathsf{KGen}, \mathsf{Enc}, \mathsf{Dec})$ be an IND-CPA secure encryption. Take the ciphertext space as $X$, and the ciphertexts of $\pi$ as $L$, Let SPHF be a SPHF on it. Let $KEM = (\mathsf{KGen}_{\mathsf{kem}}, \mathsf{Enc}_{\mathsf{kem}}, \mathsf{Dec}_{\mathsf{kem}})$ be an IND-PCA secure KEM with $KeySp = D$.

**Initialization:** The CRS consists of public keys $pk$ for IND-CPA secure scheme $PKE$ and public keys $pk_{\mathsf{kem}}$. Let PRG be a pseudorandom generator.

**Protocol execution.** Figure 1 demonstrates the execution of the protocol.

*Stage 1:* When a client $U$ (holds $\pi$) wants to authenticate to the server $U'$ (holds $\pi$), it chooses $r \leftarrow \{0,1\}^*$, computes $C = \mathsf{Enc}(pk, \pi, r)$, and sends $U||C$ to $U'$.

*Stage 2:* On receiving the message $U||C$, $U'$ chooses $k \leftarrow K$ and computes $s = \alpha(k)$ and $\mathsf{Hash}(k, C, \pi)$. It decomposes the PRG value on $\mathsf{Hash}(k, C, \pi)$ as three bit strings $r_j, \tau_j, sk_j$. It sets $\mathsf{label} = U||C||U'||s$, computes $(C', K) \leftarrow \mathsf{Enc}_{\mathsf{kem}}(pk_{\mathsf{kem}}, \mathsf{label}, r_j)$ and $T = K \oplus \pi$. Then $U'$ sends $U'||s||C'||T$ to $U$.

*Stage 3:* On receiving the message $U'||s||C'|T$, user $U$ computes and decomposes the hash value $r_i||\tau_i||sk_i \leftarrow \mathsf{PRG}[\mathsf{ProjHash}(s, r, \pi)]$. It sets $\mathsf{label} = (U||C||U'||s)$ and checks $(C', T \oplus \pi) \stackrel{?}{=} \mathsf{Enc}_{\mathsf{kem}}(pk_{\mathsf{kem}}, \mathsf{label}, r_i)$. If no, aborts else sends $\tau_i$ to $U'$ and outputs $sk_i$ which means that $U'$ has successfully authenticated to $U$.

*Stage 4:* On receiving the message $\tau_i$, $U'$ checks that if $\tau_i = \tau_j$ or not. If $\tau_i \neq \tau_j$, $U'$ aborts, otherwise $U$ has successfully authenticated to $U'$ and $U'$ outputs $sk_j$.

　　If both parties are honest and there is no adversarial interference, then the projection of the hash proof guarantees that it holds $r_i||\tau_i||sk_i = r_j||\tau_j||sk_j$. Both parties will accept and output the same session key.

**Theorem 2.** *Assume $PKE$ is an IND-CPA secure encryption scheme, SPHF is a $\varepsilon_{smooth}$ SPHF over $PKE$, and KEM is an IND-PCA secure KEM, the*

*PAKE is secure in the BPR model. In particular, let $q_e$ be the number of Execute queries, $q_s$ be the number of Send queries, and $q_e + q_s \leq t$, we have*

$$\boldsymbol{Adv}_{A,\Pi}(n) \leq \frac{1}{D} + t\boldsymbol{Adv}_{B,Enc}^{CPA} + t\varepsilon_{smooth} + t\boldsymbol{Adv}_{E}^{kem-pca}.$$

*Proof.* The proof proceeds via a sequence of experiments. Let "$G_i$" denote the sequence of experiments and denote the advantage of adversary A in "$G_i$" as $\mathbf{Adv}_{A,G_i}(n) = 2\mathbf{Pr}[A$ succeeds in $G_i] - 1$. Let $G_0$ be the experiment of BPR challenge.

The proof is separated into two phases: the first phase (from $G_1$ to $G_5$) bounds out the advantage of *Execute* queries, and the second phase (from $G_6$ to $G_{10}$) bounds out the advantage of *Send* queries.

**Experiment $G_1$.** We first modify the way *Execute* queries between two users are answered. The hash value is computed using hashing key $k$ instead of witness $r$ in the client side. This does not change anything as the correctness of SPHF. We have that $\mathbf{Adv}_{A,G_0}(n) = \mathbf{Adv}_{A,G_1}(n)$

**Experiment $G_2$.** We replace $C$ by the encryption of $\pi_0$ rather than $\pi$, where $\pi_0$ represent some password not in $D$. This is indistinguishable from $G_1$ under the IND-CPA property of $PKE$.

We first assume that only one *Execute* query is allowed. We now construct an IND-CPA attacker $B$ using a distinguisher $A$ of $G_1$ and $G_2$. In the IND-CPA game of $PKE$, on receiving public key $pk$, $B$ generates real password $\pi$ and fake password $\pi_0$ as challenge message. On receiving challenge ciphertext $C^*$, $B$ simulates the entire game for $A$, including the $KEM$ and so on (note that the randomness $r$ for $C$ is not needed now). In response to the *Execute* query, it returns the challenge ciphertext $C^*$ which is the encryption of $\pi$ or $\pi_0$. At the end, $B$ outputs 1 if $A$ succeeds. The advantage of $B$ is exactly the difference between $G_1$ and $G_2$. If $q_e$ is the bound of the number of *Execute* queries, using the classical hybrid technique, the difference between $G_1$ and $G_2$ is bounded by $q_e\mathbf{Adv}_{B,Enc}^{CPA}$

**Experiment $G_3$.** We replace the hash value by truly random elements in $\Pi$ in *Execute* query. Since when answering the *Execute* queries in $G_2$ the ciphertext in the first message is an encryption of $\pi_0$, the hash value is statistically close to uniform even conditional on $s$. Using the hybrid technique, we have that $\mathbf{Adv}_{A,G_2}(n) - \mathbf{Adv}_{A,G_3}(n) \leq q_e\varepsilon_{smooth}$.

**Experiment $G_4$.** Here, we continue to modify the *Execute* query. The key generated by $\mathsf{Enc}_{\mathsf{kem}}$ is replaced by a random key in $KeySp$.

The indistinguishability between $G_3$ and $G_4$ is bound by the IND-PCA security of $KEM$ (actually, the IND-CPA security of $KEM$ is enough). We now construct an IND-PCA attacker $E$ using a distinguisher $A$ of $G_3$ and $G_4$. In the IND-PCA game of $KEM$, on receiving public key $pk_{\mathsf{kem}}$, $D$ generates real password $\pi$ and fake password $\pi_0$ as challenge message. On receiving challenge ciphertext and key $C^*, K^*$, $E$ simulates the entire game for $A$, including the $PKE$ and so on. In response to the *Execute* query, it returns the challenge ciphertext and key $C^*, K^*$, where $K^*$ is the encapsulated by $C^*$ (corresponding to $G_3$) or a random key (corresponding to $G_4$). At the end, $E$ outputs 1 if $A$ succeeds. The advantage of $E$ is exactly the difference between $G_3$ and $G_4$. If $q_e$ is the upper bound of *Execute* queries, by the hybrid technique, $\mathbf{Adv}_{A,G_3}(n) - \mathbf{Adv}_{A,G_4}(n) \leq q_e Adv_D^{kdm-pca}$.

**Experiment $G_5$.** Here when answering an *Exacute* query, $T$ is replaced by a random string. Obviously $G_5$ and $G_6$ is exactly same.

Now the answers of *Execute* queries reveal no information of actual password. We handle the *Send* queries in the following experiments. Let $Send_0$ denote sending the prompt message that causes the client $U$ to initiate the protocol with $U'$. Let $Send_1$ denote sending the first message, $Send_2$ denote sending the second message, $Send_3$ denote sending the finial message.

**Experiment $G_6$.** On answering the $Send_2(U'||s||x||T)$ queries, we do not use $r_i$ to check $(C', T)$ but query the Dcheck oracle with $(C', T \oplus \pi)$. If $U'||s||C'||T$ is not previously used, and Dcheck returns 1, we declare the attacker successful. This just adds the advantage of adversary. We have that $\mathbf{Adv}_{A,G_5}(n) \leq \mathbf{Adv}_{A,G_6}(n)$.

**Experiment $G_7$.** On answering $Send_0$ queries, we replace $C = Enc(pk, \pi, r)$ by the encryption of $\pi_0$.

Note that the smooth hash value on instance $C$ is not needed to simulate the entire experiment now. We now construct an IND-CPA attacker $B$ using a distinguisher $A$ of $G_6$ and $G_7$. In the IND-CPA game of $PKE$, on receiving public key $pk$, $B$ generates real password $\pi$ and fake password $\pi_0$ as challenge message. On receiving challenge ciphertext $C^*$, $B$ can simulate the entire game for $A$, including the $HPS$ and $KEM$ (note that the randomness $r$ for $C^*$ is not needed now). In response to the $Send_0$ query, it returns the challenge ciphertext $C^*$ which is the encryption of $\pi$ or $\pi_0$. At the end, $B$ outputs 1 if $A$ succeeds. The advantage of $D$ is exactly the difference between $G_6$ and $G_7$.

If $q_s$ is the upper bound of *Send* queries, using the classical hybrid technique, the difference between $G_6$ and $G_7$ is bounded by $q_s \mathbf{Adv}_{D,Enc}^{CPA}$.

**Experiment $G_8$.** On answering the $Send_1(U||C)$ queries, we decrypt $C$ using $sk$ and clear success if $\pi = Dec(sk, C)$. This just adds the advantage of adversary. We have that $\mathbf{Adv}_{A,G_7}(n) \leq \mathbf{Adv}_{A,G_8}(n)$.

**Experiment $G_9$.** Here we again modify the answer of the $Send_1$ oracle. In response to a query $Send_1(U||C)$ we check whether $\pi = Dec(sk, C)$ or not as in experiment $G_9$. If so, the adversary is declared to succeed as before. If not, however, we now choose the hash value uniformly and thus $r_j, \tau_j$ and $sk_j$ at random (rather than compute these values as the output of $\mathrm{PRG}(\mathsf{Hash}(k, C, \pi))$, and then continue as before. In particular, if there is a subsequent $Send_3$ query using the correct value of $\tau_j$, the server accepts and outputs the session key $sk_j$. By the classical hybrid technique, we have that $\mathbf{Adv}_{A,G_8}(n) - \mathbf{Adv}_{A,G_9}(n) \leq q_s \varepsilon$.

**Experiment $G_{10}$.** We continue to change the answer of $Send_1$ queries. If $\pi \neq Dec(sk, C)$, the hash value is chosen uniformly as before, but after $(C', K) \leftarrow \mathsf{Enc}_{\mathsf{kem}}(pk_{\mathsf{kem}}, \mathsf{label}, r_j)$, we set $K \leftarrow KeySp$. The difference between

$G_9$ and $G_{10}$ is bounded by the advantage of the IND-PCA attack on the $KEM$. $\mathbf{Adv}_{A,G_9}(n) - \mathbf{Adv}_{A,G_{10}}(n) \le q_s \mathbf{Adv}_E^{kdm-pca}$.

In the final experiment, the adversary succeeds in four cases: (1) $Send_1$ $(U', U||C)$ is queried, such that $Dec(sk, C) = \pi$; (2) $Send_2(U, U'||s||C'||T)$ is queried, such that $\mathsf{DCheck}(C', T \oplus \pi) = 1$. (3) $Send_3(\tau)$ is queried, such that $\tau = \tau_j$. (4) The adversary successfully guesses that bit used by the Test oracle.

Note that the execution of the experiment 10 is independent of password $\pi$. $\Pr[success] \le \frac{1}{2} + \frac{1}{D}$. And so, $\mathbf{Adv}_{A,G_{10}}(n) \le \frac{q}{D}$. By summing up all the gap advantages, $\mathbf{Adv}_{A,\Pi}(n) \le \frac{1}{D} + t\mathbf{Adv}_{B,Enc}^{CPA} + t\varepsilon_{smooth} + t\mathbf{Adv}_D^{kem-pca}$. □

# 4   Instantiation and Efficiency Comparison

We instantiate the framework in Sect. 3 based on DDH assumption and subgroup membership assumptions (SGA). In case of DDH, we get a scheme with communication complexity of 6 group elements and $\log |D|$ bits; in case of SGA, we obtain a scheme with 4 group elements and $\log |D|$ bits.

Please refer Fig. 2 for the PAKE based on DDH assumption. The SPHF over ElGamal is that given in [10,12]. The KEM here is the one in [15] that improved [13] with 4-wise independent hash function rather than collision resistant hash function, and the only difference is that the length of key encapsulated is only $\log |D|$. Meanwhile, let $H_4 : \{0, 1\}^* \times G \to D$.

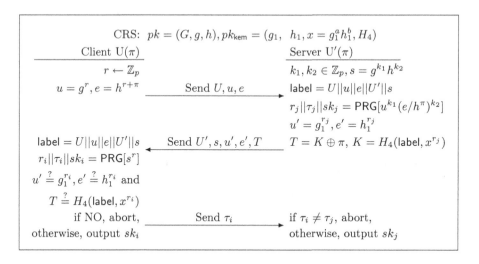

**Fig. 2.** PAKE based on DDH assumption

## 5    Conclusion

In this paper, we revisit GK-PAKE, and show that IND-PCA secure KEM is enough for PAKE. We also give concrete examples based on DDH assumptions. The instantiation based on DDH assumption need only 6 group elements and $\log |D|$ bits.

**Acknowledgement.** Haiyang Xue are supported by the Foundation of Science and Technology on Communication Security Laboratory (9140C110206150C11049) and National Natural Science Foundation of China (No. 61602473, 61502480, 61672019). Bao Li is supported by the Foundation of Science and Technology on Communication Security Laboratory (9140C110206150C11049) and the National Natural Science Foundation of China (No. 61379137). Xianhui Lu is supported by the National Natural Science Foundation of China (No. 61572495).

## References

1. Abdalla, M., Benhamouda, F., Pointcheval, D.: Public-key encryption indistinguishable under plaintext-checkable attacks. In: Katz, J. (ed.) PKC 2015. LNCS, vol. 9020, pp. 332–352. Springer, Heidelberg (2015). doi:10.1007/978-3-662-46447-2_15
2. Bellovin, M., Merritt, M.: Encrypted key exchange: password-based protocols secure against dictionary attacks. In: 1992 IEEE Symposium on Security and Privacy, pp. 72–84 (1992)
3. Boyko, V., MacKenzie, P., Patel, S.: Provably secure password-authenticated key exchange using Diffie-Hellman. In: Preneel, B. (ed.) EUROCRYPT 2000. LNCS, vol. 1807, pp. 156–171. Springer, Heidelberg (2000). doi:10.1007/3-540-45539-6_12
4. Bellare, M., Pointcheval, D., Rogaway, P.: Authenticated key exchange secure against dictionary attacks. In: Preneel, B. (ed.) EUROCRYPT 2000. LNCS, vol. 1807, pp. 139–155. Springer, Heidelberg (2000). doi:10.1007/3-540-45539-6_11
5. Canetti, R., Goldreich, O., Halevi, S.: The random oracle methodology, revisited. J. ACM **51**(4), 557–594 (2004)
6. Cramer, R., Shoup, V.: Universal hash proofs and a paradigm for adaptive chosen ciphertext secure public-key encryption. In: Knudsen, L.R. (ed.) EUROCRYPT 2002. LNCS, vol. 2332, pp. 45–64. Springer, Heidelberg (2002). doi:10.1007/3-540-46035-7_4
7. Choi, S.G., Herranz, J., Hofheinz, D., Hwang, J.Y., Kiltz, E., Lee, D.H., Yung, M.: The Kurosawa-Desmedt key encapsulation is not chosen-ciphertext secure. Inf. Process. Lett. **109**(16), 897–901 (2009)
8. Goldreich, O., Lindell, Y.: Session-key generation using human passwords only. In: Kilian, J. (ed.) CRYPTO 2001. LNCS, vol. 2139, pp. 408–432. Springer, Heidelberg (2001). doi:10.1007/3-540-44647-8_24
9. Gennaro, R., Lindell, Y.: A framework for password-based authenticated key exchange. In: Biham, E. (ed.) EUROCRYPT 2003. LNCS, vol. 2656, pp. 524–543. Springer, Heidelberg (2003). doi:10.1007/3-540-39200-9_33
10. Groce, A., Katz, J.: A new framework for efficient password-based authenticated key exchange. In: ACM Conference on Computer and Communications Security, pp. 516–525 (2010)

11. Hofheinz, D., Kiltz, E.: The group of signed quadratic residues and applications. In: Halevi, S. (ed.) CRYPTO 2009. LNCS, vol. 5677, pp. 637–653. Springer, Heidelberg (2009). doi:10.1007/978-3-642-03356-8_37
12. Jiang, S., Gong, G.: Password based key exchange with mutual authentication. In: Handschuh, H., Hasan, M.A. (eds.) SAC 2004. LNCS, vol. 3357, pp. 267–279. Springer, Heidelberg (2004). doi:10.1007/978-3-540-30564-4_19
13. Kurosawa, K., Desmedt, Y.: A new paradigm of hybrid encryption scheme. In: Franklin, M. (ed.) CRYPTO 2004. LNCS, vol. 3152, pp. 426–442. Springer, Heidelberg (2004). doi:10.1007/978-3-540-28628-8_26
14. Katz, J., Ostrovsky, R., Yung, M.: Efficient password-authenticated key exchange using human-memorable passwords. In: Pfitzmann, B. (ed.) EUROCRYPT 2001. LNCS, vol. 2045, pp. 475–494. Springer, Heidelberg (2001). doi:10.1007/3-540-44987-6_29
15. Kiltz, E., Pietrzak, K., Stam, M., Yung, M.: A new randomness extraction paradigm for hybrid encryption. In: Joux, A. (ed.) EUROCRYPT 2009. LNCS, vol. 5479, pp. 590–609. Springer, Heidelberg (2009). doi:10.1007/978-3-642-01001-9_34
16. Mei, Q., Li, B., Lu, X., Jia, D.: Chosen ciphertext secure encryption under factoring assumption revisited. In: Catalano, D., Fazio, N., Gennaro, R., Nicolosi, A. (eds.) PKC 2011. LNCS, vol. 6571, pp. 210–227. Springer, Heidelberg (2011). doi:10.1007/978-3-642-19379-8_13

# Author Index

Printed in the United States
By Bookmasters